WORLD WITHIN WORLD

WORLD WITHIN WORLD

THE AUTOBIOGRAPHY OF
STEPHEN SPENDER

FABER AND FABER
3 QUEEN SQUARE LONDON

First published in this edition 1977
by Faber and Faber Limited
3 Queen Square London WC1
Printed in Great Britain by
Whitstable Litho Ltd Whitstable Kent
All rights reserved

© *1951 by Stephen Spender*

British Library Cataloguing in Publication Data

Spender, Stephen
  World within world.
  1. Spender, Stephen - Biography 2. Poets,
  English - 20th century - Biography
  I. Title
  821'.9'12   PR6037.P47Z/

  ISBN 0-571-10212-3

TO

ISAIAH BERLIN

DARKNESS AND LIGHT

To break out of the chaos of my darkness
Into a lucid day, is all my will.
My words like eyes in night, stare to reach
A centre for their light: and my acts thrown
To distant places by impatient violence
Yet lock together to mould a path
Out of my darkness, into a lucid day.

Yet, equally, to avoid that lucid day
And to preserve my darkness, is all my will.
My words like eyes that flinch from light, refuse
And shut upon obscurity; my acts
Cast to their opposites by impatient violence
Break up the sequent path; they fly
On a circumference to avoid the centre.

To break out of my darkness towards the centre
Illumines my own weakness, when I fail;
The iron arc of the avoiding journey
Curves back upon my weakness at the end;
Whether the faint light spark against my face
Or in the dark my sight hide from my sight,
Centre and circumference are both my weakness.

O strange identity of my will and weakness!
Terrible wave white with the seething word!
Terrible flight through the revolving darkness!
Dreaded light that hunts my profile!
Dreaded night covering me in fears!
My will behind my weakness silhouettes
My territories of fear, with a great sun.

I grow towards the acceptance of that sun
Which hews the day from night. The light
Runs from the dark, the dark from light
Towards a black and white total emptiness.
The world, my life, binds the dark and light
Together, reconciles and separates
In lucid day the chaos of my darkness.

From *The Still Centre*, 1935.

INTRODUCTION

In this book I am mainly concerned with a few themes: love; poetry; politics; the life of literature; childhood; travel; and the development of certain attitudes towards moral problems.

All these are related to the background of events from 1928–1939, and their development forms the main narrative of all except the first section. Outside this decade, I have chosen only material which concerns my own story, and I do not attempt to fill in the background of the time.

I have let the main part of the narrative develop forwards from 1928 until the outbreak of the war. I say 'I have let' it do so, because this was not my original intention. I meant at first to write a book discussing my themes and illustrating them with narrative taken up at any point in time that I chose.

However, after two or three trials, I saw the advantage of having a framework of objective events through which I could knock the holes of my subjective experiences. Given this general structure, within it I could still make excursions into the past and future.

Many autobiographies have irritated me, when I wanted to read about the writer's achievements, by beginning with a detailed account of his early days, forcing me to wade through a morass of ancestors, nurses, governesses, first memories, before I get to what really interests me. Certainly masterpieces have been written about childhood, but these are chiefly important for the light they throw on childhood in general, and they are not especially illuminating as the autobiography of particular individuals. Autobiography, however, is concerned with a particular person whose childhood will interest us, if at all, chiefly as an interpretation of everything we have come to know about him. That autobiographers have to begin by plunging into their earliest memories is surely an unnecessary convention.

So childhood is like wheels within wheels of this book, which begins, and revolves around, and ends with it. It is end and beginning, introduction and explanation. In my First Section I seek only to establish the broad lines of a sketch to indicate the kind of adolescent I was until the time when I went up to Oxford in 1928.

An autobiographer is really writing a story of two lives: his life as it appears to himself, from his own position, when he looks out at the world from behind his eye-sockets; and his life as it appears from outside in the minds of others; a view which tends to become in part his own view of himself also, since he is influenced by the opinion of those others. An account of the interior view would be entirely subjective; and of the exterior, would hardly be autobiography but biography of oneself on the hypothesis that someone can know about himself as if he were another person. However, the great problem of autobiography remains, which is to create the true tension between these inner and outer, subjective and objective, worlds.

Here I have tried to be as truthful as I can, within the limits of certain inevitable reticences; and to write of experiences from which I feel I have learned how to live.

I have learned largely from mistakes, so that this book seems to be, among other things, a catalogue of errors. But I have tried hard to avoid putting these forward as if they were an example for anyone else to make the same sort of mistakes. I do not want my behaviour to appear attractive or fashionable. Nor do I offer any consoling picture of myself living now in detached philosophic calm, having survived my life like a grave illness. Most of my weaknesses, even if I have learned something from them, are still with me.

I believe obstinately that, if I am able to write with truth about what has happened to me, this can help others who have lived through the same sort of thing. In this belief I have risked being indiscreet, and I have written occasionally of experiences which seem strange to me myself, and which I have not seen discussed elsewhere.

The modern reader, in order to protect himself from taking in what he does not care to know, comes to a book armed with a whole vocabulary of defensive labels. Doubtless he will have occasion to dismiss some of my experiences by virtue of an analysis based on the evidence which I provide. But I can only repeat that I have written of what seems significant in my own life in a way which I think should be useful to at least a few readers.

Where I write of the people I have known partly as public figures, for instance as writers or politicians, I have used their real names. Where they play only a private role, I have sometimes invented names for them.

Once or twice (for example in the account of the Writers' Congress in Madrid) the narrative diverges into satire. The reader, I think, will agree that this is justified, because satire is the only means of conveying certain impressions. But characters like the Communist lady novelist are portrayals of types and not of real personalities. They do justice, I think, to the type: and to the fact that people tend to become types within certain situations.

Acknowledgements are due to the following: first and foremost, Frances Cornford, who read the whole manuscript, making numerous suggestions for corrections in manner and style: whatever improvement there may be in this over my other prose I owe to her; Mr. John Hayward, whose criticisms caused me to scrap an earlier version and start again from the beginning; Mrs. Frieda Lawrence, who, during the summer of 1947, generously lent me her ranch above Taos in New Mexico, where I wrote the pages about childhood with which the book concludes: the Hon. Victoria Sackville-West, T. S. Eliot, W. H. Auden, William Plomer, Cyril Connolly, Leonard Woolf, William Goyen, Walter Berns, T. A. R. Hyndman, Christopher Isherwood, R. M. Nadal and William Jay Smith; to Arthur Waley and to Messrs. George Allen and Unwin for allowing me to quote a translation of a poem in his *The Life and Times of Po Chu-i*; to the executors of the estate of the late Lady Ottoline Morrell for permission to quote from her letters, and to Messrs. Faber and Faber for permission to reprint 'Darkness and Light' from my book, *The Still Centre*; to Winifred Paine and to my wife for correcting proofs; lastly I thank my friend Hamish Hamilton for his patience, generosity and forbearance.

I

I GREW up in an atmosphere of belief in progress curiously mingled with apprehension. Through books we read at school, through the Liberal views of my family, it seemed that I had been born on to a fortunate promontory of time towards which all other times led.

History taught of terrible things which had happened in the past; tortures, Court of the Star Chamber, Morton's Fork, Henry VIII's wives, the Stamp Tax, the Boston Tea Party, slavery, the Industrial Revolution, the French Revolution, Bismarck, the Boer War. Weighing in the scale of human happiness against these were the Reform Act, Wilberforce, Mr. Gladstone, Home Rule, Popular Education, the United States, Health Insurance, the League of Nations. If the history books were illustrated, they gave the impression that the world had been moving steadily forward in the past thousands of years, from the vague to the defined, the savage to the civilized, the crude to the scientific, the unfamiliar to the known. It was as though the nineteenth century had been a machine absorbing into itself at one end humanity dressed in fancy dress, unwashed, fierce and immoral, and emitting at the other modern men in their utilitarian clothes with their hygienic houses, their zeal for reform, their air of having triumphed by mechanical, economic and scientific means over the passionate, superstitious, cruel and poetic past.

History seemed to have been fulfilled and finished by the static respectability, idealism and material prosperity of the end of the nineteenth century. This highly satisfactory, if banal, conclusion was largely due to the Liberal Party having found the correct answer to most of the problems which troubled our ancestors. There were still poor people in the world, but they were not nearly so poor as their forefathers had been. If there were slum-dwellers, then there were also slum workers who were kind to them, unless, indeed, they were hopeless cases. Socialists, Communists and Anarchists were fanatical idealists who refused to recognize that everything possible had been done to improve the world. Conservatives were wilful self-seekers who attacked the great fortress of Liberal morality, Free Trade. The Americans, the Boers, the Irish, the uneducated, had all had their grievances met and removed.

When I was taught about the past, I often regretted that there were no great causes left to fight for; that I could not be crucified, nor go on a crusade, nor choose to defend the cause of Saint Joan against the (then) wicked English, nor free slaves nor kill tyrants. I thirsted for great injustices.

If, lying in bed awake, there were times when I regretted not having my arms extended on a cross with rusty nails driven through my hands, there were others when I craved for a savagery, a dæmonism which seemed to have gone out of the world. I should like to have gone naked with Picts and Celts, painted in woad or clothed in pelt and rags, shameless around fires or in dark caverns.

But I was brought up with a myth in my mind of the world having resolved itself from past history, correctly, like a sum. Yet there was also, paradoxically, a feeling that the best times were over. This was not stated in history books, but it was conveyed by the tone of existence surrounding me. My parents and the servants talked of pre-war days, as poets sing of a Golden Age. I used to ask how much toffee cost before 1914, and was told – was it fourpence a pound? My mother would describe a honeymoon journey she and my father had taken to Egypt – the pyramids – thence to Florence – Giotto's Tower – in days when 'we were rich'. There were photographs of my father with a pyramid behind him, arms folded, sepia moustache trailing on each side like fox brushes, in the faded brown print; of my mother with her motoring veil, seated in the corner of a car which looked like a minute church.

The war had knocked the ball-room floor from under middle-class English life. People resembled dancers suspended in mid-air yet miraculously able to pretend that they were still dancing. We were aware of a gulf but not of any new values to replace old supports. What was new seemed negative: the immorality of the 'young people', the drinking, the short skirts, the pillion-riding, all of which my father deplored. We knew vaguely but surely that our generation would inevitably have less than his. My father supported Liberal causes of which there seemed little left but the idealism. He believed in the League of Nations, he opposed Protection. Within the Liberal Party itself he fought for Lloyd George against Asquith.

We lived in a style of austere comfort against a background of calamity. Little of our money seemed spent on enjoyment, but most on doctors and servants, on maintaining a standard of life. My mother, who died when I was twelve, was a semi-invalid, and her ill health provided the background to our childhood. We walked by her bedroom on tiptoe, knowing that to talk too loud was to give her a headache. Once, when we had been playing trains in the nursery, which was above her bedroom, the door suddenly opened and she appeared on the threshold with a white face of Greek tragedy, and exclaimed like Medea: 'I now know the sorrow of having borne children.'

I remember her lying on a chaise-longue in Sheringham complaining about debts, and telling me in a taxi in London that she was five pounds overdrawn. How strangely all spoken words are attached to scenes, like honey to the cells of a honeycomb! For it was in a 31 bus, on the blackened route that leads from Earls Court to Swiss Cottage, that my father told me (with the crowds standing outside the pubs of Kilburn) that my grandfather in his will had left us 'just enough money to keep us out of the workhouse'. And in some way I instantly surmised that this meant enough for me to do what I wanted with my life.

When my mother was not in her tragic mood she could be gay and companionable. She was always intelligent and sensitive. She recognized in me someone as hypersensitive as herself and snubbed me accordingly, being, like many sensitive people, unable to resist wounding those as vulnerable as herself, in revenge for wounds she suffered from the seemingly invulnerable. I still hesitate whenever I have to say either the word 'exhibition' or 'expedition': a scene

3

flares up in my mind. My mother is standing on the shore of the Cherwell and I am shouting to her from a punt that I am going on an 'exhibition'. To this day I hear the coldness of her reply: 'Not exhibition, but expedition.'

Childhood is like wheels within wheels of this book, which begins and revolves around and ends with it. But here I want only to establish the broad lines of a sketch of the kind of person I was before I went to Oxford.

My mother had a sense of catastrophe, but she was less afraid of life than my father. Shortly before she died, we took a family holiday at Oxford (to reach there from London we hired a lorry which we filled with members of the family, servants, dog, cat, luggage). I remember how in walks through Oxford she talked about friends, painting, travel, poetry, certain biological experiments in breeding animals, art, in a way which enabled us to share the excitement of these things with her.

She was hysterical, and given to showing violent loves and hates, enthusiasms and disappointments, which went to make us feel that our family life was acted out before a screen dividing us from an outer darkness of weeping and gnashing of teeth, immense rewards and fearful punishments. Cooks, governesses, relations, friends, were for ever entering our lives, sunning themselves in radiant favours, only to commit some act which caused them never to be mentioned again, unless with an air of tragic disapproval. The cousin who persuaded my brother Michael to let him beat his bared bottom with the back of a hairbrush, the carpenter, engaged to the cook, who was involved in a robbery, Mrs. Alger our general servant who said unrepeatable slanders – these and many others disappeared from our lives, entering a silent land of utter wickedness where I supposed them to continue openly and unceasingly the unmentionable practices, which, when we had discovered them, seemed to be revelations of their deepest natures.

My mother's painting, embroidery and poetry had a sacred, unchallenged reputation among us. If she was often moody and temperamental, her acts of thoughtfulness and her kindness to friends, governesses, school teachers, servants, expressed a touching wish to love her way into their lives, as though every stitch of some collar

4

which she embroidered were a thought directed towards the person for whom it was made. Although, at the age of twelve when I was at school, I thought of her face as agonized, and was amazed when I saw an early photograph that my mother ever could have looked carefree and beautiful in exactly the same way as brides whose photographs appeared in the newspapers: nevertheless I remember a still earlier time when before a dinner party she would bend over me, as I lay in bed, to say good night, and the amethysts round her white neck, the stiff satin of her golden dress, her scent, were a splendour such as today I would find in a Titian of some Venetian beauty.

With my father it was as though his sense of the dramatic made him inhabit a world of rhetorical situations. Everything for him was a scene in a play written by some hectic journalist. If I had to play football, he impressed on me that this was to harden the tissues of my character. His own accomplishments were to him difficulties surmounted with unflinching resolution at the cost of infinite pains. He spoke often in parables which illustrated the point that life was a perpetual confronting of oneself with vague immensities. He told me that once when he climbed a mountain, the peasant who kept a hut at the top asked him and his friends why they climbed. This why (*Pourquoi?* she had asked) became for my father the question at the centre of the universe. Whence the spirit of adventure? Why does man essay to scale the stars?

W. H. Auden, who was at school with my brother Michael, tells me that on one occasion when my father visited the school he read the Lesson: this happened to be the parable of the Prodigal Son. My brother was playing the organ and was seated in the organ loft at the end of the chapel farthest from the lectern, when my father, removing with a flourish his beribboned spectacles, and gazing up at my brother in the distance exclaimed in the voice of the father beholding his prodigal son: 'But when he was as yet a great way off, his father saw him. . . .'

My father's habit of mind created a kind of barrier between him and us, which asserted itself even in the most genuine situations. When my mother died, my brothers and sister and I were rushed home from our various schools. I remember entering a room and seeing my father seated on a chair with his head in his hands. When he saw us he raised his arms, embraced us and exclaimed: 'My little ones. You are all your old father has left.' He was genuinely stricken and there was certainly no falsity in his voice or his expression. His usual expression, indeed, was deleted with grief, like a clownish white grease paint which had smoothed out the characteristic lines. Yet he communicated a situation which put him outside us by dramatizing that we were all he had.

A few days after the death of my mother, my father took me to see the headmaster of the day school in Hampstead where it was proposed that I should be sent, in order to be (together with my sister Christine, who was also brought home) a companion to him in his widowerhood. The headmaster said something to the effect that it was a loss to children to have no mother. 'Fortunately at his age, they do not realize it,' my father said. This remark had a complex affect on me. I recognized its justice. If I felt the death of my mother at all, it was as the lightening of a burden and as a stimulating excitement. Yet I was humiliated at his demonstration of my own lack of feeling. I longed to be stricken again in order to prove that next time I would be really tragic. But the only loss which I could imagine affecting me greatly was of my father himself. For this could make me that pathetic figure, an orphan. Thus I longed for my father to die in order that I might demonstrate my grief to him, as he watched me from his grave.

Soon after my mother's death there was a change of my father's role in our lives. Until this, he had been the one who championed us in revolting against the anxious fussiness of my mother. It was he who, when we were at Sheringham, as soon as he had got us out of the house, on to the cliffs or the common, would give a sigh and exclaim: 'Away from the women at last . . .', an injunction which, for me, has never quite ceased to have its appeal. The wind blew in his hair, the lines of his forehead and at the corners of his eyes wrinkled into smiles. I watched him stride forward, with one of us on each arm, as he told us adventure stories. Sometimes he had a gun and shot at rabbits, or he hunted for things cast up on the beach after a storm, or he would pretend that we were climbing with him on the Alps, traversing glaciers, attached to one another by a rope, with the clink of an ice-axe hacking steps on the face of the ice. At such times he seemed, with his blue eyes, his sandy hair and moustache, and his chiselled nose, like a Viking.

But now, after a very brief period, during which the immediate effect of bereavement was that all controls over us were relaxed, my father's character changed. He became as anxious and concerned as ever my mother had been. My sister and I were not allowed out of the house unaccompanied, and every moment of our day was watched and worried over.

When I was fourteen, he fought in the General Election at Bath in the Liberal cause. My brother Humphrey (a year younger than I) and myself were brought down by train from London, put on the platform beside my father who made a sweeping gesture towards us, exclaiming to the audience: 'I have brought up my reserves!' We were sent round the streets of Bath in a donkey cart. The donkey had hung round its neck a placard on which was written VOTE FOR DADDY. He did not win the election.

Having been a member of the 'volunteers' in Norfolk during the war, my father had a fairly extensive vocabulary of military metaphor. Whenever one of us asked him a favour, he would hold his head down with a butting gesture, and, looking up from under shaggy sandy eyebrows, say: 'You are trying to get round my flank.'

He died when I was seventeen, certainly the age when sons react most strongly against their parents. Thus my portrait of him may be over-simplified by the fury of adolescence. To his contemporaries he may have seemed more a man of the world, more intuitive and understanding than he appears here. Nevertheless, for me his attitudes were both in a material and spiritual sense unreal. For it is no exaggeration to say that at the end his unreality terrified me. Just as Midas turned everything he touched to gold, so my father turned everything into rhetorical abstraction, in which there was no concreteness, no accuracy. It got to a stage when I was frightened of things because they were almost superseded in my mind by descriptive qualities which he applied to them. A game of football ceased to be just the kicking about of a leather ball by bare-kneed boys. It had become confused with the Battle of Life. Honour, Integrity, Discipline, Toughness and a dozen other qualities haunted the field like ghostly footballers.

He impressed so much on me his achievement in having passed certain examinations, that to gain a First, a Scholarship, Honours or a Credit seemed as difficult as scaling some great height. Indeed, to climb a real Alp would have been easier, because it would have presented a tangible difficulty, whereas the difficulty contained within Examinations seemed impalpable. I knew only that those who passed them brilliantly were mysterious Victors with Double Firsts, Scholarships, and so forth. Even answering a question in class became a problem, for the idea of some insuperable Difficulty lurking within the question distracted me from the question itself. I meditated on the idea of Difficulty: what was Difficult could not be easy; but if I knew the answer that would be easy, therefore it could not be the correct answer, and the question must conceal some hidden trap. How often at school the boy next to me, or the one next to him, gave the right answer, which I had known, but could not believe to be correct, just because it had appeared easy.

The answers handed in at examinations, and so carefully sealed and taken away, often in boxes, never seemed to me just answers. There was something mysterious, unknown to me about them, like the confidences made in the confessional, or like specimens of cerebral fluid extracted by the examiner from the examinees by the operation of examining. I could not believe that the people who got brilliant Firsts, double Firsts, and so on, for their General Essays, were just writing papers which had something in common with, say, articles appearing in reviews on some specialized subject.

I remember lying awake at night and thinking about Work, Discipline, and Thought itself, just as though all these activities were divorced from objects, and were quite abstract functionings of the mind.

I think that if, when I was young, I had been told, 'Go out on to that field and kick that ball', or 'Sit at that desk and answer that question': in a word, if I had been committed to particular tasks on particular occasions, I would have escaped a good deal of confusion. But the abstract conception of Work and Duties was constantly being thrust on me, so that I saw beyond tasks themselves to pure qualities of moral and intellectual existence, quite emptied of things.

As Work was associated with Duty, I knew that it could have no connection with enjoyment. Thus when at school I enjoyed a subject, I felt that it had ceased to be Work for me, and had become a kind of self-indulgence. It was easy, and I therefore felt that I should turn to something Difficult. At the same time my whole being revolted against my own conception of Work. I did not have the courage to enjoy myself, nor the strength to force myself to act against my inclinations.

More serious than the effect of my father's rhetoric on my school work was its influence on my ideas of morality. Discipline, Purity, Duty, became abstract concepts for me, states of pure existence almost removed from particular actions. Thus they tended to seem absolute, and individual failures to work or behave well were not just separate acts which proved little or nothing about my character in general, but proofs that I could not achieve that pure goodness of existence which I sought.

My parents impressed on us the fear of being an inadmissible, unrespectable, loveless kind of person, a moral outcast. They had a special kind of cowardice, which was a fear of finding out some final wickedness in ourselves, some unspeakable shame of ultimate depravity. In all their relationships there was the sense of something which might turn up and which could never be mentioned. Ours was a morality based on a fear of discovering something horrible about others – or even about ourselves – not on a love sternly but patiently judging every separate action within its own separateness, a love sometimes confronted with pain and failure, but never withholding forgiveness, never finally withdrawn.

My revolt against the attitude of my family led me to rebel altogether against morality, work and discipline. Secretly I was fascinated by the worthless outcasts, the depraved, the lazy, the lost, and wanted to give them that love which they were denied by respectable people. This reaction was doubtless due to the fact that I wanted to love what I judged to be the inadmissible worst qualities in myself. But such a revolt confronted me with new problems, because love, although not a discipline of fear, is also a discipline. If it accepts the reality of evil, it nevertheless tries to melt it into the wholeness of a creative purpose, and does not rest contented with what mere conventionality has rejected. Without this positive discipline, work and human relationships were no easier for me than they had been within the negative discipline of fear.

* * * * *

When I was fifteen I came under one of the most important influences of my life, that of my maternal grandmother, Hilda Schuster. My grandmother saw that my father could not understand my taste for modern painting, theatre, literature. To him, modern painting was a vast leg-pull by cynical artists, of the 'long-suffering British public'. Modern writing was largely immoral, as was the theatre. In any case, during the term, when I was in London at University College School, a day school, I was not allowed to see plays or exhibitions, as I was supposed to live under what he called a 'rigorous non-pleasure régime', which meant that I must not go to the theatre, or to art galleries.

My grandmother used, when my father was away, to take me to the theatre. With her I saw plays of Chekhov, Ibsen and Strindberg, and experimental performances of Shakespeare done by small theatre groups at Hammersmith, Barnes and Notting Hill Gate. We used to go to the art galleries and see modern paintings. She read the most recent novels in order to discuss them with me.

Towards all these works of art she brought a mind which in some ways seemed as innocent as my own. She was easily impressed, endlessly curious, excited, ready to be enthusiastic. If she did not understand something (for example, *pointilliste* painting or that kind of painting of models to look like inflated rubber dolls which was 'advanced' just then) she would say, 'I don't know what it means, but I can see that it is quite, quite beautiful.'

She was extremely influenced by a wish to share an experience of something 'new' and modern with me who was young, her most isolated grandson who most needed her. But whilst she was disposed to like what I liked, out of her loving sympathy for me (and because in some way she entered into my excitement without quite understanding the book or painting which was its object), she was also for ever anxious whether this was 'the right thing' for me.
10

Thus it became something in which opinions other than mine counted. For perhaps my uncle, J. A. Spender, or some other of her advisers would point out to her that something which I liked and which she had liked for my sake was 'not at all suitable' for me at my age. My grandmother, anxious to spare me the guilt of having liked something disapproved of by my uncle, would decide that I had not understood its meaning. Nor for that matter had she herself, sharing my enthusiasm, seen the wickedness in it. For what we had liked which had deceived us into thinking it beautiful, when really it was a bad influence, now seemed to her wicked, and she would astonish and dismay me after discussion of something which we had both praised by saying, when I met her again: 'You know, dear Stephen, I've been thinking about that book we've been reading and I've decided that although it seems so beautiful there's something nasty about it. I think the writer must really be a beastly person. Your uncle's been talking to me and I've decided that it was very wrong of me to like it so much. I don't know how I could have been so stupid.'

My grandmother's view of life was entirely personal. She loved us and she wanted us to be happy. Thus she was ready to sympathize with our every wish. But she was aware of the danger that we might wish our own unhappiness. She saw our interests and aims not as an entrance of our personalities into objective things, but as potentialities for happiness or unhappiness. A book, a poem, and a picture which I liked were, for her, only partly values justified in themselves: partly they were satisfactions of my wish to read books and see pictures. She would first sympathize with and admire the wish, and then fall to thinking that the taste for poetry and painting might bring me unhappiness, poverty, or solitude.

So with my desire to be a poet. She would sympathize, grow excited, share my own vision, with an intensity which astonished me. Then she would tell someone else, and uneasiness would assail her: very grave dangers underlay artistic life. Students painted nudes, poets drank spirits, the artist was subject to Bohemian temptations. There was no money to be made out of poetry. Of course – she was anxious to make me understand – she did not consider the artistic life immoral. But would it make for my happiness? Was it not wiser to do something else – go into the Foreign Office, for example, as my grandfather had hoped I would do. But then she remembered that, although she believed in me and thought me intelligent, I could not pass examinations; and she realized that some special kind of solution of my problems was needed after all.

The spiritual territory she inhabited was a democracy of the emotions, where she understood everything which was an appeal from person to person, for personal reasons. The sorrows of her cook could worry her for days. Fundamentally everyone to her was the same primary human being. She was a thin, bowed, passionate figure who mourned over starvation in Austria and Germany, the triumphant inhumanity of the victors over the defeated, the shrieking of hatred in newspaper headlines which haunted our childhood – 'Squeeze the Huns until the pips squeak!' She grieved over the lack of love as a guiding spirit in the world.

Her sympathy for the defeated Germans was rooted in her life, for she herself was of German origin. Her father, Sir Hermann Weber, was a doctor from the Rhineland who came to England because he wished to live in the country of Shakespeare's tongue, and who stayed there because his patients loved him and petitioned him to do so. On her mother's side of the family there was the Danish blood of the Grunings. Her husband, my grandfather, Ernest Joseph Schuster, was of German-Jewish origin, the son of a banker who derived from Frankfurt-am-Main. Thus hers was a life rent by many conflicts, as though within her own flesh, of Germans with Jews, Germans with Danes, Germans with English: and her humanity was a reconciling of these opposed causes in a protesting love, a refusal to hide from the misery she knew in her blood within the protected and privileged position which she enjoyed.

In the First World War her youngest and favourite son, Alfred Schuster, had been killed. At the same time, her family, and even the Spender family, on account of their connection with the Schusters, had been attacked by the Northcliffe Press, and by the *New Witness*, the organ of Hilaire Belloc and G. K. Chesterton, who interpreted the war as the defence of universal Catholicism against perfidious Germany and German-Jewry. My grandmother told a story of how a man, incited by universal Christian love of the Chesterton-Belloc variety, walked into my grandfather's rooms in Chancery Lane, and, finding him there, asked my grandfather how, with such a name, he could have the impertinence to allow his son to fight in the British Army. My grandfather simply handed him the telegram he had just received to announce that Alfred Schuster had been killed on the Western Front, and told his visitor he need disturb himself no longer.

That we were of Jewish as well as German origin was passed over in silence or with slight embarrassment by my family, either because, as with my grandfather, and his brothers Arthur and Felix Schuster, it was taken for granted, or because, with his descendants, it was deliberately ignored. When we were children it was not mentioned to us that we were at least a quarter Jewish, and from the conversation of nurses and governesses I gathered that Jews were a strange race with hooked noses (I imagined them to be like fish-hooks) and avaricious manners, with whom I certainly had no reason to imagine that I had any connection. When, at the age of sixteen, I became aware of our Jewish blood, I began to *feel* Jewish. At school, where there were many Hampstead Jews, I began to realize that I had more in common with the sensitive, rather soft, inquisitive, interior Jewish boys, than with the aloof, hard, external English. There was a vulnerability, a tendency to self-hatred and self-pity, an underlying perpetual mourning amounting at times to spiritual defeatism, about my own nature which, even to myself, in my English surroundings, seemed foreign. I have to admit that, although I was never antisemitic, I despised some of these qualities in myself which I thought of as Jewish, and my feeling for the English was at times almost like being in love with an alien race.

At Oxford one of my cousins told me that at Eton he had always been aware of something which made him and his brother 'different' from the other boys: and now he suddenly realized what this was, he exclaimed bitterly: 'we were Jewish'.

After this, I reacted against what I thought to be the embarrassment of my family about their Jewish blood. When editors started writing to me for biographical notes, I emphasized in these my Jewishness: so that, as a result of certain comments in the American anthologies of Modern Poetry, I am often written of in the United States as a Jew. This is not really the case, although perhaps there

13

are two ways of being Jewish: one is to be a pure-blooded Jew, and the other is to have mixed blood, a considerable proportion of which is Jewish. Certainly the only trait common to most Jews is that of feeling 'different'.

But my grandmother would say that there is no such thing as a 'pure Jew' anyway. If this is true, Jewishness becomes more than ever a state of strong racial consciousness, often emphasized by inbreeding over a long period of time with people who have a similar consciousness of being pure Jews. In my grandmother's view the difference between being a 'pure Jew' and having Jewish blood breaks down, because the 'pure Jews' are after all only people of mixed blood. It could also be argued that a person with mixed blood can cease to be Jewish simply by not thinking of himself as such. This no doubt justified the silence with which the children and grandchildren of the Frankfurt Schusters treated the subject: they were burying it in unconsciousness. But it also justified my feeling, especially during the 1930's, that I was Jewish. Having mixed blood really puts one in the position of being able to choose whether or not to think of oneself as a Jew. One has the power, more or less, to become what one thinks.

But, although sometimes we discussed these matters, my grandmother had little sense of the distinctions between peoples and classes, the respectable and unrespectable. All were blotted out for her by the great dark wailing of the oppressed. For that matter, people did not exist for her as unredeemed individuals with bad wills, dark and hidden personalities: their needs, their wrongs, their shared humanity were more important to her than what each within himself really was. If she was extremely aware of the crimes by which peoples oppressed peoples, she was extraordinarily innocent of knowledge of what makes for individual guilt. Anything bad said to her about anyone she loved, or about any member of our family, she regarded as simply incredible. If she was forced to believe it, she either excused it as the result of mental illness or intense personal suffering, or else she hardly spoke of the offender again. She was for ever surrounded by lame ducks who came limping to her with their griefs. One day a woman got into conversation with her at a railway station, declaring that my grandmother was a reincarnation of her best friend. My

14

grandmother, who was not in the least superstitious, regarded this as absurd. Nevertheless, the woman was taken to her flat, fed, clothed, favoured, written to, fussed over, and elevated to a special position in my grandmother's love. The fact is that my grandmother recognized in such a person a raw and crying need: and her own greatest need was to be needed. For her, need was more important perhaps than love, or became the same thing, because need is revealed, exposed, absolute, in a way which love but rarely is. Moreover need excuses everything, in fact, interprets all as an expression of itself, so that poverty, vice, ugliness, squalor, and other qualities in human individuals which my grandmother could not really explain or understand, can be excused as the results of need.

In railway carriages, people told my grandmother their life stories. She listened with her head bowed, her jaw dropping, her heart wrung. Yet all the time there lurked in her expression a faint suspiciousness which I grew to recognize. This was partly just the inevitable suspiciousness of a person of means, whose sympathy has been exploited by too many people too many times. It was partly shrewd intelligence of the kind by which a brilliant person is not fooled all the time. Her spontaneous sympathy was also tinged with suspiciousness which was really of herself. She knew that she was liable to like the wrong people, support someone who was unworthy, and she tried to be on guard, not against them, but against her own sympathies. As with my parents, there was always the possibility of her favourites falling from grace. They were discovered 'not to be nice after all', or even 'quite, quite horrid'.

A wealthy woman, she inhabited a corner of one room of her large Kensington flat, in which she lived with extreme simplicity, preferring to sit always on a three-legged wooden stool, eating, when she was alone, meals which consisted usually of stale bread or buns and a little cheese, wearing black dresses which were undistinguishable one from the other.

During the war she had joined the Quakers. After it, she went every day to an office to pack up parcels which were sent to Austria and blockaded Germany. This work of charity corresponded to her deepest convictions. As a result of it, she grew to hate politics and politicians. Her own remedy for the ills of society was simple: every-

15

one should love everyone else. 'Why don't the French love the Germans? Why don't we forgive our enemies and give them as much of our food as we can spare? Why don't we destroy every single arms factory all over the world?' She was for ever asking such questions. Many years later, at the beginning of the war of 1939, she approved of Chamberlain's dropping pamphlets over Germany, except that she thought he should have dropped things more useful. 'We shouldn't drop just leaflets, but every scrap of food we can possibly do without.' Then she added, with a show of practicality, 'On parachutes.'

When I was sixteen, my attachment to my grandmother was so great that I count it as the earliest of those friendships through which I have at various times identified my own situation with that of another person. We discussed everything, including art, religion and sex. So long as we were together she was quite unshocked by anything I said, though the moment I left the room she was likely to have qualms and to ask someone's advice as to whether our conversation was all right or 'quite, quite wrong'.

'Dear Stephen, say something quickly to shock me,' she would exclaim sometimes when I came into the room. Then I risked telling her something which she would at once communicate to my uncle, J. A. Spender, in order to obtain his approval of our conversations. My uncle was profoundly disturbed at my having spoken of coarse things to my grandmother. I was to discover that there was a trace of duplicity in my grandmother's nature. Like many highly intelligent but naïve people, she was not so guileless but that she did not sometimes exploit her own innocence in order to gain confidences and assert her power. So it is not impossible that sometimes she 'drew me out' in order then to consult about me with my uncle.

Her icy-cold flat in which the bedrooms were never heated and in which, to save electricity, little oil lamps burned along the corridors, depressed me. These lamps were by no means the least of her economies, the most impressive of which was that she retained from the First World War small squares of sweetened paper, used as a sugar substitute, which she continued to put in her tea right up to the Second World War. She often used to eat her lunch, consisting of a roll picked up at tea from a Lyons Restaurant, on a bus, on her way to Friends' House.

At the teas to which we went every Sunday there were always stale cakes, relics of some bygone day when cakes and buns were new. Nor could we well avoid eating these, because if, when one of us was handed a plate, he attempted to choose the least mildewy, my grandmother who was watching from her corner would immediately cry out: 'No, darling, take the one nearest to you. It's the stalest, and was put there on purpose.' Breakfasts and luncheons were full of orders such as, 'Eat that orange, darling, it's going bad,' or 'You must eat every one of these lovely, lovely scones. My sister sent them from the country, and they won't last.'

Yet her economies could strike no one as mean. Indeed, they were one aspect of an enormous act of generosity of a woman who not only gave much away, but who, out of a sense of the wretchedness of humanity, lived in some ways less comfortably than the poor.

At this time, just before and after the death of my father, I had several illnesses. It seems to me now that these periods of sickness were like a sharing of my grandmother's ascetic, emotionally charged existence, in which she was so conscious of suffering all over the world that sometimes she would cry out that the world was terrible and life not worth living.

These illnesses were also a means of escape from certain problems. They were a plunge into depths of my own weakness, until at last I attained a place where I knew I must either be ill or really well.

The most mysterious of them was an unidentified fever. I had supposedly a mild attack of German measles. Since my father was at this time in the first stages of what proved to be his last illness, it was decided that I should go to the London Fever Hospital. I was given a room in an isolation ward. The window of this room opened on to a vista of depressing buildings, among which were several churches, whose bells seemed to toll endlessly through the decayed-looking sky which resembled the cracked yellowing varnish of an old painting. I lay in bed reading those tales of science and mystery in which H. G. Wells displays the feverish poetry of an inspired though literal-minded man: stories of the one-eyed man in the Country of the Blind, of termagant ants attacking a band of human explorers, of a man cast into a huge furnace of an iron foundry – forebodings of the nightmares of contemporary science. Suddenly one of these stories seemed to open out on to a terrifying reality. The room in which I lay had expanded enormously, so that arched mouldings in the walls close to the ceiling became great openings leading into naves of a Roman bath or a Gothic cathedral. I was simply lost in this uncontrollable immensity of the room ever growing larger and more comfortless. But also I was in the world of my grandmother, mourning for ever over the wrongs of humanity, and I imagined that she came to visit me here (though afterwards I learnt she had not been permitted to do so). With her imagined form beside me, I experienced a vision. Now I entered a world which was no longer that of H. G. Wells, but of Blake's illustrations to Milton's *Paradise Lost*. I travelled an immense journey through darkness inhabited by the beautiful figures, innocuous in their incandescent nudity, neither male nor female, of Blake's angels. At last I came to an arching of the sky which contained a brilliant light, and I knew that this was a shadow cast by the unseeable light of God.

My father's dying seems merged into this dreamlike period of alternating health and illness. He himself was unaccountably ill. The doctors thought at first there was something wrong with his teeth, then his feet. At one time he had an inflammation of his eyes, which caused him to have to lie in bed with leeches placed over them. During this period, in my merciless adolescence, I was at times contemptuous, triumphing over him; at times humiliated by his needs; at moments only, sympathetic. He dramatized his illness, as he did everything else, and was apt to add weight to his utterances by prefacing them with: 'These are the words of a dying man.' Because he had difficulty in bending down, he used sometimes to make me tie and untie his shoes. This seemed to me a symbol of subservience. But once, when we were in a taxi going to a tea party, I noticed that there was a rust-coloured froth of saliva on his lips, and I very gently wiped his mouth.

At last an X-ray photograph revealed that he had an internal growth necessitating a major operation. Before he had this operation he took me with him for a walk in Kew Gardens. It was a beautiful day of early spring, with buds of green leaves and blossom gleaming like brittle glass in a milk-white misty air suffused with a kind of singing light. It seems to me that we walked through the gardens,

18

saying little, as though in a trance. But during that walk an understanding seemed to have been reached between us that he had to die. He gave me later an envelope in which were ten one pound notes (more money than I had ever had at any time before) and told me to go away on a walking tour with my school friend, Maurice Cornforth. Cornforth and I walked on Dartmoor. I told him that we must aim to arrive at a certain post office on a certain day, in order that I might receive the telegram to say that my father was dead. This amazed him, as neither of us had any reason to think that the operation would prove fatal.

The walking tour was through the country near Dartmoor. There were the woods with the drops of pure sunlight filtering through high up rustling boughs, falling on to streams below, which rippled above brown stones, slate and roots. We came to a hillside covered with turf and ferns, through whose green the pinkish baked clay earth showed. As though precipitating all its grass and flowers into the water, the cliffless field fell down to the great plain of the sea, flat and steely, engraved with lines as though by keels and winds as sharp as diamonds across glass. Far out on this sea one motor-boat chugged and filled the morning with a spreading flower of sound.

I carried Shakespeare's sonnets in my pocket. Cornforth explained to me the importance of Buddhism, and shouted at the huge mongrel which accompanied him on all his hikes. We were both traversing crises in our adolescence. We made frightful confessions to one another which left me shaken, as though with sobbing. All this was completely absorbing, a passionate mingling of beauty and wickedness and nature and world, in which I plunged my intensified living while my father was dying. But the telegram arrived, and I took the train home. I was in such a calm, equable mood when I reached Paddington that my godfather, who met me, thought I could not have understood the significance of the telegram. When I said that I realized that my father was dead, he was shocked.

The feeling that the death of my father was arranged at a time when his life had become intolerable to us did not leave me. I went home at once, prepared to begin a new and freer life. Yet perhaps I was more shocked than I realized, or perhaps the shock was distributed over a long period, previous to and following his death, for soon after this I underwent the worst of the succession of my illnesses, rheumatic fever. This caused me to be almost completely paralysed in both legs for some weeks. The illness was in its own way a revelation: not the least in showing me that to the person who is paralysed it is a miracle to be able to walk. I used to lie in bed looking out of my window up the hill of red-brick Frognal, and wondering how people walked, and still more why those who were able to do so were not everlastingly grateful simply that they could put one foot in front of the other. Another revelation was that I had real friends. For boys from University College School, a few hundred yards from our house, used to come to my room after class and talk and play with me. Most gratifying of all, they used sometimes simply to ignore me and talk with each other, or play with the kitten, while I dozed in bed. They were not bored by me.

The death of both my parents, in the middle of their lives after operations, gave me a sense of death as an almost voluntary act within a tragic family relationship. My father failed to meet the situation in our family after my mother's death. Therefore his death seemed a function of our living. We flourished after it. For example, I myself, when I had recovered from the illness which was surely an epilogue to my relationship with him, proceeded to enjoy perfect health. This has given me a sense of the life-and-death nature of intimate human relationships. It is difficult for me not to believe that people who are involved in one another's lives are not also involved in their deaths. Such a conviction means that intimacy has terrors for me.

After the death of my father I was at a troubled period of my adolescence. My grandmother's attitude towards my brothers, my sister and myself now changed, just as my father's had after the death of my mother. She became conscious of the necessity of carrying out my father's wishes. She anxiously consulted other people as to how she should treat us. Her purpose was to protect us from temptations and physical dangers by supervising as much as possible of our time.

In order to carry out this policy, my grandmother had the assistance of friends who observed our actions. She always saw a great number of people and she would cross-examine these as to whether they had seen any of her grandchildren. Her lame ducks – ladies dressed in clothes, every stitch of which, including stockings and hats, seemed to have been knitted by themselves of the same muddy wool – were a hydra-headed all-pervading tribe who provided information. My grandmother showed her power of surveillance by introducing into her conversation sentences such as this: 'Dear boy, I hear last week you were at Kew Gardens. Why, oh why, didn't you tell me you were going there? Of course, I don't mind you going where you want the least little bit. But why do you young people never tell me anything?'

We went for a holiday in Switzerland, and my grandmother's great energy, at her advanced age, equated with my reduced energy after my illness. This meant that I was never out of her sight for a moment. She accompanied me on every walk, trailing after me in her black dress and carrying a black umbrella instead of a sunshade. She never seemed to tire of asking me questions about my philosophy of life, my plans for reforming the world, my literary projects and my personal relationships. A good meal of the kind that Swiss hotels provide was anathema to her, and if ever we happened to be in the hotel lounge when the luncheon bell went she would announce that it would be more pleasant to eat some rolls which she had saved from breakfast, in the hotel garden. Soon, instead of wanting to tell her everything, I began to fear that there was nothing I could hide from her.

My grandmother's closest control of us was through two sisters, Bertha and Ella, who ran our lives in the Hampstead house. Berthella, as they were compositely called by my mother, who had a talent for nomenclature, had been with us ever since our childhood in Sheringham. Even before they were with us I remember them. For when we lived in Sheringham they were employed by a family called the Henekers. While we were playing on the beach with our buckets and spades, they would sit on a bench on the sea wall against the cliffs and the grey wall of sky, like two birds on a spray, nodding, and watching us with their bright eyes. Ella was mild and patient, smiling always with an air of waiting. Bertha, her elder sister, was reckless and opinionated, a leader and example and judge.

Ella indeed had something saintly about her which we mocked a little as we grew older, but which we could not but admire and revere.

She lost her fiancé in the war (my mother wrote a poem called *To Ella with a Hairbrush* about this). Several years later she told no one of her engagement to the postman who delivered the evening letters along our street in Hampstead, not wishing to leave us when we still needed her, and still less wishing to leave Bertha working for us alone. With suffering, overwork and illness, her sweetness acquired a passive, disappointed, slightly martyred air, and it was this at which we smiled. She hardly ever answered a rudeness, and if we offended her, she went about the house quietly with what we called her 'pursed lips' look. But however inconsiderate we had been to her at evening, she always called us cheerfully in the morning, drawing back the curtains with a clatter and calling out: 'Wake up! It's a lovely day!' 'Oh, but it's raining, Ella', or 'foggy', one of us might say. 'Never mind. Rain before seven, clear before eleven,' she would answer, because she could not believe that a morning would not resolve itself in sunshine. If we failed to wake up at once she would recite some lines of a poet who perhaps attracted her because she had the same first name – I mean Ella Wheeler Wilcox:

> 'Rise, for the day is passing,
> And you lie sleeping on.
> The others have girded their armour
> And forth to the fight have gone!'

Two people could scarcely have been more different than these sisters, who were yet strangely one in their devotion to each other, their warm-heartedness and their care for us. They seemed most one when, for example, the cat died, and they went about the house with tears streaming down their faces. That is to say, they wept when we were at an age when such things could make us weep also. As we grew older, they in some way grew with us and no longer mourned so over the loss of dogs and cats, puppies and kittens.

In other ways their reactions were quite different. When I was determined to be a painter, Ella consented to be my model for hours on end, and when I showed her the murderous caricature, with a great vermilion slash like blood across her neck which I produced, she smiled and said she thought the nose and the chin were very like. But when I showed Bertha my best efforts she looked at them sourly and then said: 'Tell me what you want me to say, Stephen, and I'll say it.'

Again, if Ella and I quarrelled and then in a mood of penitence I tried to atone to her, her reproaches dissolved at once and turned to kindness. But Bertha felt that attempts at reconciliations were a bribe. Once, after a terrible row (for sometimes we staged passionate rebellions against the Berthella régime), I bought Bertha a present which I thought would particularly please her. It was very much in her style: a 'girdle' made of wooden beads to fasten round her waist. But when I gave it to her she tore it up with a passionate gesture, throwing the two hundred or so beads across the kitchen floor.

Bertha was the dominating sister of the two, and was in fact an intellectual woman who, in different circumstances, might have become a Member of Parliament or head of some institution, or perhaps a lady novelist. She read Dickens, Thomas Hardy, Galsworthy, Wells, and Bennett in my father's library. She told stories of her own childhood and youth and experiences 'in service'. When we had the wireless, she listened to the symphonies of Beethoven and would speak with tears in her eyes of some passage, like 'human speaking voices' when the flutes replied to the violins. She went to a performance of *Othello* and came home saying how true it was about the 'green-eyed monster jealousy'. She reviled snobbery, but at the same time she regarded Socialism as affectation. She took her political opinions from the *Daily Mail*. She was outspoken, and spiced her conversation with anecdotes of slips of her tongue which 'popped out without her knowing it' when she told someone some bitter home truth. 'I could have bit my tongue off, but you know Bertha,' would be the finish of a story deeply humiliating to a third person in which she had got off with a triumphant example of one of her 'accidents done on purpose'.

Berthella slaved for us over a period of about fifteen years. They were so completely part of the family that they did not care for holidays. To them we were 'home' and they made 'home' for us. If other domestics were introduced into the household to help, they soon floated away on a flood of tears produced by some verbal tripping up of Bertha's tongue.

Ella was our companion on our walks, on buses, in the tube, for we were hardly ever allowed to go out unaccompanied. She was patient and mild, but in the background was Bertha, with her strong views, her racy conversation, her moods. The combination of the two sisters added up to what we called 'the Berthella point of view'. The virtues of this were that work and loyalty and gratitude were all-important. More dubious was an insistence on the superlative value of cleanliness, physical and moral. Berthella hated houses which had twisting corridors and unexpected corners, because such dwellings were 'harbourers of dust'. They liked the plain, the solid, the sensible. And so with people who visited us. They had an unfailing eye for unwashed ears, and a darkness round the necks of friends which they said was not just produced by shadow. They considered nearly everyone we knew to be dirty, physically or morally, and perhaps both. The very names of some of our best friends caused Berthella to look pained and purse their lips. They were suspicious of physical beauty in people as in architecture, for somewhat similar reasons. A man who married a pretty woman was a fool who had fallen into a trap. Bertha had a deep contempt for nearly all other women, whom she considered as a kind of spiders weaving webs for men, stupid flies. 'Well, she's got her man,' was her frequent comment on the happy ending of romance.

They had no tolerance for petty ailments. One was either ill or not ill, and that was that. Everything between definite illness, registered with a doctor and treated with proper respect, and good health was 'imagination'. They had a contempt for imagination in all its aspects. When Humphrey remarked once that he had a headache, Bertha said acidly: 'We all have headaches in the kitchen.'

We were somewhat intimidated by Berthella. Unless I was in some desperate predicament, or suffering from a certified illness (in which case they became angels of mercy), to ring a bell for one of them seemed *lèse-majesté*. Gradually we got into the habit of going into the kitchen, knocking at the door, and asking politely for what we wanted. In a late, rather Byzantine stage of their régime, after my father died, we had a bell fixed at the bottom of the well of the stairs which rang upstairs when one of them wanted any of us.

Berthella's almost absolute control over us did not extend to my

24

brother Michael, who had managed at a very early age to establish a legend that he was independent of all rules applying to his sister and brothers. They accompanied the rest of us everywhere, and paid out of the household accounts for everything, so that it was not necessary for us to have any cash except sixpence a week pocket money. At a later time, when we went out alone, they would sit up all night waiting for us, rather than let us have latch-keys. My grandmother telephoned to them every evening. But they imposed a censorship on what they told her.

After the death of my father, my grandmother decided that, now we had no parents, we (in particular Christine) should have some companion in the house apart from Berthella. She was at a loss to know who would be suitable, but one day the thought popped into her mind: 'If I had died when my own darling children were young, there is no one in the world whom I would have so wished to look after them as dear Helen. . . .' 'Dear Helen' was Miss Helen Alington. Unfortunately, though, being a contemporary of my grandmother, Helen Alington was now well over seventy. Although my grandmother always insisted that to be seventy was not to be old, nevertheless she did think that my sister should have someone a little nearer her own age as companion. Then she remembered that Helen Alington had a niece called Caroline. She had only known Caroline as a little girl, but so great was her confidence in some hereditary virtue of the Alingtons which qualified them to look after her grandchildren, that she promptly wrote to Caroline.

Subsequently Caroline described to me the circumstances of her arrival at our house in Hampstead. The next two pages are paraphrased from this description. The contents of my grandmother's letter, which she received when she was working at a temporary job in Lausanne, completely baffled her. However, she was intrigued by the account of Michael, aged nineteen, who had just got a scholarship to Balliol, Christine, eighteen, who was studying at a domestic science college, Stephen, seventeen, and Humphrey, sixteen, both still at school.

Caroline returned to London, and after a few days met Mrs. Schuster by appointment at the Piccadilly Circus Underground. Mrs. Schuster escorted her to 10 Frognal, explaining en route: 'Michael is very clever, oh, so clever; Christine is a sweet girl, but oh, so shy; Stephen is a dear and writes the most lovely poetry; and Humphrey is so charming. The two maids, Bertha and Ella, known as Berthella, are wonderful people: Bertha does all the housekeeping and organizes everything and Ella nurses the children simply beautifully when they are ill. . . .'

They reached the house and the door was opened by Ella, who greeted them with a most friendly smile. (Caroline noted that it was an ugly house in the Hampstead style, as if built from the box of bricks of a nineteenth-century German child. It was surmounted by an abortive tower at one corner, to vary the regularity of the roof. There was a stone-tiled hall, long and high, out of which doors led to a dining-room containing massive furniture, and to Harold Spender's book-lined study, which had a roll-top desk. Upstairs was a drawing-room, painted grey, and furnished in a style reminiscent of Mrs. Spender's *art nouveau* phase. Above this there was a floor which contained several bedrooms.)

Caroline was introduced to Christine, who was 'almost ill with apprehension and shyness', and to Stephen, 'who gave her the limpest of handshakes'. They went in to tea and Mrs. Schuster destroyed whatever was left of Christine's self-control by saying: 'Of course you must pour out tea, dear Christine, and don't drop the cups, and, oh, be careful, you're spilling the milk', etc.

Mrs. Schuster soon got up and went home and Caroline was left alone with Christine, almost in tears, and a 'bored Stephen'. Very soon Stephen murmured something about fetching a book from the library and vanished to put on his coat. The coat was never put on, for out of the kitchen rushed Ella, saying: 'No, you don't, sugar, you don't go out with your cold.' Caroline, who had not noticed that he had one, was impressed: still more to see that he really hung up his coat again.

After supper there was a game of cards. Then suddenly Stephen, as if he could keep silence no longer, began: 'When we played this game at Aunt May's . . .' and proceeded to give such an absurd account of Aunt May and her game that everyone started laughing, and Caroline felt that she would take the job.

The lines on which the house were run Caroline found fantastic.

Mrs. Schuster telephoned her orders every morning from her flat in Kensington not to Caroline but to Berthella, and every evening Berthella phoned back to her a detailed report of the day's events.

Every Sunday, Caroline walked with Christine and Stephen across Kensington Gardens to take lunch and tea with Mrs. Schuster, when they were subjected to a cross-examination of all their doings.

Michael was at Oxford and Humphrey at boarding school, so that Christine and Stephen were alone with Caroline during the first few weeks.

After a short time, my sister and I began to like Caroline with an intensity which was perhaps rather dangerous. She was sensitive and sensible and cultivated and kind. She was perhaps the first person we had known who treated us as reasonable human beings and who did not act towards us in order to carry out the supposed wishes of my father, or my mother, or my grandmother. With her we escaped from the atmosphere of moral compulsiveness, which my grandmother had gradually acquired since my father's death and which was certainly part of the 'Berthella point of view'. With her we did not feel guilty.

My sister and I simply fell in love with her. This was most unfortunate for my sister, more painful for Caroline than for me, perhaps. To me this was inevitably a transitional stage, a growth of my interest in other people, which travel and Oxford must soon inevitably develop. To my sister it was a period of agitation which led to disappointment. To Caroline it must have been more than she had bargained for. She had, as it were, acquired a son six months before he went out into the world and became independent.

To state my taste for poetry, painting, and friends at this time was an act of passionate self-revelation. One day, in the fruit garden of a house in Surrey, I told Caroline that I liked Michelangelo and the Elgin Marbles. It was the trembling revelation of a terrifying truth.

Caroline was highly strung and had a strong, almost masculine intelligence. A passion for independence had prevented her ever marrying. She told me once that the idea of sharing a bedroom with a man, night after night, for her whole life was quite intolerable to her. It gave her a sense of claustrophobia. Half-French on her mother's side, she passionately loved France, Italy, the Alps. She did not share my grandmother's enthusiasm for Germany. As at this time I was reacting against my grandmother I reacted against Germany also.

Caroline disliked businessmen and officials. She had a detached almost amoral attitude on sexual subjects. She had a splendid free habit of generalizing about what she did not like. After my uncle, J. A. Spender, who was the legendary 'great man' of the family came to visit us, she sighed: 'A typical businessman,' rather unjustly. Taking up a newspaper, glancing down the columns, she would say: 'Everyone's mad nowadays.'

Caroline had only been with us for six months when it was decided by my grandmother that before going to Oxford I should spend some time abroad to learn a useful language. She wished me to go to Germany. But now, of course, I was set on France. This was to my grandmother a terrible decision. France represented to her the traditional enemy of all our German relations (in so far as she was capable of nationalist feelings she hated the French and blamed them for everything that had miscarried in Europe since the war). Moreover she considered the French to be immoral.

However, soon she remembered the existence of some French Quakers who had belonged to the committee for helping the Viennese. They came from Nantes. She made inquiries and discovered that Nantes, the centre of French Protestantism, was nice and 'quite, quite different' from Paris. Her Quaker friends arranged for me to stay in the house of the Protestant *pasteur* of Nantes and his wife.

There was still the possibility – my grandmother reflected – that on my way to Nantes I might be waylaid by the 'nasty' French, perhaps when I was changing trains in Paris. To obviate this she accompanied me on my journey, taking my brother Humphrey with her.

Nantes was a grey stone provincial town, with a third of its population always dressed in mourning for some far-removed deceased cousin. It seemed as respectable as my grandmother could have wished, but for a very strong local wine which affected drinkers so potently that they lay about the streets near the harbour, completely overcome with it. I remember my grandmother, dressed entirely in black, striding past prostrate drunkards, resolutely ignoring them, as she exclaimed in a firm voice 'how perfectly delightful' – for now that we were at Nantes she was determined to see no ill.

My life with the *pasteur* was sad. He was an unhappy man with an enormous parish. His visits into the Breton countryside were made tormenting for him by the fact that he suffered from hay fever. He sat through meals with tears streaming from his sore, red eyes. Occasionally he would look at me and, out of respect for my love of poetry, recite: '*O pâle étoile de soir. . . .*'

Often tears were streaming from my own eyes also, but for a different reason. I was afflicted by an indescribable anguish of homesickness. I lived at this time for the letters discussing books and art which I received from and wrote to Caroline. I wrote these letters on a table in the *pasteur's* garden among leaves which seemed to stifle me. Sometimes I went for walks on the outskirts of Nantes, along white dusty roads through a factory landscape, until I came to the poignant green reaches of the Loire, a river crossed often by lightly built wooden bridges which vibrated and made a noise like rolling drums when traffic crossed them. I would buy cherries from some toothless old peasant and stuff them furiously into my mouth, or drink wine which made me feel as if I had been struck down by the glaring of the sun on white dust, water and leaves. As I walked in the dangling, lost, isolated way of my adolescence along the dusty roads through the cruelly beautiful foreign landscape, suffering from a homesickness which was the exact opposite of that of Joachim du Bellay for the Loire when he was in London, I would populate the scene with passionate fantasies: of a bare-throated poet, as beautiful as Shelley, approaching me with a book under his arm which he wished to open between us, like the unfolded wings of a bird, as we lay under a hedge. Or of a handsome couple whom I would meet in a copse, of whom the husband would say: 'Monsieur, we have a great sorrow. I cannot give my wife a child. Therefore I implore you to sleep with her behind this hedgerow, then get up and walk out of our lives for ever.' Or I imagined that I met a youth who wished to learn English and to teach me French. We began by naming all the parts of the body, beginning with the head and working downwards: until this anatomy of the bodies entered into the anatomy of the language and became a passionate love-making of French with English.

I attended history classes at the Lycée Clemenceau where the professor was giving a course on the Napoleonic wars. Whenever he had to mention a British victory or defeat, he would turn to me, bow, and apologize for the unpleasant truth which duty obliged him to teach. In front of me the French boys, feverishly living up to my grandmother's idea of them, furtively passed from hand to hand newspaper cuttings about women's complaints and menstruation. In my state of idealist hypocrisy I forgot about my own fantasies and felt unspeakably disgusted.

By sending me to Nantes my grandmother had certainly triumphed. She had cured me of France for a great many years. She had also taught me the important truth that France – outside Paris – is the most bourgeois country in the world. I implored to be sent to some other place. Caroline recommended Lausanne, and the association of the place with her made me wish to go there.

So I was sent to a pension above Lausanne, looking down on the Lake of Geneva. The pension was on the mountainside with a view across the lake to the mountains, which seemed on a hot summer day like coals burning in the azure fire of the lake below them.

Here there was an English boy of my own age, well-bred and ignorant, delicate and uncultivated, beautiful and vapid. He was far from being André Maurois' Shelley, Ariel, but his capacity to dismay me, and mine to shock him, resulted in our feeling a mixture of attraction and repulsion one for the other. In the end I almost loved him, for his beauty, and out of a deep insight into his weaknesses. I discovered how difficult it is to distinguish between love, and a certain kind of sympathetic understanding and forgiveness which seeks vainly in another person for any cause of hatred. Our relationship remained at a stage of mutual frustration and irritation, because we were both afraid.

It was a passion as far as it went. When it was at its most intense I received a letter from Caroline to say that she was gravely ill and must have an operation. This was my first experience of the feeling that I had betrayed my love of one person, by being too deeply involved with another. What distressed me most was to realize that even when I cared most intensely for Caroline I was not released from my obsessive fascination for D——. The surgeon's knife in the flesh of someone I loved could not purify my heart. I longed, though, to leave Lausanne at once and be with Caroline. I suffered for her and was torn with anxiety. Yet my life at Lausanne was the questions, criticisms, confidences and betrayals of D——, who behaved to me like a spoiled favourite towards a mad prince.

By the time I had returned to London Caroline was better. I was already preparing to go to Oxford. New experiences, and the expectation of still newer ones, had weakened the intensity of my relationship with her, which had been the most important one in my life until now.

On the verge of the University, I was intensely self-conscious, guilt-laden, undisciplined, curious, inspired, and naïve. Sometimes, when I walked down a street, I felt as though every eye of every passer-by were a knife twisted in me. I seemed to walk upon pavements of fire and through air of ice. I was held in cages of time which seemed infinite and which I believed never would pass – the time at Nantes, the time at Lausanne, the time it took me to walk down the road when every eye seemed to look mockingly at me.

I hoped always to be received into some smiling and forgiving companionship within which I would effortlessly, without guilt, among loving companions, flower. I imagined that Oxford would be a mixture of the Symposium and the youth of the Renaissance in Florence.

Looking back at myself as I was at the age of nineteen, across a gulf of more than twenty years, it seems to me that my problem was that of the idealist, rather than the innocent. The innocent can retain his purity throughout life, without deceiving himself or being deceived by others. To be innocent, he does not have to believe in a guileless world. But the idealist expects too much from himself and from others. He is like an artist who cannot relate inspiration to form, because the shift from vision to the discipline of form involves him in conscious deliberation – for him, a kind of disillusioning.

Thus in all my attitudes I had already, at the age of nineteen, arrived at a point where fulfilment seemed only possible through compromise, and compromise meant self-betrayal. In love, I wished for a transcendence of physical desire, an escape from the real. In politics, I wished for a social revolution which would achieve justice without introducing new injustices into the methods used to make the revolution. In poetry, I wished to achieve a purely inspirational kind of writing which rejected the modern life of day-to-day living.

I could not forsake any of my ideals without loss. The cure for my idealism was to accept loss, and plunge myself in living, in the hope that after a period of aberration I could recover integrity of purpose, based, though, on an acceptance and not a rejection of reality.

II

OXFORD was not as I had imagined it would be: I soon discovered that I was a new boy among public-school boys, who thought that not to come from a public school was as ridiculous as to be a foreigner. To them, my interest in poetry, painting and music, lack of interest in games, and eccentricity in dress and personal appearance, were symptoms of insanity. Prince Radziwill from Poland, Count Czernin from Austria, Bergen Evans, an American Rhodes scholar, and myself were regarded as strange fauna who had wandered out of unpublic-school zoos.

In my humorless adolescence, I was incapable of being interested in my fellow undergraduates just for themselves. I wanted them to be interested in me and in what interested me – in that order. When I found that they cared only for games, drinking and girls, I was disappointed. Worse than this was their intolerance of everyone not like themselves.

I took revenge on them for disappointing me, by becoming self-consciously their opposite. I became affected, wore a red tie, cultivated friends outside the college, was unpatriotic, declared myself a pacifist and a Socialist, a genius. I hung reproductions of paintings by Gauguin, Van Gogh and Paul Klee on my walls. On fine days I used to take a cushion into the quadrangle, and sitting down on it read poetry.

Affectation is an aping of hidden, outrageous qualities which are our real potentialities. I aped my own exhibitionism, effeminacy, rootlessness and lack of discipline.

One day the other freshmen decided that the time had come when they should break up my rooms. They decided this not out of enthusiasm but on principle, because it was the correct thing to do. I was sitting in a chair reading Blake when about a dozen of them trooped in, equipped with buckets and other clanking instruments of room-breakers and throwers-into-rivers. I could not decide on the most suitable way of receiving them, so I went on reading, very conscious of course that I was reading poetry. They were as embarrassed as I. They stood about in an awkward semi-circle. One of them said: 'What's the big idea, Spender?' For reply I read aloud a few lines of Blake. I achieved the result: they simply changed their minds and left the room, shrugging their shoulders as though to indicate that I was too crazy for their treatment.

This scene lacked conviction. I was playing the role of the mad Socialist poet, they that of the tough who breaks up such a man's rooms and throws him into the river.

All we could any of us do was to create a mental vacuum within which our actions seemed affected, even to ourselves. My paintings, my love of poetry, my Socialism, all became empty gestures, and I think their 'heartiness' was equally empty.

I used to wear a scarlet tie. After I had left my rooms on the night of the room-breaking, someone came back and, finding this, cut it into little fragments which he hung over the frames of my Gauguin, Van Gogh and Klee reproductions. Such an action might well have been justified as a protest against what was merely a pose in my political views. For probably most of the ex-public-school boys got to know – in the course of their games, hunting and pub-crawling – more about the workers than I, who found it impossible to overcome my shyness even to the extent of going alone into a pub. All the same, I had an attitude towards the workers different from theirs. They believed in class differences and in the inequality of man as devoutly as they believed in anything, despite their being as little embarrassed with the workers as with one another. I believed that even if there were differences between men, these were not reflected in the arbitrary distinctions of class. They felt unembarrassed with the workers (whom they regarded as stage 'characters'), because they were sure of their own social position. I was embarrassed because I felt guilty.

I may be asked: 'How can you portray the Oxford of your time as a community dominated above all by the consciousness of class? Were there not many working-class students, and even dons of working-class origin?' There were, indeed: but tendencies which ran counter to the public-school snobbishness became either absorbed into it or isolated. Few of the public-school majority of undergraduates had their view of life altered in any way by the presence of the scholars who came from working-class homes.

The power of the University to ignore the proletarianization of European life which was going on everywhere outside it (even within the city of Oxford itself) was reinforced by the hierarchy of colleges. For some colleges were considered by most undergraduates as superior and more characteristic of 'being at Oxford' for those who were there than others. There was a feeling that to be at certain colleges (for example, Keble and Brasenose, in my time) was as though not to be at the University at all. We thought of the University as consisting pre-eminently of New College, Balliol, Magdalen, Christ Church, and a few respected smaller colleges such as Wadham, Corpus Christi and Oriel. Then there were the middling colleges, such as Worcester, Hertford, Queen's, St. Johns and Univ.; and, last, the colleges which simply did not count.

The strongest social tendency of the University was therefore to create a hierarchy, and this hierarchy reflected and supported, on the whole, the idea of the superiority of the students from the best public schools over the others. Thus the University was very far from moving towards the idea of a classless society, and the giving of scholarships to grammar-school boys did not alter this, any more than did the existence of a University Labour Club. In many cases the working-class students were simply the most obscure, most ground-down members of their colleges. They were often so poor, so exhausted by the effort of winning scholarships over a period of many years, so much involved in the long grind of their lives, in which Oxford was only an episode, so little able to meet the public-school boys on equal terms, that they remained secluded in their poverty and their work. If they overcame these difficulties and obtained Fellowships, generally they became absorbed into the Oxford hierarchy.

Money played a decisive part in fixing the boundaries of one's

Oxford career. To have an income of three hundred pounds a year meant that one could take part in most University activities, joining the clubs, playing the games, choosing friends who did not entertain extravagantly and going for walks with them. But to have much less than this was to be excluded at Oxford from Oxford. One of my friends, the brilliant son of very poor Scottish parents, came to Oxford with no money except that which he gained from scholarships. During his first year he had about two hundred pounds. This meant that he could take part in almost no University activities outside the college, could not entertain or be entertained, could not join any clubs, was forced to scrape and save even to go to the cinema. The poor scholarship student at Oxford led a kind of slum life in his college. The very rich student, on the other hand, led an equally segregated life at the other end of the scale.

The social snobbery of the English public-school boys was a revelation to me. One day when I visited my cousin, who had just come up to New College, I found him surrounded by six fellow Etonians, all of them hilarious over an excellent joke. This was to have found on arriving at New College that the senior scholar of their year was the son of the proprietor of the confectionery shop at Eton, a boy called Richard Goodman, whom they had laughed at during their Eton careers. Goodman, who became a close friend of mine, never adjusted himself completely to being the butt of his fellow Etonians who were not his fellow Etonians. He was disconcerted and unsure of himself; and, without my meaning to do so, my influence helped him to despise the one thing he was most sure of: his scholarship.

After the room-breaking episode the attitude of my fellow freshmen towards me altered and I became more or less tolerated. It was as though in an absurd moment a spark of good will had crossed the barrier between us. The next day an undergraduate called Marston (of whom I shall write more) said, 'That was a poor show last night,' with an air of being ashamed. One or two other of the undergraduates who had been there were markedly friendly. Their way of demonstrating affection was to tell me things about themselves which they would not tell one another. It was as though I had involuntarily demonstrated to them that living was more complicated than they realized: and they ran to me with examples from their lives to confirm

36

this. On my side, I began to realize that under their horsey laughs and crude expressions they were more afraid, less happy and confident, and more in need of affection than they appeared to be.

Yet although it was a relief to discover that I could be tolerated by, and like my fellow freshmen, Oxford had not come up to my expectations. Here the ideal of the educated man did not resemble that of Rabelais, or of Castiglione: a man in whom the outdoor world of sport and the indoor world of learning and music and poetry are interwoven, like flesh with spirit, like outer with inner, to accomplish the harmony of a mind and body moving through a world of intelligence and art into a world of nature, like the figure of a horseman in an ancient tapestry. Oxford was not even the Oxford of Ruskin and William Morris, with young men caring for beautiful things, and caring also for social justice, considering themselves trustees of a beautiful and just modern society, the key of which they would hand over to the workers. It was not even the Victorian forum, with puny Gladstones and Asquiths hammering their way to the premiership via the Oxford Union, which was the University of my father's and my uncle's imaginations.

Instead of any of these, it was a place where most undergraduates chose in their own minds to belong either to the category 'hearty' or 'æsthete'. Of these, the overwhelming majority were the hearties, devoting themselves to rowing or rugger, beer-drinking, back-slapping, furtive love affairs, and a dully dutiful attempt to get through their 'schools', and then take some job for which they were not entirely unqualified. Very few of these young men brought any sense of vocation to the problem of what they were to do with their lives.

The hearties despised the æsthetes, and regarded anyone who showed any tendency to interest himself in the arts as an æsthete. At Univ. the two or three college æsthetes were certainly sickly young men. They called one another 'dear' and burned incense in their rooms.

Naturally there were many exceptions in this community. Indeed, since a large proportion of the most promising young men of the English middle class were sent either to Oxford or Cambridge, it was inevitable that little groups of people who were lively and intelligent should spring up every year. Oxford provided a meeting-ground for

37

youthful genius, and that, apart from its vast machinery of learning which was accessible to those who wanted it, was perhaps its most useful function.

At Univ., whoever did not conform to the 'hearty' pattern felt himself exceptional. There were several exceptions amongst men in their second and third years. These sought for support among the freshmen, and soon after my arrival they did me the privilege of 'discovering' me.

One was the half-Russian Alec Grant, a young man with a waxen complexion and an interest in D. H. Lawrence. Another was Archie Campbell, timid and pale, with enormous eyes in the face of an eighteenth-century Scot, a Boswell. Another was an ecstatic philosopher, Sidney Thorp. He had little logic but a passion for Santayana. When he took his finals his examiners were in doubt whether to give him a fourth class for his arguments, or a first for his visionary style. They gave him a first. Drinking much beer, arguing late into the night, I was opened up by the drunken, obscene, witty conversation of my Oxford friends, like a tin by a tin-opener.

Looking back on it, I think the atmosphere at Univ. was very strange and that really it would need a Dostoevsky to describe it. The 'hearty' public-school boys lacked conviction and there was a certain hysteria about their athleticism. One rowing man, who encouraged so many Univ. men to row that at one time six members of the Oxford Eight were from Univ., was impelled to a fanatical athleticism by fear of venereal disease. There were a few brilliant scholars and eccentrically intelligent students, who became in this atmosphere coarse and drunken, as though they would not admit the fineness of their sensibilities. The Master of the College, Sir Michael Sadler, was a famous educationist whose interest in education seemed to stop or to be arrested when it came to governing his own college. He was despised by most members of his own Senior Common Room, because he happened to have a very fine collection of French Impressionist paintings. Univ., known then as 'the pub in the High', was claustrophobic. A student was not well thought of if he had to do with members of other colleges.

During my first year I had a room on the High. At night I was sometimes kept awake by the heavy traffic of the industrial city of

Oxford, which had grown of recent years. The part of the town known as Oxford to members of the University was a little archipelago of colleges, churches, halls and a few old buildings, surrounded by the flooding red-brick tide of industrial Oxford, on which lorries and cars floated like the craft of a new era among Greek islands. This lumbering, roaring traffic of a town, whose existence dons and undergraduates scarcely recognized, gave me a peculiar sense of the impermanence of the Oxonian culture.

In this room I led my artificial existence. I covered reams of paper with ungrammatical incoherent sentences which I imagined to resemble the style of James Joyce in *Ulysses*. I read Shakespeare, the Elizabethans, the Romantics and the Moderns – little else. I used to go for long walks and bicycle rides into the hilly, tree-scattered, river-winding countryside.

I did not study methodically what I was supposed to study for my Schools. At the back of my mind I clung to the idea that I was a creative writer and that what I needed was not study nor discipline but experience of life. Whatever presented a difficulty or could not be immediately grasped or understood seemed to me an intrusion of dead, rigid, and indigestible material on my sensibility. I feared that if I studied the things which interested me along the lines laid down by the University, my interest in them would become academic. Thus instead of studying English in which I might have excelled, I entered the Schools firstly of History, then of Politics, Philosophy and Economics. History oppressed me with its facts and dates which so easily obscure its lines of development. Politics, Philosophy and Economics made demands on me of sustained, abstract, logical thinking, of which I was incapable, and also afraid, for the reasons I have stated.

I do not know whether it is usual to teach philosophy as I was taught it. In the first lesson we were told that J. S. Mill's *Utilitarianism* meant the greatest happiness of the greatest number and that, for Mill, happiness was the criterion of moral value. In the next tutorial we were told that Mill was wrong because he had forced himself into the position where, according to his criterion, a very happy pig might be considered morally better than a moderately happy human being. Obviously this was outrageous. Mill himself realized that it was unthinkable; accordingly he introduced standards

39

of higher and lower kinds of happiness into his philosophy. Here he was caught out, because, if you talk of a higher happiness, your criterion which qualifies happiness is not happiness but something else. Next please. The next philosopher is Locke. We were told what he thought and then why he was wrong. Next please. Hume. Hume was wrong also. Then Kant. Kant was wrong, but he was also so difficult to understand that one could not be so sure of catching him out.

This might be described as the Obstacle Race way of teaching philosophy. The whole field of human thought is set out with logical obstructions and the students watch the philosophers race around it. Some of them get further than others but they all fall sooner or later into the traps which language sets for them. It soon occurred to me that it was useless to enter a field where such distinguished contestants had failed.

If I had been clever or wise (I was neither) I would have done what W. H. Auden did: decide clearly in my own mind what to take and what to reject of Oxford. Auden regarded the University as a convenient hotel where he stayed and was able to read books and entertain his friends. But I had neither his sense of objectivity nor his vigorous independence of spirit. My temperamental aversion from any kind of discipline was increased by dread of this particular Oxford discipline.

I was dominated by emotions. These were so strong that they overwhelmed any impulse to think clearly, to plan a way of life or even a piece of work. I was confused, yet the forces within my confusion were so pressing, driving me from person to person, poem to poem, that out of my confusion I acquired experience: and through experience I was sometimes able to see beyond my confusion.

Oxford was in some ways for me a period of my life having little connection with what went before or after it. There was a sense of unreality, of living in a vacuum. I found soon that there were other students who felt that, apart from their academic work, nothing which they did could possibly have any value outside Oxford. It was all labelled 'undergraduate' and therefore not to be taken seriously.

One of my friends, Tristan, the son of a philosophy don, felt this strongly. He and I used to go for long walks, during which he expounded his views: 'We're just little piddling undergraduates and everything we do or feel is without any importance. If we write, we write undergraduate stuff; if we fall in love, we're just undergraduates in love. Whatever we do or think has been done or thought by under-graduates hundreds of times before through hundreds of years. What's so nice about you is that you're so naïve, Stephen,' he would wind up affectionately, grasping my arm with a grip which seemed to put me in my place, very finally. He laughed, looking at me sadly out of his grey eyes in their big, sad, pale sockets.

My relationship with Tristan was of a tormenting and English kind – he liked me on condition that he might despise me. Occasion-ally, as a concession, he would admit that he knew of a few under-graduates – W. H. Auden, Dick Crossman, Rex Warner – who really were exceptional. 'You'd better not meet them,' he'd say. 'They wouldn't understand you; they'd think you embarrassing. But what I like about you is that I feel you're like me. We aren't clever, we aren't brilliant, we're just ourselves, and we know we're just little undergraduates.'

I realized from the sorrowful look on Tristan's face that if I said that I did not accept this view of myself I would be making an out-cast of him. For some reason, what I could give him was an ordinary warmth which he divined under my pretensions. So I clung to my belief in myself but kept it a secret from him. After all, in a way he was right, because my 'extraordinariness', if I had it, did not lie in my being exceptionally clever or even gifted. It lay in a strong grasp of my uniqueness in time and space, in my simplicity. I was aware that I was different from everyone else in the same sense in which everyone is different from everyone else.

Tristan's fears expressed, though, my own fear of entering too fully into the life of the University. I would rather be nothing and know nothing than be so impressed by Oxford attitudes that I should come to think of myself simply as an expression of any of them. His special kind of melancholy, with which he punished me, was that he did not feel real at all. He and I, he said, were unreal because we were 'little intellectuals' who cared about experiences at second hand through books and art rather than directly through contact with 'life'. He would argue that the 'hearties', the athletes, were 'real' because when they rowed or kicked footballs around they 'became

41

in their minds that which they did with their bodies': thus they lost the self-consciousness which was the reason for our being 'unreal'. Tristan would turn on me during a walk and say: 'You never look at anything. You don't become a tree or a field when you are in the country. You just go on thinking your own thoughts while you are absorbed in your inner world. Or else, when you do look at something, it becomes a description of itself in your mind. Now when Dick Crossman goes into the country, he climbs a tree and spits into the wind. Dick is always at one with nature.' We thought that perhaps being a working man, or perhaps even making love with a prostitute, was to be *real*. We wanted to write poetry, we wanted to believe, we wanted to love, we wanted to live without excuse or evasion, and we felt that the power to do these things was taken from us.

If we put the problem of being real to the students of philosophy, they answered: 'What do you mean by "real"? Why do you consider that it is realer to participate in one activity than another? Why is it realer to be a worker than to be an undergraduate? Surely there is nothing realer about living with your body than with your mind? And it is just as "real" to think as to act', etc. These considerations persuaded us that perhaps we should dismiss the word 'real' from our vocabulary, but they did not remove our uneasiness.

It was perhaps symptomatic of Oxonian jealousy at the very suggestion of a reality not included in the curriculum of the Schools, that nothing infuriated my tutor more than mention of a 'subconscious' or an 'unconscious' mind. 'If there is an *unconscious*, how can I know unless I am conscious of it, and if I am conscious of it how can it be unconscious? Read Broad on this,' was his answer to Freud. 'Yes, sir,' I dared, 'but what about dreams?' 'Well,' with a pitying smile, 'No doubt there may be parts of my dreams which I do not remember when I am awake. But if I do remember them, then they become conscious.' 'Have you ever read *The Fantasia of the Unconscious* by D. H. Lawrence, sir?' 'Is that the book in which he writes of "the lotus growing out of the navel"?' He pulled his pipe out of his mouth and suddenly gave a brilliant and boyish smile. 'That seems to me *extraordinarily* funny: *the lotus growing out of the navel.*' Then he chuckled to himself for a few moments, rather ostentatiously, I thought.

We were earnest, solemn, self-dramatizing; but however much we wished to be so, it seemed impossible for us to be *serious*, because Oxford, by cutting away the connections of activity within ourselves with the world outside, had deprived us of the convincing sense of our own identity outside Oxford. The greatest achievements of the best Oxford minds filled me with admiration coupled with a certain dismay. During my last year as an undergraduate a poem was published which was the supreme product of an Oxford poet in this century: Robert Bridges' *The Testament of Beauty*. In this poem great powers of invention have been used to create a new style which yet seems archaic. A sensuous contemplation of nature produces the effect of the poet having a platonic love affair with the country round Boars Hill. The thought, created in crystalline language, resembles the most high-minded Senior Common Room conversation or a brilliant paper written on æsthetics for Greats. If one compares Bridges with writers such as Hopkins, Joyce or D. H. Lawrence, one sees the petrifying effects of an isolated culture which has too little communication with any life outside that of the University.

* * * * *

Through my brother Michael, I knew a group of undergraduate scientists who were his contemporaries at Balliol.

My brother was a physicist studying engineering. At the extremely early age at which people make the most fateful decisions, Michael had decided that efficiency and definiteness were values providing a strong, factual path away from the emotional disturbances of my mother, the imprecision and rhetoric of my father. This attitude gained him an ascendancy in our family life which I have already indicated. At an early age he succeeded in persuading my parents that he had reduced the 'margin of error' in his activities to a minimum. He could be relied on to be punctual, exact and capable in all circumstances. Already at the age of nine he had established his independence, and was given freedoms withheld from us until we were sixteen or seventeen. He achieved this somewhat at our expense, emphasizing his own 'efficiency' and our 'inefficiency'. Occasionally he produced withering scientific *mots* from his vocabulary of the laboratory. At home, we had one of those rotating

43

servers in the centre of the table which is called a dumb-waiter. My youngest brother Humphrey, turning this too rapidly, caused a jam-pot to fly off. 'What made that happen?' he asked. 'Centripetal energy,' said my father. 'On the contrary,' said Michael, 'centrifugal action due to lack of centripetal force.' I was very tall. One morning, when I came down to breakfast, Michael looked closely at my ankles and said: 'Of course Stephen could be expected to wear socks with vertical stripes which emphasize his verticality, rather than horizontal ones to subdue it.' When I was thirteen, he analysed a spot of my blood and gravely announced that it must be classified in a very inferior category. A year later he produced an even more depressing report on my skull, which, he declared, reverted to the Neanderthal.

Perhaps my brother, wielding his scientific bludgeons, showed more humour than we realized. He seemed rather lacking in humour. On one occasion he certainly astonished my Uncle Alfred, J. A. Spender, with a surprising come-back. My uncle has been portrayed by Sir Osbert Sitwell, 'with, enwrapping him, a spiritual aura of soft white wool that matched his hair'.* His hair might also be said to resemble a moss. Uncle Alfred had been brought in by my grand-mother to reason with us, and he was saying sententiously: 'You young people, like all the Spenders, are rolling stones,' when my brother Michael, staring intently at Uncle Alfred's hair, said: 'Well, at any rate, rolling stones gather no moss.'

Michael, being convinced that he was always making advances in acquiring information, took no interest in his own past, which to him consisted of developments which had been superseded by more ad-vanced ones. Years after the time of which I am writing, he spent some weeks in being psychoanalysed. He found that he could remember little of his childhood, which he wholly despised and had set his back on. So he persuaded the analyst (who was a Jungian) to agree to the unusual arrangement that I should attend an hour of his analysis to remember his childhood for him. This I did. In the course of the hour I discovered that Michael, for as long as he could remember, had dismissed our parents from his mind as 'totally incompetent'. After this he had given them as little thought as possible. The analyst inquired of him what his attitude to me had been, and I told about

* *Laughter in the Next Room*, Osbert Sitwell (Macmillan and Co.)

44

his analyses of my skull and blood. He then asked Michael whether he might not perhaps have been envious when he analysed my anatomy so unfavourably. Michael said no: rather to my surprise, he remembered the incidents, which he considered examples of objective judgment. He said that he could not remember ever having held a subjective opinion. The analyst then invited Michael to draw my skull as it had been when I was fifteen. Without hesitation Michael drew a monstrosity. For he genuinely believed that he moved from objective phase to objective phase, and that he was incapable of subjectivity.

There was certainly rivalry between us, but perhaps he was right in saying that, on his side, he was not motivated by envy. It must have seemed to him that he had saved himself from the confused emotions of our home life by the strongest measures of self-discipline and self-defence. He had gained his own freedom and become respected at school and home for his competence, reliability and brilliance in examinations. His first intellectual decision – having in his personal life an importance corresponding to that of the discovery of the wheel or of fire in the history of the human race – was that everyone at home was 'inefficient'. His whole system was built up on this rejection of us: not only his wonderfully salvaged, shining cleverness, but also what he called his 'scientific attitude', which consisted of the belief that reason, competent work and effective instruments were the answer to every problem.

Therefore the emergence of any of us from the gloomy chaos of unreason and emotional despair into which Michael (no doubt unconsciously inspired to some extent by his name of leader of the hosts of warring angels) had hurled us, disturbed the radiant order of his array of scientific facts. His feelings when I crawled out of the family abyss, bearing my first volume of poems, must have resembled those of God when he discerned Satan emerging from the bottomless pit. For of all our family, I was the one who most strikingly represented irrationality to him.

Our first nanny related a story which illustrates vividly the earliest relationship of Michael and me. When we were aged he five and I three, apparently I was always victorious in our nursery brawls. But one day, when Michael lay recumbent under my puny feet, nanny said: 'Get up, Michael, and knock Stephen down' – which Michael promptly did. And for ever after this, to the joy of nanny and all her successors, he always did.

Possibly this was Michael's initial victory in his struggle for independence – in a way, perhaps the most decisive victory of his life. From now on he required of me that I should play a mythological rôle in his world of pure reason. He wanted me to be the Caliban to his Prospero, not because he envied me, but since, because I represented certain subjective attitudes, I served his scientifically rational universe by playing this grotesque part.

That Michael was by no means merely envious, is confirmed also by the fact that when we were at Oxford, and afterwards, he began to realize that he must take account of my position and relate it to his own, disturbing as it was to him to do so. He took the line that poetry was an achievement of a kind which he had not happened to explore but in which it was quite possible to be 'competent'. So he was prepared to respect me for a sudden burst of efficiency in this field. When I had published one or two volumes and a few articles, he said to me one day: 'Of course, if I wrote a book it would have a far greater effect than any of yours.' This remark did not offend me, or even seem conceited. Indeed, I was touched by it, because that he made it at all was an act of recognition and of confidence. Moreover it was true that if ever he had written the volume he planned, of speculations of an explorer, about his experiences in Greenland, the Himalayas and on the Great Barrier Reef, it would have been very remarkable. He wrote well, and he had wonderful material for such a book.

All the same there was a side of life from which Michael, with his faith in 'science', had put himself out of touch. Often he seemed to me like a person who had neglected to develop one of his faculties, until at last he arrived at a stage when he saw that his view of reality would be incomplete and even distorted without just this. What was lacking was awareness of the irrational in life. He suffered from a kind of spiritual astigmatism. But he gradually became more and more conscious of what he lacked, until his suffering itself became a form of spiritual experience.

When he was with other people, Michael sometimes gave me the impression of one who, however talented and brilliant, and however much respected by them for these qualities, did not see something which they were seeing: and they stared at his failure to see it. There was that about him which at times was like an object more seen than seeing, or like a blinkered animal, looking narrowly in one direction, but looked at from the blinded sides. He talked in an embarrassed way, as though forcing himself, in what we called his 'pebbly' voice. He sometimes began sentences with the phrase: 'Speaking strictly as a scientist.'

When Michael had realized what was lacking (which was perhaps during his first term at Oxford) his life became a pilgrimage, a search for the Holy Grail of the Unconscious. His relationships with women, as well as his travels, had this character of a search for something primeval. On the first of the expeditions which he undertook, to the Great Barrier Reef, he fell in love with a young woman who was a fellow explorer. The other members of the expedition were surprised when he had a fever which gave him hallucinations about his relationship with her.

He came back from the Himalayas with a profound respect for Tibetan civilization, which he considered superior to the European. In Greenland he admired the Eskimo, perhaps because their way of life seemed to him a perfect fusion of the efficient, which he understood, with the instinctive, for which he was in search. 'An Eskimo can point out a place in the ice, exactly six feet below which you will find, when you have hacked a hole, a fish,' he said, blinking.

In Berlin, when we were sitting at the Romanisches Café, Michael said to me one evening: 'There isn't a girl sitting in this place who hasn't got scars on her wrist where she has cut her veins in an attempt to commit suicide.' This was said in his statistical tone of voice, as though to show that he retained the scientific spirit, but with a look of dazed admiration as though at last he had really found something.

At Oxford, Michael and I made one of those spasmodic attempts to draw closer together which embarrassed us both during certain periods of our relationship. Michael professed an admiration for the poetry of a school friend of his, who was then an undergraduate,

W. H. Auden. 'He's an extremely able technician, and I admire a chap who can do a technical job efficiently,' he said. Michael's face, when he said things like this, had a peculiar, shut-in, almost hunted expression. His eyes were deep-set, and sometimes his suffering spirit in his bony head under his sunk eyes reminded me of a diver deep under the ocean.

Michael's scientific friends were extrovertly masculine: they had a passion for women, combined with an almost complete inability to understand them. To me, the most sympathetic of these was Christopher Bailey, a great, bear-like man of a certain genius. Bailey, with his straight bristly hair more like a hairbrush than like hair, his meaty hands, and his very charming smile, inhabited lodgings which were like an animal's cave. Here he surrounded himself with theses, musical scores, beer bottles and parts of gramophones. He made machines which produced what he called 'high-quality production', spoke of electric pick-ups and sapphire needles before I heard anyone else do so. The commonest word in his vocabulary was 'definitely' which gave an air of romantic precision to everything he said. 'Are you going to town?' someone would ask. 'Yes, quite definitely,' he would answer, scratching his head, and the adverb made the answer sound as exact as a surgical operation.

They researched into life, pretending that their behaviour was an inquiry yielding results, like experiments in laboratories. My brother would say that he had made the experiment last night of drinking several whiskies in rapid succession to see how soon he became intoxicated. 'Oh,' Bailey would say, creasing his brow, 'what quantity did you consume within what space of time?' And then, 'what exact symptoms did you have? A giddiness and a diffused blur, or a sense of exhilaration, or a definite double image?' Once Bailey told me that another friend Y——, who had been in love with a girl called Polly, of whom more later, had weighed himself over the course of some days and had 'quite definitely' lost ten pounds at an average loss of – I forget how much – a day.

The scientists talked about music with an air of complete familiarity with the scores, and with the lives of the composers. Bailey liked nothing better than to get on his huge motor-bike – Boanerges – with a heap of scores on the carrier, get off under some country hedge,

48

and there read Beethoven. The composers seemed to them much like themselves (as perhaps indeed they were), a technical, clever, virile, beer-drinking and coarse-mouthed race.

Bailey treated me with a gentleness which revealed a delicacy in his nature. As a matter of fact, we had been for some terms at Old School House, the junior school of Greshams School, Holt, together, and there once, when I was blinded with misery and tears, at the age of nine, he – being ten – had taken me for a walk and kindly explained to me how a motor-car functioned. The tone of voice in which he said, 'Now, if you were going downhill, would you press down the foot-brake or pull the hand-brake at your side?', in order to cover up my misery with his gentle examination, still showed in the way he spoke to me at Oxford. His ostentatious rudeness could never cover up his good nature. As once, when I had shown him a poem I had just typed out, he handed it back with his kindest smile and said: 'Your typing has definitely improved.'

*   *   *   *   *

My brother, Bailey and Tristan were all roads which led me to, and blocked me from, Auden. Michael and Bailey had been at school with him; Tristan carried on with him some variation of the mildly tormenting and tormented relationship which he had with me. In the snubbing Oxford social atmosphere all these people talked to me of Auden, but none of them wanted us to meet. My brother's relationship with him was in any case slight, and he obviously feared that in producing me he would be playing the weakest card in his hand. Tristan's fears were more complex: his principle in general was to keep all his friends apart. He was afraid of their getting together and pooling, in some way that would be dangerous to him, the thin trickles of relationship, like Chinese tortures dropping water into each separate neurotic heart, which he had carefully established. If all his friends got together, he might be swept away in a torrent. Bailey, who was avuncular and benevolent, regarded meeting Auden as a treat which should be withheld from me until the last possible moment.

All of them told me a good deal about Auden. Bailey said 'just to go into his room and see his books gives me definite symptoms of inferiority.' Tristan said that although Auden was far and away the

49

cleverest man he had ever met, and a creative genius by comparison with whom he and I were just little Oxford intellectuals (for nothing was worse in his vocabulary than an intellectual), he was at heart extremely kind and simple.

When Auden and I did meet it was not, of course, through any of these, but at a luncheon party given by Archie Campbell. Campbell, being a Scot, did not play the Oxford game, which he regarded with a mixture of detachment and amused cynicism. This first meeting appeared to be a humiliating failure. During the greater part of the meal, Auden, after having cast a myopic, clinically appraising glance in my direction, did not address a word to me. When coffee was served, he jerked his head with a gesture which pulled his chin up, and said: 'Who do you think are the best poets writing today?' I answered nervously that I liked the poetry of W——. Auden said: 'If there's anyone who needs kicking in the pants, it's that little ass.' When he left, to my surprise he asked me to come and see him at his room in Christ Church.

Calling on Auden was a serious business. One made an appointment. If one arrived early one was liable to find the heavy outer door of his room, called 'the oak', sported as a sign that he was not to be disturbed. When with him, one was liable to be dismissed suddenly and told the interview was at an end.

On the occasion of my fulfilling my first appointment, he was seated in a darkened room with the curtains drawn, and a lamp on a table at his elbow, so that he could see me clearly and I could only see the light reflected on his pale face. He had almost albino hair and weakly pigmented eyes set closely together, so that they gave the impression of watchfully squinting. He jerked his head up and asked me to sit down. There followed a rather terse cross-examination in which he asked me questions about my life, my views on writing and so on. In all this there was on my side an element of self-betrayal. I tried to please, gave away too much, was not altogether sincere. 'What poets do you like?' he asked again. 'Blunden,' I said. 'Not bad. Who else?' I mentioned another name. 'Up the wrong pole.' Another. 'Written ravishing lines, but has the mind of a ninny.'

He then told me who was good. These included Wilfred Owen, Gerard Manley Hopkins, Edward Thomas, A. E. Housman, and, of course, T. S. Eliot. He had an excellent verbal memory and could recite poems with an intonation which made them seem obscure, and yet significant and memorable. He had the power to make everything sound Audenesque, so that if he said in his icy voice, separating each word from the next as though on pincers, lines of Shakespeare or of Housman, each sounded simply like Auden:

> 'No, I am that I am and they that level
> At my abuses reckon up their own.
> I may be straight, though they themselves be bevel
> And by their faults my faults may not be shown.'

or:

> 'In gross marl, in blowing dust,
> Beneath the drowned ooze of the sea
> Where you would not lie you must
> Lie you must and not with me.'

The poetry which he loved most had this monosyllabic, clipped, clear-cut, icy quality.

He told me that the subject of a poem was only the peg on which to hang the poetry. A poet was a kind of chemist who mixed his poems out of words, whilst remaining detached from his own feelings. Feelings and emotional experiences were only the occasion which precipitated into his mind the idea of a poem. When this had been suggested he arranged words into patterns with a mind whose aim was not to express a feeling, but to concentrate on the best arrangement that could be derived from the occasion.

Auden derided most contemporary poets and admired few beyond those I have mentioned. He thought that the literary scene in general offered an empty stage. 'Evidently they are waiting for Someone,' he said with the air of anticipating that he would soon take the centre of it. However, he did not think of himself as the only writer of the future. He had the strongest sense of looking for colleagues and disciples, not just in poetry but in all the arts. He looked at a still life on the wall and said: 'He will be The Painter.' This was by Robert Medley. His friend Isherwood was to be The Novelist. Chalmers was another of the Gang. Cecil Day Lewis was a colleague. A group of

51

emergent artists existed in his mind, like a cabinet in the mind of a party leader.

At our first meeting he asked me how often I wrote poetry. Without reflecting, I replied that I wrote about four poems a day. He was astonished and exclaimed: 'What energy!' I asked him how often he wrote a poem. He replied: 'I write about one in three weeks.' After this I started writing only one poem in three weeks.

I took to showing Auden my poems. I would arrive with my pockets stuffed with manuscripts and watch him reading them. Occasionally he would grunt. Beyond this his comment was restrained to selecting one line for praise. I showed him a long poem, after reading which he said:

' ' 'In a new land shooting is necessary,' '

is a beautiful line,' and immediately the line entered as it were his own poetic landscape of deserted mines, spies, shootings – terse syllables enclosed within a music like the wind in a deserted shaft.

After I had known him six weeks he must have approved of as many of my lines. Therefore it was rather surprising to discover that he considered me a member of 'the Gang'. Once I told him I wondered whether I ought to write prose, and he answered: 'You must write nothing but poetry, we do not want to lose you for poetry.' This remark produced in me a choking moment of hope mingled with despair, in which I cried: 'But do you really think I am any good?' 'Of course,' he replied frigidly. 'But why?' 'Because you are so infinitely capable of being humiliated. Art is born of humiliation,' he added in his icy voice – and left me wondering when *he* could feel humiliated.

Doubtless Auden influenced me at this time. I absorbed many of his remarks and attitudes, which impressed me even more deeply than I was aware of then. Here I should perhaps repeat that I am writing of a time when I was nineteen, and he not yet twenty-one. Yet his intellectual attitudes were very developed, and he was explicit about them. For my part I had, as I have explained, a reluctance to follow philosophical arguments. I even lacked the vocabulary to understand always what he was saying. That I absorbed so much, while labouring under these disadvantages, goes to show what a hold

Auden had over my mind. But it follows also that when I paraphrase his views, I may have modified them, or even reformulated them, out of what I came to understand later. Conversations I quote consist, however, of phrases little altered which have stuck in my memory.

For his Oxford contemporaries the most impressive thing about Auden undoubtedly was that, at such an early age, he was so confident and conscious a master of his situation. Not only did he hold very definite views about literature, but he also had a philosophy of life which, if juvenile, at least explained to him his own actions and those of his friends. He saw himself – as I then envisaged him – with certain potentialities and talents, certain desires, certain attitudes of mind, living within a community governed by certain rules and traditions, and consisting also of people with different potentialities, desires and attitudes. His aims were to fulfil his potentialities, obtain satisfaction for his desires, and maintain his attitudes, without prejudice and without accepting any authority outside his own judgment. At the same time he avoided coming into unnecessary conflict with the interests and views of those around him. As a youth he was outrageous, but he was not a rebel. His clinical view of living, whereby he regarded life as an operation performed by a surgically minded individual upon the carefully analysed and examined body and soul of the society round him, was amoral. He rejected, quietly and without fuss, the moral views of both his preceptors and his fellow undergraduates. The only generally accepted virtue which he himself accepted was courage: because courage was required by anyone wishing to achieve his own independent development. The extreme edge of his youthful philosophy was that he accepted suicide as the 'right of choice' of an individual who, having failed in what he set out to do, wished to end his game with life.

Self-knowledge, complete lack of inhibition and sense of guilt, and knowledge of others, were essential to the fulfilment of his aims. Unless one knew oneself, one could not know what one wanted and plan to obtain it; guilt and inhibition stood between oneself and the satisfaction of one's needs; knowledge of others was necessary for the purpose of entering realistically into their lives, and fitting one pattern of oneself into a larger psychological pattern of surrounding people.

At this early age, Auden had already an extensive knowledge of the theories of modern psychology, which he used as a means of understanding himself and dominating his friends. His self-knowledge, combined with this key to the understanding of his contemporaries, certainly made his the ruling pattern in his relationship with most of them. He knew what he wanted and he seemed to understand himself, which made him stand out amongst his intelligent but dazed and un-self-knowing friends.

Probably I exaggerate his self-awareness and self-confidence, though I do not, I think, exaggerate the impression he made on others. I assume, though, that no one is quite so sure of himself as the person I have just described. To admit this is perhaps to put a finger on a weakness in his position. For to know oneself and others too well is a form of realism which risks defeating its own ends. The doctor who knows all about us can easily become the person who least knows, because we are intimidated by our awareness of his perception and therefore he does not know us as we are among other people, or alone. Auden, despite his perceptiveness, lacked something in human relationships. He forced issues too much, made everyone too conscious of himself and therefore was in the position of an observer who is a disturbing force in the behaviour he observes. Sometimes he gave the impression of playing an intellectual game with himself and with others, and this meant that in the long run he was rather isolated. His early poetry also gives the impression of an intellectual game – a game to which the name Clinical Detachment might be given. It is a game of impartial objectivity about catastrophes, wars, revolutions, violence, hatreds, loves, and all the forces which move through human lives. But this attitude of the young poet with a bird's-eye view on human calamity in a world of wars and dismantled works runs the risk of becoming facilely inhuman. Auden himself was too human, moreover, for it to be an attitude which he could for long maintain in the face of experiences that wrung his heart. After all, the young poet does become involved, he cannot regard justice and injustice, love and hatred, life and death, with exactly the same impartiality, tracing them with icy precision, like the features of a frozen landscape. But although Auden ceased to be detached, joined movements, wrote love poetry, accepted the Angli-

54

can creed, I am not sure whether he completely broke away from the isolation in human relationships which was simply the result of his overwhelming cleverness as a very young man.

His later work is distinguished from his earlier by the attempt to find answers to what, in the earlier, he is content to state as tremendous questions. In an early, exceptionally autobiographical poem, he describes himself walking with a friend who speaks of injustice; of someone being murdered, of someone else being 'thrown downstairs', and so on; and Auden describes himself listening to this, preserving his attitude of detachment in the face of the account of human injustice 'till I was angry, said I was glad'. It is enough to state behaviour; one must not protest, affirm, hold opinions, try to find an answer. But perhaps this attitude only existed because the young poet was not near enough to the problems stated. For in the next phase an answer is rather promiscuously provided: and this answer is Love. However, the love which is supposed to save both the individual who is aware of his own subconscious depths, and the society which has repented of its evil exploitation – 'the sovereign touch Curing the intolerable neural itch' and which connects 'new styles in architecture' with a 'change of heart' – is too analytic, too adaptable and adjustable to every occasion, too sterilized, too much the love in a psychoanalyst's room. So with the other answers: from psychology to Communism to Christianity; they remain a little arbitrary: and perhaps the root of this arbitrariness is the poet's own isolation. But if Auden's answers, which have been psychoanalysis, political revolution, universal love and Christian dogma, have never quite lost their arbitrary, experimental quality, as though they were repeated attempts to understand the nature of a problem, and to solve it by the arrangement of its elements according to certain hypotheses, nevertheless the problem itself is ever more profoundly understood and brilliantly illustrated. And the problem is Man in this Century. Auden is certainly an intellectual poet: but to say this in a way which would imply that he has only an intellectual grasp of things would be to underestimate him. He has an intellectual understanding of situations which he states with his heart as well as his intellect, and if the solution which he offers to the problem seems intellectualized the problem itself is completely realized.

55

But to return to 1928, when we were together at Oxford.

At our very first meeting there was an incident which demonstrated my ignorance. I told him that I had liked a poem of his which I had read in an Oxford magazine. 'Why did you like it?' he asked. As I had not understood the poem I was at a loss to explain why. I said: 'I like the climatic part,' thinking that the word 'climatic' referred obliquely and mysteriously to the climax. I could imagine Auden himself say that Eliot's *The Waste Land* was 'symptomatically climatic', by which I would have understood him to mean that it was a poem full of a sense of everything coming to a climax in a way characteristic of this epoch. 'What do you mean by "the climatic part"?' he asked curiously. 'I don't remember anything in it about the climate.' Neither did I, so I was silent. Fortunately, though, Auden could drop a subject. He would look down for a moment as though he were registering some impression, and then look up again and talk of something else.

He used a vocabulary containing words drawn from scientific, psychological and philosophical terminology. At the same time he avoided the jargon in which articles by political journalists, economists, psychologists and scientists are usually written. He used these technical words with a certain effect of mysteriousness which communicated itself excitingly, as Milton uses names of heathen gods, with an intellectual awareness of what they signify and yet like a kind of abracadabra.

It is scarcely possible to reproduce passages of conversation which mystified me when they were said twenty years ago. I did not so much listen to Auden's conversation as absorb his tone of voice, his gestures, the attitudes behind the words, until all these became part of my own experience which I now think about. I possess in my library a copy of *Oxford Poetry*, 1927, with an introduction written by him which recalls the matter and manner of his conversation at this time. Here is a paragraph from it:

'A tripartite problem remains, and may be stated thus: (a) The psychological conflict between self as subject and self as object, which is patent in the self-consciousness and emotional stultification resultant from the attempt to synchronize within the individual

56

mind the synthesis and the analysis of experience. Such appears to be the prime development of this century, our experiment in "the emergent evolution of mind". Emotion is no longer necessarily to be analysed by "recollection in tranquillity": it is to be prehended emotionally and intellectually at once. And this is of most importance to the poet: for it is his mind that must bear the brunt of the conflict and may be the first to realize the new harmony which would imply the success of this synchronization.'

This passage shows the abstract nature of Auden's thinking. Basically, I think his grasp of a situation is nearly always abstract. But he combines with this an extraordinary power of creating the images which illustrate the situation contained in the abstraction. Abstractions for him are not deductions and generalizations: they are experiences directly apprehended. He seems to have some sense which reacts to an abstract conclusion as other people do to a sunset or a mountain. Reading a little further in his introduction, the abstract solemn language suddenly acquires a buffoonish, half-absurd, half-serious quality:

'Those who believe that there is anything valuable in our youth as such we have neither the patience to consider nor the power to condone: our youth should be a period of spiritual discipline, not a self-justifying dogma. As for the intelligent reader, we can only remind him, where he experiences distaste, that no universalized system – political, religious or metaphysical – has been bequeathed to us: where pleasure, that it is but an infinitesimal progression towards a new synthesis – one more of those efforts as yet so conspicuous in their paucity.'

The mixture of the austere with the extravagant, the kind of burlesque and self-mockery, the pleasure in abstract phraseology mouthed so as to suggest a kind of incantation, in this passage, recall Auden's conversation. 'So conspicuous in their paucity', I can imagine him saying with an upwards jerking movement of his head. He would hold the vowels between the consonants as though in steel forceps.

Perhaps the passage I have quoted shows more recognition of emotional values than I had allowed for in my account of him. This is true, and may explain what puzzled me, why Auden accepted me and my work.

Indeed, the situation between us as I have described it is simplified. Inevitably Auden must have felt more than I realized. Equally, I was more intellectual than I knew.

Yet the differences between us remained more striking than the resemblances. One difference, in which I did not at all challenge him, was in the altogether superior brilliance of his gifts over mine. This I need not discuss.

What may be valuable to discuss is the difference of our minds. He, in his manner of knowing exactly what he was about, criticized my attitudes. But I did not realize until later that the difference between us was not just of his cleverness and my ignorance: that there were certain of my own positions which I could defend, and that I did have good reasons for rejecting some of his.

One significant difference was the use to which each put his memory. Auden, as I have described, knew much poetry by heart. I knew almost none. The difference here was not just of his good and my bad memory. It was one of our having different attitudes towards remembering. I resisted learning poems by heart, because in recollecting them I did not want to hold them word by word in my mind, in exactly the same form as when I read them. I wanted to remember not the words and the lines, but a line beyond the lines, a sensuous quality which went, as it were, into the lines before they were written by the poet and which remained after I, the reader, had forgotten them. Poetry could thus become in my memory qualities which I could separate from the words themselves. The *feeling* of a poem which I did not completely remember seemed to put me in touch with the poet's mind in a way which the exactly recollected poem itself could not do. In this way, also, I could relate his poetic impulse to my own, because it was no longer tied to words and a form which, belonging to his time and circumstances, could not apply to mine.

The difference of Auden's and my attitude towards memory is, indeed, perhaps the most important difference of all. For memory is the root of creative genius. It enables the poet to connect the immediate moment of perception which is called 'inspiration', with past moments in which he has received like impressions. This relating

58

of the immediate impression with past ones enables the poet, through the moment, to strike a kind of chord across time, made up of notes which are similar impressions felt at different times and connected with one another in a simile within which all are contemporaneous.

The quality of a poet's memory, and the way in which he uses it, are what chiefly distinguishes him from other poets. There are two main categories of memory: one is what might be called overt and conscious memory, the other is hidden and unconscious. Overt and conscious memory is memory of impressions which at the time of their being experienced have been formulated in the mind as ideas. Hidden and unconscious memory is memory of impressions which have not been consciously formulated when they were experienced, so that remembering is like creating them anew, or like experiencing them for the first time.

Auden's kind of remembering was overt. He had at his command at every moment an incredible store of impressions vividly recorded as ideas, which could serve to illustrate some thesis to which they were related. I had a buried memory, and to remember past impressions was for me a more or less involuntary process, whereby some immediate particular experience called into being similar experiences out of the depths of the past.

When Auden said at one of our earliest meetings, 'The subject of a poem is a peg to hang the poetry on,' he had indicated what I gradually realized to be another basic difference between our attitudes. For I could not accept the idea that the poetic experience in reality, which led into a poem, was then, as it were, left behind, while the poem developed according to verbal needs of its own which had no relation to the experience. My poems were all attempts to record, as truthfully as I could, experiences which, within reality, seemed to be poetry. Whenever the poetry, for the purpose of ending satisfactorily a poem, seemed to require something which was not true to my own experience, I abandoned it. For example, I frequently abandoned love poems because I felt that perhaps after all I was exaggerating and not stating the truth about my feelings, or because the person to whom the poem was addressed behaved in some way which seemed inconsistent with my poetry.

To the reader who is not initiated into the controversies of modern

59

poetic schools, it may seem that what I am trying to say here is that my poetry is more 'sincere' than that of other poets. But this – I should warn him – is the most superficial aspect of the problem which my attitude towards poetic truth touches on. What I am really doing is to put myself outside a very general movement amongst modern poets to develop philosophies, embrace creeds, join movements, not because they have arrived at a stage in their personal experience where they are converted, but because they have arrived at a point in their writing where they need a myth, a faith, or some external impulse which takes them beyond the limits of their personal experience. Just as a poet who writes love poetry might find that, for the purposes of realizing his gift, it was necessary for him to invent some idealized lover, so they find at a certain stage of their development that it is necessary to invent a belief in some faith:

> 'Consequently I rejoice
> Having to construct something upon which to rejoice.'

It may be that the poet who, out of a poetic necessity, embraces a lover, or a creed, or a mythology, or even a political movement, creates a truth for himself in his poetry which ultimately becomes true also in his life. His poetry leads back into his life at a point where his life has failed to lead into his poetry. The nature of the faith which he adopts will obviously have a good deal to do with deciding whether or not this is the case. Moreover, the reader's confidence in the 'truth' of the poet's faith will also be influenced by the reader's own beliefs. To a Catholic reader, a poet like Verlaine who introduces Catholicism into his poetry will have discovered the Truth, and therefore the question of whether his lived experience influenced his poetry, or a necessity of his poetry reflected back on his life, will seem irrelevant. But W. B. Yeats, who became a spiritualist attending séances, who dabbled in Indian and neoplatonic philosophies, and who built a structure for his immensely powerful poetry out of a dozen fragments of esoteric beliefs, raises the question of whether much of his thought was not a deliberate artifice constructed for the purposes of creating his poetry. Yet the result was great poetry.

So, in stating my own position, I am stating my limitations, not advertising my poetry as 'sincere'.

60

Auden's life was devoted to an intellectual effort to analyse, explain and dominate his circumstances. Mine was one of complete submission to experience, which I approached with no preconceived theoretic attitudes. I could not, like him, see other people from above, as though their behaviour formed part of a psychological pattern which I could interpret with my knowledge. There was something withdrawn, inaccessible and unexplained to me about the motives of others, which I imagined to be more disinterested, less obsessive and clearer than my own. When I attempted to write about others, it was not in the spirit of illustrating my knowledge of them but of exploring the unknown. I had no confidence in myself as a dominating intellectual force, but a secret and profound belief in myself as someone acted upon by experiences and capable of revealing the truth of my feelings about them. I combined immense faith in myself with immense doubt. In what I created I could be what I was.

*   *   *   *   *

After I had known Auden only a short while, I showed him a manuscript which I thought might amuse him as a psychological document. This was a narrative I had written when I was eighteen years old, immediately after I left the pension at Lausanne. It was an exact account of the relationship I have described with the English boy D——.

When I next went to visit him in his rooms he said: 'This is pure poetry. Listen.' He recited in his flat, expressionless way, which in the reading of words produced somewhat the effect of atonality in music, the following lines:

'His whole life had probably been a pilgrimage to this moment. Or, rather, if not his whole life, one portion of it, divided into sections: little closed-in beads of lust running on a chain of days and weeks through years: till now, that which had been furtive, cried to be let out, would burst its way through.'

The lines stirred me with a peculiar kind of excitement, at the centre of which was recognition, though it was difficult to recognize anything said in Auden's voice. 'Who wrote that?' I asked. 'You did.'

Now when I saw my own creation transformed through the medium of his mind, I felt the pleasure and relief which the writer feels on very rare occasions. The letters are a dance; living signs on the glossy page. They seem capable of being touched by the mind's eye like the ferrule of a stick running along a fence. With the feel of warm blood in his cheeks the writer knows there was a moment when he was justified.

Next day we went for a picnic. Auden told me now that he had changed his mind about my work. I should not write poetry, but autobiographical prose narrative.

He walked very fast on flat feet, with striding angular movements of his arms and legs and jerkings up of his head. Once he had been told by a doctor that he must walk as little as possible, so he immediately began going for thirty-mile walks. He had a theory that the body is controlled by the mind. He would explain a headache, a cold or sore throat in what are now called 'psychosomatic' terms.

We came to the open country, crossed fields and climbed a hill, where we opened our luncheon baskets and ate, lying on the grass. Auden talked about 'the poet'. 'In a revolution, the poet lies on his belly on the top of a roof and shoots across the lines at his best friend who is on a roof-top of the other side . . . of course, at heart, the poet's sympathies are always with the enemy,' he added darkly. '. . . When he is in love the poet always hopes that his loved one will die. He thinks more of the poems which he will write than of the lover . . . the tragic, at its greatest, is always funny: "*enter Lear with Cordelia dead in his arms. Lear: Howl, howl, howl!*" Or that scene in *War and Peace*, where Pierre rushes into the burning building to save a baby and the baby turns and bites him.'

Auden told me that I should drop the 'Shelley stunt'. 'The poet is far more like Mr. Everyman than like Kelley and Sheats. He cuts his hair short, wears spats, a bowler hat, and a pin-stripe city suit. He goes to the job in the bank by the suburban train.'

And so on. . . . Such lectures by one young writer to another, with their mixture of sense and nonsense, fun and portentousness, malice and generosity, compose a secret language among a circle. They are the witches' brew from which a literary movement is made.

This conversation took place on a very fine summer day, which remains in my mind as the most English day of our relationship.

From the field on top of a hill in which we had our picnic, there was a wide view of the undulating countryside. The monumental trees, among green cornfields and dark hedges, were like old, thick, impregnable walls, with fissures and crevices between their dense-leaved boughs, like crannies between massive stones. The landscape seemed polished by innumerable suns rising in the island sky, which seemed to have preserved intact through many centuries such a day as this, where two undergraduates lay in a high field, talking about poetry, as they might have done in Elizabethan times.

Auden came to stay with us at Frognal during the vacation. He was not a great success with Berthella, though Caroline and he became very friendly. I got to know him better, but we never repeated quite the feeling of communion which we achieved during the walk I have just described. The relationship was prevented from developing partly by my own uncritical admiration, which kept me always in the position of being a disciple. Partly also I regarded him as a kind of public entertainer I had hauled into my home, whom I must perpetually applaud. When he was amusing – as happened often – I laughed to the point of hysteria. When he was dull or exhausted, I was dismayed and discouraged. It seemed to me that if Auden was not vital always, when we were together, something terrible must have happened.

At this time Auden had fantastic fads. He was extremely particular about food, grumbled outrageously if everything was not arranged as he wished, sometimes carried a cane and even wore a monocle. Generally he organized the people around him where he stayed to suit his whims, but he kept his hosts in a good humour. He was not witty. His humour was of a buffoonish kind and consisted partly of self-mockery. 'I have a face of putty,' he said, 'I should have been a clown.' Or, 'I have a body designed for vice.' He smoked, ate, and drank cups of tea all in great quantities.

I have always had difficulty in working with concentration. Auden used to shut me in a room and tell me to write. He had a simplicist view of things which did me good. One day when I said I was un-happy he replied: 'You have no reason to be unhappy. You have sufficient money, you are talented and you are in love.' This was a remark made at the right moment. I realized that it was true. Yet twenty years later I can now see that at the age of twenty I had days when I was seriously unhappy because I could not see then that unhappiness, unless it has a permanent physical or economic or psychological cause, is only a mood.

*   *   *   *   *

The particular cause of the unhappiness to which Auden referred was my relationship with an undergraduate, whom in several poems I called Marston. Marston was someone with whom I had few interests in common. He was not talented or intellectual or even strikingly intelligent. What was extraordinary about him was the purity of his ordinariness. In the Oxford world, where even athleticism had to a great extent become self-conscious, here was a person who quite simply was what he was, unaffectedly pursuing his interests in games and flying – for he was already training to be a pilot.

Marston had little consciousness that he was different from the other athletes. But he preserved a certain aloofness towards them. He was like someone islanded within qualities supposedly common to many people but which with him had acquired such a purity that they actually isolated him from everyday life.

I first noticed him – I remember – in the train to Oxford, at the beginning of my second term. He was with a crowd of the other 'hearties', but there was something watchful, withdrawn, in his attitude which made him seem separate from them. Sometimes he smiled to himself with the secret jauntiness of a very modest person who does not realize that his modesty makes him different from the others.

At that moment I made a decision to get to know him, when I quite well might not have done so. There was a moment of pure arbitrariness when I thought: 'I need not do this, but I will do it.' This decision remained like a core of emptiness at the very centre of everything I felt afterwards, however strong the feeling might be.

After this, I chose every opportunity to see Marston. I called on him in his rooms, which he shared with a friend, and I made great efforts to interest myself in his boxing, skiing and flying. I tried to behave like the hearties by whom he was surrounded, because a pretence of heartiness gave me opportunities to behave demonstratively.

All the same, there was something fussy and old-womanish about my pursuit of a person who met my enthusiasm with quiet politeness, and my own behaviour at times repelled me. For I only succeeded in embarrassing and boring him, and I bored even myself with the false relationship I had fabricated between us, kept going by indelicacy on my side, delicacy on his.

The most painful episode of this relationship was a walking tour along the River Wye on which I went with him. I attached great importance to this arrangement which I had planned for many months, inviting him so long before the date of the tour that I knew he could not possibly have a previous arrangement. The tour itself was a depressing failure. I walked by the side of this young man who looked unassuming and yet dazzling. We walked along the river bank in April, through a countryside of low green hills on which the trees had boughs flushed red and chestnut brown, bursting at the ends into flame-like leaves. I soon realized that for him the walking was just walking, so I tried to transform myself into the kind of indifferent companion I imagined he would want for such an occasion. I talked about games and machinery, of both of which I knew nothing. Once I discussed for a whole morning whether razor blades remained sharp or grew blunt if they were left unused. I imagined that a practical topic of this kind would interest him. One morning he felt ill, and at this my attachment took the form of guilty anxiety with which I surrounded him, until he told me not to fuss over him 'like an old hen'. When he said this, I had a grotesque vision of myself fluttering by his side like Charlie Chaplin in *The Gold Rush* when his starving companion imagines Charlie as poultry. I then apologized overwhelmingly. With all my desire to obliterate my own tastes in order to please him, nevertheless I clung to a faint hope that I might convert him to poetry. When we reached Tintern Abbey I explained to him that Wordsworth had written a poem about this scenery. He expressed a mild interest, so while he sat among the ruins, with cloudless eyes set under a forehead of a kind of stony Englishness not so unlike the arched stones of Tintern themselves, I read him Wordsworth.

My only contact with him was really a power gradually to get under his skin, to explore certain vanities and weaknesses, to make him self-conscious. I began to realize that there was potentially something corrupting about this relationship, and secretly I sided with him when he was against me. Soon I gave up all attempt at communication on my own terms, and while I attempted to speak his language in the way I have described, I interpreted also from him secret signs by which I would know whether or not he cared. When we had returned from the walking tour, we travelled from the bus terminal in London to our homes, on the tube. He had to get out at a stop before mine. The sign I had been waiting for was whether or not he would turn round and look at me through the window after he had left the train. He did not do so.

A crisis finally occurred. I decided it was necessary to write him a letter stating my feelings towards him. He was upset but he did not refuse to have anything more to do with me. He wrote back saying that we should meet. When we met he explained that he in no way responded to my emotion. Nevertheless, he said that he would like me to explain matters and make him understand. When I had done so, he looked at me with a dazed expression and said naïvely: 'Do you know, old son, this is the first time you've ever talked with me that I haven't been completely bored?'

I insisted that we should not meet again. However, as we were of the same college, not to do so proved impossible. So now we used to meet at intervals, usually in teashops in Oxford or London, and talk seriously, with a kind of sadness. He used to confide in me at length and with a certain effort all the worrying details of his life: his affairs with girls, his loneliness, his failures in his work, his fears when he boxed or flew. I never knew whether he did this out of a real need to confess, or out of an admirable desire to compensate me for a loss by making me a present of his hidden life. This uncertainty gradually became intolerable. I realized that the relationship could not develop further, and I allowed it to lapse through neglect on my side.

It is easy to say that this friendship was immature. What is more important is that it influenced my life. Immediately after the walking tour I began to write poems different from any others I had done. A concrete situation had suddenly crystallized feelings which until then had been diffused and found no object. A relationship which had thus acquired a significant place in my development continues to exist in my mind now that I have developed beyond it. Thus I often think of this one-sided friendship as being still part of me, side by side with other relationships which came afterwards.

Moreover, the friendship with Marston was one phase of a search for the identification of my own aims with those of another man. For, different as we were, there was a kind of innocence and integrity in him which was present also in my poetry.

I leave it to the reader to apply the psychiatric labels to the various relationships which I have to describe. Yet I have come to wonder whether many contemporaries in labelling themselves do not also condemn themselves to a kind of doom of being that which they consider themselves in the psychological text-book. For example, I suspect that many people feel today that a conception of friendship which can be labelled homosexual, on account of certain of its aspects, excludes normal sexual relationships: and conversely that the heterosexual relationship should preclude those which might be interpreted as homosexual. As a result of this tendency to give themselves labels, people feel forced to make a choice which, in past times, was not made. It also follows that since a relationship of the highest understanding can be between two people of the same sex, some who have experienced this relationship renounce a normal way of life.

Yet when we look into the lives of men and women in the past we see that relationships which today would be labelled abnormal existed side by side with the normal. Men labelled themselves less and adjusted themselves more. Thus Shakespeare's sonnets are today often labelled declarations of a homosexual passion. Many of them certainly do express the love of Shakespeare for a young man. But what does Shakespeare say to his lover? Get married and have a child. It is true that in the middle sonnets (perhaps addressed to another young man) the passion becomes less disinterested, but even here the poet reproaches the young man for stealing the poet's mistress, there is talk of the two men sharing a mistress, and so on. At no point is there the acceptance of the idea of the poet and his

friend belonging to a world of men of a third sex, which is characteristic of much literature in the twentieth century.

So I learned that, although I had to accept certain limitations in
myself, I should try nevertheless to go beyond those qualities which
isolated me from commonly shared human experience, towards the
normal. Here when I use the term 'normal', I mean that which is
generally considered to be so. It is true, of course, that what is
'normal' for the individual is simply to conform with his own
nature. But what I am concerned with here, is adjusting my acceptance of my own nature to the generally held concept of the normal,
though this may be a rarely attained ideal. For individuals judge
themselves normal or abnormal in relation to this standard. A complete inability or refusal to conform with it, is to put oneself outside
a concept which has a saving value of sanity in most people's
minds.

For the artist to feel cut off from this warm flow of the normal
general life, is to cut himself off from what absorbs other people,
perhaps also to place himself too much in the company of those who
feel cut off in the same way. For a writer, such isolation is a grave
disadvantage.

The exception, even while remaining exceptional, and accepting
himself as such, should, as far as is possible to his nature, enter into
a whole point of view, and not remain fixed in a partial, negative
one. Wholeness is everything.

*   *   *   *   *

During this period of late adolescence, older people guarded me
from having any love relationship with a woman. The first occasion
when this might have arisen was when I was sixteen. An extremely
attractive nurse looked after me when I had measles. As I recovered
I grew fond of her, and without consciousness of the implications of
what I was doing (my illness had in some way released me from inhibitions), I used often to pull her on to the bed beside me and cover
her with kisses. The nurse suggested to my father that, to complete
my convalescence, I should go to the seaside where she had a cottage,
and stay with her there. This suggestion was, of course, quashed, and
I do not blame my father for not pursuing it. Yet it is difficult not to

feel that later on I paid a heavy price for having been guarded so carefully from women.

I was saved from a similar entanglement at Oxford. In writing of my brother's scientific friends, I mentioned a girl called Polly, who was an object of their fervent experiments. Polly – it will be recalled – had caused one of them to discover that during the week or ten days when he was in love with her, he definitely lost ten pounds in weight. They all, to a greater or less degree, fell in love with her; measuring the while, in their 'objective', scientific way, her effects on their glands, secretions, weight, etc. Polly was so stimulating that at one time her efforts moved her scientific admirers right out of the field of biology into that of the comparatively recent science of psychology. Amongst one or two of them, quite irrational symptoms of jealousy were observed.

Polly grew bored with science and turned her attention to the Oxford poets. She was one of those girls whom the universities excite to a peculiar degree. She seemed literally bathed in the warm admiration of young men. Her cheeks were always flushed, her eyes were bright and had a laughing, watchful expression as though she were anticipating at every moment the emergence of a new admirer, a renegade from the puritanical undergraduate ranks. There was a recklessness about her which was quite rare: for most girls in her situation simply led the young men on and then refused to give themselves: they were cold tarts. But Polly was a brave little pirate flaunting the flag of her promiscuity.

She was a scholarship girl who came from a poor family. Her father kept a confectioner's shop somewhere, she told me. She was extremely honest about all her interests. Sex was the chief of these, but with her making love was a preliminary to taking a genuine interest in men's minds. She knew all about scientists, and now she wanted to know about poets. She had yellow hair which fell over her flushed forehead and contributed to the general effect of embarrassed excitement. She laughed often and warmly but not distastefully. Her thighs showed above her stockings and looked like hot marble.

Polly showed an interest in me, and I liked her. After a certain time I invited her home to meet Caroline. It was a warm summer evening, and all I remember apart from this was that at a certain moment

69

Polly suggested that she and I should go out into the garden. Immediately it seemed as if the trees were filled with terrifying nightingales. Caroline intervened and made some excuse to keep us indoors. So I never went into that garden.

At this time my relations with Caroline were rather strained. The affectation, excesses and emotional upsets of my two years at Oxford had tried her a good deal. A few days later, in a conversation during which she reviewed our friendship bitterly, she said, speaking of Polly: 'Well, at any rate I saved you from that!'

She was right, of course, not to think of Polly and me as being entirely suited to one another, yet perhaps at this stage I could not be saved for something better but only for something worse. I had driven myself and had been driven into a kind of sexual slum.

Until I went to Oxford I had responded to Caroline with a fervour which completely absorbed me and which I wished to absorb us both. However, when I lost this first enthusiasm, I simply exploited her sympathy, in order to test her reaction to things which I still confided to no one else. She was shocked by the change which took place in me at Oxford. To explain her annoyance with me to myself, I adopted the facile view that I exasperated her because she loved me, and I tried to persuade her also to accept this explanation. At one time she was so angry with me that she made a bonfire on which she burned all the letters I had written her from Nantes and Lausanne. Fortunately, our relationship traversed this crisis and we really succeeded in becoming friends.

* * * * *

Auden left Oxford a year before I did. Without his dominating presence, my life there changed a good deal. I made more and more friends outside College, and I became one of a circle of contemporaries who had interests in common.

Among my friends were Louis MacNeice, Bernard Spencer, Humphry House and Arthur Calder Marshall – all of them later to become well-known writers. One of my friends was Isaiah Berlin. Isaiah was by origin from Riga. He had an interest in other people's lives which was strengthened by the conviction that he himself was detached from the passions which moved them. Human behaviour was for him a subject of fantastic enquiry into motives and actions, reminding me of Henry James's many-branched speculations over the characters in his novels. Berlin excelled in descriptions of people by metaphor. 'X——,' he said to me one day, speaking of a contemporary essayist, 'is like a man who at a certain stage in his career decided that his talents were worth exactly so many pounds. So then he went and changed himself into threepenny bits. He has been publishing threepence a week ever since.' Berlin and I shared a passion for music. This took us to Salzburg during my last long vacation, in the very early days of the music festival. We heard there the operas of Mozart conducted by Bruno Walter. I learned to care now for the posthumous quartets of Beethoven as I cared for the tragedies of Shakespeare. In lines like

> 'Peace, peace
> Dost thou not see my baby at my breast
> That sucks the nurse asleep?'

I found a burning away of the human condition contained within the dramatic situation, and then a penetration into a world of pure imagination beyond it. And in Beethoven's posthumous quartets there was the exploration of a universe of pure melody, beyond suffering, oppression and difficulty.

Even the side of Beethoven which had something which falls short of his aims and is *manqué* made me love him. No opera moved me quite so much as *Fidelio*, whose first act is like a series of humble, deeply touching exercises in the search to understand and state the material of character and subject matter of the opera, whilst the second and third scenes, with the Prisoners' Chorus and the Quartet in the prison cell of Florestan, scale the greatest heights of Beethoven's humanistic piety. Here certain simple concepts such as Light, Love, Hope, Freedom – especially Freedom – are raised by the music from the point where they touch humble human experience to that where certain things, such as the piece of bread which Leonora gives to Florestan in his cell, or the key with which the cell gate is unlocked, become sacramental symbols; and that which makes the music from a certain point of view undramatic, but which, from another one, moves towards a new conception of operatic drama, is

71

that the action becomes arrested, even frozen at these points, and produces a kind of drama which is statuesque, immobile, rather than fluid.

Isaiah Berlin and I shared this enthusiasm, he entering fully into the passion for the Beethoven quartets and *Fidelio*, but pointing out to me, none the less, that *Don Giovanni* was a sublimer work than *Fidelio*. With him, I enjoyed a relationship as between equals, which was in contrast to my relationship with Auden, where I was in the position of a pupil learning from a schoolmaster.

Immensely clever as Berlin was, he did not dominate me in the way in which Auden had dominated his friends. Immensely as he talked, in a monologue where sometimes all the words seemed joined together into one huge word, he was not dogmatic.

So during this last year at Oxford I met new friends. Even Tristan became easier. He seemed to think that, now all the clever people had left, we could be happy and enjoy our inferiority together to our heart's content. He called me 'dear old' Stephen; adjectives at once of humour and contempt, like golden chains which have become honourable symbols of the spiritual manacles which keep another human being in his place.

*   *   *   *   *

Long before my life as an undergraduate, when, at the age of seventeen, I was staying with my uncle, J. A. Spender, at his house at Marden, he announced one morning that a poet was coming to tea. This was Frank Kendon, then quite a young man. He was the first poet I ever met.

Of Mr. Kendon's work, I knew a long poem, *Judas Iscariot*, the opening of which, if I remember rightly, describes Judas in his boyhood meeting with a snake, amid sun-bright stony Palestinian scenery (my memory of the poem may be inaccurate: the point is to be faithful to my impression. I also remember the binding of the book with a 'stuck-on' label bearing the title, and the look of the printing on the clean page). The rest of the poem tired me, but I did not blame Mr. Kendon for this. In those days I found it difficult to sustain interest in a long poem, though I had read most of *Paradise Lost*, the whole of *Paradise Regained*, and ten Cantos of *Don Juan*. So that

72

when I could not get through a poem, as happened to me not only with Mr. Kendon's, but also with Keats's *Endymion*, I assumed – what may have been true – that there was something wonderful in it beyond my comprehension.

Mr. Kendon was for me a maker of crystalline miracles, a lord in that country of the imagination, where above all things I longed to have an existence. It was my ambition to write one line, or, at most, one poem, really 'poetry', which might appear in print and whose words would produce the ravishing sensation of being at once airy, fantastic, and solid as concrete, like a branch of coral extended in the reader's mind. Mr. Kendon represented liberation from all that I felt fretting the life of my uncle. I remember how my uncle would say, blowing out his small white moustache as he leaned back in his chair, or perhaps as he tramped the dusty road of the weald through miles of hop fields and cherry orchards (whilst I watched with fascination the perspiration at the back of his neck melt away the starch of his white collar): 'Poetry! Well, when I was at your age I used to make patterns of words which fascinated me, but of course that was in Latin, which was more difficult. Believe me, I would still like to write something purely literary, if I had the time and leisure to amuse myself in that way. But you see,' glancing at my prodigious Aunt May, 'I have to sing for my supper.' When my uncle spoke in this way he seemed to me a benevolent journalist gaoler, his drawing-room groaned with invisible chains, and my little secret ambition suddenly became a bomb concealed in the room, timed to go off in a few years. I longed to say: 'But for me poetry is not just a game of words. It is the most serious aim in life.' Looking round his room, with all the heavy furniture, the framed water-colours by Cotman and De Wint, the chests and sacks ransacked from her beloved 'The East', by Aunt May, I felt like crying out what I still know to be a real question (though now it turns mockingly against myself): 'Why, if you can create something literary, do you have to sing for your supper? Why don't you live in a garret and be neglected and starved, so long as a line of yours may be remembered for a hundred years?'

Kendon, my uncle told me, *was* poor and neglected. 'A poet is lucky today if he sells four hundred copies of a slim volume of verses.'

Then my uncle would go on to say that the public was not to blame for the neglect of the moderns because none of them was 'great'. They were all *petits maîtres*, not to be compared with Tennyson, Browning and Swinburne, who, in their heyday, sold in tens of thousands. If some modern poet, such as that young fellow T. S. Eliot, attempted to write verse which was not all about skylarks, then he only succeeded in being fashionable. 'And believe me, in my time, I have seen any number of literary fashions become the talk of the town and then fade away.'

When Frank Kendon came, I could only look at him. He had (I think) sandy hair over an unassuming face, and he was dressed in tweeds. He sat quietly in a chair, did not look at me, and ate cake. He was silent and my uncle had to question him for him to talk at all. When he did talk, it was to discuss literary life in London. The names of Jack Squire, Walter de la Mare, John Freeman, thrilled through the drawing-room, but not as I imagined them, like king-fishers and humming-birds; for they were spoken of somewhat banally as ordinary people, in terms of what they were doing, whom they were seeing, how they were making a living. Knowing of them as poets who, in their poems, preferred being herded by the shepherd Nod into the land of dreams to sitting in an editorial office, or who, when they saw a blade of grass in a factory yard, declared that they wished it to possess the power to strike down and destroy all the useful commodities manufactured by the factories in the world, and who, when they went into the countryside, found in every breeze a naked nymph who sat upon their knees; knowing all this, I was a little puzzled by the rather materialist literary back-chat of my uncle and Mr. Kendon.

But my uncle had a more sensitive perception than I of the real yearning which underlay Kendon's remarks: the yearning of the young literary man to get away from here, to get to London. My uncle knew all the men of whom Kendon spoke, for when he edited the *Westminster Gazette* he had published their poems in corners of the weekly edition of that paper – the *Saturday Westminster* – and he had given them reviewing work with which they supplemented the few guineas they turned from their verses. His view of poets was from the editorial angle. He saw them as impecunious weavers of words, and he knew how nearly all of them were driven sooner or later to his office to beg for a little reviewing.

He had a deep, almost tender sympathy for the younger ones, and when Kendon was gone he sighed: 'How I pity that young man.' 'Why?' I asked, astonished. 'Because he is eating his heart out here in the country. He longs to be in town with his Freemans and Squires and other fry.'

I was a little disappointed that Kendon had not looked at me, not even when my uncle had explained to him that this young nephew also fancied himself as a maker of patterns of words. I had prayed for a sympathetic glance of recognition, I had hoped that he would, while accepting my obeisance, see the halo of my own idea around my head. However, before the end of the afternoon, my vision of Kendon was reaffirmed. For shortly after his visit had ended, my uncle and I went for a ride in a hired car (my uncle, like my father, was always in a position in which he could not 'afford' a car: and he was obliged to hire one at enormous expense) and, just outside Marden, we passed Kendon on the road. When we had driven by, I saw him standing alone there in the cloud of dust we had raised, stick in hand, absorbed in his thoughts, and I felt as though his imagination possessed the whole landscape. The trees and oaks and the hopfields leaned against his skull and entered into his brain through his eye sockets, changing there into a branch of coral which he, the poet, created, a branch of coral and an interior world, where he was able to remain indifferent to the conventions and creeds and needs of the external world. 'He doesn't want a lift. He doesn't want to be disturbed by us. He has his thoughts,' said my uncle. I realized at that moment that he, who had denied his own dreams, could enter the dreams of others.

My uncle was decidedly a man of the world, who had interviewed kings, been the confidant of prime ministers, and the patron of writers. He had a taste for life, and a twinkle in his eye which was yet rather wistful, as though he half-regretted the Bohemia he had renounced. He was sensitive to any suggestion that he was a Philistine. Before the war of 1914 he had sent Rupert Brooke to America to write a few articles in the form of letters for the *Westminster Gazette*. Henry James, writing later a preface to these, indicated in that later manner of his which resembled a steam-roller spinning out filigree, that the editor who recalled Brooke did not understand the needs of his sensibility. Twenty years later my uncle was still hurt by this, and took the trouble to explain to me that James had not understood the real reasons for bringing Brooke home. My uncle, who had enjoyed the friendship of Henry James, Robert Louis Stevenson, and Oscar Wilde, regarded art as an extravagance on the part of the artists, like champagne or taxis.

In this amiable worldliness, my uncle differed greatly from my father who, as I have described, regarded modern art as a huge, perverse, obscene, blasphemous practical joke. An exhibition of paintings by Augustus John held at the Alpine Club, of which my father was a member, threw him into a state of public indignation which he directed at all of us at meal-times. Reverence for God, the human form, and nature, were, he said, lacking in modern art. The only pleasure I ever saw him get out of a modern painting was once when we went to the Tate Gallery and saw Henry Lamb's large portrait of Lytton Strachey seen through an open window sinuously reclining in front of a toy-like landscape. My father stared at this in silence for a long time. Then hatred for the painter suddenly clicked in his mind with hatred of the most irreverent and iconoclastic of modern essayists, as he said in a loud voice: 'Well, Lytton Strachey deserves it! He deserves it!' And he strode away, meditating on the poetic justice which had ordained Henry Lamb to place Lytton Strachey in the inferno of those rooms which my father labelled 'the lunatic asylum' in the Tate.

In our house at Frognal the names of Augustus John, Bernard Shaw, Lytton Strachey, Van Gogh, stood for a diabolic, cunning depravity, a plot of bearded demons against all which should be held sacred.

My uncle did not share my father's prejudices, but he had a kind of Philistinism of his own. He only saw a contemporary manner, never a contemporary vision. Thus, when he spoke of Cézanne, it was of someone who had introduced a new style which 'you young people are all wild about', but which would soon be relegated to its place. He spoke of Proust and Joyce as though he had seen a dozen such pass out of fashion in his day.

My uncle was famous for his balanced point of view. At the time of which I am writing (when he was nearly seventy) it had become so balanced, that the act of balancing seemed rather automatic. One had only to offer an opinion for him to balance it with a counter-opinion of exactly the same weight, as a grocer puts a pound weight against a pound of sugar. When I said that I had a friend called Auden who seemed to be a poet of brilliant promise, my uncle assured me that in his time he had met hundreds of young poets of brilliant promise and none of them had come to anything: as though weighing Auden against a heap of miscellaneous nonentities. When, in the 1930's, I said that I thought there was going to be a war, he said that in his time he had seen Germany a menace which recurred at regular intervals: but the other powers always cancelled it. Once I told him how a friend of mine, appointed a magistrate in the Indian Civil Service, had resigned, because he found that, unless he condemned political prisoners on what he regarded as insufficient evidence, the police always appealed to a higher court, where the prisoners were inevitably given a harsher punishment than my friend would have given even had he believed them guilty. My uncle replied that if one took 'a bird's-eye view' of the whole of India, one would find that such injustices were rare and that on the whole the justice of British rule cancelled out the injustice, etc.

It always seemed to me that the Great War had made singularly little impression on him. He believed that we lived in an age of improvements, and not even that holocaust had shaken him in this belief. 'If one thinks about it,' he once said to me, 'in spite of everything, the little group of comfortably-off middle-class people in the world today, to which we belong, enjoys the most fortunate situation in the whole of history and on the entire globe. Think how unlucky it would have been for us as individuals to have been born in almost any other time or in any of a thousand of other places. We really enjoy an incredible gambler's luck in being born here and now.' This firm view was the centre of my uncle's vision.

He was a European Liberal who belonged to a time in which Europe was governed by a fairly small number of initiated monarchs, professional politicians and their professional advisers. It was a world in which, even though there were wars and revolutions, a new political ruling class was always willing to come to terms with the old one. He would point out that the Germany of Bismarck, despite the Franco-German war, had worked within the concert of Europe. He conceived political responsibility to be a spirit of co-operation among political opponents, national leaders and journalists; they agreed to preserve the existing political order, even if they largely altered it. What he feared above all was that 'wild men of the Left' (like my Oxford economics tutor, G. D. H. Cole) would break into politics without understanding that the essence of the political game was that it should be played by experts who respected one another's political existence.

My uncle's philosophy as a journalist could be summed up in the word 'discretion'. He thought of the newspaper editor as a confidential adviser to the responsible political leaders (by 'responsible' he meant non-revolutionary). The editor would criticize and even attack politicians, but he would not give away their secrets and thus perhaps prevent them carrying out their policy. Nor would he attack them in a manner which might make the public lose confidence in politicians as a class. Thus my uncle was utterly opposed to the kind of journalism which gives away the terms of negotiations between opposing groups while these are still under consideration.

Two examples will indicate the way in which discretion was for him a matter of the highest principle. He told me that in the earliest years of this century, when he was first an editor, there was an ambassador of a great power in London who was never sober when he made a public speech. The London editors, realizing this, agreed among themselves that whenever this ambassador appeared at a banquet they would take it in turns to invent and communicate to one another what he might be supposed to have said, had he been sober. This fictitious speech appeared in the London newspapers; not one of which ever published a report which made evident the ambassador's condition.

The other example concerns my uncle's relations with the man he most hated, Lloyd George. On one of the occasions on which the two branches of the Liberal Party were meeting with the aim of reuniting, my uncle was Chairman of the conference. As Chairman he was asked by Lloyd George to circulate a highly confidential document amongst the inner committee of the conference. My uncle even had to emphasize that under no circumstances must the contents of the memorandum be divulged. It was always my uncle's firm belief that Lloyd George, taking advantage of the editor's absence, had seen to it that the document reached the newspaper. He therefore found himself faced with a choice of denouncing Lloyd George or resigning from the chairmanship of the Liberal Federation. Sooner than make public what he regarded as an act of betrayal of the first order by a leading Liberal politician, my uncle resigned. Which may well have been exactly what Lloyd George wished him to do.

From my uncle's point of view, these were examples of the highest journalistic integrity. But from another, they might seem to reveal a kind of honourable corruption, peculiarly English, but justified if it really did serve the public interest. In the case of the ambassador there seems little doubt that the London editors were right. But in the case of Lloyd George, who had already practised similar tricks a dozen times on his colleagues, the wisdom of my uncle's action seemed to me more doubtful.

When my uncle, who was a friend of Asquith and Grey, talked about Lloyd George, I began to wonder whether this statesman was not a demonic spirit nurtured within the soul of the Liberals, like the frightful nightmare of some maiden aunt. My uncle would tell how this terrible man whose real name was not Lloyd George at all but just plain George, who had not been to Balliol and knew no Latin or Greek, had by a series of betrayals gained the most powerful position in the Liberal Party and then destroyed it, gaining at the very moment of destruction, control over the Party funds. To my uncle, Lloyd George was a politician of the calibre of Horatio Bottomley, and had simply cheated his way through political life. When I asked why he had not been exposed like Bottomley, my uncle explained that to expose him would be to destroy confidence in political leaders.

My uncle's malice about Lloyd George's utter ignorance of geography, history and economics knew no bounds. He swore that at the time of the Treaty of Versailles it was evident to the journalists at Paris that Lloyd George often did not know the position on the map of countries which he cut up and dismembered, and knew still less of the history of the people living there. George, he said, could never understand the arguments for and against Free Trade, and had to be coached in these whenever he made a speech defending this bastion of Liberal policy. When George was first in Liberal Party or Coalition Cabinets the Asquithians would keep him in his place by quoting Homer and Virgil at him. But George, when he became Prime Minister, took revenge by holding up Cabinet meetings while he quoted verses from the Welsh bards 'in a language which no civilized person has ever understood or wanted to understand,' my uncle would exclaim ferociously. Speaking of George, my uncle became fiery. I could not resist asking him once why, if he felt so strongly, he had not exposed L.G. 'Oh, but I have,' he said and took down from the shelf a volume of his *The Public Life*, in which he showed me the following example of his balanced manner:

'What Birmingham was to Chamberlain, Wales was to Lloyd George, and for the early years of his career, he was above all things the man from Wales, the young man who spoke for its ardent youth, and who better than any other expressed both its religious and its political aspirations. His detractors said that Wales could produce a score of others like him, and as good, but he alone was where he was, a Parliamentary figure while still in his thirties, claiming to speak for his countrymen, who apparently endorsed his claim.'

My uncle's hatred of L.G. astonished me the more because to my father – who was a Coalition Liberal – Lloyd George was a kind of saint. My father had been a friend of Lloyd George when they were young men, had climbed mountains, and visited Germany with him. Later, he had written his biography which was cited by reviewers as a striking example of hagiography. My father even looked like Lloyd George, with flowing white hair, a domed forehead, rather small chiselled nose, shaggy eyebrows, and eyes which had something of the expression of the public performer. To my father L.G. was the crusader who had defended the dockers, had introduced his scheme of health insurance, and who finally had won the war by exposing the scandal of munitions in 1916. Nearly all my father's stories about Lloyd George were enlivened by impersonations which had the

80

passion of love. There were stories to illustrate L.G.'s brilliant re-
partees in dealing with interrupters in the earlier days of his career.
For example, at a great meeting in favour of Home Rule, in the early
part of the century, Lloyd George had made a speech advocating
Home Rule not only for Ireland but also for other parts of the Empire. 'I would like to see Home Rule in Ireland, Home Rule in India,
Home Rule in South Africa,' he declaimed, when he was interrupted
by a voice from the gallery shouting coarsely: ' 'Ome Rule for 'Ell.'
At this Lloyd George with a pointing gesture of his digit finger, a
creasing of the lines of his forehead, and an expressive movement of
his eyebrows (all of which my father most vividly performed), picked
out the interrupter and said: 'Yes, Home Rule for Hell. I like every
man to speak for his own country.'

I remember well my father coming into our nursery after a great
speech on the subject of peace, made by Lloyd George at (I think)
the Albert Hall. He described how, before the immense audience,
L.G. embarked on a rhetorical gesture which caused my father some
anxiety. For, lifting his hands one above the other to imitate the
climbing of successive rungs of a ladder, L.G. spoke of peace conference following disarmament conference, disarmament conference
peace conference, as a progression of steps climbing to world peace.
While he made this movement of his hands, my father was left wondering what he would do when he arrived at the top rung, whose
height was limited by his rather miniature capacity for self-extension.
Wondering, too, I asked: 'What did he do?' 'He just dropped them
to his side,' said my father imitating the Prime Minister's gesture
with a sublime expression.

To my father Asquith was as sinister, as Lloyd George was abomin-
able to my uncle. In my father's mind, the keynote of Lloyd George's
career was a saintly simplicity. He was the Welsh cobbler's son who
had put down his hereditary last and heard the voice which called
him to the highest duty. He had married a simple country girl, lived
a model domestic life, and suffered, like other prophets, from being
misjudged by his people. Asquith, on the other hand, was a cunning,
worldly, designing, sneering, snobbish plotter. When Lloyd George
and his family were singing their humble Methodist hymns after eating kippers for high tea, Asquith was dining with the élite and, at the

orders of his worldly social wife, leaving the House in the middle of a debate on world affairs to make up a fourth at a bridge party of divorcées and divorcés.

So I was brought up to think of the battle of Asquith and Lloyd George as something which resembled a mixture of the conflict of Protestant with Catholic, and Tweedledum with Tweedledee.

Only once in my childhood did I come near to meeting one of the participants in this struggle, and this encounter was by no means edifying. It was, however, prophetic of my relations with the political world.

My father did not actually see much of Lloyd George except at one period, after 1918, when he was writing his biography. (My uncle, on the other hand, always was in a close relationship to Asquith. This difference is important to an understanding of the two brothers.) But just after the war he went often to Downing Street. On one of these occasions he took me in a taxi with him. It was a memorable journey for me at the age of ten, because it was not only a visit to the shrine of a living and reigning deity, but also the first time I had been to the centre of London after dark. It was a drizzling, foggy winter evening. The lights of Piccadilly Circus shot up through the fog like rockets against a thick green-black wall turned to blurred bright golden-red and other colours, where the lettering and the crude symbols of the advertisers stood in the night. To me, a wine bottle made of ruby electric bulbs, perpetually filling a ruby wine-glass, was not an advertisement for anything: it was a gasp of wonder high above the black wet streets.

When we reached 10 Downing Street, my father told the taxi driver to wait and me to stay in the taxi, while he went into the door beyond which there was Lloyd George. I waited in the damp downpouring darkness for what seemed an infinite time, at the end of which I became more and more conscious of a physical need which, in the childhood of a boy taught to be ashamed of his body, can be so memorably agonizing as to outweigh far more honourable kinds of suffering. For a long time I debated in my mind whether or not I could 'hold out'. After this, there was a more desperate debate as to where I could 'go'. How could I ring the front-door bell of 10 Downing Street and ask whether I might use the lavatory? By now it was as though thought had become an agonizing physical sensation,
82

pressing its way against my body between my thighs, and in so far as I had any mind it was left with wonder that I could suffer so much for so slight a cause; suffer to a point where it became incredible to think that by a mere act of physical release I could restore myself in a few seconds to the same state of ease as I had enjoyed an hour before. I noticed then that the fog had thickened, providing me with a kind of smoke-screen, while at the same time the noise of the rain caused a diversion. So I let down the window of the cab very softly and relieved myself out of the window. I had scarcely finished, and, trembling, was crouching on the back seat, when the driver poked his head through the window and asked: 'Did you see what I see?' 'What?' 'Just now. Didn't you see him go by?' 'Who?' 'The Prime Minister.'

Perhaps if I had told my father this story on his return he would have laughed. Perhaps he would have been horrified. Probably he would have been kind and serious about it. It is unlikely that he would have been amused, because his attitude towards physical things was that they were never funny. Once I was amused at Dickens's description of how Mrs. Gamp had developed a water-works in her eyes so that they could manufacture tears at will. My father told me that there was a regrettable coarse strain in Dickens and that I should remember that the human body was at all times, in all its aspects, very serious, and never to be laughed at.

So now years later, after my father's death, I was astonished to discover that Lloyd George, the god of my childhood, was in the eyes of my uncle just 'that scoundrel George'. One day I asked my uncle how it was possible that my father could have admired such a man as he described. 'Your father considered George to be a genius,' said my uncle, 'a kind of demi-god: and just as on Olympus the gods are allowed to do things which would appal men who worshipped them if their fellow beings did those things, so your father permitted every latitude to his god.'

I saw little of my uncle during my father's life-time, but when both my parents had died, he, having no children of his own, would have been glad, I think, to have us spend our holidays with him. My Aunt May, however, incapable of liking anyone, was most capable of disliking us, and most of all me. The relationship with our family began badly when Michael was sent down to Marden as a forerunner and was returned by my aunt the next day with mumps, in a hired car. Berthella were acidulous about a woman who was capable of dealing with a sick nephew in such a way.

Aunt May, on the other hand, was sour about the commonness of a nephew who could contract a childish ailment at the age of seventeen. Shortly after this, when I went to Marden, my aunt declared to me that I was to be her favourite nephew. A honeymoon period of our relationship ensued during which she extracted many of my confidences. She then began to tell me that she discerned I was in danger of becoming an artist, a poet, or a novelist. She spoke with grief of the terrible misfortune which had befallen General X and his wife, neighbours at Marden: their son had published a novel. My aunt never lost an opportunity of lecturing me on the depravity, animality and irresponsibility of artists. It was true that she admired Rudyard Kipling's *If*, but Kipling had not confined himself to writing poetry. Rather psychic, one day she had a prophetic vision: she came downstairs knowing that I was doomed to marry an actress.

Next to artists, she hated Lloyd George. She was a crude expert at insulting people, and this gift exercised among the delicate fissures of the Liberal Party – which my uncle was for ever trying to heal – made her a kind of perambulatory human chisel on the occasion of Liberal reunions. She insisted on attending these junketings, where she would push herself forward, declaring in a loud voice: 'Let me meet Mr. George!' Having been brought to Lloyd George she would then say in the indignant tones of one exposing a plot: 'Good afternoon, Mr. George! Good-bye!' Then, deeply satisfied with herself, she would turn her massive back on him.

She hated any tender emotion with a thoroughly English intensity, only understood by novelists like Trollope and Henry James, who have portrayed such women. On one occasion we went to visit friends of my uncle's at Tunbridge Wells. At this party there happened to be two young people, newly married, whose liking for each other was so vibrant that it filled the room like music. In the presence of their happiness I felt the assurance that my own adolescent problems would one day melt away, liquify in a passion like theirs. But they filled my aunt with a fury she could hardly conceal. As we went home

84

in the hired car afterwards she burst out: 'How disgusting! How selfish! How horrible! Fancy insulting *Alfred* by introducing him to those people! Of course, *I'm* used to every kind of horror after what I went through at the hospital during the war, but Alfred ought to be spared!' And so on. She went on to say how selfish, how venal, how immoral the young were nowadays. Just then she was interrupted by seeing the new moon through the window of the car, a misfortune which diverted her attention; for she was extremely superstitious. For despite her ferocious barking at a pair of lovers who seemed miraculously to have slipped by a back door into the Garden of Eden, my aunt had something about her of a frustrated earth-goddess worshipping the East, familiar with ghosts, and ruled by signs and seasons.

Although she disapproved of happy lovers, she had some conception of love as an examination which had to be passed at some time in one's life, a kind of ritual which savages impose on adolescents, like circumcision, terribly painful but a final seal on maturity. She acknowledged grimly a torture which she called the Fiery Furnace of Loving and she had deep reserves of scorn for those who had not been through this. 'Do you know what is wrong with Bernard Shaw, Arnold Bennett, H. G. Wells and so many others?' she asked me with that grimly indulgent glance which implied that I would certainly go wrong here, too (and that she would go right). 'They have never, any of them, been through the Fiery Furnace of Loving.' 'Who,' I asked timidly, 'has been through it?' 'Robert Louis Stevenson, Robert Hichens, Sir Ian Hamilton, and, of course, your uncle,' was the reply, uttered rather darkly. It was not until later that I heard the legend that my aunt had been courted by these, so she apparently considered her relations with people productive of ferocious heat.

My aunt used sometimes to take me into her garden where, under the pretext of our pulling out the weeds (inevitably she loved gardening), she would lecture me on my future. 'Don't choose the *easy* way of Art and Bohemianism. Choose the *hard* way as your uncle has done. Of course, if he had liked he could have been a great 'cellist, a great poet, or a great painter, and won the empty admiration of the mob, as you are tempted to do, and married some feather-brained actress as you will do, if we aren't all very careful.'

Sometimes she talked to me about the East (which she called *her* East) for which she had a Great Passion. She was excellent at Early Morning Bedroom Scenes, when she would summon me to her room and, after explaining that she was in bed because the snares which surrounded me had kept her awake all night, she would tell me her Night Thoughts, full of forebodings on my account. After one of these occasions, I wrote at the age of seventeen a poem opening with lines which capture, I think, a little of my aunt's vigour:

> 'Madam, your face half-hidden by your hair
> Which hung in tousled patterns from the fair
> Massively active flesh, surrounded by great pillows,
> You were the largest of your bed's huge billows!
> Reclining there, incarnate confidence,
> You chid me for my lack of competence
> In the half-curtained room. Warm shadows fell
> Round you, like guardian ghosts. I did not tell
> You of them, being sure that you
> Would think this an æsthetic thing to do.
> And most æsthetic was the mad March wind
> Which rashly rapped against the window blind. . . .'

My uncle had in his book-lined study a parrot with whom he held long conversations. It used to sing to him, or rather, he used to sing to it, a song called 'Cock o' the North'. At moments when he had his head bowed towards the bird which he cajoled, my uncle himself seemed like an old bird caught in a cage, who clutched at the back of his eyes a glimpse of a long-lost exotic landscape.

*   *   *   *   *

The seed of poetry was planted in me when I was nine years old. At that date my parents took us on a summer holiday to a place called Skelgill Farm, near Derwentwater. The journey was long and taken in stages, every one of which I remember vividly. We spent a night in an hotel at Leeds – the first hotel where I had ever stayed. Here I disgraced myself by allowing the large yellow-striped hairy caterpillars, which I always carried about in a box with me, to escape in the lift, from where they got on to the clothes of our fellow guests.

86

As soon as we arrived at Skelgill Farm which is below the side of a mountain called Catbells, which separates it from Derwentwater, we four children scrambled up the side of the mountain with my father to view the lake.

I remember the rainy lakeside days, and how, after the rain, great raindrops would cling on to the serrated leaves of brambles like hundreds of minute lenses, through which the sun, emerging in a rinsed sky, would gleam with a new-seeming whiteness. I remember the long black slugs on paths wrinkled by many torrential downpours, and the smell of the earth, and how on our walks we found rock crystals on the stones like lost enjewelled caskets. The countryside was as honest as in those epochs in English history when a noble lady could leave a bracelet on a hedge and no one take it. When we went on walks and the weather seemed set fine, our governess used to leave her bright yellow mackintosh by the wayside, and we would take it up on our return.

This countryside is fused in my mind with my first sustained experience of poetry. For here my father used to read to me the simple ballad poems of Wordsworth, 'We are Seven', 'A Lesson to Fathers', 'The Lesser Celandine'. The words of these poems dropped into my mind like cool pebbles, so shining and so pure, and they brought with them the atmosphere of rain and sunsets, and a sense of the sacred cloaked vocation of the poet.

In the warm evening while I lay in bed at Skelgill Farm, I heard the murmuring of my father's voice as he read the Longer Poems of Wordsworth to my mother. The voice flowed like a river through the landscape, above which the mountains grew into the sky.

After this, the mystery and the pleasure of poetry remained. When I was aged eleven, at a preparatory school in Worthing, I used to look through the grammar books for the quotations in verse:

> 'The Ettrick Shepherd was my guide',

and immediately the varnished deal wood walls and the poky, asphalted backyard with a privet hedge separating it from the road, which were the surroundings of this school, seemed to disappear and it was as though I stood in a green valley through which ran a river.

The idea of being a poet faded though, when my ambition became a projection of my father's disappointment. For my father, himself a second son, was a disappointed man, and thought of me, I believe, as the son who would mysteriously redeem his failure. Sometimes he would say: 'You are the one who will surprise them all,' and while attaching me to my failure, by calling me 'the black sheep' and 'the fool', he also filled my mind with an ambition to be a black sheep who grew a golden fleece, a goose who became a swan, a fool who amazed his brothers and sisters. How, in his terms, should I do this except by being Prime Minister? It was to this which all my fancies turned. I imagined myself addressing the House, being acclaimed by crowds who whispered as I passed, 'It's He', making decisions on which the world waited, and always astonishing everyone by the simplicity and naturalness with which I spoke to quite unknown people whose names never appeared in the newspapers, as though they really mattered. For even my greatest ambition merged into the fantasy of utterly generous love. I wanted to be above all in order to be equal, to have in order to give, to be covered in order to be revealed. Beyond every goal there lay another – friendship.

I could not bear to wait, and often I lay at night wondering whether it was possible for a Boy Wonder, a virtuoso of politics, to become Prime Minister at the age of eleven or twelve, with all the House listening to him in silence while he told the quarrelsome elder politicians to set aside their petty points of view and put country before party.

I might have continued to believe in this political vocation, had not various events cast doubts on the political life, on the sagacity of my father, and on the nobility of Lloyd George.

The first of these occurred when my father stood as Liberal candidate for Bath in 1923. During the election, before that occasion I have described when my brother Humphrey and I were the 'reserves' my father summoned from London, I went for a walk with my grandfather, Ernest Joseph Schuster, whose judgments I instinctively respected, as did everyone who knew him. (We used always to walk on Sundays at eleven o'clock from Frognal to Albert Court behind the Albert Hall. We walked along a route plotted by my grandfather, down Avenue Road and across Primrose Hill, then along Baker Street to Marble Arch, and across Hyde Park and Kensington Gardens. During our winter walks the sun would sometimes show through the fog like a red balloon above fields of frosted glass.)

On this walk I asked: 'Will Daddy win the Election?' and my grandfather said something abrupt to the effect that he hadn't a chance, and shrugged his shoulders with a movement of heavy impatience. There was something in this gesture which made me see that my bearded grandfather regarded my father's politics as a childish and profitless game. At my grandmother's flat at luncheon that day there was conversation about Lloyd George. My grandmother said that he was a demagogue who had won an election after the war on the slogan of 'Hang the Kaiser'. She went on to say that he was responsible for the blockade of Germany which had caused the starvation of thousands of people, and that by his own political methods he had encouraged the worst instincts of the worst people and been obliged to obey them himself.

This was mere politics to me and I simply thought that my grandmother was wrong. All the same a doubt had been planted in my mind. When I went to Bath I found the Election being fought in an atmosphere of ebullient confidence by my father's supporters, whose slogan was *Vote for a Wise and Careful Spender*. But probably Humphrey and I were the only people who in our innocence were convinced that he would win. When the results showed that he had lost by a substantial margin, I was utterly surprised, vaguely disillusioned, and I wept bitterly.

At this time I adored my father. While he read to us in the evenings from Dickens, Thackeray or Tennyson, I used to sit drawing him, and the proportions of his features assumed in my mind the authority of the measurements of some classical head of Apollo or Hermes. His forehead was high, a feature exaggerated by the receding hair. The space from the highest point of the forehead to the bridge of the nose equalled that from the bridge of the nose to the base of the chin. The nose itself was of the type which I still think of as nobly formed, with a notched bridge. The chin was deceptively firm. A handsome moustache concealed his mouth. His eyes were very light blue, and looked Scandinavian. There was indeed something pronounced and dominant about his type which is marked in all the Spenders (which Bertha calls 'That ginger look'). Now, it seems to me that the well-formed nose emphasizes a certain limit to our imagination and sensibility. It verges on the stupid and evades the religious. To me this nose is like the boundary line of a spiritual province.

My intensive, fanatical study of my father, whom I sought to understand as he in a secret way understood me – our link being a hidden and frustrated longing for public success – gradually led me to realize that he was a failure.

After the death of my mother, he liked taking me to small pietistic gatherings of Nonconformist Youths, which took place in the drawing-rooms of certain members of the congregation of Lyndhurst Road Congregational Church. One evening, after our arrival, our host offered up a voluntary prayer which went something like this: 'We thank thee, O God, for having brought among us today the distinguished lecturer and author, Harold Spender, whom Thou by Thy everlasting mercy hast privileged to travel in many far countries. We pray that we may learn and benefit from the wisdom which he now brings to us' – a form of chairmanly introduction which shocked me more than it seemed to surprise my father. On another occasion, when my father himself was delivering a homily to some gathering of devout youths, in the darkness of the chair-crowded room I suddenly realized that they were all sniggering at him. Something in their manner told me that even before we came they had already anticipated his speech as an entertainment in a different sense from that which he intended. I felt outraged and indignant and at the same time I experienced a sense of pity. But my attitude towards his public appearances, which until then I had regarded as spectacular successes, was for ever changed.

The simple realization that he failed led me on to see that the public values which he admired were shallow. His conception of politics was confined to high ideals, having our name in the newspapers, and journalistic discussion of political personalities. Unlike my uncle, he had little conception of the task of being a public administrator or of the responsibility of pursuing a realistic policy.

When I realized that the desire to be Prime Minister was in itself only a thirst for notoriety, I shifted my ambition. Instead of wanting the fame that makes people discussed in the news, I looked to that which lasts for many years. I turned back to poetry. But although I

90

wanted a truer fame, I cannot deny that I have never been free from a thirst for publicity very like that of my father. Even today it often disgusts me to read a newspaper in which there is no mention of my name.

My conception of the poet had now shifted from my boyish idea of the simple nature-loving Wordsworth to that of Milton, with the 'last infirmity' of his noble mind, the thirst for fame. The poet now became for me someone whose mind rejects the preoccupations of the day, news, struggles for material gain, the machinery of society and even the apparatus of scholarship, by which men add stature to themselves, and who makes for himself a world out of timeless things, nature, and the beauty that he can create with his own imagination. He creates by virtue of the power that comes from the fullest realization of his own being. He does not add anything external to his personality: only that which will develop his inner life. However, my view of the poet was not solipsist. For I remember the thought striking me that to realize oneself to the fullest extent of one's powers means an entering into that which is beyond oneself. So it seemed to me that the point of my writing poetry might be to understand other poetry, to enter Shakespeare's mind as it were across the threshold of lines and images of my own creation which at some point were simply 'poetry'. If I could write a line which was 'poetry', then it would be like a key by which I could enter into the poetry of Shakespeare as far as the limits of my imagination enabled me to go. And after all, what can the aim of life be, beyond attaining, at certain moments, the height of oneself so as to gain a view of heights attained by minds in the past?

At these best moments a great humility fused with a great ambition: to be only what I was, but to the utmost of what I was, in order to enter into the being of the poets. And if I could not do so, to accept that I had failed after I had tested my own being against that of others, upon the level of naked existence.

When I was young I did not like the poems of every poet, and I recognized that some were better than others. Yet I had nothing which could be called critical sense. I assumed that every poem published in anthologies like *The Oxford Book of English Verse* and *Poems of Today* was good, because competent authorities had selected them. It was my own fault if I did not appreciate all the poems which editors

91

admired. Often my excitement about the idea of poetry created, as it were, a poetry beyond the words themselves, so that words which conveyed little to me were surrounded by the aura of what others had found in them. Thus:

> 'Charm'd magic casements, opening on the foam
> Of perilous seas, in faery lands forlorn',

conveyed no attractive picture to me. But that they were often quoted as 'pure poetry' illuminated them nevertheless, and just as getting out of a boat at a quayside and seeing some ships, I was later one day to cover my disappointment by saying to myself, 'This is France', bringing my whole conception of France to bear on my glimpse of Calais or Dieppe, so when I read these lines, I said to myself: 'This is poetry.'

Other poetry, as soon as I had read it became identified with an experience which seemed already to have existed unconsciously within myself. When I read certain sonnets of Shakespeare, Wordsworth, Keats, I seemed to know them at once as though I had known them before: and yet I had not done so. The inevitability of the words in the poetry had such force that it created in my mind an illusion of its own past history there. What is meant by 'inevitability' in poetry is surely a time-illusion produced by a certain order of words, which, while striking one as original, seem at the same time to have been said, and said in this way, always. This illusion exists also in music: Mozart can open a symphony or quartet with a tune which seems quite fresh and yet eternally familiar.

Some poetry, which I should have liked, actually repelled me: Milton's *L'Allegro* and *Il Penseroso*, Gray's *Elegy*, Wordsworth's *Ode on the Intimations of Immortality*, Dryden's Odes. What repelled me about these wonderful achievements was that the poetry in them seemed to strive to become monumental. I felt barred out of these great architectural constructions.

I liked much that was bad. The young accept the bad, not through bad judgment, but through lack of experience. They like the good as well as the bad, and they cannot distinguish between an effect which a writer indicates that he is trying to make, and one that is actually made. Thus although I was conscious of the ravishing beauty of the

92

poems of de la Mare, I thought his virtue lay in a dream-like atmosphere which he shared in common with other writers. I did not understand that this very vagueness was achieved by methods of as precise as those by which a watchmaker screws the jewels into a watch. I was deceived by the will to make a thing of beauty which betrays itself in some poems by the excessive use of words such as 'beauty' itself.

The thread which led me through the maze of poetic experiences to a truer sense of poetry was the concern, which I have already mentioned, with the single line. For what I remembered were not whole works, but lines – 'His silver skin laced with his golden blood', or 'The multitudinous seas incarnadine'. Gradually I came to see that such single lines crystallized an image which was the very core of the poetry: and to realize that there is a difference between the poets who allow their imaginations to lead them into a pleasant garden of poetic phrases, and those who use language as an instrument to hew a replica of their experience into words. I began to realize how much audacity, patience and solitude are required to express one's experiences. For the imagination suggests to the poet the undefined sensation of a metaphor which explains to him the quality of some experience. But to feel his way beyond this vague sensation to the exact image of the metaphor, to pursue it through solitude to places where it is hidden from all that has been put into words before, and then to mould it within all the hazards of language, reconciled with grammar and form, is extremely difficult. Most writers allow their ideas to lead them back from terrifying solitude to the consolatory society of approximate and familiar phrases. An experience to them is the beginning of a journey where they soon arrive at already expressed ideas. The writer who clings to his own metaphor is facing his own loneliness; in fighting to distinguish a new idea from similar ideas which have already been expressed, he may find that his most hidden experience brings him in conflict with current ideas among people surrounding him, and face to face with the terrifying truth of his own isolated existence. For he is revealing a fragment of the ultimate truth of his loneliness.

Gradually I saw that the true poets are not just 'poetic'. They also have an audacity of the imagination which enables them to pursue an

93

idea even when it may seem unpoetic, a desperateness in clinging to their own vision wherever it may seem to lead. This realization prepared me for the moderns. Thus while I was still at school I read *Troy Park* and other early volumes of Edith Sitwell. I was immediately attracted by a poet who transforms everything into pure hard images. Edith Sitwell wrote of the 'stalactites of the hard rain', light in one of her poems 'brays', and when a kitchen maid holds a candle in her hand the flame is compared with a carrot.

Until I met Auden, my idea of poetry remained still that of a separate poetic world apart from the real world. I thought of it as word-pictures and word-music outside everyday life. You look out of a window on to a lawn: beyond the lawn there is a stream running parallel with the house and the horizon, and, barring the horizon, rising like a pillar whose top is dark against the fiery wheel of the moon, is a poplar tree whose leaves, absorbing the darkness, are filled with the music of nightingales. My idea of a poem was the imitation of some such picture. It was the extension within music and imagery of the great 'O' of pure invocation.

Once, many years after this, when travelling in Greece, I dined out of doors at a restaurant on a small island which lies in the Bay of Chalcis. The tables were under the stars, and a few yards from them lay the sea like a black flapping flag, beyond which in a vast ring around the waters the mountains stood like huge green-grey transparent stones. At the table next to me sat a young Englishman – whose face I could not see – and with him a girl. After we had eaten, this young man pushed his chair back from the table, and, without affectation, looking up at the stars, recited lines which began with a great 'O'. Some vague recollection from my school days told me that these were the address of the watchman to the night in the *Agamemnon*. I did not understand the lines, but the Greek words in the clear English voice were filled with the stars, the seas and the mountains. This is the effect which was my idea of pure poetry, an invocation which one understands imperfectly but which is yet expressed exactly, filled with the stars, the mountains, the tables, and the chairs.

When I was at Oxford, I changed my view of poetry. I ceased to think of it creating a special world in which the poet enjoys Keatsian imaginings shutting out the real word. Nor did I think of the poet

94

as a kind of shadowy prophet behind the throne of power, Shelley's unacknowledged legislator of mankind. Instead, he was now a translator of the world which man projects around him through the actions of his will, back into language of the inner life of dreams and phantasy which has projected this materialistic external actuality. I believed now that everything which men make and invent is to some degree a symbol of an inner state of consciousness within them, as they are conditioned by their generation. Poetry was a use of language which revealed external actuality as symbolic inner consciousness.

I began to realize that unpoetic-seeming things were material for poetry. What seemed petrified, overwhelming and intractable could be melted down again by poetry into their symbolic aspects. The fantasy at the back of actuality could be imagined, and the imagination could create its order.

What excited me about the modern movement was the inclusion within new forms, of material which seemed ugly, anti-poetic and inhuman. The transformation of the sordid scene and life of the Dublin of Stephen Daedalus and Bloom into the poetic novel whose title, *Ulysses*, sets its aim beside that of the most timeless epic; the juxtaposition of scenes of European decline with ones recalling the greatest glories of the past tradition, in Eliot's *The Waste Land*: these showed me that modern life could be material for art, and that the poet, instead of having to set himself apart from his time, could create out of an acceptance of it.

Some of the writers who now came to interest me were: James Joyce, T. S. Eliot, Virginia Woolf, Robert Graves, Laura Riding, Ernest Hemingway, Osbert, Edith and Sacheverell Sitwell, Ezra Pound, Henry Green, Herbert Read – to name a few. What I admired was their hard clear imagery, their boldness of experimentation, and their search for means of expressing complicated states of consciousness and acute sensibility.

At Oxford I started writing poems containing references to gasworks, factories and slums. I understood the significance beneath the affectation of Auden's saying that the most beautiful walk in Oxford was that along the canal, past the gasworks, and that the poet must go dressed like 'Mr. Everyman'. I used to try experiments in prose to

95

express several levels of consciousness going on at the same time. For example, my taking up a book of history or philosophy and beginning to read a paragraph of facts or abstract speculation whilst all the time a part of my mind was thinking of a conversation with a friend. I studied how such a double layer of two streams of thought flowing simultaneously could be expressed.

Joyce, Virginia Woolf and Hemingway revealed to me areas of sensibility of which I had hardly been conscious before reading them. For example, the sensibility which can enable one to think about what one is thinking while one is thinking it. Hemingway made me aware of a quality and texture in the words upon a page which are like the rough surface of a plaster wall.

What differentiated these from previous writers seemed, above all else, to be that they drew attention to the processes of thinking and perceiving. Other writers have made their readers aware of the significance of a stain on a wall. Virginia Woolf makes them aware of the moment in which an observer becomes conscious of the stain: the stain is made vivid by the description of the state of mind of perceiving.

The tendency of these writers was to extend the material of literature and at the same time to clarify the processes whereby the outside world becomes an inner world within the mind of the individual. On the whole, the result of their writing was to direct the literary sensibility inwards. It was as though the twentieth-century writer had extended the range of his material, but in so doing had made the external world an object of interior sensibility. He had cast away the husk of its outwardness in attempting to digest it in his mind, and he had often become sick in the process. The hero of this literature was inevitably the exceptionally sensitive person, that is to say he who was most capable of receiving a wide range of impressions, most conscious of himself as a receiver of impressions, and most likely to make use of his impressions as a means of cultivating himself rather than of acting upon the world. Joyce, Proust, Eliot and Virginia Woolf had turned a hero or heroine into a passive spectator of a civilization falling into ruins.

One writer whom I began to read at Oxford challenged the passive sensibility which was characteristic of this literature. He was D. H.

Lawrence. Lawrence, despite his artistic defects, wrote poetry and prose which turned outwards from himself towards men and women, and towards nature. He had an abhorrence for the isolation of certain modern writers within their own highly developed sensibility. He had a sense that the distinctions between outer and inner are sacred: that whilst the inner life should meet the outer, the outer world should not become the inner world of the writer. To him the idea of the separateness of perceiving from what is perceived, of man from nature and from other men, is sacred. Meeting is a dark mystery, a kind of godliness, and even within the fusion of the sexual act the separateness of man and woman remain. This paradox of a fusion of existences which cannot become one another is for him the creative mystery. For from the contact of the individual with what is outside him, with nature, and with other people, there is a renewal of himself.

No attempt to resume Lawrence's ideas can explain the influence he had over me. This was an immediate reaction when I read a page of his descriptive prose, or one of his poems. At once I was aware of nature as a life-and-death force, existing independently of man's existence but containing energies capable of renewing him. Lawrence's birds, beasts and flowers were marvellously themselves, marvellously outside Lawrence, even where his intuition of them had an uncanny animal or vegetable quality. They stubbornly refused to become ideas or to be coloured by his own mental preoccupations. Lawrence could not have cerebralized the sea in the manner of Joyce calling it the 'snot-green sea'. Nor could he, like Eliot, have described the evening sky as 'a patient etherized upon a table'.

Lawrence, besides opening my eyes to a world that was just not potential literature, also seemed to challenge my own existence, my mind and my body. I felt the force of his criticism of his contemporaries and did not feel that I myself was spared his condemnation of Oxford undergraduates and namby-pamby young men. Worst of all, I felt that my work must suffer from that which was lacking in my own physical and mental being.

This lack of confidence in the quality of my own nature was reinforced later by Communism. Perhaps I was the type of cerebral modern writer condemned by Lawrence, or perhaps the bourgeois serving the interest of a class which imprisoned me in its own decadent social environment, condemned by the Communists.

*   *   *   *   *

During my last year at Oxford I became secretary of the University English Club. This enabled me to enlarge my acquaintanceship with writers by inviting, amongst others, Walter de la Mare, Edmund Blunden, J. C. Squire, Humbert Wolfe, William Plomer, to speak. I began to realize now that the poet is, amongst other things, a man who has to have another job, tired, overburdened, who cannot live on his poetry and who is in danger of clinging to it out of self-esteem. Most of these poets and writers, with a great sympathy for youth, were most cordial in revealing themselves. Generously overlooking the wrong information I had given them about the trains from London to Oxford, they delivered their sad advice on the literary life which I was now just about to enter, like ghosts in purgatory, conscious of the relative failure of their illusions, but still glowing with the faint effulgence of a vision. When he heard that I wished to write poetry, Edmund Blunden exclaimed: 'Whatever you do, don't review books as I did,' as Paolo and Franscesca relate that it was reading a book which led to their downfall. J. C. Squire, at the end of a rather convivial evening, eyed me with a wavering severity to ask: 'What do you intend to do with your life, young man?' 'Write poetry.' 'Then you will be like me,' he sighed, as one of those ghosts warns before surrendering himself to the flames. 'You will write poetry until you are twenty or twenty-one. Then you will fall in love with a fair young girl and you will write more poetry. Then you will marry that girl and you will write reviews and journalism. Then you will have a fine young strapping baby and you will write more reviews and journalism. Then, when you are my age, you will look back and think: "Well, perhaps after all, to have married that girl and had those children is worth more than to have written four hundred sonnets." '
Humbert Wolfe said: 'If you have a job in the Civil Service – which there is no reason you shouldn't have if you get a First like me – and if you are able to sell ten thousand copies, as I did of my last volume, you will be able to write poetry,' and he continued to talk of the books he had sold, in the transparent tones of one who buries his

98

critics under his public. J. B. Priestley advised: 'Well, it's not at all a bad idea to start with a little poetry if you want to write something serious later on. Now I myself . . .' and he went on to explain how, as a consequence of his early poetic discipline, trains were at that moment being loaded with copies of *The Good Companions*.

Walter de la Mare, perhaps because he had already so much the air of being an inhabitant of the shades, seemed confident in his modesty and modest in his confidence. In his charming way, de la Mare can make admissions about himself far more damaging than those of other writers. 'It's strange, isn't it,' he said, 'that I have a kind of sixth sense by which if my name is printed in a newspaper I know at once and turn immediately to it.' De la Mare has the child-like profound innocence which accepts and wonders at every pheno-menon and is not shocked. Many years after this, I met at his house a young American, a poet and story-teller and grandson of a famous presidential candidate, who told me a story of how he had met a sailor in London who had gone home with him and stolen his money and clothes. De la Mare listened, asked questions, smiled, as though it were a narrative from the realms of dreams. All the time we were sitting in his drawing-room, sipping tea out of cups of thin china as though in the house of some maiden lady in one of his rhymes for children. Later I saw something of this American who perhaps liked de la Mare and myself because we both understood him, though for different reasons: de la Mare from enchantment, I from disenchant-ment. When, after being thrown in and out of prison, he took his life, de la Mare and I entered into some correspondence about his literary remains. It was not, though, until I read a passage of insight in the introduction to de la Mare's anthology *Love*, that I realized how profoundly this most dreamy and unworldly of poets had accepted and understood the underlying actuality of the whole epi-sode. Recently I heard a story about de la Mare which charmed me. An old friend had been to visit him and was a little disconcerted because he asked dozens of questions throughout the whole after-noon without ever waiting for an answer. As he was leaving, the friend reflected sadly: 'After all, de la Mare is getting old.' At the door de la Mare said: 'I know I have asked many questions this afternoon, and never waited for an answer. But don't you agree that it's much more important to ask questions than to answer them?'

During this early period of my meetings with the Great, I experienced those agonies of longing for their friendship which can hardly be explained to those who do not understand what it is for a young man to start trembling when he recognizes in a crowd the face of someone who means to him, Poet.

At this period, to receive proofs of a poem or article I had written for some University magazine, to buy the magazine and see my own name in print at the beginning or end of article or poem, agitated me for days. They were the days of waiting for the fulfilment, there was the moment when with trembling fingers I turned over the pages, and then there were the hours when, covertly, I reconstructed the scene of first opening the review, like a crime, opening it as if by chance and falling on my own work, re-experiencing that astonishing sense of newness, of rebirth – myself in print.

On such occasions I was able by an act of self-projection to imagine myself as another person, an unknown reader, who opened the pages and read what I had written with eyes not my own. 'Astonishing! Amazing!' this I-not-I would exclaim, as he saw the words for the first time express in black characters on the white page some inmost thought or image of his own mind.

Although such a mood of self-intoxication may seem uncritical, paradoxically it was now, in the role of this other self-amazed-self that I could see an error with the same clarity as I could recognize a certain rightness. Even today, when I may become so familiar with something I have written that I seem unable to detach myself so as to judge it at all, I find that if I give the work to a friend I can look at it with his eyes as though for the first time.

What could be a greater change than from the days when to receive the proofs of a poem or article was like getting a love letter, to those when they became merely a tiresome interruption of new work with a reminder of work already put aside? What more different than from those when I regarded other writers as deities in whose presence I trembled, from those when I began to regard all but a few of them as the more successful, the more respectable, or the more wretched members of a nagging family, of which I myself was one?

*   *   *   *   *

During my last year at Oxford I already began to belong to a world outside the University. Feeling that I wished to devote myself entirely to writing, I tried to persuade my guardians to take me away from Oxford. But they were unwilling to do this.

Two things had brought about this change. The first, which belongs to the next chapter, was a summer vacation spent in Hamburg. The second was the beginnings of my friendship with Christopher Isherwood.

I first met Isherwood in Auden's rooms at Oxford at the end of the previous year. Auden had spoken of Isherwood in a way which made me think of him as The Novelist, who applying himself with an iron will to the study of material for his work, was determined to live the life of The Ordinary Man, going to the office in the train, dancing in dance halls at seaside resorts, dressing with a studied avoidance of every kind of distinctiveness, and so on. Isherwood, according to Auden, held no opinions whatever about anything. He was wholly and simply interested in people. He did not like or dislike them, judge them favourably or unfavourably. He simply regarded them as material for his Work. At the same time, he was the Critic in whom Auden had absolute trust. If Isherwood disliked a poem, Auden destroyed it without demur. Should he select one line for praise and condemn the rest, then Auden skilfully inserted this one line into a new poem. According to this principle, some of Auden's early poems are composite constructions made out of the fragments of parts of poems approved by Isherwood, and skilfully woven together.

Just as, for a long time, I had not been considered worthy by Bailey, my brother Michael or Tristan, to meet Auden, so now Auden withheld the privilege of meeting Isherwood from me. Tristan was introduced to him first, and tormented me a good deal with remarks to the effect that 'Christopher is awfully nice because he's just a quiet ordinary chap', and that it was pleasant to meet him, though personally he, Tristan, could never understand why anyone should want to meet anyone, and he feared that the desire to meet famous people was a great weakness of mine.

As a matter of fact, Isherwood was not famous at this time. He had published one novel, *All the Conspirators*, for which he had received an advance of £30 from his publishers, and which had been

101

not very favourably reviewed. It is curious that before I knew Isherwood and before I had read a word by him, I had been so convinced by his legend, that I read these reviews with an indignation which makes me still recall them better than I can reviews of my own books.

Tristan who, when he was with me, poked a certain amount of fun at his gods, partly as a means of asserting our mutually accepted inferiority, drew my attention to the fact that just as Auden seemed to us the highest peak within the range of our humble vision from the Oxford valleys, for Auden there was another peak, namely Isherwood, whilst for Isherwood there was a still further peak, Chalmers. Tristan quite gloated over our smallness in relation to heights beyond our visioning.

Perhaps I would never have been introduced to Isherwood had not Auden one day shown him the story about the pensionnat to which I have already referred. This made him want to meet me. Our first meeting was in Auden's rooms on a bright sunny afternoon. As Auden hated the daylight, all the blinds were drawn and the electric light was on. Seated at a table covered with manuscripts were Auden and Isherwood. Auden wore a green shade over his eyes, and looked like an amateur chemist. Isherwood looked like a schoolboy playing charades. The manuscripts were their respective books. Auden looked up abruptly when I came in and said: 'You're early. Sit down.' Isherwood giggled, and while I sat down he turned to Auden and said: 'But really I don't see the image of a "frozen gull flipped down the weir"': it sounds like cold storage.' Auden flushed and struck out the lines with a thick lead pencil.

When they had finished, Isherwood made me a quite formal little speech saying he had read my manuscript, and that he regarded it as one of the most striking things he had read by a young writer for a long time, and so on.

After this I saw Isherwood in London. He simplified all the problems which entangled me, merely by describing his own life and his own attitudes towards these things. He told me how, when he was at Cambridge, he and Chalmers had isolated themselves completely, remaining almost entirely in one or other of their rooms, writing the stories about a fantasy world called Mortmere (later he described all this in *Lions and Shadows*). When the time came for him to take

102

his tripos, Isherwood answered all the questions in limericks and blank verse. In this way, he achieved his aim of getting himself sent down.

Isherwood had a peculiarity of being attractively disgusted and amiably bitter. If I said, for example: 'After all, at the Universities you get to know the most intelligent minds of your generation,' he would look into the distance, and in a voice which seemed as far away as a tree on the horizon, say: 'Oh yes, of course the best minds of one's generation. Certainly one meets them there.' But while he said this the lines from his nostrils to the corners of his mouth would deepen with a kind of inexpressible pain which yet had something smiling about it.

After he had met Tristan, he spoke of him as a person who played one friend against another and gave extremely little to anyone. I explained that Tristan had psychological problems which I then described: he said, 'Oh yes. Of course, problems! How tired I am of people with problems,' in a way which made me realize that he did not mean that he had no sympathy with personal difficulties, but that he thought too many people used their problems as an excuse for exploiting the feelings of others. After I had introduced him to Marston he merely remarked: 'I see. You like people who are indifferent to you.'

I walked with him one night in Hyde Park when the day was darkening and the lights began to appear. Beyond the branches of the plane trees, on which the leaves hung in the gilded summer-late-light like old brocade (a fabric which seemed that it would fall if it were touched), the silhouettes of the houses of Park Lane and Knightsbridge lay like battleships. We walked around the Serpentine and it was as though Christopher were making circles round my world. The weak centre of this was that I did not do what I wanted and I did not ask what I needed. I wasted my time at Oxford when I wanted simply to write. I involved myself in situations with other people which were frustrating and which probably I myself created because I was afraid of a more intimate relationship.

Isherwood hated the dons for being divided between their academic-ism and the provincial gossip which is the social life of Oxford and Cambridge: the undergraduates for their snobbishness and exclusive-

103

ness. The whole system was to him one which denied affection: and which was based largely on fear of sex. His hatred extended, though, beyond Oxford. It was for English middle-class life. He spoke of Germany as the country where all the obstructions and complexities of this life were cut through.

But there was a positive as well as negative side to his beliefs. He spoke of being Cured and Saved with as much intensity as any Salvationist. He talked like some Christian Scientist *maudit* of people who were so Pure in Heart that they never contracted illnesses. Psychological cures were – according to him – effected by revolutionary methods. For example, he himself had cured a kleptomaniac by the simple method of accepting and organizing his kleptomania. Together, he and his patient had kept a large account book in which they noted down everything the kleptomaniac stole. This made stealing seem unromantic, because it had ceased to seem exciting and extraordinary.

By the end of our conversation on the edge of the Serpentine, I was longing to be cured by this method of being allowed to do whatever I liked, though I secretly doubted whether my desires, if fulfilled and even organized, would be less agitating.

When he talked, his words had an effect on me like the end of *Alice in Wonderland*. All the players in my game seemed suddenly to turn into a pack of cards. I was determined now to leave Oxford, to write and to live. A few months later, when I went to Hamburg, the opening words of a journal which I kept at the time were:

'1929. July 22nd. Hamburg.

Now I shall begin to live.

Resolution for the Long Vac. To do absolutely none of the work set for me by my Oxford tutor. Now I am away from England, I shall begin my own work, and whether I stay at Oxford or not, from now on I shall continue to do that and no work but that.

My own work is to write poetry and novels. I have no character or will power outside my work. In the life of action, I do everything that my friends tell me to do, and have no opinions of my own. This is shameful, I know, but it is so. Therefore I must develop that side of me which is independent of other people. I must live and mature in my writing.

My aim is to achieve maturity of soul. . . . After my work, all I live for is my friends.'

III

At the side of a lake there is a city which in the gloom suggests a vast construction of many forms, all shaped like gallows. Buildings, some of which are only blackened façades with broken windows, rise from its shores. An outline of the town's centre still exists, with churches, offices and hotels. Indeed, some of the buildings are remarkably unscathed, just as in a corpse some flesh seems perfect and even flushed with life. But that astonishing and total change, that incalculable shift from a soaring to a sinking motion which distinguishes a dead body, has taken place in Hamburg.

This is Hamburg as I saw it in August 1945. All legends of the living city have been superseded by the legend of the dead one. In a great air raid, when fire bombs were dropped in a ring around the centre of the city, the immense heat of the fire caused a whirlwind in which flames rushed from building to building, and thousands of people were roasted alive.

Dusk fell as I walked along the end of the lake in the late August evening. The water of the lake became a soft blue gauze wrapped round the plough of stars reflected in its surface.

In all my memories of Germany these great wrecks rise up between me and my past. They are the more insistent because they were implicit in their own past: and now it is difficult for me to think of my first evening in Hamburg (which now seems joined to present evenings by an axle of bright stars reflected in the diaphanous lake) without remembering that then I was conscious of a wrecked city in the future, as now I am conscious of an undamaged one behind today's ruins.

In July 1929, I walked along the shore of the lake with my host whom I had met in Oxford and who invited me to stay with him at Hamburg – the pale, rather intent, young Jew, Dr. Jessell – and he made a watchful, attentive guide. As we walked I started whistling. 'What tune are you whistling?' he asked. 'The scherzo of the Eighth Symphony.' 'So. Then you like music. We have many tastes in common.'

For the first time I noticed the scent of lime trees, which in Hamburg is like a screen along the roads by the lake. Sixteen years later it was a running trail, nostalgic scent of a past life, through the ruins. Between the road and the lake were grassy banks planted with occasional weeping willows. Their trailing branches made a Chinese calligraphy upon the paper-blue lake. Triangular sails floated across the water as softly as petals. It was like the music of Debussy. 'I have written poems in French and German, but I do not quite know whether my English is idiomatic enough,' said Dr. Jessell at my side. 'You can help me a great deal in things like that. I anticipate much from our friendship.'

My host introduced me to his friends, who invited me to parties in their bed-sitting-rooms and studios. We went swimming in the lake and for excursions in canoes. To these young Germans, who had little money and who spent what they had immediately, the life of the senses was a sunlit garden from which sin was excluded. Perhaps they thought that their generation had been purged of the bourgeois ideal of accumulated property by the great inflation of 1923. Now their aims were simply to live from day to day, and to enjoy to the utmost everything that was free: sun, water, friendship, their bodies.

The sun – symbol of the great wealth of nature within the poverty of man – was a primary social force in this Germany. Thousands of people went to the open-air swimming baths or lay down on the shores of the rivers and lakes, almost nude, and sometimes quite nude, and the boys who had turned the deepest mahogany walked amongst those people with paler skins, like kings among their courtiers.

The sun healed their bodies of the years of war, and made them conscious of the quivering, fluttering life of blood and muscles covering their exhausted spirits like the pelt of an animal: and their minds were filled with an abstraction of the sun, a huge circle of fire, an intense whiteness blotting out the sharp outlines of all other forms of consciousness, burning out even the sense of time. During their leisure, all their powers of thought were sucked up, absorbed into the sun, as moisture evaporates from the soil.

I went to the bathing places, and I went to parties which ended at dawn with the young people lying in one another's arms. This life appeared to me innocuous, being led by people who seemed naked in body and soul, in the desert of white bones which was post-war Germany. Yet I walked through all this curiously unscathed. There was something about my appearance at this time, so inhibited, pre-occupied, and physically nervous, that it prevented these young Germans from being drawn to me as they were to one another. They looked at me and said: '*Nicht schön, sondern interessant,*' or '*unschuldig.*'

Their lives flowed easily into the movements of art, literature and painting, which surrounded them. Everything was 'new', deceptively so. There were buildings, with broad clean vertical lines crossed by strong horizontals, which drove into the sky like railroads. There were experiments in the theatre and opera, all in a style which expressed with facility the fusion of naked liberation with a kind of bitter pathos, which was characteristic of this Germany. I once saw a movie which contained sequences of scenes with trams and bicycles going along the street. Music had been used to give these sequences a certain unreality. The bells of the trams and bicycles, the noises of the traffic, were woven into themes expressing a kind of tragic yet gay recklessness. This skilfully conveyed the nihilism, sophistication and primitive vitality which was so dangerously attractive in the beginning of the Weimar Republic.

Modernism in this Germany was (within certain limits of which I was not then aware) a popular mass-movement. Roofless houses, expressionist painting, atonal music, bars for homosexuals, nudism, sun-bathing, camping, all were accepted, and became like bright, gaudy, superficial colours in which the whole country was painted. Surrounded by this superficiality there were also serious artists, indignant Protestants, vengeful nationalists, Communists, many private tragedies, and much suffering. But such intense expressions of will and feeling were obscured by the predominant fashionableness of advanced attitudes. It was easy to be advanced. You had only to take off your clothes.

I was so intoxicated by my first weeks in Hamburg that I felt too creative to write very much: as when the conception of a book so overwhelms a writer that he can scarcely bring himself to work on it. I used often to leave the house of the Jessells with whom I was staying, and walk along the shore of the lake, with the grass and willow trees on one side of the broad road, the clean fronts of houses behind lime and plane trees on the other, whilst the road surface itself throbbed like a drum-skin under the traffic. On these walks I had a tremendous sense of release, of having got away from Oxford and home. Drums and flags seemed to march through my brain: it was as though my blood were a river of music. An embrace of recognition seemed celebrated between my inner life and the hot, green, throbbing world outside. When I had reached the centre of the town, I would go to some café and look at the poem or the novel I was then engaged on. I would drink an iced coffee crowned with thick cream.

Dr. Jessell had introduced me to several of his friends. Gradually I found myself detaching myself from him and spending more and more time with them. The two I liked most were called Joachim and Willi. Joachim had a large studio flat, of which he was extremely proud, on the outskirts of Hamburg. One night he invited my host and me to a party.

We climbed up four flights of stairs and I found myself in a large simple, airy room, like an attic, lit by a skylight and by slits of windows looking over Hamburg. The room was L-shaped, so that one part of it could not be seen from the other. At each end were beds which were mattresses, and bare modernist tables and chairs made of tubes of steel and bent plywood. The main part of the room formed a large space which had been cleared for dancing. The room was lit by lamps of tubular and rectangular ground glass.

We arrived late for the party. The other guests were already there. Joachim was tall, with a rather Mexican appearance, a sallow complexion, black eyes, raised, sensual, expressive nostrils, brushed back hair. As soon as he saw me, he took my arm and showed me all the

109

objects in the room: the bowl of rough-cut glass, the Mexican mat, the modernist crockery, and the massive books printed in heavy clear-cut modern types which indented the rag-paper pages.

He talked English with a faint American accent, telling me he had bought these books shortly after he had left school, but that he didn't read much now. He liked beautiful things, but he preferred 'living' to having things. Living was bathing, friendship, travelling, lying in the sun. 'I like the sun mostly and doing things with my friends: not reading.' I admired a drawing pinned on the wall. He said that he had done it long ago but that now he had given up drawing. He did, however, take photographs, and giving me a handful from a shelf under the Finnish table, he strolled off to greet other arrivals.

The photographs were like an enormous efflorescence of Joachim's taste for 'living', a great stream of magnificent young people, mostly young men, lying on the sand, standing with their heads enshadowed and pressed back as though leaning against the sun, rising from bul-rushes and grasses, swimming in seas and rivers, laughing from verandas, embracing one another. (I imagine all these photographs now, sodden under sweet-smelling rubbish from which weeds grow behind broken window frames: and where is this army of the young?) About the appearance of them all and about the very technique of the photography, there was the same glaze and gleam of the 'modern' as in the room itself and the people in it: something making them seem released and uninhibited yet anonymous, as they asserted them-selves by the mere force of their undistinguishable instincts.

A door out of the main room led to a little scullery, and here I found Joachim's friend Willi preparing drinks. He was quite different from Joachim, blonde, blue-eyed, Scandinavian and always smiling. A lock of his hair flopped over his blue eyes. He pushed this back from time to time across his forehead with his hand. His conversation showed his utter devotion to his friend, whose tastes and furniture and photographs he thought the most wonderful in the world. There was a kind of sadness, though, about this admiration. When I left Willi and went back to the main room it was filled with other guests. They were bronze-skinned and they dressed with a simplicity which suggested leaves and summer. The boys seemed girlish whilst the girls seemed masculine.

110

There was dancing, and when I danced with a girl called Irmi, who was slim and boyish, she danced in an inviting way, pressing her body close to mine, and holding her warm brown face almost against my lips. This seemed natural and so simple that the questions which would have arisen before me at Oxford did not arise.

After the dance, she left me and went towards Joachim, threw her arms around his neck and kissed him: that she should do this after having just embraced me also seemed natural. I seemed to be moving in a trance of sensuous freedom where everything was possible and plausible and easy. Irmi wore a short skirt like a kilt, and plaid socks with little tabs stuck into them. Her knees were bare.

A film was shown of another party just like the one at which I was now present and with some of the same people. Then there were pictures of sun-bathing, swimming. It was as though this Germany were a series of boxes fitting into one another, and all of them the same.

In the picture Joachim was now on board ship under a sky almost black with heat. Iron shadows lay on the sun-bright deck. Joachim leaned on the railings as he stared out to sea, his brow corrugated in a squinting smile which seemed to carry a great burden of pleasure. An instant later he was playing deck-tennis, laughing and gesticulating in a gayer mood than I had yet seen him in. Now on the screen there was a party here in this very room, and people dancing. The camera passed through moving figures, surveying the room, occasionally pausing as it were to examine someone's dress or figure. Boys and girls were lying on the ground embracing and then rolling away from one another to turn their faces towards the camera's lens. Willi lay stroking the head of a girl beside him. He turned, his face white in the light, and then he kissed her, the shadow first, and then his head, covering the light on her lips. I heard Willi laugh beside me.

After the film was over, people rose up with gestures as though they were yawning, and then stood quietly around with a strained excitement. Only one light, in the centre of the room, was turned on. The corners of the room were in darkness. Two or three couples started dancing, softly, to no music in the half-darkness, and then they seemed to swoon away together, prostrated in silence and shadow of corners of the room.

Dr. Jessell came up to me and said: 'I think it's about time we went home.'

'All right,' I said. 'But I want first of all to say good night to Willi.'

'He's just gone out of the room, I think.'

Dr. Jessell gazed at me with a scrutinizing smile which seemed posted like a sentry at the outskirts of his face, ready to open fire at a sign from me. He went away and came back with Willi. 'What do you want, Stephen?' Willi asked, smiling broadly. 'I only want to say good night to you, Willi.' 'Oh, is that all!' he burst out laughing and took my hand. 'How very funny! Good night!'

I walked back through the streets with Dr. Jessell, whose presence always forced me behind barriers of impassivity. I stopped walking when we came to a bridge over a stream flowing sluggishly into the lake. As I looked down onto the lake I noticed that something was happening to the sky. Dawn was beginning. There was no sun as yet, but the sky was no longer quite dark. A faint light seemed to cover the town, slowly filling it like water filling a tank. Below the liquid air I saw the heavy foliage, massive, without detail, over the river and the lake.

In the evenings in Hamburg, I used sometimes to go down to the district of San Pauli near the port, where there were cafés and bars for sailors, labourers, and tourists. Most of these *Lokalen* were situated on either side of a broad road brightly lit with signs, opposite a park dominated by an enormous statue of Prince Bismarck, looking like a monstrous pepper-pot carved out of granite.

Deep down by the quays of the harbour, as though plunged below the city into its black waters, there was the strangest of these places, a den kept by an old sailor who had a square unshaven chin, bristling hair and bulging Mussolini eyes. He had collected in his den the souvenirs of Arabian Nights' Voyages. From the ceiling hung stuffed alligators. Huge bats were clamped like scutcheons to the wall. One end of the bar was fenced with prairie grass and bamboo, overgrown with withered poison ivy. Under the chair on which Joachim sat, a porcupine spread its quills.

Another *Lokal* had the air of a parish hall decorated for Christmas with tinsel stars, paper ribbons, coloured crêpe and brightly lit

112

coloured electric bulbs. The dancers here were poorly dressed, and men danced with men. Several freakish febrile men were dressed as women. Singing weirdly, rolling their eyes, chucking staid citizens seated at their tables under the chin, these lolled from table to table. Most of the guests sat quietly at their tables drinking their beer, taking all this quite for granted. Leaning against the platform at one end of the room, or standing together in talkative groups, were working boys wearing their peaked caps, and a few sailors.

At one table not far distant from ours was an old man with a long beard, staring with eyes of unwavering desire at a young couple dancing together, whilst with young-seeming nervous fingers he touched the rim of his glass. There were men who stared into the centre of the room as if from a drugged sleep.

Amongst the dancers was a young man who danced alone. He had pale features. He wore pince-nez and the drab clothes of a bank clerk. He seemed, from the way in which he held himself, to suffer from some kind of partial paralysis. He was a little drunk now, as he threaded his way through the dancing couples waving his hands to and fro with an angular distorted movement like a parody of wings.

None of this seemed to me ugly or terrible or shocking. I saw it, rather, as a kind of play in which the ways in which people sought for happiness – and suffered – were revealed. And the fact that everything was bare and there were no pretences made even ugliness seem beautiful and exhilarating to me.

The reverse aspect of this decadence was the swimming, the sun-bathing, the rather facile pleasure in beautiful things. Once some friends drove me in their little car to a small modern house in the countryside near Hamburg. After dinner, we lay in the garden listening to gramophone records of Mozart's flute concerto played on a portable gramophone. I have never before or since heard this music sound at once so ethereal and yet so earthly, as though the flute passages moved amongst the orchestra like a white and secret stream pouring through roots of plants in dark, scented flower-beds, on a summer night. When it was quite dark we lit a bonfire in the garden, and as the light shone on to the house and wandering sparks drifted with the smoke into the warm upper air, the wife of our host came out on to the veranda. She was a beautiful young woman,

113

far advanced in a pregnancy which added radiance to her beauty. In the light reflecting upwards from the fire she looked Rembrandtesque, a ripe glowing figure painted in shadows and gold, bathed in flickering light.

But even here, in one of the most beautiful moments of my first visit to Germany, a certain heartlessness at the centre of it all raised questions in my mind. Our host, a very Nordic-looking blonde young man with self-consciously liberated and advanced views which were almost an orthodoxy here, explained that he had determined to go for a long bicycling tour by himself in Holland during the last days of his wife's pregnancy, as it was quite unnecessary for a modern husband to be near his wife at the time of childbirth. What happened in the hearts of these people who gave themselves so easily to so many things? If any of them had deep feelings, were these not bound to be hurt and disappointed?

Joachim was a dominating character who drew me into his orbit. He regarded himself as the commanding predatory captain of his own world, one who knew what he wanted, was not influenced by others, ruled over a court of those who loved him. He had organized his life in a way which seemed to him admirable. He worked for several hours a day in the great Hanseatic business of his family, which was selling coffee. He prided himself on being a good businessman: yet at the same time not dominated by business. He assiduously organized every moment of his day towards the pleasure which he called 'living'. The luncheon hour, which for him extended from one to four, was devoted to a simple vegetarian meal with friends, followed by swimming in one of the baths at the centre of the town. In the evening he went to the *Lokale* of San Pauli, or canoeing on the lake with friends, or to some party. The most intense experience of his life was what he called '*Une grande passion*'. By this he meant a passion which to some extent was outside his control, for someone whom he might want to see when that person did not want to see him. It was a variant on his feeling that people were willing objects invoked to satisfy a temporary state of desire.

He regarded me as an ally. He would meet me at luncheon at Hamburg's vegetarian restaurant (which was rather fashionable) and discuss his affairs, and explain his philosophy of 'living'. He often

114

had stories to tell which were amusing, and although what he took for smartness in his dress was a little vulgar, his self-confidence gave him a certain style. His black eyes shone, he had the big slow smile of the cowboy, and he wore broad-brimmed hats which recalled American travels.

In the late summer, Joachim invited me to go with him for a walking tour on the Rhine. In beautiful weather we walked along that part of the river where the shores are most mountainous. At nights we would stop in some little town with a boulevard looking out over the wide river. Here the people, dressed in their fancy dress costumes, seemed to have gaping mouths into which grapes were pressed. The boys in leather shorts and the girls in their billowing skirts stood gazing out over the river in the evening, when the darkness seemed inwoven with heavy scent, and it was as though they dissolved into the dragonish sensuality of the Rhine landscape.

Joachim in his dynamic arrogant way strode amongst the groups of girls and boys, with an expression as though one magnetic look could extract anyone of his choice from a crowd and bind him to Joachim for ever. One evening, when I had gone by myself for a walk after dinner, I returned to the inn where we were staying, to find Joachim drinking with one of the youths who stared across the waters as though waiting for an arm to rise out of them with a gleaming sword. Joachim gave me a burning look and said: 'Heinrich, this is Stephen.'

The next morning he told me that Heinrich was to accompany us on our tour. Heinrich and Joachim walked along in an exalted mood, singing in turn the songs of Hamburg and of Bavaria. (Heinrich was Bavarian.) I could not join in these songs and I realized that after all there was something exclusive about this Germany which included the bronzed, the athletic, the good-looking and the smart, but shut out the old, the intellectual and the ugly.

Heinrich, though, was very friendly. During the next days, often he came to me as though with a message from Joachim, put his arm round my shoulders and said in broken English: 'I like you; you must like me.' His body was like carved polished wood, rather emaciated and yet strong and lithe. He seemed some saint made by an artist who has fallen sensually in love with his own carving, and pro-

115

duced a pagan instead of a Christian image. Forehead, mouth, chin, and even hair, gave the same impression of carved wood, varnished by many suns, a product of Bavarian folk-art. Yet in this carved face there were almond-shaped, greenish, extremely watchful eyes, which did not leave your face when he was talking to you.

Joachim soon told me that his relationship with Heinrich was the great attachment of his life, as, indeed, rather surprisingly, it almost proved to be. Even in those first few days I would sometimes notice a strange expression in Heinrich's eyes: not just shrewd or calculating, but vengeful and spiteful. At the same time I learned something of his history – the folk story of the workless wanderers in the Germany of 1929. It was nothing more than a story of wanderings, misfortunes, bad beginnings, in which his own disasters were inseparably confused with those of all the other boys who were his comrades. It was a fragment of the saga of all this German youth which had been born into war, starved in the blockade, stripped in the inflation – and which now, with no money and no beliefs and an extraordinary anonymous beauty, sprang like a breed of dragon's teeth waiting for its leader, into the centre of Europe.

So impressed was I that I wrote a poem in which I described the young bank clerk with 'world-offended eyes' who stood naked with the 'new German', and 'myself, being English', prepared to build his world out of our bones.

We ended our walking tour at Cologne, which in the light of that summer lay on each side of the river, like two great turbines, one the cathedral, the other the modern concrete buildings of the exhibition: the two of them connected by arches of great bridges like folded wings. (When I crossed the river at Cologne sixteen years later, in 1945, it was on a pontoon because the bridges had fallen into the river. Two uniformed public-school boys were with me: and the city, where it had not been completely broken, was torn and scratched over as if by claws.)

After this walking tour I returned to England for my last year at Oxford. As I have explained, I simply neglected my studies during this last year. I spent the remaining part of the long vacation printing a little volume of the *Poems* of W. H. Auden, an edition of thirty copies which is sought after today.

When I had left the University, I returned to Hamburg. But I no longer lived in the great house of the Jessells at the end of the lake. I had a bed-sitting-room in a boarding-house. At one *Lokal* I met an unemployed young man called Walter, in whom I rather arbitrarily decided to take an interest. Walter had large clumsy hands, an intent expression of his eyes in his pale face, under the cloth cap which he nearly always wore. I used often to go with him to the amusements arcade. He would put his heavy fingers on the handles which controlled silver balls, in those games where illuminated numbers appear, bells ring, balls disappear down holes, and if you achieve a victory reckoned in an enormous sum, you get some money back. Walter was for ever explaining to me that he needed money for some journey which would take him to his mother or a brother or an aunt from whom he had been separated for many years. Several times I gave him the money, but his journey was one of those frustrated voyages which are never made, because it always happened that he lost his money before he got on to the train: and then, when I was lying on the bed of my bed-sitting-room, my bell would ring and there he would be, with gravely shining eyes under his peaked cap, explaining in his Hamburg dialect that before taking his ticket to the station he had been so tired that he had lain down to sleep in the waiting room, where he had been robbed: or that he had lent his money to that friend, of whom I had already been told, whose girl must have the abortion. At the advice of Joachim, I finally bought Walter a ticket and put him on to a train which presumably took him to his relatives.

Now I look back with amusement at the episode of Walter. Yet at the time I took his problem seriously, and I tried to believe the stories he told me. If I had not tried to believe him, or if I had not thought that his stories were ways of expressing a need for money with which I could sympathize, the relationship would have been more cynical. Because it was not so, I can still think of it as a friendship in which there was something more significant than a kind of mutual exploitation. I cannot just dismiss Walter as part of my very gullible past when I allowed myself to be victimized by a tramp. For in this relationship there was a grain of real affection of a kind which I had not had before. It is as though I was in need of some precious ore and had been driven to seek it in the smallest quantities and the roughest

117

places. What my friends – and even I myself, at moments, saw – was that I returned with clothes tattered, and having been robbed and degraded. But as a matter of fact I did have a little of the precious ore: there were moments when in the middle of cheating me Walter trusted me, and when I gave him more than money. With him I escaped to some extent from the over-spiritualized, puritan, competitive atmosphere in which I had been brought up, to something denser, less pure, but out of which I could extract and refine little granules of affection. From such experiences I gradually learned a feeling which I could later bring to the highest relationships.

Through Walter, I imagined the helplessness, the moral weakness, the drift, of unemployment. I imagined, I suppose, that something which I was now beginning to call in my mind 'the revolution' would alter his lot, and I felt that as a member of a more fortunate social class I owed him a debt. If he had robbed me I would have felt that he could never rob me sufficiently of advantages which society had given me over him: for I was a member of a class whose money enabled me to benefit automatically from its institutions of robbery, to assume automatically its disguises of respectability. To my mind, it appeared that there are two classes of robbers: the social and the anti-social.

Although this attitude embodied a certain truth, I was being sentimental. I had allowed a sense of social guilt to put me in a position where I was unable to criticize a thief or a blackmailer. This meant that I was a potential exploitee, because I could never feel within myself the rightness of a social situation which would rebuke the wrongness of others. So I allowed my time, energy and money, all of which I should have spent to the advantage of my talent, to be wasted. Or did I? For after all, what seemed, and may still seem, inexcusable wasting was at least in part a flowing in of life through silted, muddy channels. What was really bad, was that my attitude prevented me from being able seriously to help Walter. For I saw his faults as projections of my own guilt, and not as problems which he must deal with for his own interests, within his own situation. I should have been tougher and more cynical, accepting my own position in the world, and expecting others to accept theirs, or more prudent, or else perhaps more fanatically idealistic, giving up my advantages, so that

118

I was able to speak to outcasts as one who had made himself an outcast. But although I had comparatively little money, my whole position of independence depended on it. Without it, I would not ever have gone to Germany and lived the life in a bed-sitting-room. It was not the quantity of what I had which was striking, but the quality of what I could do and be by virtue of having a little. The difference between having twenty thousand a year and three hundred is as nothing compared with that between having three hundred and none.

Because I projected my own weakness on to those around me, I was fascinated by those with no qualifications for adapting themselves to their circumstances. Such people are forced into a certain detachment from aims and conventions by being neither rulers nor workers, but victims. Their existences are marginal, registering as delicately as the needle of an instrument, booms and slumps, when they are unemployed or thrown into unemployment: periods of social decadence, when they are demoralized: of upheaval, when they become the crude material of revolution: wars, when they may suddenly become heroes. The unemployment of the 1930's produced tens of thousands of such hapless, workless people, all over the world.

At this time my prevalent social attitude was one of pity. This, and sympathy with weakness, showed in my work and behaviour. These were attitudes of what Yeats calls 'passive suffering'. They were the projections of a mixture of strength and weakness: strength, to the extent to which I was master of my own kingdom of the creative imagination, my own work wherein I might create as I chose. Within this inner world even weakness could become a kind of strength. It isolated me and disqualified me from other kinds of work than poetic writing. I needed only the strength of my own weakness to say that I had no other responsibilities than simply to exist in order to write. It enlarged my sympathies by leading me down paths where people were insulted, oppressed, or vicious. It saved me from having to judge them by conventional rules of conduct, since I did not observe these myself.

The danger, which I did not avoid, was of identifying the weakness of him who really does nothing, with that of the poet who sometimes appears to do nothing, but who, in a way which mystifies his fellows, redeems himself by turning a meaningless or depraved or idle

119

life around him into the significant material of his poem. I detected in others qualities which I shared, and I thought they might share mine, so that there were moments when it would not have surprised me if someone like Walter or Joachim had produced from his pocket a poem, magical with the mystery of the lights and silver balls of amusement arcades, or smouldering with the passion which chooses a different bed-mate from the pavements every night. I held back my energies, in order not to disturb the precarious happiness of those whose lives I shared by revealing that there was in me this difference, this *deus ex machina*: the poem.

During these months in Hamburg, I discovered a terrifying mystery of cities which fascinated me in the way that one reads of people in the past being fascinated by the Eleusinian Rites. This is that a great city is a kind of labyrinth within which at every moment of the day the most hidden wishes of every human being are performed by people who devote their whole existences to doing this and nothing else. Along a road there walks a man with a desire repressed in his heart. But a few doors away there are people utterly devoted to accomplishing nothing but this desire. What has been crushed, never spoken of for generations by his family, revolves there night and day like the wheels of a machine. He has only to know a secret word, open a door, and he may enter into this continuity of things which are elsewhere forbidden. He has only to shut the door again and walk out of the house, and he is again in the locked street where things are scarcely mentioned and unseen. Yet he has in his hands this magic key of entrance into a perpetual stream of fulfilment which he can use whenever he wills. When he even no longer feels desire, he can in an idle, abstract and unwishing kind of way prove to himself, almost for no reason except a mysterious and remote compulsion to reaffirm that it is so, that the hidden life of forbidden wishes exists in extravagant nakedness behind mazes of walls.

When I discovered this, I was almost tempted to think that I had stripped bare my deepest wishes and found that others shared them and that even if this were a kind of hell, perhaps it was my destiny.

At the same time there was a desire to save myself for work. I realized the danger of there being a place beyond which the fulfilment of the senses becomes an automatic activity too complete

120

and devouring in itself for one to want anything else or be able to work.

Nevertheless, during the year or so when I was living a life dangerous to myself and impossible to justify to others, I was writing my best early poems.

*   *   *   *   *

After I had been in Hamburg only a few months, Christopher Isherwood, who was in Berlin, invited me to live near him there.

At this time he was not the successful writer and well-known personality he has subsequently become. He was comparatively poor and almost unrecognized. His novel, *All the Conspirators*, had been remaindered, and he was working on a second, *The Memorial*. During the years when I was often in Berlin, he lived in various poor parts of the town, of which the best was in the neighbourhood of the Nollendorfplatz – a grand-shabby square dominated by a station of the overhead railway – the worst, that of the Hallesches Tor, an area of slum tenements. He lived very poorly, scarcely ever spending more than sixty pfennigs (about eightpence) on a meal. During this time, when I had meals almost every day with him, we ate food such as horse flesh and lung soup, which for some years ruined my digestion, and for all time my teeth, as they had long ago ruined his.

Very soon my relationship with Christopher fell into a routine. I would leave my bed-sitting-room, situated in the slightly more luxurious Motzstrasse, and walk past its grey houses whose façades seemed out of moulds made for pressing enormous concrete biscuits. Then I would come to the Nollendorfplatz, an eyrie of concrete eagles, with verandas like breasts shedding stony flakes of whatever glory they once had into the grime of soot which caked the walls of this part of Berlin. The bridges, arches, stations and commanding noise of the overhead railway had taken possession of the square and of the streets leading westwards through Tauenzienstrasse and Wittembergplatz, and eastwards to the ever more sordid tenements which never yet quite lost some claim to represent the Prussian spirit, by virtue of their display of eagles, helmets, shields and prodigious buttocks of armoured babies. A peculiar all-pervading smell of hopeless decay (rather like the smell of the inside of an old cardboard box) came out of the interiors of these grandiose houses now converted into pretentious slums.

I turned out of the Nollendorfplatz down the Nollendorfstrasse, yellowing parody of the Motzstrasse, to the still more sordid street in which Christopher lived. I climbed up two or three flights of stairs, the walls of which had an even stronger odour than the street outside. Then I rang the door-bell of the flat where Christopher had his room. The front door was opened by Christopher's landlady, Fräulein Thurau, with pendulous jaws and hanging breasts, the watch-dog of the Herr Issyvoo world; and now I had entered one of Christopher's stories, Fräulein Thurau, with a *'Guten Tag, Herr Spender'* of a cordial kind which recognized that I was one of those friends of Christopher whom she did not reckon a blackmailer or a wastrel, perhaps even that I was a 'good influence', would add '*Herr Issyvoo ist noch nicht fertig*' with a rolling of her eyes, or '*Herr Issyvoo hat Besuch*', with a sombre humorousness which suggested a double meaning. I would then be shown into the room which was the very centre of the Fräulein Thurau universe, reception room, dining-room, entrance hall, as one might choose to regard it, with faded tapestried and oaken furniture, out of which the doors of other rooms opened. Here on a wide chair large enough to seat two people, in front of the table covered with a wine-coloured velvet table-cloth which had been affected by a kind of mange so that it looked like a skin of a huge cat of the same colour, I would sit amongst the tassels, the pictures of Blücher's yellowing victories, the wreckage of Fräulein Thurau's mythical grandeur, waiting an unconscionably long time for Christopher to appear. Whilst I was waiting, one or other of the characters of his as yet unwritten novels would dart out of one of the rooms opening into this one. Perhaps Bobbi the bar-tender would shoot fish-like through this central tank and escape into another room, or perhaps Sally Bowles would appear, her clothes dishevelled, her eyes large onyxes fringed by eyelashes like enamelled wire, in a face of carved ivory. Christopher lived in this apartment surrounded by the models for his creations, like one of those portraits of a writer by a bad painter, in which the writer is depicted meditating in his chair whilst the characters of his novels radiate round him under a glowing

122

cloud of dirty varnish, not unlike the mote-laden lighting of Fräulein Thurau's apartment.

After some time Christopher would appear, probably in his shirt-sleeves, razor in hand, to say that he was extremely sorry but last night had been terrible, he had not slept, but now he would be ready in a few minutes. Ten minutes later he would reappear, remarkably transformed, with a neatness of the cuffs emphasized by the way in which he often held his hands extended, slightly apart from his body. His hair was brushed in a boyish lick over his forehead, below which his round shining eyes had a steadiness which seemed to come from the strain of effort, as though their feat of balancing themselves in Christopher's face at the same time balanced the whole world which they saw. They were the eyes of someone who, when he is a passenger in an aeroplane, thinks that the machine is kept in the air by an act of his will, and that unless he continues to look steadily in front of him it will fall instantly to the ground. These eyes were under sharp-angled eyebrows which added to the impression of his being a strained school leader. The mouth, with its deep vertical lines at the corners, was that of a tragi-comic Christ. He was well aware of these effects. Perhaps if we decided to go to Insel Ruegen from Berlin in the summer, after discussing other possibilities, he would say: 'Well, to the North,' and assume the bleak wrinkled look of a pilot steering through arctic seas with icicles hanging from sandy eyebrows. Once when we were eating an execrable meal, I implored him, with that exaggerated concern I had in those days for any annoyance to a friend with whom I was, to eat something better. But he waved the suggestion away in bad German which, with his gesture, absurdly recalled the Greek of the New Testament: '*Was ich habe gegessen ich habe gegessen.*'

My morning call at Fräulein Thurau's was always the time for grave pronouncements. 'That is the last time I ever go to *that* place I went to last night again. They can sink or swim without me.' Or: 'Do you know what that bitch Sally said to me last night?' 'No.' 'Perhaps, one day, Christopher darling, you will write something really great, like Noel Coward.' Or: 'Mr. Norris has been caught.' Or: 'I have given Fräulein Thurau notice. I will not live under the same roof as Bobbi an instant longer.'

123

I entered so completely into Christopher's moods that, although I was in part entertained by these pronouncements, they also filled me with a certain apprehension, and, as we went down the stairs into the street, I felt the oppression of the silence which follows fateful news. Secretly I was disappointed that Christopher's dramas rarely ended with complete catharsis. All the people who had fallen into disgrace were sooner or later taken back into favour, for Christopher, so far from being the self-effacing spectator he depicts in his novels, was really the centre of his characters, and neither could they exist without him nor he without them.

We would then have a meal consisting of watery soup followed by some frightful meat. Eating such food was a penance for Christopher to which he attached an unstated but disciplinary importance. When sometimes, if I was alone, I went to one of those pleasant restaurants with outdoor gardens in the Kurfurstendamm, and had a meal costing one mark fifty, or if, still more self-indulgent, I went to one of the excellent Russian restaurants which were a feature of Berlin, with my friend the American composer, Roger Sessions, or my brother Michael, I felt as though I had betrayed him.

After lunch there was a relaxation of our régime, for we then walked to a shop near the Bahnhof-am-Zoo where we bought a packet of toffee. So regular were our appearances at this shop, that on seeing us enter a girl assistant would rush behind the counter, fetch the packet of sweets, hand it to us and receive one mark in payment, all without a word. Perhaps it was the influence of Christopher which had this effect, because I do not believe it would have happened to me had I been alone. In fact, in his own neighbourhood, Christopher had trained most of the shop people to spring into automatic, swift, silent action as soon as he appeared at the shop door, as though he were a switch and they machines running on electric rails. When a certain grocer refused to act in this way, Christopher took revenge by buying his groceries at a store a few doors away, having them packed as bulkily as possible, and, thus laden, walking slowly, bowed down with his purchases, past the erring grocer's shop, hoping thus to break his spirit.

It may seem that there was an inconsistency about his extreme economies and the purchase of the sweets. This is true. But I think

124

that Christopher regarded the sweets as being in their way another penance, an excess ruining his teeth. What he would have regarded as inexcusable would have been a 'balanced diet', for at that time Auden and he were in full revolt against all forms of hygiene. If you were 'pure in heart' you could not catch a disease with which you came in contact. But iced coffees and toffee had an exorbitant place in our budget, so that once Christopher said to me when he was complaining about money: 'If I could suddenly see now in front of me the Niagara of iced coffees which I have drunk during the past year, then I would understand where all my money goes.'

Eating our toffee, we would then, if the weather were fine, take a train to the Grünewald where we would walk among the pine trees or along the shores of the lake. We walked a great deal, and my memories of the stories which Christopher told me – of his family in the house near Manchester, of Chalmers, of meeting Auden when they were both at the same preparatory school – are mingled with impressions of the sandy Grünewald and the streets of Berlin. The architecture of Berlin was unlike that of any other town. It had a unity amid its diversity, and was like (as it was meant to be) an ideological expression in stone, granite, and concrete, of certain ideas. The streets were straight, long, grey, uniform, and all their ornaments expressed the idea of Prussian domination. There were a good many squares, but these had little positive character. They were just places where several streets halted and had a rest before going on with their uniformed march, at the exact opposite side of the square from where they had left off. They were more like spaces in time than in place, intervals in which the passer-by was able to breathe before resuming the logic of the street. Certain parts of Berlin were characterized by what seemed a relaxation of régime, or by a rise into higher ranks, rather than by a change of style. The streets grew wider, there were more frequent intervals between houses, more trees and gardens, and the squares, when one came to them, were larger. Other parts of Berlin represented wild fantasies, as though the architects who had restrained themselves when they designed the more austere neo-classical buildings of the Unter den Linden had gone mad when they came to design the cathedral and the palace. Moreover, Unter den Linden and its environments were connected to the West End of the

125

Kurfurstendamm by roads and bridges laid like twisting cables over chaotic parts of the city, consisting of railway lines, stations and canals. Lastly, nothing expressed the cynical relationship between the grim architecture and the feckless population more than the belief of the Berlin population that one of the stone lions outside the palace at the end of the Unter den Linden roared whenever a virgin walked by.

When we had got out of our train and were walking through the Grünewald with the flat, white, Moroccan-looking modernist houses gleaming behind the brown and green pine trees, and with the sun-bathers lying in profusion on the flint-grey grass – the relentlessly handsome German youths with their arms round their doughy girls – Christopher talked. He told me the plot of a novel he was planning, to be called *The Lost*. Day after day, against the background of the pine trees, lakes or streets, I witnessed that transformation taking place in his mind, where the real becomes the malleable, the people who are garrulous and shabby in life become the crystal entertainers of fiction.

Like most vital people, Christopher could be depressive, silent, or petulant. Sometimes he would sit in a room with Sally Bowles or Mr. Norris without saying a word, as though refusing to bring his charac-ters to life. Sometimes he was in a Dostoevskian mood of gloom, or a Baudelairean one of debt and failure. About once a fortnight he was hypochondriac and I would accompany him to the doctor, both of us imagining that he was about to be sentenced to a fatal disease. Sometimes he was broke and we would force ourselves to think up ways of earning money. He gave English lessons, he translated, occa-sionally he even did a little journalism, but in Berlin in 1930 you not only had to work very hard to earn very little, you also had to be a financial genius to get paid.

In the early stages of our friendship I was drawn to him by the adventurousness of his life. His renunciation of England, his poverty, his friendship, his independence, his work, all struck me as heroic. During months in the winter of 1930, when I went back to England, I corresponded with him in the spirit of writing letters to a Polar explorer. I thought of him in the centre of the northern European plain, gripped in icy cold, across the stormy and black channel. His

126

letters were of a besieged person, facing creditors, the elements, and the breakdown of a civilization, surrounded by a little loyal crew: 'the position is absurdly terrible. The ice is cracking on the capitalist Wannsee like pistol shots and the doomed skaters in tights and Hessian boots are at least a kilometre from the beer house on the shore.' And: 'My financial troubles are worse than ever before. Chalmers left the sinking ship this morning,' he wrote. I was sometimes an emissary from Isherwood in Berlin to editors and publishers in London. We both thought of London as a kind of province on which we unfortunately depended, to which I had been sent. 'I am praying to God to soften the heart of Virginia Woolf,' he writes. 'An appropriate greeting to Mr. Lehmann if he is still with you.' Then there is the bulletin of Berlin disasters: 'Sally goes into the clinic tomorrow. Last night I was drunk.' And there is always the note of his consciously overacting his own role: 'A telegram handed to a porter at Liverpool Street is sufficient notice for me.'

About three years of my life, I realize now, were lived precariously off the excitement of being with Isherwood. I told him everything, I showed him every letter of any interest I received, I looked to his judgment of my friends and activities.

Sometimes, as in the case of my friendship with a girl called Gisa Soloweitschik, I seemed to be offering my own feelings on an altar of Christopher's domination. Thus I encouraged, even if I did not provoke, in him characteristics which he probably did not care for in himself. Gisa Soloweitschik was of Lithuanian origin. I was an undergraduate and she was seventeen when I first met her whilst ski-ing in Switzerland. I introduced Christopher to her in Berlin. Her parents used most generously to invite us each Sunday to their flat in Wilmersdorf where they gave us a large meal, at the end of which they used to send us away with our pockets stuffed with fruit. They called Christopher Shakespeare and me Byron. Gisa was studying *Kunstgeschichte*. She would fill her rooms with volumes opened at pictures which she showed us, saying: 'Look! That is beautiful. Isn't it? Yes!' Or she would suddenly stop the conversation with a command: 'Listen! This is beautiful! I think you need it!' And play what was her then favourite piece, the adagio of the Beethoven Violin Concerto, on her portable gramophone. Christopher would listen to the music in silence, a polite but sour smile on his face. Gisa said: 'But do you not find it beautiful?' 'Oh, yes. Beautiful. Exquisite,' Christopher said and then sighed, leaning back against his chair. 'I understand!' exclaimed Gisa. 'You do not like music! You are stone-deaf. Stone-deaf or tone-deaf, do you say? Which?' 'I like music very much, and particularly that concerto, which I happen to know very well. As a matter of fact, it may interest you to know that I was secretary for some time to a violinist, André Mangeot. You may have heard of him,' said Christopher rather acidly. Somewhat on these lines a struggle went on between them, with Gisa standing for Art and the things of the spirit, Christopher for human relationships and for war against all self-conscious æsthetic and intellectual pretensions. In his mood of hating intellectualism, he disapproved of my going to concerts, was bored when I attempted to discuss ideas, and was cold about friends with whom I shared intellectual interests.

He soon found out that there was an Oriental sense of untouchability in Gisa. She could not drink from a glass if anyone else had drunk from it; she hated even to be touched. The result of the conflict was that although Gisa and Christopher were always at one another's throats, within a few weeks he knew her better than I had done in seven years. I realize now that I myself had engineered this result, so great was my desire to know people through his knowing them. Partly I was surrendering my relationships to him; partly I just wanted to see my friends live in his conversation.

Perhaps my greatest debt to Christopher is the confidence he gave me in my work. He was more than a young rebel passing through a phase of revolt against parents, conventional morality and orthodox religion. He also recognized that nearly everyone wanted something out of life which he or she had been taught to conceal. He was on the side of the forces which make a work of art, even more than he was interested in art itself, and on the side of the struggle towards self-realization more than he was interested in the happy ending or the success story. He simply believed in his friends and their work, and in his own judgment of them. His judgment might be wrong but it would be himself who would decide this. No institutions with their standards or examinations, no citing of conventions and past examples, no criticism, would affect this. His hatred of institutions of
128

learning and even of the reputation attached to some past work of art, was really hatred of the fact that they came between people and their direct unprejudiced approach to one another. Of course Christopher's judgments were not always just. But what is true is that a creative writer can be enormously encouraged by the complete support, without conditions and without reference to any other judgment, of a fellow writer.

     *   *   *   *   *

Meanwhile the background of our lives in Germany was falling to pieces. There was a sensation of doom to be felt in the Berlin streets. For years the newspapers contained little news but of growing unemployment and increased taxation necessary to pay reparations and doles. The Nazis at the one extreme, and the Communists at the other, with their meetings, their declamatory newspapers, their uniformed armies of youths, their violence against the Republic and against one another, did all in their power to exacerbate the situation.

Brüning had abandoned the attempt to govern through the yelling mob of members of twenty-nine different political parties, which was the Reichstag (broadcasts of whose howling debates, punctuated by a tinkling bell, were a feature of the German wireless), and, using emergency powers under the Constitution, governed by decree. Every decree, accompanied by dissenting cries of 'dictatorship' from the extreme Right and the extreme Left, produced an impression of the Brüning Cabinet as a little boat manned by a hopeless crew, trying to navigate an unending storm.

The feeling of unrest in Berlin went deeper than any crisis. It was a permanent unrest, the result of nothing being fixed and settled. The Brüning régime was neither democracy nor dictatorship, socialism or conservatism, it represented no group nor class, only a common fear of the overwhelming disorder, which formed a kind of rallying place of frightened people. It was the *Weimardaemmerung*. Tugged by forces within and without, by foreign powers and foreign money-lenders, industrialist plotters, embittered generals, impoverished landed gentry, potential dictators, refugees from Eastern Europe, it reeled from crisis to crisis within a permanent crisis.

In this Berlin, the poverty, the agitation, the propaganda, witnessed

129

by us in the streets and cafés, seemed more and more to represent the whole life of the town, as though there were almost no privacy behind doors. Berlin was the tension, the poverty, the anger, the prostitution, the hope and despair thrown out on to the streets. It was the blatant rich at the smart restaurants, the prostitutes in army top boots at corners, the grim, submerged-looking Communists in processions, and the violent youths who suddenly emerged from nowhere into the Wittembergplatz and shouted: ' *Deutschland Erwache!*'

Germany had been pushed down to that level where the members of every group were conscious of themselves as a political interest. The prosperity of some was the direct result of the inflation (there was a row of luxurious new houses in Hamburg, known to the population as *Inflationstrasse*) which had been the ruin of others. Almost no one had interests above and outside the immediate day-to-day political situation. Not only were nearly all thus conscious of being politically involved, persecuting and persecuted, but events wore the same political aspect. When, for example, the Darmstadter National Bank failed, there was an atmosphere of general collapse in Berlin for a few days. The Nazi newspaper *Der Angriff*, trying to push the Republic over the abyss, came out with the headline: '*Alles bricht zusammen.*' A spell of intensely cold weather, by increasing misery, throwing workers out of employment, and thus adding a burden to the dole, became a political crisis threatening the Government, and welcomed by the Nazis and Communists.

Thus the whole of Germany was politicized in a way which divided it against itself. The depressed and partly ruined middle classes attributed their downfall to the Jews and to the Polish refugees who had poured into Berlin after 1918. The aristocrats and generals considered themselves to be fighting for the survival of the noblest German tradition against foreign elements and proletarianization. In the course of their self-righteous struggle, General Schleicher, the Hindenburg family, von Papen and the rest, made strange allies and corrupting compromises. The Jews and intellectuals, attacked by the Nazis and Nationalists, were fighting for survival. The workers were class-conscious, but wooed by Communists and Nazis: and some of them remained staunch Social Democrats. The young, finding themselves thrust into a world of unemployment, were enlisted by Parties which

130

promised them a future of work and prosperity, and which even gave them present opportunities to strut about in uniforms and feel important.

Christopher and I, leading our life in which we used Germany as a kind of cure for our personal problems, became ever more aware that the carefree personal lives of our friends were façades in front of the immense social chaos. There was more and more a feeling that this life would be swept away. When we were on holiday at Insel Ruegen, where the naked bathers in their hundreds lay stretched on the beach under the drugging sun, sometimes we heard orders rapped out, and even shots, from the forest whose edges skirted the shore, where the Storm Troopers were training like executioners waiting to martyr the naked and self-disarmed.

In 1929 I had first heard of Hitler when, in between the singing of Bavarian songs, Joachim had told me of an orator from Austria, who had a power of speech which those who listened to him called hypnotic, whilst realizing that he talked nonsense. Hitler was regarded as a kind of wonder whom one did not have to take seriously. But two years later in Berlin, the Soloweitschiks were beginning to make grimly comforting jokes to the effect that the Jews had nothing to fear; for every Nazi, although an anti-semite, had his favourite Jew whom he wished to spare from persecution, and that made up as many Jews as all the Nazis. In the summer of 1932, a friend of Christopher's, Wilfrid Israel, came to stay with us in Sellin. One day, he and I went for a walk together through the forest. He was an elegant, distinguished, dark-eyed young man, whose family owned one of the great department stores in East Berlin. Wilfrid Israel surprised me, during our walk, by outlining a plan of action for the Jews when Hitler seized Germany – an event which he seemed to anticipate as certain. The Jews, he said, should close their businesses and go out into the streets, remaining there, as a protest, and refusing to go home even if the Storm Troopers fired on them. It was only such a united action, within a hopeless situation, which would arouse the conscience of the world.

Nearly all the German intellectuals whom we knew accepted and practised a kind of orthodoxy of the Left. This attitude influenced the theatre, the novel, the cinema, and even music and painting. So great

131

was the unanimity of opinion that it occurred to me once that perhaps these people, just because they appeared to have arrived at their political views so easily, might be wrong. After all, the Nazis, whom they so hated, claimed to be socialists and were opposed to the treatment of Germany by the Allies, which I was opposed to also. Possibly Germany was in a position where socialism could only be achieved by a virulently nationalist party. I decided that I must study the Nazi point of view: so I bought the Nazi programme and a good deal of the literature of Goebbels and the other Nazi propagandists. I found that they were written with a blatant cynicism and brutality which could deceive no one. So far from pretending to believe their own propaganda, or even doing their followers the service of trying to deceive them, the Nazis openly proclaimed that the purpose of propaganda was to state, without any regard for truth, lies which served their cause. After I had read this literature, I knew that I hated the Nazis.

One day Isherwood told me that he had received a letter from his greatest Cambridge friend (whom he has called Chalmers in his autobiographical sketch, *Lions and Shadows*), saying that Chalmers had joined the Communist Party. We regarded this as an extraordinary action. Communism to us was an extremist, almost unnatural cause, and we found it hard to believe that any of our friends could be Communists. However, Chalmers' action deepened our interest in Berlin politics. We discussed them with our friends, went to political meetings, read the newspapers and a good deal of political literature attentively. Whenever we could, we went to see those Russian films which were shown often in Berlin at this period: *Earth*, *The General Line*, *The Mother*, *Potemkin*, *Ten Days that Shook the World*, *The Way into Life*, etc. These films, which form a curiously isolated episode in the æsthetic history of this century, excited us because they had the modernism, the poetic sensibility, the satire, the visual beauty, all those qualities we found most exciting in other forms of modern art, but they also conveyed a message of hope like an answer to *The Waste Land*. They extolled a heroic attitude which had not yet become officialized; in this they foreshadowed the defiant individualism of the Spanish Republicans. We used to go long journeys to little cinemas in the outer suburbs of Berlin, and there among

132

the grimy tenements we saw the images of the New Life of the workers building with machine tools and tractors their socially just world under the shadows of baroque statues reflected in ruffled waters of Leningrad, or against waving, shadow-pencilled plains of corn.

Upon us in this restless and awakening mood came Isherwood's friend Chalmers, on his way back to England from an Intourist Tour of Moscow. Very much the emissary of a Cause he seemed, with his miniature sensitive beauty of features, his keen-smiling yet dark glance, his way of holding the stem of his pipe with his finely formed fingers of a chiseller's or wood-engraver's hand. He was not unlike the smiling young Comsomol hero who saves the boys in the reform school in one of our favourite films – *The Way into Life*. Two days after his arrival, he and I went for a walk. I remember that we went through that part of Berlin where roads connect the Tiergarten, the Bahnhof-am-Zoo, and the Gedaechtniskirche – a church on a road island, with the traffic streaming all round it. The pressure of what Chalmers said to me was not just his words, but a consciousness of Berlin, of unemployment and Fascism, and, dimly beyond that day, of the day fifteen years later when I would walk along the same road and see the Gedaechtniskirche, which had looked (on the occasion of our walk) like an absurdly ornate over-large inkstand set down in the middle of the traffic, transformed into a neo-Gothic ruin, having about it something of senile dignity. What Chalmers was really asking me was (as though we both looked through the transparent traffic on to the ruin) how to stop this happening? How prevent this Europe being destroyed in the war which – as he analysed the situation – was certain to arise from recrudescent German nationalism, supported by American and British capitalism, and flung (as he thought it would be) against Russia? I gave my stumbling answers: I desired social justice; I abhorred war; I could not accept the proposition that to resist evil we must renounce freedom, and accept dictatorship and methods of revolutionary violence. Chalmers who had listened intently, smiling slightly to himself, observed quietly, when I had finished speaking: 'Gandhi.'

My vaguely distressed consciousness now began to formulate itself along lines laid down by Marxist arguments. The essential ideas

133

which moved me were: firstly, the inevitable development of social situations resulting from analysable material conditions; secondly, the division of the world into two interests, the bourgeois and the proletarian, which represented not just political views, but also influenced the whole pattern of behaviour and thought and culture of everyone who belonged to them.

Until now I had, I suppose, thought of myself as being a member of society in the same way as a passenger thinks of himself belonging to the ship on which he is carried. The very fact of my being in Germany, a country where I was a foreigner, emphasized my outside position to myself. I pitied the unemployed, deplored social injustices, wished for peace, and held socialist views. These attitudes were emotional, and I used them as a way of proving my own values to myself and testing my sincerity in some hypothetical situation. The opposite feelings to pity and sympathy and well-wishing would not have done me credit in my own eyes. The hypothetical test was to ask myself whether I was really prepared to make sacrifices if socialism 'happened', and I found myself a member of a classless society. The answer to this question was that, on the whole, I thought I would. But a more significant fact was that I thought of socialism as 'happening' outside me within a society of which I did not think of myself as a part.

In general, I thought of public events as happening more or less incalculably, as the result of clashes of interests, economic factors, the influence of outstanding personalities in political life. The future was always uncertain: and this made it unreal to me. For example, I could not think that in 1931 a war which would take place eight years later existed within the structure of events, like the foundation stone beneath a building, or like past history; that unless the structure was altered the war would inevitably take place; and that, in order to alter it, methods would have to be used which could really achieve the alteration. As all political events, solid as they might seem today, appeared to liquefy in the uncertainty of tomorrow, it seemed to me enough that I should preserve a guileless attitude in relation to them.

But during the coming years I began to appreciate the seriousness of the political situation: that within today there were not only all the injustices of the day – producing unemployment, poverty and ex-
134

ploitation – but also the victims of tomorrow, buried as it were within its structure: all the shot-down pilots, the inmates of concentration camps, and participants in war – a generation then at school, training, if one viewed things in this way, to be shot down by machine guns. This Berlin contained within a pattern, partly its own and partly imposed on it by the folly of the victors of the war of 1914–18, its own ruins and the ruins of the European cities, exactly as if buildings and their ruins co-existed; for they already were within the political situation. And now I saw that a personal self-righteousness whereby I secretly washed my hands of social guilt had no objective value.

A debate which still continues had begun in my mind. I was impressed by the overwhelming accusation made by Communism against bourgeois society, an accusation not only against all its institutions but also reaching deep into the individual soul.

When I considered the existing injustices and the future destruction which were involved in the system in which I lived, I longed to be on the side of the accusers, the setters-up of world socialism. But at this stage, having shifted the centre of the struggle within myself from the bourgeois camp to the communist one, I failed to find myself convinced by Communism.

Even when I had accepted in my own mind the possibility of having to sacrifice everything I gained by living in a bourgeois society, I still could not abandon my liberal concepts of freedom and truth. The Marxist challenge, thrown out in the Communist Manifesto, that the opponents of Communism were concerned only with *their* freedom, *their* truth, and that all their ideas were rationalizations of their interests, made me think out for myself the position of the freedom of the individual. It became extremely important to answer the question – was my sense of my own individuality simply an expression of the class interest which I, unknowingly and instinctively in everything I thought and wrote and did, represented? If this was so, must I accept the argument that to alter my position I must make myself its exact opposite – a function of the proletariat?

When I had admitted to myself the force behind the Marxist arguments, I still found in myself a core of resistance to the idea that if I was a Marxist my conceptions of freedom and truth must simply be

135

behaviour and facts dictated by Marxist expediency. This hard core was the point in my self-examination when the rather abstract phrase 'freedom of the individual' became replaced by the more concrete one, 'independent witnessing'. However much a projection of class interest the mind of the individual may be, I was persuaded there was a point where he chose simply to witness truths which served no interest.

Another objection to Communism which I could never overcome was to what I called in my own mind the world-provincialism of Marxism. I can explain this best by a hypothetical illustration. Suppose that in a corner of Africa there are two tribes, A and B, interlocked in a historic struggle. In such a conflict, Marxism assumes that each must think entirely in terms of its own interest in asserting itself and overcoming the other. Suppose that tribe B is in a state of historic decline, has been wasting its own resources and compensating for this by raiding and enslaving tribe A, so that historically it is doomed to exhaust not only itself but, owing to its internal contradictions, tribe A as well. Then the historic task of tribe A is to throw off tribe B and establish a system with a political and economic future. This means that the whole view of life of everyone in tribe A must be directed towards this aim. Whatever does not serve this end, is not truth for tribe A. The story that there are white men living beyond the furthest mountain ranges and having factories and great ships is only a myth serving the interests of tribe B, by distracting the attention of the warriors of tribe A from their historic task.

This stifling provincialism is the communist attitude applied to the class struggle of the whole world within history and the universe. Philosophic speculation, unpropagandist art, and even scientific research which do not serve the interest of the workers, are labelled idealistic, untruthful, escapist, and reactionary.

The insistent philosophic materialism of the communist dogmatists struck me as characteristic of their way of over-reaching themselves, in order to achieve concentration of purpose on immediate aims, by depriving their followers of a moral attitude which has anything in common with that of the rest of humanity. To divide humanity into irreconcilable groups with irreconcilable attitudes, having no common language of truth and morality, is, ultimately, to rob both groups of their humanity. They will be inhuman first to one another, and lastly to their own followers.

From 1931 onwards, in common with many other people, I felt hounded by external events. There was ever-increasing unemployment in America, Great Britain, and on the Continent. The old world seemed incapable of solving its problems, and out of the disorder Fascist régimes were rising.

There was the feeling through all these years of having to race against time to produce a book or a poem. Not only was this disturbing to the stillness of attention necessary for creative work, but the life itself out of which the work grew was being borne away from under us. No wonder that the literature of this period is time-obsessed, time-tormented, as though beaten with rods of restless days.

From notes which I kept at this time – notes of such urgency that they even interrupt the manuscript sketches of poems – I find that there were two things which incessantly preoccupied me. One was the problem of the freedom of the individual, which I have just discussed. The other was the problem of the sense of guilt. For if, on the one hand, the Communists told me that my sense of freedom was only a projection of the interest of the bourgeois class, there was also a Freudian argument which told me that I only troubled about these things out of a sense of guilt. Rid myself of guilt, and I would no longer worry about my privileged position in society.

What I gradually came to see is that there is not just one guilt but many guilts, and that we must learn to distinguish between these, discarding useless guilt and making use of that kind of guilt which, so far from inhibiting us, releases us. For example, it was useless guilt which prevented me criticizing my Hamburg friend Walter, because, feeling myself involved in a gigantic lie of my whole social heritage, I could not criticize his small dishonesties. On the other hand, in discarding the attitude which prevented me from helping Walter, I would have been mistaken to discard also what was valuable in this attitude: the realization that my own position did rest on a social injustice.

Thus although guilt may create for us a kind of stumbling darkness in which we cannot act, it is also the thread leading us out of a labyrinth into places where we accept, instead of being overwhelmed by, the responsibility of action.

*　　*　　*　　*　.　*

In 1932, Michael Roberts edited an anthology of poems called *New Signatures*, published by the Hogarth Press. This he followed a year later with a second volume, containing prose as well as poetry, called *New Country*. These two anthologies revealed the existence of a new, for the most part socially conscious, group of young writers. Of these, W. H. Auden, William Empson, Cecil Day Lewis, Rex Warner, William Plomer, A. J. S. Tessimond, John Lehmann, Julian Bell and myself made the greatest impression. These writers wrote with a near-unanimity, surprising when one considers that most of them were strangers to one another, of a society coming to an end and of revolutionary change.

In 1933 my volume, *Poems*, was published. It followed on Auden's *Poems* and Day Lewis's volume, *Transitional Poem*. Immediately, the names of Auden, Day Lewis and Spender were linked together by the critics. In fact, we were very different talents. Auden was a highly intellectual poet, an arranger of his world into intellectual patterns, illustrated with the brilliant imagery of his experience and observation. His special achievement was that he seized on the crude material of the unconscious mind which had been made bare by psychoanalysts, and transformed it into a powerful poetic imagery. He showed great technical virtuosity. Day Lewis was a more traditional talent, a writer steeped in the work of his immediate predecessors, the 'Georgians', much as Yeats had, when a young man, been steeped in the *fin de siècle*. Day Lewis to some extent corrected the blurred quality of the Georgians by introducing images drawn from factories and slums and machinery into his poetry. This modernism had a slightly willed quality in his early work, and as he developed further he tended to drop it. He had a metrical strictness and an intellectual sternness which were impressive and refreshing. As for me, I was an autobiographer restlessly searching for forms in which to express the stages of my development.

Why then should the work of these three poets have been linked

138

together? Partly, I think, on account of the influence of Auden, which was responsible, for example, for much subject matter of the early poems of Day Lewis. My own work showed his influence in certain imagery, the tone of certain lines. What we had, then, in common was in part Auden's influence, in part also not so much our relationship to one another, as to what had gone immediately before us. The writing of the 1920's had been characterized variously by despair, cynicism, self-conscious æstheticism, and by the prevalence of French influences. Although it was perhaps symptomatic of the political postwar era, it was consciously anti-political. If there was one principle the writers of this generation shared, it was that they considered politics alien to literature. During the First World War, some English poets, for instance Osbert Sitwell and Siegfried Sassoon, had satirized war, and after it they had turned to Left-wing politics. But this phase had been followed by one of abandoning political faith entirely.

Perhaps, after all, the qualities which distinguished us from the writers of the previous decade lay not in ourselves, but in the events to which we reacted. These were unemployment, economic crisis, nascent fascism, approaching war, which I have described. The older writers were reacting in the 'twenties to the exhaustion and hopelessness of a Europe in which the old régimes were falling to pieces. We were a 'new generation', but it took me some time to appreciate the meaning of this phrase. It amounted to meaning that we had begun to write in circumstances strikingly different from those of our immediate predecessors and that a consciousness of this was shown in our writing. According to this familiar use of the phrase 'new generation', every important historic change produces its generation of young talent whose sensitive reactions to a new set of circumstances separate their work from what has gone before. In this century, generation succeeds generation with a rapidity which parallels the development of events. The Georgian poets were a pre-1914 generation. The war of 1914-18 produced a generation of War Poets, many of whom were either killed by the war or unable to develop beyond it. The 1920's were a generation to themselves. We were the 1930's.

Rather apart from both the 1920's and the 1930's, was the group of writers and artists labelled 'Bloomsbury'. Bloomsbury has been derided by some people and has attracted the snobbish admiration of others: but I think it was the most constructive and creative influence on English taste between the two wars.

The label 'Bloomsbury' was applied to people more by others than by themselves. Nevertheless if one examines the reasons for regarding Bloomsbury as a serious tendency, if not as a self-conscious movement, the label is meaningful.

The names most usually associated with Bloomsbury are Virginia Woolf, Roger Fry, Lytton Strachey, Clive Bell, Vanessa Bell, Duncan Grant, Raymond Mortimer, and perhaps David Garnett. E. M. Forster and T. S. Eliot are associated with it rather than 'belonging' to it, if 'belonging' may be said of a free association of people with similar tastes and talents.

Bloomsbury represented a meeting of certain influences and an adoption of certain attitudes which became almost a cult.

Not to regard the French impressionist and post-impressionist painters as sacrosanct, not to be an agnostic and in politics a Liberal with Socialist leanings, was to put oneself outside Bloomsbury. For this reason Eliot was too dogmatic in religion and too Conservative in politics to fit in. It is more difficult to say why Forster does not quite fit. He was perhaps too impish, too mystical, too moralizing.

But the positive qualities of Bloomsbury were shared not only by Forster and Eliot, but by nearly all the best talent of this period. Roger Fry, Lytton Strachey and T. S. Eliot, in their different ways, introduced the influences of French impressionism, French prose, and in poetry the French symbolists. All these writers were pre-occupied with re-examining and restating the principles and aims of art and criticism. They were interested in experiment, and were amongst the first to discuss and defend James Joyce and Proust. Their attitude towards an easy-going conventionality masquerading as traditionalism was critical: at the same time, they were deeply concerned with traditional values which they studied and restated with a vigour which made the old often have the force of the revolutionary. They insisted on the necessity of expressing past values in the imagery and idiom of today.

Most of these writers had begun writing before 1914, though they did not become widely known until after the war. They had sympathized with pacifism. Leonard Woolf, an intellectual Socialist who was at heart a Liberal, Maynard Keynes, the economist who denounced the Treaty of Versailles, Bertrand Russell and Harold Nicolson, were amongst their friends and colleagues who discussed politics, economics, philosophy, history and literature with them. In this way Bloomsbury was like the last kick of an enlightened aristocratic tradition. Its purism was founded on a wide interest in ideas and knowledge of affairs. Reading the essays of Lytton Strachey, Virginia Woolf, Clive Bell, Raymond Mortimer, and even Forster, one sees how inevitably they interested themselves in the eighteenth-century French salons and the English Whig aristocrats.

Like a watered-down aristocracy they made moderate but distinct claims on society. They were individualists who asked for themselves (and usually by their own efforts, from themselves) the independence in which to do their best work, leisure for reading, and pleasure. In order to produce a few works which seem likely to live, and a great many witty, intelligent and graceful conversation pieces, they needed to nourish themselves on a diet of the arts, learning, amusement, travel, and good living. They certainly were not malicious exploiters of their fellow men, and they expected less reward than the bureaucratically favoured Soviet writer receives today. At the same time, their standard of 'five hundred pounds a year and a room of one's own' (Virginia Woolf's formula in a well-known essay) made them decidedly unwilling to sacrifice their independence to the cause of the working-class struggle. They were class-conscious, conscious even of a social gulf which divided them from one of their most talented contemporaries – D. H. Lawrence, the miner's son. Despite their Leftist sympathies the atmosphere of Bloomsbury was nevertheless snobbish. They were tolerant in their attitude towards sexual morals, scrupulous in their personal relationships with each other.

To them there was something barbarous about our generation. It seemed that with us the thin wall which surrounded their little situation of independence and which enabled them to retain their air of being the last of the Romans had broken down. A new generation had arisen which proclaimed that bourgeois civilization was at an end, and which assumed the certainty of revolution, which took sides and which was exposed even within its art to the flooding-in of outside

141

public events, which cared but little for style and knew nothing of Paris.

*   *   *   *   *

I spent about six months of each year from 1930–1933 in Germany, and the remainder in London. When my book of poems was published I began to lead a literary-social life of luncheons, teas, and week-ends at country houses.

Nothing could have been more different from the atmosphere of Berlin than this way of living, which had hardly been shaken by the war or even by the economic crisis. It is true that the Slump had caused a certain uneasiness, and the fall of the pound still more. But with the recovery from these disasters, during the years of the Baldwin Government, not only were these forgotten, but English middle-class life was characterized by a refusal to contemplate further disasters. The middle years of the 1930's were symbolized in England not by Hitlerism or even the Spanish war, but by the Royal Jubilee.

Most of the writers I knew regarded the Continent as a refreshing well of culture, not as a storm centre. My friends deplored my spending so much time in Germany and wished that I went more often to France: but to them France was still the France of Proust and the French Impressionists, not the France of the Front Populaire.

The English were passing through a phase of isolation not just of place but also of time, so that there was a refusal to recognize problems which affected England very deeply if these appeared disturbing to the very narrow vision imposed by Baldwinism and the Jubilee. All that the English permitted themselves to see of Europe was characterized by the Salzburg Music Festival, French Impressionism, the Lake of Geneva, and of course the museums and art galleries.

The idea that the future of the British Empire was being decided in Europe between 1933 and 1939 was absolutely intolerable to all classes. It was characteristic of the English attitude that when I published in 1936 a book called *The Destructive Element* in which I analysed the deep consciousness of destructive forces threatening our civilization, which was to be found in the work of Henry James, James Joyce, T. S. Eliot and some more recent writers, a reviewer wrote that if I had not gone abroad so much, but had stayed in

142

England during the year of the Royal Jubilee, I would realize that England could not possibly be affected by forces of chaos which disturbed continental countries.

One of the writers with whom I often stayed was Rosamond Lehmann, whom I had met already while I was an undergraduate. She had then the beautiful Ipsden House in the Chilterns, which had once belonged to Charles Reade, the novelist. It had a garden partly surrounded by a screen of trees, through gaps in which the whale-like grey-green Berkshire downs could be seen. The house and garden sheltered by the trees had their own closed-in atmosphere of lawn and paths and old brick walls, in which some windows survived from the Elizabethan period, in a Georgian façade.

Rosamond was one of the most beautiful women of her generation. Tall, and holding herself with a sense of her presence, her warmth and vitality prevented her from seeming coldly statuesque. She had almond-shaped eyes, a firm mouth which contradicted the impression of uncontrolled spontaneity given by her cheeks, which often blushed. Her manner was warm, impulsive, and yet like her mouth it concealed a cool self-control, and the egoism of the artist. At this age she seemed at the height of her beauty: yet when I look at photographs of her then it seems to me that her features were in fact too rounded, too girlish, and that years confirmed a sculptural quality which one felt then in her presence but which later showed in her features. So that she was one of those women in whom even greying hair was a kind of triumph, a fulfilment of maturity which her youth had promised.

Wogan Philipps – to whom Rosamond was then married – was at this period a painter. He used to paint with a fanaticism which later he brought to politics. The house was full of his wild, somewhat childish paintings, amongst which were many portraits of Rosamond. Although these were not good portraits they brought out something grandiose, almost Byzantine, mosaic-like about her appearance.

Rosamond and Wogan would often take me with them when they drove to see friends in the country or at Oxford. One of their not-too-distant neighbours was Lytton Strachey. Strachey, with his long russet-brown beard and his high, squeaky voice, was certainly the most astonishing of the Bloomsbury group. He combined strikingly

143

their gaiety with their intermittent chilliness. Sometimes he would play childish games such as 'Up Jenkins', which we played one Christmas. Often he would gossip brilliantly and maliciously. At times there was something insidious about his giggling manner; at times he would sit in his chair without saying a word. He was delicate and hypochondriacal. Wogan Philipps, who was given to Celtic exaggeration, told me once that Strachey had an arrangement by which the wires of his bed under the mattress were electrically heated: so that lying in bed he was agreeably grilled all night long.

Thus I began to enter into this civilized world of people who lived in country houses, pleasantly modernized, with walls covered with areas of pale green, egg-shell blue, or pale pink distempering, upon which were hung their paintings and drawings of the modern French school, and a Roger Fry, Vanessa Bell, or Duncan Grant. They had libraries and good food and wine. They discussed few topics outside literature, and they gossiped endlessly and entertainingly about their friends. In my mind these houses in the south and south-west of England, belonging to people who knew one another and who maintained approximately the same standards of living well, talking well, and believing passionately in their own kind of individualism, were connected by drives along roads which often went between hedges. At night the head-lamps would project a hundred yards in front of us an image of what looked like a luminous grotto made of crystal leaves, coloured agate or jade. This moved always in front of us on the leaves and branches. Delight in a vision familiar yet mysterious of this kind was the object of much of their painting, writing and conversation, so that when we drove in the country at night, and I watched that moving brilliant core of light, I felt often that I was looking into the eyes of their sensibility.

One house where I stayed sometimes was Long Barn in Kent, where Harold Nicolson and his wife, Victoria Sackville-West, then lived. Nicolson had interested himself in a small volume by me called *Twenty Poems*, which Blackwell published at the end of my last year at Oxford, selling all the copies of a limited edition to cover the cost of other copies which I gave to friends. At that time he was reviewing for the *Daily Express* and he kindly asked me whether I would care for him to notice this book in his columns. This offer I refused on

144

the grounds that the book was only a limited edition and not for public sale: but really out of pride and for no other reason.

Nicolson was a strange combination of contradictory qualities: idealism and cynicism; unworldliness and love of the world; satire and sentiment. When he told me that he had kept a diary every day of his life since his boyhood, I thought these contradictions were exactly those which make a diarist. For he never lost his passionate desire to enter into other people's lives, to be with people who were at the centre of events, nor his capacity to be affected personally by these. I was reminded of what Auden had said about the poet thriving on humiliation.

Now when I look back on these days when I was twenty-one, I see that I missed opportunities of friendship which were offered to me. I had so strong a sense of the busy, filled lives of people like the Nicolsons that unless they asked to see me I never dared ask to see them. But to them it perhaps seemed that I did not respond to their kindnesses. But one unspoken friendship I always felt confident in, though little was said between us: this was with Vita Sackville-West. Working always in her garden, caring for her friends, her flowers and her poetry, modest and never interesting herself in literary disputes, her friendship had the freedom of silence and watchfulness about it, and I often think of it with gratitude.

Nicolson discussed Communism with me (as he did other problems of my life) sensibly and seriously, recommending me to see a Labour M.P. of the extreme Left who had disagreed with the Communists, for reasons which Nicolson thought I would take seriously. To the Nicolsons I confided the kind of discouragement I sometimes felt which made me think I would not go on writing, and they said: 'You are describing exactly what every creative writer feels.' When I sent to Vita Nicolson the copy of a poem which began, 'O young men, O young comrades', she wrote back saying that she was dazzled by it, that nevertheless my attitude horrified her.

When I was twenty a friend had sent some of my poems to T. S. Eliot, and a few weeks later I met him for the first time at one of those London clubs where I have met him so often since. His appearance was grave, slightly bowed, aquiline, ceremonious, and there was something withdrawn and yet benevolent about his glance. When

145

Eliot orders a drink or inclines over the menu to consider a meal the affect is such as to produce a hush. It is a priestly act as he says in a grave voice: 'Now will you have a turtle soup (I doubt whether it will be made from *real* turtle) or green pea soup?' But he is also a connoisseur who has strong views about wines, and still more, cheese.

On the occasion of one of our first meals, I disturbed him a little by announcing that I would choose smoked eel to eat. I was surprised to hear him say: 'I don't think I dare eat smoked eel,' thus unconsciously paraphrasing Mr. Prufrock who asks himself: 'Do I dare to eat a peach?' This incident suddenly became illuminating for me shortly after I had recorded it in a draft of this book when, having tea one day with Eliot, he refused cake and jam, saying: 'I daren't take cake, and jam's too much trouble.' Then I noticed that the effectiveness of the line, 'Shall I part my hair behind? Do I dare to eat a peach?' is precisely that it is in the poet's own idiomatic voice.

Eliot's conversation is gravely insistent. It does not give the impression of exceptional energy, but it has a kind of drive all its own, as it proceeds along its rigid lines. He cannot easily be interrupted or made to change the subject. I say it is a fine day, and Eliot replies gravely: 'Yes, it is a fine day, but it was still finer yesterday—' with a faint hint in his voice that when I used the word 'fine' of today I was not choosing the word altogether exactly. However, he continues about the weather: 'If I remember, this time last year the lilac——' and then it is quite likely that if I have gone on listening carefully, out of this dry climate, there will suddenly flash a few words of poetry like a kingfisher's wing across the club room conversation. His voice alone, grave, suggesting a bowed gesture, almost trembling at moments, and yet strangely strong and sustained – his voice alone is Eliot. Again, the observation of the obvious becomes here suggested. For despite its intensity the line of Eliot's poetry is relaxed and natural. It is near to conversation made rhythmic.

At our first luncheon he asked me what I wanted to do. I said: 'Be a poet.' 'I can understand your wanting to write poems, but I don't quite know what you mean by "being a poet",' he objected. I said I didn't only want to write poems, but also perhaps novels and short stories. He said that poetry was a task which required the fullest attention of a man during his whole lifetime. I said I wished to be poet and novelist like, say, Thomas Hardy. He observed drily that the poems of Hardy had always struck him as being those of a novelist. 'What about Goethe?' I asked. He replied that he thought the case of Goethe was rather like that of Hardy, only on a greater scale.

This dismayed me, in part because it gave me a sudden moment of insight in which I realized that I could not devote myself entirely to poetry. My problem is that which this book must make apparent: what I write are fragments of autobiography: sometimes they are poems, sometimes stories, and the longer passages may take the form of novels.

At this first meeting I asked him a crude question such as I suppose only someone as young would confront him with so soon. 'What,' I asked, 'do you think is the future of Western civilization?' He indicated that politically he thought there was no future 'except' – I remember the phrase because I did not quite understand it – 'internecine conflict'. I asked him what exactly he meant by this, and he said: 'People killing one another in the streets.'

This marked a difference in our attitudes. Towards social and political action his was one of negation and despair, or, at best, he thought that one should do what one could within a conviction of despair. I think he continued to feel like this until the war, but the war modified his attitude by convincing him that there was a Western cause to be positively defended. And after the war there was a Germany to be brought back within the Western tradition.

I am now forty, the same age as Eliot was when, at the age of twenty, I first met him. He seemed to me then exactly as old as he does now. I am not so much surprised that he should seem no older now as that he should not have seemed younger then. Perhaps we do not notice people who are older than ourselves getting older, but only our contemporaries or those who are younger. Yet perhaps being mentally old, being adult, living always a few years beyond his age, has been part of his art of living and writing. For at the age of twenty he was writing the Prufrock poems which surely express the sensibility of a man of forty. Shortly after the time I met him, when he was in his early forties, he was to liken himself in *Ash Wednesday* to an 'agèd eagle'. He has always exercised some privilege of post-

147

dating his age. This must have helped him to elude his contemporaries and perhaps even to avoid some of the problems which arise from people being the age they are.

Eliot, in his capacity of a director of the firm of Faber and Faber, was one of my publishers. Just as we conducted a relationship which, after all, meant a good deal more than I realized, under the surface of meetings in clubs, so we conducted a correspondence under the surface of business letters. Looking over these now, I am surprised by a considerateness, a friendliness, a concern, which at the time I must have ignored because I could not believe it to be there, in the same way as I failed to cultivate the kindness of the Nicolsons. Occasionally I wrote questioning Eliot's views on his religion, which I crudely imagined to be an 'escape' from social tasks. I attacked him because I felt that in doing so I was discussing a public issue where he himself met his public: I would not have dared approach him on some more private matter.

He replied that religion was not such an effective escape as I seemed to think: and he pointed out that the great majority of people find their escape in easier ways, by reading novels, looking at films, or driving very fast on land or in the air, 'which makes even dreams unnecessary'. He went on to say that 'what matters is whether I believe in Original Sin'.

This letter I remember reading in the bright spring sunlight in the Hofgarten at Munich. There I felt sure that I did not believe in 'Original Sin'. I supposed, even, that it was wrong to do so. Nevertheless, I felt guilty and disturbed at the back of my mind when I read this letter, which was an answer to mine disputing his pamphlet, *Thoughts after Lambeth*, in which he maintained that what the young need is to be taught 'chastity, humility, austerity, and discipline.'

Quite early in our relationship I wrote a review of Eliot's essays, criticizing his political attitudes and certain implications of his traditionalism. After this had been published, it grieved me, and I sent a copy of the review to him, together with a letter of explanation. Eliot wrote back an answer which, while disagreeing with one or two points in my review, was gentle. He ended by saying that I must always write exactly what I felt when I criticized his work and that our public relationship had no connection with our private one.

148

At about the same time as I received this letter, Harold Nicolson told me of a painful experience he had after unfavourably reviewing the novel of a friend. Grieving as I had done, he wrote a letter of explanation and apology. A few days later he got the answer which ran (as I remember) something like this: 'Little as I can forgive you for stabbing me in the back in public, I can forgive still less that you should apologize in private.'

William Plomer, whom I have already mentioned meeting when I was English Club secretary at Oxford, became my close neighbour when we both lived in Maida Vale. This was a part of London which almost rivals Berlin in its atmosphere of decay. Along the banks of the canal were the rows of stucco houses, whose doors and windows, flanked with yellowing, peeling Corinthian or Ionic columns, 'tactfully struck a soft Egyptian note, varied by a Greek one,' as Plomer pointed out to me. Steam rose from the canal, covering the lower parts of the houses and washing everything in sweat, as though this part of London were a Turkish bath. But at the back of the sinister row of houses (drawn out like a bow directing an arrow against Paddington) called Randolph Crescent, in which I lived, there was a very large garden with lawns and trees and flowers, stretching for hundreds of yards and totally unknown to all except the inhabitants of the houses around it, by which it was completely surrounded.

Often people relate the most revealing things about themselves when one first meets them, so that the subsequent relationship becomes the development of a theme already indicated at its opening. I first met William Plomer (before I had invited him to Oxford) at the flat of my friend, Réné Janin. I remember how that evening I said little , but listened to Plomer tell Janin stories of life in Japan. Plomer spoke of the necessity of presenting a mask to the world, and his clear-cut features, his smoothly brushed-back fair hair, the faintly ironical yet sparkling smile on his lips, had something of the mask, a certain impassivity imposed on most unoriental features. Through that slightly bronzed face, hewn as it were from a hard light-coloured wood, very clear blue eyes looked out at the world. During the coming years I was to see how the effect of his 'mask', which concealed his feelings, was to give him exceptional sympathy for the difficulties of others and a capacity to ignore his own troubles or, if they were

149

discussed, to treat them with a lightness which had the effect of objectifying them.

Plomer, when he came to Oxford for the English Club Meeting, was accompanied by his friend Anthony Butts. Tony Butts looked like a malicious and naughty boy who had gone completely bald. He had eyes of a china blue which stared out of their façade of a slapstick face, with a solemnity which would suddenly collapse in laughter. A portrait of one of his ancestors in an eighteenth-century family group, which hangs in the National Gallery, contains a boy who looks exactly like him. One could fancy that his head was bald, because, belonging so much to the eighteenth century, his skin instinctively anticipated a wig. Tony Butts was a master of the absurd who, when he was at Oxford, bought a large motor-cycle, got on to it without having learnt how to drive, managed to start it and then could not stop. He drove straight out of Oxford, and found no place where he could turn until he got to Blenheim. The story runs that there he drove round the back of the palace, past the private grounds in which a tea party was taking place. The guests were extremely surprised to see a young man on a motor-bicycle rushing along the private drive. Noting their astonishment, Tony Butts waved his hand with a courteous gesture and continued – as he had to – on his way. This story, like most of those which depend on the vivacity of the protagonist who relates it himself, now has a somewhat faded air. In any case it would be impossible for anyone to tell it with the baroque extravagance, the ribbons and trimmings, of Tony's conversation. His one book, published anonymously after his death and edited by William Plomer, contains some of his stories about his family. It is a book which has found a small band of enthusiasts, in the way that Firbank found admirers. Some critics complained that the incredibility of the adornments to the stories robs them of a good deal of interest. However this may be, I have indicated – all too briefly and flatly – the story about the motor-cycle, because the picture of the wigless young eighteenth-century beau rushing through the country on a motorcycle which he cannot stop is so like Tony Butts's own life. He was one of those extremely talented people who do not know how to direct their gifts. During one promising period of his life he became a painter, and was for a time a pupil of Sickert. Sickert told Plomer that Butts was the best talker he had known since Degas. Later he stopped painting and began writing plays (I never knew what happened to these). He wrote also the memoir, from whose disordered drafts Plomer edited the volume I have mentioned. At a time when fashions were becoming surrealist, he and William Edmiston, a young man with ideas almost as extravagant as his own, started a business for designing fantastic hats. At an early age he contracted a serious illness, and he died during the war, leaving a few paintings and manuscripts.

*   *   *   *   *

The group of people whom I describe here, look, at this distance of time, and through this frame of European ruins, like a large loosely knit family, most of them under the rather remote guardianship of their parent of Bloomsbury. At the centre of Bloomsbury was Virginia Woolf, whom I constantly heard discussed by the Nicolsons, and Rosamond Lehmann and Wogan Philipps.

Sometimes I dined with Leonard and Virginia Woolf at their house in Tavistock Square. They lived in the upper half of this, the lower half being occupied by the offices of their publishing firm, the Hogarth Press. Their drawing-room was large, tall, pleasant, square-shaped, with rather large and simple furniture, giving, as I recollect it now, an impression of greys and greens. Painted panels by Duncan Grant and Vanessa Bell represented mandolins, fruit, and perhaps a view of the Mediterranean through an open window or a curtain drawn aside. These were painted thickly and opaquely in browns and terra-cottas, reds and pale blue, with a hatch work effect in the foreground with shadows of the folds of a curtain. These decorations were almost a hall-mark of Bloomsbury. Similar ones were to be found in the house of Lytton Strachey. They represented a fusion of Mediterranean release with a certain restraint and austerity. Looking at them, one recollected that Roger Fry was of a family of Quakers, and that Virginia Woolf was the daughter of Leslie Stephen.

When her guests arrived, Virginia Woolf would be perhaps nervous, preoccupied with serving out the drink. Her handshake and her smile of welcome would be a little distraught. Now when I recall her face it seems to me that there was something about the tension of the

151

muscles over the fine bones of the skin which was like an instrument tautly strung. The greyish eyes had a sometimes limpid, sometimes wandering, sometimes laughing, concentration or distractedness.

When we had gone upstairs and had sat down to dinner, she would say to William Plomer (we were often invited together): 'If you and Stephen insist on talking about Bloomsbury, I shall label you "the Maida Vale group".' 'Really,' Plomer said, raising his eyebrows and laughing. 'I am not aware of having talked of Bloomsbury, but you know how much one has to write these days. . . .' 'Well then, if it's not you, it's Stephen!' 'Oh, Stephen. How like him! But still, please don't include him with me; I can assure you we are very different kettles of fish! Still, I can imagine nothing more charming than an essay by you, Virginia, on the Maida Vale group.' Then the conversation wandered a little. Perhaps the name of a critic who ran a small literary magazine in which he had made a scurrilous attack on her would be mentioned, and she would say aciduously: 'Why do you mention that name? Surely we have more interesting things to discuss.' The uncomfortable moment passed and she answered, with a warmer interest, someone's question whether adverse criticism annoyed her: 'Of course it annoys me for the moment. It is as though someone broke a china vase I was fond of. But I forget about it afterwards.' Then another name was dropped into the conversation, that of a poet, later to become a supporter of General Franco, who had written a satire directed at two friends whose crime was that they had lent him for an indefinite period a small house in their garden where he might work. 'What ungrateful people writers are!' she said. 'They always bite the hand that feeds them.' She looked pensive. As I write this it suddenly occurs to me, by the kind of intuition which remembering things across a gulf of years brings in the very act of writing, what she may have been thinking at that moment. For the people who had been ungratefully attacked were the Nicolsons: and her novel *Orlando* is a fantastic meditation on a portrait of Victoria Sackville-West; and in this novel there is an account of a poet who comes to stay with Orlando, accepting his/her hospitality and then writing a cruel satire on the visit.

Did she say that when she wrote *Orlando* she began writing the first sentences without at all knowing how she would continue? Or

152

am I thinking of something else? How Julian Green told me that he wrote his novels without in the least knowing how the story would develop? Or how Vita Sackville-West, who owned the manuscript of *Orlando*, showed me, written across the first page, a brief note explaining the idea for a novel, whose hero-heroine should live for three hundred years of English history, experiencing half-way through this life a change of sex, from hero into heroine. The excitement with which she embarked straight from this note on to her voyage of three centuries of English history, is shown by the letter which she wrote to Victoria Sackville-West the same day: 'I dipped my pen in the ink, and wrote these words, as if automatically, on a clean sheet: *Orlando, A Biography*. No sooner had I done this than my body was filled with rapture and my brain with ideas. I wrote rapidly till 12.'

In recalling Virginia Woolf there is something which causes my memory to become even more a kind of reverie than most of what I write here. It is necessary to remind myself that often she served the meal herself efficiently, and that she cooked it well. The dining-room was a lighter, perhaps more successful, room than the drawing-room. There was a pleasant table of painted wood, the work of her sister, Vanessa Bell, who also had designed the dishes. The pink blodges, small black dots, lines like brackets, characteristic of this style of decoration, were extremely successful on the creamy white surface of the china. Then Virginia described the beginning of the Hogarth Press, and at the age I then was, I listened like a child entranced. Her husband, Leonard Woolf, had won a prize in the Calcutta Sweepstake. With this they had bought a printing press and some type, and in the house where they then lived at Richmond they had printed stories by Virginia herself and by Leonard Woolf, T. S. Eliot's *The Waste Land*, and several other small volumes. She described how they had done this with little thought except to please themselves, and then one book (I think it was her own *Kew Gardens*) had been well reviewed in the *Times Literary Supplement*. She described running downstairs and seeing the door-mat deep in letters bringing orders for more copies. They then had to farm out the printing of a second edition with a local printer: and hence they found that they had become not amateur printers who sold their own work privately, but The Hogarth Press, a small but flourishing firm which even produced a few best-sellers.

From publishing the conversation turned to writing. She asked: 'How do you write, William?' 'How do I write?' 'Yes, what do you do when you write? Do you look out of the window? Do you write while you are walking in the street? Do you cross out a lot? Do you smoke when you are writing? Do you start by thinking of one phrase?'

When William and I had both been examined, we would ask her how she wrote. She came out with something like this: 'I don't think there's any form in which the novel has to be written. My idea is to make use of every form and bring it within a unity which is that particular novel. There's no reason why a novel shouldn't be written partly in verse, partly in prose, and with scenes in it like those in a play. I would like to write a novel which is a fusion of poetry and dialogue as in a play. I would like to experiment with every form and bring it within the scope of the novel.'

She said that no one should publish before he or she is thirty. 'Write till then, but scrap it or put it aside.' She herself had covered reams of paper with what she called 'just writing for the sake of writing,' and she had scrapped it all. She said she believed that prose was more difficult to write than poetry.

Then after dinner we would go down to the drawing-room again, and Virginia would smoke a cheroot. There would be talk perhaps of politics, that is to say, of war. For Leonard and Virginia were among the very few people in England who had a profound understanding of the state of the world in the 1930's; Leonard, because he was a political thinker and historian with an almost fatalistic understanding of the consequences of actions. So that when, in 1934, I asked him whether he thought there would be a war he replied: 'Yes, of course. Because when the nations enter into an armaments race, as they are doing at present, no other end is possible. The arms have to be used before they become completely out of date.' Virginia had also a profound political insight, because the imaginative power which she shows in her novels, although it is concentrated often on small things – the light on the branches of the tree, a mark upon a whitewashed wall – nevertheless held at bay vast waters, madness, wars, destructive forces.

154

While Leonard was talking about war, labour, League of Nations, Virginia would fall silent. There was often after dinner this kind of political intermezzo. She had a little the air of letting the men talk: still more that of listening to Leonard.

The conversation passed from politics to gossip about personalities, quite possibly to Hugh Walpole. Now some stories seem so familiar to me that they have become inseparable from this life of literary London, as though it were woven out of them. For example, the story of how Hugh Walpole sat up all of one night reading an advance copy of Somerset Maugham's *Cakes and Ale*, to recognize himself in the cruel analysis of the career of the best-selling novelist.

Virginia had a passionate social curiosity, about the 'upper', the 'middle', and the 'lower' (I think these distinctions of class were sharply present in her mind). The Royal Family was a topic of intense interest to her. This preoccupation could be embarrassing – if one is embarrassed by snobbishness. Yet her interest in royalty was largely due to the fact that royalty, surrounded by an atmosphere of radiant adoration as though bathed in a tank of lambent water, were peculiar and exotic in precisely the way in which people are strange and luminous in her writing. The little episode in *Mrs. Dalloway* where a chauffeur extends a small disc to a policeman, and the car shoots on ahead of the stopped traffic, exactly expresses like a minute phrase in a descriptive symphony what fascinated her – the privileged special life sealed off in the limousine whose driver has a pass. Indeed, her Mrs. Dalloways and Mrs. Ramsays are by nature queens shut off from other people who gaze at them with wonder, as through a window. The wonder of life is a wonder of royal self-realization, which has something akin to a gaping crowd staring at a lady dressed in ermine. When she writes – in her essay in *The Common Reader* – of Dr. Johnson, and Fanny Burney, and the Elizabethans – one is staring at exotic fish swimming in their tank.

'Why are we so interested in them – they aren't so different from us?' she would exclaim after the talk on the Royal Family had bordered almost on tedium. The answer was 'because they are held up to our gaze', or 'because they are like a living museum of flesh and blood dressed in the clothes of past history', or 'because after all, their heredity does make them extraordinary'.

There was a division between her and other people which she attempted – not quite satisfactorily perhaps – to bridge by questions. She enquired of everyone endlessly about his or her life: of writers how and why they wrote, of a newly married young woman how it felt to be a bride, of a bus conductor where he lived and when he went home, of a charwoman how it felt to scrub floors. Her strength and her limitations were that she didn't really know how it felt to be someone else. What she did know was how it felt to be alone, unique, isolated, and since to some extent this is part of universal experience, to express this was to express what many feel. But she was lacking in the sense of a solid communal life, divided arbitrarily into separate bodies, which all nevertheless share. What bound people together escaped her. What separated them was an object of wonder, delight and despair.

She seemed as detached from herself as from everyone else. Thus she would talk about herself with an objectivity which was unambiguous in her but which in others would have seemed uneasy. She was simply interested in the point she was making or the story she was telling, and the fact that she herself might be deeply involved in it seemed irrelevant. Once the conversation having turned to Rupert Brooke, she said: 'He was very keen on living "the free life". One day he said, "Let's go swimming, quite naked".' 'And did you, Virginia?' William asked. 'Of course,' she answered, and then she added: 'Lytton always said that Rupert had bandy legs. But I don't think that was so.' She said that Rupert Brooke was writing at this time his poem which begins 'These have I loved', in which he lists a catalogue of sensations which had given him pleasure. She said that he was quite external in his way of making this list and that he surprised her by asking what was the brightest thing in nature, as he needed a dazzling image for his poem. She looked up at the sky and saw a poplar tree with white underleaves rotating to shimmer against the light. She said: 'Bright leaves against the sky.'

She seemed to hate her dinner parties to come to an end. Sometimes they would go on until two a.m. She gave her guests an impression of gaiety which could plunge at any moment into the deepest seriousness. She would tell stories of things which amused her until the tears ran down her cheeks. Usually these stories concerned one

156

or two people who played a kind of jester's role in her life. There was a trace of cruelty in her feeling towards them. One of these was Hugh Walpole, concerning whom I have quoted one of her stories, and another, Dame Ethel Smyth. There was always some new item about Dame Ethel. Once, when Dame Ethel was already eighty-four, Virginia had just received a letter from her, announcing that she had become attached to a lady aged eighty who lived next door. 'And to think that we have been close neighbours for five years,' Dame Ethel's letter complained, 'and that we might have met when she was seventy-five and I only seventy-nine.' Dame Ethel was a highly eccentric character. On one occasion the Woolfs invited her to dine at their house at Rodmell near Lewes, Sussex. Dame Ethel bicycled the twenty miles from the village where she lived to Rodmell, dressed in rough tweeds. About two miles from her destination she decided that perhaps she was not suitably dressed for a dinner party. She thought that possibly corsets were required to smarten up her figure. Accordingly, she went into a village shop and asked for some corsets. There were none. Distressed, she looked round the shop and her eye lighted on a bird cage, which she purchased. About twenty minutes later, Virginia went into her garden to discover Dame Ethel in a state of undress in the shrubbery struggling with the bird cage, which she was wrenching into the shape of corsets and forcing under her tweeds.

Virginia Woolf was a most scrupulous artist who demanded high standards of artistic integrity from others. Once I submitted to The Hogarth Press a novel which was rejected. It interested her and she spent some part of an afternoon discussing it with me. As she made several favourable comments, I asked how I could re-write it. 'Scrap it!' she exclaimed with force. 'Scrap it, and write something completely different.' When she said 'Scrap it!' I had a glimpse of the years during which she had destroyed her own failures.

She composed, I imagine, like a poet. That is to say, her writing proceeds from the organic development of images growing out of her subject matter. These become symbols in a discussion which often takes her beyond the subject itself. I have in front of me an essay called *The Leaning Tower*, which is the written version of a lecture given in 1939. The essay develops from the apparently simple image of a writer sitting in a chair at his desk. This image proliferates into

157

further ones of the pen, the paper, and the writer's chair even: and these all become symbols of the writer's high calling, expressed in terms of the simple machinery of his trade, scarcely altering through the ages, and joining him to past writers. Within this symbolism there is a further symbol of the hand holding a pen: and through the veins of the hand there flows the blood which is the whole life of the literary tradition joining the writer, sitting at his desk, with Shakespeare. Such writing, dependent for its truth on the inter-relation of ideas in the structure of thought, developed parallel with the inter-relation of the images: the chair, the desk, the pen, etc., can only 'grow' like a poem. And I have heard that there were as many drafts of some of Virginia Woolf's essays as most poets make of a poem.

But just as my lack of belief in Original Sin divided me from the views of Eliot, so my attitude to politics divided me from Virginia Woolf. Not that we disagreed about the political issues themselves: for she hated Fascism, sympathized with the Spanish Republicans, and held much the same political views as we did. But she objected to the way in which our writing was put to the service of our views, and she discerned that my generation were 'sold' to a public sometimes more on account of their views than for the merit of their writing. Indeed all of us irritated her in this respect, and she sometimes showed her irritation. It occurs first in the *Letter to a Young Poet*, where she quotes Auden, Day Lewis, John Lehmann and myself in order to criticize us for our impatience, our preoccupation with external social factors, and with our desire to set the world right. She returns to the assault, less directly, in *A Room of One's Own*, where she discerns in George Eliot and Charlotte Brontë a desire to preach (though she excuses this as being the result of the position of women in their time). At the beginning of the war, in the essay I have mentioned, *The Leaning Tower*, she returns to the attack more directly. She felt that though we were aware of the calamitous condition of the world, we reacted to it with our intellects and wills, before we had experienced it fully through our sensibilities. 'You have to be beaten and broken by things before you can write about them,' she once said to me. To hold strong views and feel deeply about what, however significant and important, was outside the range of one's experience, was not enough. I might have replied – though I did not – that, often passing Edith Cavell's monument near Charing Cross, with its inscription of *Patriotism is not enough*, I reflected that I would like to have *Sensibility is not enough* engraved on my tombstone.

She and her circle formed a group of friends who shared the same ideas and who, within a common appreciation of high values, had a deep loyalty for one another. Living in their small country houses, their London flats, full of taste, meeting at week-ends and at small parties, discussing history, painting, literature, gossiping greatly, and producing a few very good stories, they resembled those friends who at the time of the Plague in Florence withdrew into the countryside and told the stories of Boccaccio. Our generation, unable to withdraw into exquisite tale-telling and beautiful scenery, resembled rather the *Sturm und Drang* generation of Goethe's contemporaries, terribly involved in events and oppressed by them, reacting to them at first enthusiastically and violently, later with difficulty and disgust.

This Boccaccio-like group, together with others who did not belong to it, had a pre-eminent hostess in whose house and garden they often met. This was Lady Ottoline Morrell. The house was Garsington, near Oxford. At the time I knew her she no longer lived in Garsington, but only in Gower Street in London. Long before I had been invited to her London drawing-room, the Nicolsons, who were exact prophets of my future, told me that I would inevitably meet this extraordinary great lady who dyed her hair purple (I think they said purple, though when I met her it seemed dark red). She had, they said, made the most bizarre impression on those who accepted her hospitality: as was shown by the portraits of her in books by D. H. Lawrence, Graham Greene, Aldous Huxley, and several others.

She interested herself in the work, plans and ideas of these friends, helped them, interfered with their personal lives, was loved and hated by them.

Bertrand Russell, Augustus John and D. H. Lawrence were the means by which she had escaped from the Dukeries and discovered and entered into a world of exciting ideas, ideals, and passions. An evangelist fervour went into her social life, and to say that she was a great hostess and patroness would be to give an inadequate idea of

159

the role she played in the lives of her friends. Her guests undoubtedly revealed to her the highest quality of friendship. She had an exalted devotion to what she took to be the True, the Good, and the Beautiful.

Her intensive idealism was complicated by a great inquisitiveness. Thoroughly incapable of being shocked by anything human, she wished her friends to contribute their most intimately dramatic qualities to the *commedia* which was her home. 'Does your friend have *no* Love-Life?' she complained once to a poet who had brought a somewhat reticent friend to tea.

Early in 1934 an invitation arrived for me on hand-made writing paper, scented with a powder which she used for drying ink. This ink itself was of a rust colour, as though it had been manufactured out of nails left a long time in water. The hand-writing was almost vertical – perhaps it sloped a little backwards – and very fine. It was prolific in shoots, tendrils, and loops which blossomed at every curve or even with the crossing of a 't'. These forms were purely ornamental, having an extraordinary natural grace and no utilitarian purpose whatever. They must have made writing a slow process and they did not help towards deciphering it.

When I entered Lady Ottoline's drawing-room, I saw an enormous quantity of objects: pictures, looking-glasses, small boxes, vases, armchairs, sofas, large and small tables, beautifully bound books. On some tables, bowls were placed which contained heaps of pomanders. These gave out a musty odour, making the room smell like the inside of an Oriental cedar box. Long damask curtains hung on either side of tall windows which, at the back of the house, looked out on to a garden. In a prominent position on the wall there was a misty spiritualist painting by the Irish poet A.E., and there were other paintings by Sickert and Henry Lamb, and early Augustus Johns of figures in front of landscape.

In the dining-room, which had a long table, was a large portrait of Lady Ottoline by John. The pose recalled Reynolds' portrait of Mrs. Siddons, whilst the head itself with smudged lips was like a Velasquez portrait of one of the Hapsburgs.

The eighteenth-century style which Augustus John had indicated was most evident in her dress. She affected the tradition of its aristocratic eighteenth-century shepherdesses. She wore creaking silks and
160

satins and she carried a crook when she walked in the Bloomsbury squares.

In the last years of her life (which was when I knew her) she always had the air of falling apart, with hair like a curtain suddenly dropping over one eye, or a bodice bursting open. On one occasion, when she was in the middle of a sentence, a large ear-ring fell off the lobe of one ear and dropped into her tea-cup. Without interrupting what she was saying, she fished it out and attached it to her ear again. I once or twice saw far worse things happen, but she was not at all embarrassed as, with a diving, pulling motion, she set herself to rights. Sometimes her lipstick was askew; and she had rheumy eyes. Yet all these things were incidental to her grand manner, and they even partook of her grandeur. Had not Augustus John smeared the line of the lips in his portrait of her? What would have been slovenly in others, acquired in her a kind of audacity.

When Lady Ottoline went out, she had attached to her, or to her shepherdess's crook, by ribbons, two or three pekinese dogs. She never ceased to be surprised that people stared at her in the street. Having heard of my socialist sympathies, she explained to me once that she had much sympathy for the workers – was prepared to love them – but there was this difficulty – they would stare so. For example, only two days previously, she had boarded a tram (Bloomsbury was a district where trams were indigenous) – she loved sailing through the streets in a tram – such a beautiful, billowing motion – on a London tram she felt like Queen Elizabeth floating down the Thames in the royal barge. But, of course, she had to be helped with her pekinese on to the top by the conductor, and then of course she liked the front (or was it the back?) seat . . . and everyone had stared so . . . and 'there was a man who I think must have been slightly under the weather who made a *rude* remark, and some rather silly children. . . .' She was prepared to be *most friendly*, but she had met with *such concentrated hostility* that it was impossible not to be impressed by the fact that she was *not* welcome among them.

She talked with many underlinings, in that way which is so consciously verbal with some women that it is their idiom, as a special timbre of blank verse distinguishes each Elizabethan dramatist. My Aunt May, for example, had a style which underlined certain words

161

with an effect of hammering spikes into each sentence with great blows. But Lady Ottoline's underlinings were often only of syllables. The syllables which she unerringly chose to emphasize changed speech into horn-like blasts which were peculiarly her own. Her conversation was interrupted by these significant trumpetings. One listened to her not so much for words as for an operatic aria, where the real meaning is in the music, though the words may also be understood.

Just as the opera demands that the idiom of the libretto should be adapted to the musical expression, so she had created for her own music a librettist's form, with a syntax different from prose. Sentences consisting of single words, whose separate syllables were trumpeted, were a feature of this special language. But where there were sequences of words, these were broken by dashes and pauses, a use of punctuation which was really the libretto modifying itself to musical notation and phrasing.

Even her letters were written in a style which reflected the demands restricting her conversation to very short sentences. Her handwriting, which I have already mentioned, in a way echoed her style of talking. For, just as in talking, her words became swallowed up in a sound like amplified sighing, so in writing, her more expressive words passed beyond mere letters into a realm of pure ornament where the words which look most beautiful on a page are in fact the most illegible, becoming a mass of waving tendrils and exquisite loops like convolvuli. On the written page, a sentence such as the following resembles the effect of her conversation:

'Venice needs sun . . . & shadow . . . & creeping round corners – and sunsets & Barges . . . with pomegranates and grapes. And Melons.'

Greece, Italy, Plato, Phidias, Michelangelo, Shelley were for her pure evocations of Truth, Goodness and Beauty. Eliot's dislike of Shelley and paganism were to her more distressingly blasphemous than her own pantheism would seem to most Christians.

'I saw T.S.E. again . . . he was ever so Nice – but – I think he is very queer. . . . I showed him photographs of Greek IVth and Vth

Century Statues and he said they gave him The Creeps. They were so akin to "Snake Worship". Now of all Art. Phidias/ the Time of . . . seems to me to be Sublime – & – Not Corrupt. Don't you think it odd of him – I feel he has Demons . . . on the Brain——'

Lady Ottoline's Thursdays were often very crowded. Some of the guests attended them regularly, in particular two Irish poets, George Russell (A.E.) and James Stephens. George Russell gave the impression of living within his brown bushy beard like a luminous spirit haunting a dark forest. He talked of Indian mysticism, but paradoxically, what made people speak of him with awe was that he was supposed to be an excellent economist. James Stephens was gnome-like and very loquacious. Not only did the Irish as well as the English writers and poets attend on Ottoline, but the scientists and philosophers as well. Julian Huxley and his wife Juliette came often. Bertrand Russell was one of her oldest friends. Here I met Aldous Huxley, who, remarking that I was about the same height as himself, looked at me meditatively and said: 'You and I are the wrong height for the work we wish to do. The great creative geniuses are short and robust "pyknic" types with almost no neck to divide the nerves of the body from the centres of the brain. Balzac, Beethoven, Picasso, did not have great stooping bodies to lug around. There was no gulf to divide their minds from the immediate communication of their physical senses.'

There were also teas on days other than Thursdays, for smaller groups. On one of these occasions I was invited to meet W. B. Yeats. Yeats, at the age of seventy, had something of the appearance of an overgrown art student, with shaggy, hanging head and a dazed, grey, blind gaze. On the occasion of our first meeting he looked at me fixedly and said: 'What, young man, do you think of the Sayers?' This took me aback and I murmured that I had not read any. 'The Sayers,' he repeated, 'the Sayers.' Lady Ottoline then explained that he was speaking of a certain troupe of speakers who recited poetry in chorus. I knew even less of these than of detective fiction and had to admit so. Lady Ottoline, who had arranged for us to have tea with very few people present, saw that I was a failure. She left the room and telephoned to Virginia Woolf to get into a taxi and come round

163

from Tavistock Square *at once*. Virginia, highly amused, arrived a few minutes later.

After tea, I listened, relieved not to have to take part in the conversation, while Yeats sat on the sofa with Virginia Woolf and explained to her that her novel, *The Waves*, expressed in fiction the idea of pulsations of energy throughout the universe which was common to the modern theories of physicists and to recent discoveries in psychic research.

I heard no more of this, as other guests arrived, but later Yeats was kind enough to talk to me again, and this time we discussed his attitude towards the writing of poetry. He told me how, when he had written *The Tower*, he took the manuscript to Rapallo. From his hotel there he sent it to Ezra Pound, with a note explaining that he had not written poetry for some years; that he was writing in a new style; that if this were not an improvement on his past work, he was too old now to hope to develop in another direction. For these reasons he was very anxious to know Pound's opinion of them. A day or so later he received a post-card with written on it the one word: 'Putrid, E.P.' Yeats told me this story with amusement, and he went on to talk of Pound's kindness which resulted in his discovery at all too-frequent intervals of new literary geniuses, and his introduction into his house of many stray cats.

(Fifteen years later, at the hospital where he was confined at Washington, D.C., I went to visit Pound. The American poet Robert Lowell and I were allowed to talk to him, seated round a table in the ward of the hospital. As we talked, other patients wandered through the ward. Here, amongst the lunatics, Pound seemed a genial and benevolent host, receiving us with the same courtesy as he might have done at his home in Italy, and talking of literature and personalities. I asked him whether he remembered the visit of Yeats to Rapallo. He looked at me and said: 'If you want me to talk about Yeats I shall do so, but you must give me twenty-four hours' notice, as the top layer of my mind is gone.')

Yeats went on to criticize the Imagist poets for the lack of movement in their poetry. Pound's own poetry, he said, when I asked him for his opinion of it, was static, like a tapestry. For his part, he felt that poetry should always have an underlying lilt, as simple as
164

Byron's: 'So we'll go no more a-roving, /So late into the night.' He said he was brought up in an environment of æstheticism and artificiality. He had striven all his life to simplify his diction. Yet he did not think that to write free verse was a solution of the problem. He wanted to write starkly and yet not sacrifice the Byronic lilt.

Then he spoke about the political views in the writing of my friends and myself, contrasting it with his own interest in spiritualism. 'We are entering,' he said, 'the political era, dominated by considerations of political necessity which belong to *your* people. That will be bad enough, but there will be worse to come. For after that there will be an age dominated by the psychologists, which will be based on the complete understanding by everyone of all his own motives at every stage of his life. After that, there will be the worst age of all: the age of *our* people, the spiritualists. That will be a time when the separation of the living from the dead, and the dead from the living, will be completely broken down, and the world of the living will be in full communication with that of the dead.'

Yeats expressed these ideas in a half-prophetic, half-humorous vein, and I may have distorted them in recording them. But certainly he spoke of the three ages to come, of the political, the psychological, and the spiritual: and he affirmed that the last would be 'the worst'. It is difficult to understand how seriously to take such a prophecy. What is clear though, is that he saw spiritualism as a revolutionary social force as important in its power to influence the world, as politics, psychology, or science.

Of all that Yeats said, I remembered most his words about Shakespeare. 'In the end,' he said, 'Shakespeare's mind is terrible.' When I asked him to expand this, he said: 'The final reality of existence in Shakespeare's poetry is of a terrible kind.'

There were other occasions when I met Yeats at Lady Ottoline's. Once he came to a 'Thursday' when there were even more people than usual on those crowded afternoons. He told amusing stories of George Moore and Edward Martyn. His worst malice was directed against George Moore who, in *Ave atque Vale*, brings out the most ridiculous (as well as the best) aspects of Yeats. But to some extent he also saw himself in a ludicrous as well as a noble light. In his poems he refers often to his own folly and absurdity. Also, he was

165

conscious of a pose, a mask, which it was necessary to assume for the purpose of meeting other people. After one of these parties Anthony Butts, who had been there, said: 'I didn't realize that Yeats had a——' 'Shanghai belly', did he say? or 'Singapore belly'? – at any rate some sobriquet to describe the curious way in which the poet's stomach jutted out. Another irreverent spirit – Mark Gertler – used to entertain his friends with descriptions of the hush which Lady Ottoline imposed on her guests at Garsington, when Yeats, seated in the drawing-room, was supposed to be composing. This also shocked me a little at the time. Yet now it seems to me that there was certainly something in Yeats which called out to be mocked at. Virginia, on the way back from the party I have described where I first met him, said that when he had finished with talking about *The Waves* he went on to speak of the carved wooden head of a baby on a pillar at the foot of a staircase, which Yeats said had spouted Greek to him. She went home impressed and elated and amused and mocking. When, many years later, I read a poem describing a meeting with Yeats by a solemn poet who had recorded with the utmost seriousness some of Yeats's most nonsensical generalizations – I suddenly thought of Anthony Butts laughing at Yeats's protruding figure – then the vision of Yeats blazed vividly before me.

*   *   *   *   *

There was a sense of fulfilment in meeting these people. I was accepted by writers whose names were still surrounded for me by a sacred glow. Although I became used to meeting them, I never lost the feeling of awe for those who had written work which I continued to admire. A sentence of Virginia Woolf's, beginning 'A great beast stamps its foot', a line of Eliot, 'The awful daring of a moment's surrender', and, at a later date, a description of a rock pool by Cyril Connolly – all these seemed to be beyond the writers themselves, as the sceptre and crown lie beyond the man who is a king. To know the writers themselves was never to give me an insight deeper than that which had come to me through their single lines, but there were moments when I saw in the conversation of Virginia Woolf, Eliot, Isherwood, Auden, or Cyril Connolly, the working of the characteristic sensibility of each.

166

What can I feel but gratitude that I was taken into this great wave of the talent of my time? When I had been bathed in it, I was imperceptibly changed. That strange feeling which I had had at the age of eighteen when I walked down a crowded road and felt a wall of ice surrounding me and shutting me out from the people who shared my own preoccupations was now melted away. There are moments when one can be grateful for disaster. At this moment I am almost grateful for the war and the losses which followed, because they have put a part of my own life into a distant perspective, where I can praise wholly the lives of the people I knew then.

Really, I suppose, this life gave me what I had failed to obtain from the University. For Bloomsbury was largely a product of King's, and its interests had already begun among a group of people who were together at Cambridge. I should add to those whom I praise the name of E. M. Forster, the best English novelist of this century, and one of the most acute of its moralists. But Forster's strange mixture of qualities – his self-effacingness combined with a positive assertion of his views, his whimsicality combined with a great precision, his almost pagan amorality combined with his minute preoccupation with moral issues, his love of freedom combined with an impressive self-discipline, would make it wrong to describe him in connection with a group, even of his friends. He is one of the most comforting of modern writers, and at the same time one of the most uncomfortable.

*   *   *   *   *

The London meetings I have here described were part of a literary social life, which inevitably consisted of week-end parties, luncheons, dinners, teas. I fairly soon fell into a manner of living in which whole days were wasted. In London it often takes an hour to get to a luncheon, which lasts perhaps till 3.30. It then takes an hour to return home, and at 6.30 you may have to leave again for a dinner engagement. I was always extremely bad at saying 'No.' If I was asked whether I was free at a certain time, my response was to look in my diary, and if I had no engagement to say truthfully 'Yes.' Having once said 'Yes' I felt it would be terrible to let my hosts down by excusing myself, or in the case of a cocktail party, simply

167

not appearing. I had an exaggerated sense of social obligation. To this day it still torments me to remember an occasion when I forgot a dinner party. I did not actually enjoy social life, but I felt a strong compulsion towards it. As I have said, I never lost the sense that to meet certain people was a wonderful privilege. Moreover, I had always the romantic hope that one day I should meet someone, perhaps at such a party, who would alter my whole life.

Meeting people, receiving a large number of letters and invitations, and feeling under an obligation to reply to them, these are perhaps greater dangers to the writer than debauchery. For debauchery is a sleep-walker's activity, an attempt to act out fantasies within an obscure reality. Its danger is that it may become an end in itself more significant than creative activity, and more exhausting, and therefore destructive. However, this is a problem which lies within the writer's own personal development, whereas social life and public life are external factors which easily get outside his control. They mean entering into obligations with other people to fulfil engagements, undertaking loyalties which may prevent him saying what he feels about this very life which has become so large a part of his experience, and accepting the standards of some kind of social group. The fact that these may be lax, or eccentric, or Bohemian, does not make any difference to the confusion which they may cause in his pursuit of his own standards.

Social life is all the more dangerous because it is to some extent necessary to him. It is one of his main doors of entrance into the life of other people; unless indeed he happens to be one of those solitaries who can gain nothing from others. Of course, there is no great problem for those who have sound judgment and strong wills. But one can be talented without having either. And the writer is peculiarly dependent on his own judgment and will – made dependent by his very freedom. He is not protected by having an office and office hours. Unless he fights hard against them he is constantly exposed to interruptions.

Another danger of social life is that it is exhausting. People who move energetically in society put a greater strain on themselves than many of those who work. All the hostesses I have ever known have had something about them of the athletic champion – the Channel

168

swimmer or the Olympic runner. The hot rooms, the standing up, the dinning of voices, the alcohol, the late hours, all absorb time and energy.

Thus whilst I met people in London whom I wanted to know, I also worked less than when I was leading an unrespectable life in Berlin. Several of my friends realized what was happening and reproached me for being so sociable. William Plomer, in his affectionate, mocking way, chided me for going out so much. He himself controlled every moment of his day, refused to be on the telephone, only saw a small number of people, and made all his friends conscious of the value of his time. My friends always seemed to think that all my time was available to them; and I myself wished them to think this. For a matter of principle was really involved. I did not want to wear a mask, to exert my will, to choose among people, to judge before I knew them, whom I should see and whom not see; I felt that any such attitude would inevitably result in a kind of hardness from which my work would suffer, and which would be a far more serious sacrifice than the loss of time.

Therefore I solved the problem by simply running away from England. I went abroad six months a year and during these months I lived a more solitary life.

Shortly after my half-dozen poems appeared in *New Signatures*, a publisher wrote asking me to contribute an essay on Coventry Patmore in a collection discussing Nineteenth-Century Poets. This reached me when I was at Sellin on Insel Ruegen. The publisher offered me what then seemed the large sum of ten pounds for an essay of 3,500 words. I regretfully replied that I knew nothing of Patmore and was far from libraries. The publisher wrote that Patmore's poems could be sent to me, and that I could then form an opinion of them. But I was in that state of literary innocence when I thought that even if I read Patmore I might have nothing to say about him, so I refused. How little I knew myself.

After this, editors wrote asking me to review books, and publishers to write a biography. There was a great hunt after biographies at the beginning of the 'thirties, and the only question was to find some past figure who had not already been debunked in the manner of Lytton Strachey. The candidature of Lady Hester Stanhope was pressed on me. I thought (quite rightly) that I would never know enough about anyone to write a biography, so I refused.

However, I got into the habit of writing reviews. I do not think I reviewed much better or much worse than most reviewers, and I tried to be fair. On looking back, I see that often in reviewing a book I was too ready to take up certain points I agreed or disagreed with, and make them the subject of my review, instead of considering the book as a whole. If I read a book with the idea of writing a review, I approached it with a different attitude of mind from when I read it out of simple curiosity. As a reviewer, when reading I was, as it were, interrupting what the writer had to say, with the pressure of my need to write my few hundred words, and this had much the same effect as not listening to someone's remarks because one is thinking how to answer them.

Once I had become deeply involved in the literary profession, I could not help approaching the works of all but a very few of my contemporaries either in a spirit of rivalry or in one of identification of my aims with theirs. Gone were the days when I read every new book which had been recommended to me, as it were, open-mouthed, and expecting manna to fall. Now that I myself had appeared in print, my attitude began to resemble that of the owner of a race-horse, who watches the field not only with an eye on the performance of his own entrant, but also with a sharp sense of the methods of other trainers, which he often judges as mistakes into which he has avoided falling.

It never occurred to me that anything I wrote might annoy the author I was reviewing. That he or anyone else should attach importance to my opinions appeared to me so unlikely that in my early days I often overstated them. But at a later date I knew so many writers and had experienced their hurt sensibilities so often that I had a kind of loss of nerve, and found myself unwilling to criticize the work of those I knew personally: not that I was frightened, but because I did not see how to do so without a certain awareness of the writer's personality entering into my writing which would destroy its objectivity.

A part of my literary experience was not just reviewing but being reviewed. Here I showed all the vulnerability which I believed other

170

writers could not show. The good reviews which I received sometimes gave me a sense of being recognized with that warmth which is truly encouraging, but more often that of having scraped, with all my glaring faults, by the reviewer's defences. Adverse criticism was a terrible blow to me in my early days, and I still find it extremely discouraging when it is made of my poetry. In fact, I think that it is more difficult for a poet than for other kinds of writer to 'take' criticism. It is impossible to 'prove' that a poem is good, and a refusal to enter into the illusion created by a poem demonstrates that there is a failure of the poet to communicate, at least with the reviewer. A poem succeeds completely or not at all. Every weak place in a poet's armour is an opening for a fatal thrust.

Gradually I came to realize that the reviews which a writer receives are less his business than that of anyone else. They are a kind of conversation which goes on behind his back, which happens, though, to be published. Reviewers do not address themselves to writers but to readers. To overhear conversations behind his back is more disconcerting than useful to the writer; though he can perhaps search for criticism which may really help him to remedy faults in style. But he should remember that the tendency of reviewers is to criticize work not for what it is but for what it fails to be, and it is not necessarily true that he should remedy this by trying to become other than he is. Thus, in my own experience, I have wasted time by paying heed to criticisms that I had no skill in employing rhyme. This led me to try rhyme, whereas I should have seen that the moral for me was to avoid it.

At first the money I earned from writing was only useful pocket money, for I found my three hundred a year enough to live on. But soon, with increased responsibilities, my earnings became an addition to my income which I could not do without, until at last I became almost completely dependent on what I earned, for supporting a family.

Economically, I found that there is much in common between the career of a writer and that of a gambler. Work of the same quality and even about the same subject-matter sometimes does not pay at all or sometimes pays extremely well. A poem of mine, 'I think continually of those who were truly great', which was refused by

171

several literary editors to whom I sent it, was subsequently chosen to represent me in every anthology, and has made more money than any other poem I have written. On the whole, it holds true that a writer is paid best for doing his worst work: although sometimes, as in the case of the poem I have just mentioned, he may, almost accidentally, express in a form which attracts a wide public, some idea which is very significant to him. Today, a special temptation of writers is that they can live largely by giving their views about subjects of which they know nothing. Because there is a popular idea that the writers are 'wise', and since the public is not interested in the particular form in which this wisdom is best expressed, they are expected to be omniscient about those subjects, such as Higher Education, Euthanasia, and the Atom Bomb, which interest the public. A Brains Trust of misapplied Brains is the prevalent idea of the function of writers, and this is encouraged by editors, Talks' Directors of Broadcasting, governmental organizations for cultural propaganda, and an enormous machinery for misdirecting creative energy.

I became involved in obligations to editors and publishers, accepting suggestions as to what I should write, instead of carrying out my original plans for novels, poems and stories. I began in my own mind to divide my work into three categories: poetry, my vocation; books about things which interested me, the subjects of which were sometimes suggested by publishers; journalism, which I often wrote hurriedly.

This division of labour was not really satisfactory, for the reason that a creative writer should always write out of the inner necessity of a unique occasion. Not to do this is to risk paying a price. The labour which he puts into studies not essential to his inner development, and the shoddiness of journalism, overflow into his creative work by widening his experience too much and confusing his sensibility. Or if these things do not happen, his best work becomes too obviously hedged off and separated from the rest.

Circumstances combined to make me attach too much importance to my opinions. For my views as critic, as journalistic observer, and as amateur politician, were all in demand, and sometimes the pressure to express them was not just economic, but came from events themselves, such as the need to take sides against Fascism.

172

I found that my own views, however strongly held, bored me as soon as they were uttered. I realized that they concerned things which other people could express better, or that they arose out of the irritation of the moment, like an angry telegram. The effect of publishing too many opinions was like an inflation of the currency of my reputation, not only before others, but – which was more serious – to myself. Before I published a line I felt a kind of awe at the idea of my own writing. Later I lost a good deal of this, and only recently have I determined to act so as to regain it. My resolution was rather banal: to take much greater pains over everything, including journalism, and to publish no poems for several years, so that I could keep my poetry in a kind of isolation away from my other activities.

There is something about the literary life which, although it offers the writer freedom and honour enjoyed by very few, at the same time brings him a cup of bitterness with every meal. There is too much betrayal, there is a general atmosphere of intellectual disgrace, writers have to make too many concessions in order to support themselves and their families, the successful acquire an air of being elevated into public figures and therefore having lost their own personalities, the unsuccessful are too spiteful and vindictive and cliquey, and even the greatest, when they are attacked, reveal themselves often as touchy and vain. I think that almost every writer secretly feels that the literary career is not worthy of the writer's vocation. For this vocation resembles that of the religious.

Perhaps, though, the writers belong to an order which is not only plunged in the world, but actually belongs to it and has to do so. Literature has its purists, both in work and life, but it would grow devitalized with more than a few of these in each generation, and some of the greatest writers (Dostoevsky, Balzac, even Yeats) have involved themselves in controversy and journalism in their time.

If success is corrupting, failure is narrowing. What a writer really needs is a success of which he then purges himself. The writer's life should, in fact, be one of entering into external things and then withdrawing himself from them. Without entering in, he lacks experience of the world; and if he cannot withdraw, he is carried away on the impulse of literary politics, success, and the literary career.

*   *   *   *   *

My London life was the occasion of a break with Christopher Isherwood, which led to my leaving Berlin.

In the winter of 1932, Christopher came to London at the same time as myself. He met most of my friends, shortly before or after I had met them. He found that I had already told them most of his stories, and that I had been indiscreet. Moreover, he disliked seeing me transformed from his Berlin disciple into a London literary figure. Our quarrel was, on the surface, as simple as this. Underneath, Christopher had better reasons than these for being annoyed. I had lived vicariously on his life in Berlin, and later in London I had taken up a proprietory attitude towards it. He had accepted my dependence in Berlin, only to discover that all the while I had a life of my own in London. He felt cheated, irritated and even betrayed.

One day Christopher and I were together at the house which William Plomer then shared with Anthony Butts. At this party, Christopher showed so clearly his irritation with me that I decided I must lead a life which was far more independent of his. So the next day I called on him at his mother's house in Kensington, where he was staying. I explained that I had noticed I was getting on his nerves, and that when we returned to Berlin we should see nothing, or very little, of each other. He said that he was quite unaware of any strain, and that of course we should meet, exactly as before. I went away not at all relieved, because I thought he was refusing, more out of pride than friendship, to face a situation which he himself had made obvious. Moreover, he had expressed his views in the accents of ironic correctitude with which Auden, Chalmers and he could sometimes be insulting. Next day I received a letter from him saying that if I returned to Berlin he would not do so, that my life was poison to him, that I lived on publicity, that I was intolerably indiscreet, etc.

The result of this letter was that I decided not to return to Berlin. It made me break with my habit of dependence on Christopher. Most important of all, it made me realize that at the age of twenty-four I had still succeeded in forming no intimate human relationship. It was true that I had new friends, but it was clear that in every case they had friends in their lives who played a more significant rôle than I. There was no one whom I could ask to travel with me or share a flat.

Christopher went back to Berlin. We immediately made up the quarrel by writing to one another frequently, and by meeting often when we happened to be in the same place. All that occurred was a slight readjustment of our relationship, in a way that was inevitable. Christopher was at fault, perhaps, in not simply accepting my offer that we should agree to see less of one another. But I had been seriously at fault long before this, and doubtless my attempt to manipulate a change in our relationship, after my prolonged and deceptive docility, was irritating. The way in which people recognize a change which is inevitable, can often be the cause of quarrel, and at this distance of time I can assume that my way was a bad one.

I did not want to live alone and I did not consider marrying. I was in the mood when people advertise for a companion in the news-papers. I used to enquire of my friends of their friends in case they knew anyone suitable. So when by chance I met a young man who was unemployed, called Jimmy Younger, I asked him to live in my flat and work for me.

Jimmy came from a small town near Cardiff where his father kept an hotel. He had run away from home at the age of eighteen, and been in various jobs, including, for three years, the Army.

He was pleasant-looking, friendly, quickly intelligent in certain ways, and capable of learning. He read a good deal and had a re-sponse to poetry which often astonished me. For example, he under-stood without apparent effort, by a kind of immediate apprehension, passages in Auden which I found difficult. When I had known him a short time, I was also surprised to find that he knew most of my own poems by heart. He wrote excellent letters, and at a time which I will describe later, when he was in the Spanish war, moving ones.

When we first met, there was a certain mutual suspicion of em-ployer and employed between us. He was accustomed to be treated rough, and he expected that I would behave like his past em-ployers. When I did not do so he was disconcerted and felt that in some way I was gaining power over him as no one had done before. Quite early in our relationship, when we were at Levanto on the Italian coast, he said: 'I want to go away. You are very nice to me, but I feel that I am becoming completely your property. I have never

175

felt like that before with anyone, and I can't bear it.' I said that he could go away at once, if he wished to, that he could leave me entirely, or he could go back to London, and when I returned continue to work for me. Actually, when I said this I was stating what I was giving him, and how little I expected in return. Inevitably, this made it difficult for him to leave me. I realize now that this was one of the most important moments in our relationship. He knew that what I said was true, and he did not notice the element of self-deception in it. He could leave at any moment he wished, and he was under no obligation to me. By saying this, I had deprived him of any reason for wishing to leave.

I really did not need a secretary, and I find it difficult to force someone who is living on equal terms with me to work. Moreover, to make Jimmy work seriously, meant attempting to discipline a person who had already been disciplined by harsher employers than I could ever hope to be. He had been shouted at by sergeant-majors, locked up in guard rooms for some trivial offence, and so on. As with most soldiers, the army had disciplined him at the price of breaking down any power of self-discipline which he might once have possessed. Outside the Army he seemed lacking in will and purpose, because these had been forced upon him by punishments and drills.

We painted our Maida Vale flat, Jimmy cooked, I worked, we entertained and were entertained. Occasionally we quarrelled, largely because I was furious with him for having so little to do – then I repented because I realized that there really was very little he could do. There were days when I did not notice him, and then when I looked up and saw him moving about the flat, I felt extraordinarily touched, and I felt also a kind of pity for the burdens which my way of life imposed on him – the weight of which he could surely scarcely understand. There was real affection, real happiness, real interest in our life together: but also a sterility which sometimes affected me so much that I would lie down on my bed with a sensation I have never known before or since, as though my mouth were full of ashes.

At this period, I sometimes asked myself whether I shouldn't be doing him more good by turning him out, than by keeping him with me. In ordinary circumstances it would certainly have been better to force him to stand on his own feet. But the question was made rather theoretical by the fact that if he had left me he would simply have been thrown amongst the millions of the unemployed.

I asked it partly because our life together, despite our bonds of affection, was a strain. Often I realized that the pressure was greater on him than on me. For it was he who was living my life, not I his. He met my friends, listened to our conversation, entered a world which was alien to him. He was successful when he simply drew on his natural intelligence. He was sympathetic and amusing, and he could tell a story well. Yet for him this life was a kind of perpetual examination in which he felt that he ought to be answering the questions which he did not understand. There came moments when he was involved in some fairly difficult argument about politics or literature. He had the Welsh passion for arguing about things of which he knew little. This, coupled with the fact that he was out of his depth sometimes, made him lose his head. It was then that I would be at first most irritated with him, and finally most sorry. The irritation and the sorrow cancelled one another out. For if I started to blame him I recollected that I had much more than he to blame myself for.

The strain on my side came from the impression of being with someone whose life was empty, and who was living in a way which seemed to lead to no better future. The uncreativeness of Jimmy's life often left me with a feeling that my own work was a kind of disloyalty to him, the exercise of an unfair advantage. The emptiness of his day filled my imagination. If his restless desire to amuse himself made me impatient, what really depressed me was the realization that he had no other way of filling his time, which without me would have been even more wasted. There was certainly a sense in which I could see that this very arbitrary decision of mine to take him as a companion, having once been made, became a social phenomenon, as though in him I had taken into my home the purposelessness of the life of the Depression outside.

In the spring of 1933 we travelled in Italy. After a few days in Florence, we went to the beautiful little town of Levanto which I have mentioned. In the following year and the year after that we stayed at a small village called Mlini, near Dubrovnik on the Jugoslav coast. Mlini consisted simply of two or three pensions, a church, and a pier for steamers. It had one enormous tree which created a

177

monumental effect of shade and quiet, and gave the village a curious quality as though it had brought within a few yards from the coast, the peace of a place far in the interior. The pension where we stayed had tables out of doors a few yards from the water. Opposite Mlini was one of the many islands of which there are hundreds in this part of the Adriatic.

Dubrovnik, a few miles from Mlini, is a little off-shoot of Venice, with marble streets, Venetian palaces and a wall surrounding it. Two other walls stretch out into the sea like a mailed hand, opened out to form the harbour.

There was a walk along the coast from Mlini to a ruined palace in a garden where all the flowers ran wild. Above the village was the coastal road, and beyond it the mountain-side rose to a jagged crest of jutting rock, from which one saw range after range, all the stony mountains of the interior. The coastal road led to Montenegro where it twisted with many hair-pin bends to the top of the mountain, from which there was a great view of the Bay of Kotor like an immense mirror under the mountain.

This country with a riviera which is still wild, where many villages in the valleys lie half in ruins from Turkish invasion, where in the mountains a field is like a jewel set in a ring of stones, where there are half a dozen races, fascinated me. Some of them, the blonde, often tall and blue-eyed Montenegrins, were among the most beautiful people in the world. But when, in 1935, we sailed south to Greece, I saw how Jugoslavia, though beautiful, was perennially savage, whereas Greece, though wild, was intrinsically civilized. Jugoslavia lifted against the sky its cargo of crags and ruins. Occasionally the light and the sea wonderfully made many islands look like transparent scattered agates; this happened one afternoon when I looked northwards from the hill on which there is the famous cemetery of Cavtat. Nevertheless Jugoslavia remained Balkan, stormy, resistant of light, heaped with the wrecks of past quarrels and populated with dissident races. Greece was a country chiselled out of its own light. For what is that architecture, that columnar marble, except an invocation of light? The stone is cut into, with the aim of making a column look subtly straight against the sky, and shadows lift their darkness upwards like wings.

178

It seems to me now, thinking about our travels, that I could almost describe Jimmy Younger's character by recording his reaction to the places we visited. Levanto passed off almost without incident. He liked the life of swimming, bathing, and the conversation of pensions both there and at Mlini. He enjoyed the adventure of journeys in ships and motor-buses in Greece. In Austria he was probably happiest, because the architecture of Vienna was dramatic in a way which raised no question in his mind, and because the scenery of green mountains and lakes, like solid rock-crystal, pleased him. There was also something close to the Austrian in his *gemuet-lich*, easy-going, lax temperament, which entered easily into enjoyment and conversations, and was easily discouraged.

But his reaction to two places, Venice and Toledo, was something like panic. Venice he was mentally unprepared for. This overwhelming flesh of marble with arteries of water, which he had been told was the most beautiful place in the world, simply dismayed and depressed him. All he noticed was the dirt and the smells. Toledo discouraged him in a different way. We took a bus across the great plain outside Madrid, which had the quality of miles and miles of leather, like the hide of a great slaughtered bull. Then we came to that extraordinary river-encircled, mountain-cresting city of Toledo, of a merciless perfection with a cathedral rising from it like a great embossed candlestick. There was something about the city itself as alien and uncompromising as its inhabitants, whose attitude to tourists was either to stare at them with hostility or to beg from them with an insulting flagrancy.

Even the idea of certain places fills the minds of most people with a kind of sacred joy, not unconnected with the sense of prestige of having been there. To say therefore that Jimmy did not enjoy Venice and Toledo may sound like accusing him of an inability to comprehend the obviously beautiful. But actually going to places is not like appreciating diamonds into which all that is valuable has been concentrated into the hardest possible stone: nor even paintings in which the painter has selected his visual experiences in order to create his form. Travel is an art which has to be created by the traveller. It requires the piecing together of experiences of the places visited, until we have discovered for ourselves Paris in Paris, Vienna

179

in Vienna, Rome in Rome, Athens in Athens. A re-creation of these places in our minds is an art by which we fuse our conception of their pasts with our scrappy experience of their present. To do this we have to reconcile with the past a great deal of fragmentary contemporary material.

How well I know the dirty brick and rusted iron railway station, situated amid a desert of sidings and sheds, which is like a projection from many hundreds of miles away of an equally sad point of departure; the stuffy bed-sitting-room smelling of bugs and looking out on to a narrow courtyard in a district which seems to be situated nowhere, and refuses absolutely to offer the serene comforting assurance, 'You arrived where you set out to be; the architecture stretches out its cool, classic, famous arms to take you in'; the smell of homesickness which rises from nostalgic gutters even in the most beautiful places; the lamps in tenement windows seen from the gliding window of a train, which seem to say, 'Stranger, this is not your home——' – the glimpse of double beds and then the drawing down of blinds; the untidy, squalid secrets of tins and bits of wood and rubber, laid out on the wide sand of the famous resort when it is 'out of season'; the immensely serious and purposeful buildings in the centre of famous cities, which shut out with their hard edges glimpses of the crumbling Crusaders' tower or the cathedral; the hurrying contemporaries in dark suits and Homburg hats who pursue the affairs and politics which rise from all cities like a dense smoke enveloping the modern world; the squinting mountaineers in leather shorts and with flowers embroidered on their braces, with their minds like little caves of calculating darkness which the light-reflecting snow has never penetrated; the dismay felt at the edge of deserts and glaciers; the beggars who show their sores on the steps of buildings which are the wonders of the world, diseases which have not been cured by the most privileged scenery; the pimps who offer their sisters, so insolently sure are they that the traveller is a hypocrite who has come for this and not for the sake of art; and the guide who offers dirty post-cards to those who have travelled across the world to see a statue or a painting or a building.

How thoroughly I learned this lesson; that everywhere I went I took myself dressed in my clothes which at home were ordinary, but
180

abroad were the uniform of the English tourist. Arrived at my room, I first propped my books up on the mantelpiece and set my notebooks out on to the table, and then I went out into the streets to start on the chase of the historic town through the modern town. But then I often was in turn chased through these by my fears and my desires; these demons had more in common with what I had left behind than with anything new which I found. And always the threat of war lay over all these places like the meshes of one huge net.

Is travel then the mirage where the real itself becomes mirage, a mirage of mirages? When we are in Rome or Athens, do they evade us, lost under the scurrying modern life imposed on them, an ancient ghost behind a modern ghost? Do we meet always and everywhere nothing but ourselves? Or are there, in Florence, for example, moments when the emanation of the past stamped on stone and bronze surges up above the present, with a greater order perhaps than it ever had in the past? This is surely so when, from Fiesole, we see the dome of the cathedral like a shield made of rust-coloured petals guarding the city. Or is travel only a collecting of distinct memories, shade by shade, and colour by colour, like the paints upon a palette, so that on the canvas of the mind we paint for ourselves a picture of the world, laying the ruggedness of Jugoslavia against the clear light of Greece, or the transparency of Italy, where each olive tree stands up, minutely observed leaf by leaf, against a terraced hillside reflecting light?

Certainly I think the chief purpose of my own travelling was to form a gradually enlarging picture in which the countries were the paints which went to form the world.

Several years after the time of which I am now writing, I added, as it were, the sky to my picture of the world. For in travelling frequently to and from and across the United States, I went almost always by air. Then I discovered the great joy of being high above the clouds, where the flat outstretched wings of shining silver metal move in an enormous calm space of blue, alone with the sun. I came to understand the far longer time through which an immensely fast aeroplane seems to move than the slower trains and cars on land, so that in the air there seems to be an almost unchanging scene of sky and clouds, and sea, mountains or fields below. The highest

181

mountains, or the jagged lines of coasts, or the curves of great rivers, provide all the scenery: except when the atmosphere itself displays range on range of cloud, through whose summits the aeroplane moves, as though an alpinist swum through a mountain peak which had suddenly become a river.

I can well understand now that the journeys which were also an escape from London and a search for a place where I could work, as well as an education, were a strain on Jimmy. Sometimes they brought out attractive aspects of his character. As when we first went to Italy, he wrapped his greatcoat round him and dossed down on the floor of the compartment, or when in our room of the hotel on the island of Tinos, he burned hundreds of pieces of paper in an effort to discourage the mosquitoes.

I have never had so many quarrels with anyone as with Jimmy. They went on because he was completely unable to give way in an argument, because he liked arguing for its own sake, and because I was equally unable to give way on what I thought to be a matter of principle, and nearly everything between us became for me a matter of principle. These quarrels arose from unbelievably trivial causes. One of the worst was because I told him one day to buy a tin of roast chicken. Immediately he denied with indignation that one could possibly buy such a thing; that I should have thought so became a symbol to him of a certain vagueness in me which irritated him. So years before, as a boy lying in my bedroom at home, I had been irritated by the vague way in which my father shuffled his feet as he ran down the path in front of our house. For Jimmy had really become the son whom I attempted to console, but of whom I was the maddening father. However, I was convinced that I had in fact seen a picture of a sizzling farmhouse chicken entire on the outside of a chicken-sized oblong can. Therefore Jimmy's assumption that I was being vague in a particular instance, when I thought I wasn't, outraged me. Thus the smallest differences rapidly became illustrations of the weaknesses which annoyed us in each other. There was, of course, a further reason for these quarrels. They were the means by which Jimmy broke through the barriers of self-protection surrounding me. At such moments we really were ferociously together, revealed to one another, with all defences down. What we heard was

182

Jimmy's real voice, under his irrelevant angry voice, saying: 'You have helped me at the price of taking away all possibility of my having any self-respect. I have been moved into your world where everyone must think of me as your creation, and no one as having an existence independently of you. When I realize this, I want to get away from you.' And mine, which said: 'Your complete dependence on me, your lack of any life of your own, your indolence, sap my work. When I write, I am away from you. I only exist when I am free of you.'

Yet the morning after such a scene he would insist that he had not meant a word of what he said, that I should forget it all, that he could imagine no happiness apart from his life with me. This was indeed quite true; for his mind spoke with two voices; one was the voice of the enjoyment of living from day to day, of adjusting himself to situations as they arose; the other was the voice of an inner despair which told him his life with me was hopeless. But even if, as I came to think, the despairing voice was the true one, casting him out into a society where he had already been unemployed did not solve the problem. His position with me was perhaps the best he could get in any case; and now it once more sometimes seemed to me that the most eccentric and intimate factor in Jimmy's life – his hopeless dependence on me – for which I was responsible, was also a social phenomenon with an entirely public aspect.

Though I was not reassured by Jimmy's telling me that everything was all right, I had my own faith which was perhaps almost as shallowly optimistic. This was that our affection, our need of one another, formed a situation in which there was a meeting of two human beings, and this transcended our separate characteristics, which I regarded as superficial. But gradually I came to see that in the moments of our quarrels and the making up of them, when we were most completely and terribly together, there was something in each which wanted to destroy the other. My character undermined his belief in himself; his dependence and lack of anything to do threatened my creativeness.

There was perhaps another reason for the failure of our relationship. We had come against the difficulty which confronts two men who endeavour to set up house together. Because they are of the same sex, they arrive at a point where they know everything about each

183

other and it therefore seems impossible for the relationship to develop beyond this. Further development being impossible, all they can do is to keep their friendship static and not revert to a stage of ignorance or indifference. This meant in our case that loyalty demanded, since the relationship itself could not develop, that neither of us should develop his own individuality in a way that excluded the other. Thus a kind of sterility was the result of the loyalty of each to the other; or rather of his loyalty to the relationship itself which he did not wish to grow beyond.

It might be said (and indeed I often argued this with myself) that if Jimmy and I had had interests in common, we ought to have been able to grow side by side, without this feeling that having arrived at the furthest place of knowing one another we had reached sterility. Yet – superficially at least – it seemed to me that a relationship with an intellectual equal would have been even more open to the same objection. For the differences of class and interest between Jimmy and me certainly did provide some element of mystery which corresponded almost to a difference of sex. I was in love, as it were, with his background, his soldiering, his working-class home. Nothing moved me more than to hear him tell stories of the Cardiff streets of Tiger Bay, of his uncle who was in the Salvation Army and who asked for his trumpet to be buried beside him in his grave, so that when he awoke on the day of judgment he might blow a great blast of hallelujah on it. When Jimmy talked of such things, I was perhaps nearer poetry than talking to most of my fellow poets. At such moments, too, I was very close to certain emotions awakened in childhood by the workers, who to us seemed at the same time coarse, unclean, and yet with something about them of forbidden fruit, and also of warm-heartedness which suddenly flashed across the cold gulf of class, secret and unspoken. As I write, many instances of this unfold before me in all their original unsullied excitement. One especially: of an air-raid alarm on the Norfolk coast when I was seven. A soldier carried me in his arms from our house at Sheringham to some dug-out on the cliffs. As he did this, he held me to his heart with a simplicity which my parents with their fears for health and morals, and their view that any uninhibited feeling was dangerous, could scarcely show.

184

My relationship with Jimmy had therefore made me realize that if I were to live with anyone it could not be with a man. Through this very relationship I began to discover a need for women, to think about them, to look for them. At the same time I did not lose my fundamental need for the friendship of a man with whom I could identify my own work and development, even the need for women. But I did not now need this friendship on the same terms as before. Then, when I thought I had arrived at a goal, I was only at an early stage of a difficult journey.

The things I am now writing of are difficult to explain. Very few people dare to have a clear view of their own complexity. They would prefer to simplify themselves even at the expense of condemning their way of life rather than maintain complex and perhaps contradictory attitudes towards it, from which a harmony might finally be achieved.

At this time, then, I became vividly aware of an ambivalence in my attitudes towards men and women. Love for a friend expressed a need for self-identification. Love for a woman, the need for a relationship with someone different, indeed opposite, to myself. I realized that self-identification leads to frustration if it be not realized; destruction, perhaps, if it be half-realized; a certain sterility if it be realized. The relationship of a man with the 'otherness' of a woman is a relationship of opposite poles. They complete, yet never become one another, never reach a static situation where everything which is possible to be known between two people is known, every gesture a repetition of one already performed, where little development, except the loss of youth, seems possible beyond this. As I understand Goethe, he defined creative human energy as the action of male force, energizing, intelligent, constructive, upon the receptive body of that which is outside it – *das Ewigweibliche* – the eternally feminine. I could not develop beyond a certain point unless I were able to enter a stream of nature through human contacts, that is to say, through experience of women. Yet I never lost the need for camaraderie also, my desire to share my creative and intellectual adventures with a man, whose search was the same as mine.

The two needs, while existing side by side, seemed to some extent to be mutually exclusive, so that whilst I was with a friend it might seem that I had renounced a whole world, of marriage, of responsibilities, and I had been received into another where everything was understood, where work, ideas, play and physical beauty corresponded in the friend's life with my own. On the other hand, when I was with a woman, it was as though I had shed my other personality, left it in some other room, and that instead of reflecting and being reflected by my physical-spiritual comrade, I had entered into the wholeness of a life outside me, giving to the woman that in myself which was not contained in her, and taking from her what was not in me. At the same time, I was afraid of losing too much by this exchange, afraid of becoming something different from what I was. One curious result of this was that I felt less immediately present with a woman than with a man. So that when I had shared some experience with her, there was a time-lag, and my moments of deepest feeling often occurred after I had left her.

IV

I WAS in Vienna in July 1936 when the newspapers reported the beginnings of the Spanish Civil War. Here I was in contact with a group of Socialists who had been driven 'underground' ever since the liquidation of the Austrian Socialists by the Dollfuss Government in February 1934. This small group used to meet in the flat of a great friend of mine, an American woman, whom I shall here call Elizabeth.

To these Austrian Socialists the Spanish war was at first more a subject of amazement than of hope. They felt that Vienna had been abandoned, almost without protest, by the Socialist and Liberal forces in the world. Cut off in Central Europe, they concluded that Republican Madrid would go the same way, and at first they followed the Spanish struggle with only an academic interest.

But within a few weeks Spain had become the symbol of hope for all anti-Fascists. It offered the twentieth century an 1848: that is to say, time and place where a cause representing a greater degree of freedom and justice than a reactionary opposing one, gained victories. It became possible to see the Fascist-anti-Fascist struggle as a real conflict of ideas, and not just as the seizure of power by dictators from weak opponents. From being a pathetic catastrophe, Spain lifted the fate of the anti-Fascists to heights of tragedy. Since the area of struggle in Spain was confined, and the methods of warfare comparatively restrained, the voices of human individuals were not overwhelmed, as in 1939, by vast military machines and by propaganda. The Spanish war remained to some extent a debate, both within and outside Spain, in which the three great political ideas of our time – Fascism, Communism, and Liberal-Socialism – were discussed and heard. At first the Republicans were men of very different opinions, and it was only at a late stage of the war that the Communists succeeded in forcing their unified ideas upon the others.

*   *   *   *   *

To hundreds of people, of whom I was one, the most significant happenings in Europe between 1933 and 1936 had been the triumph of dictatorship and the consequent accumulation of fury. Like many others, I had watched the bases on which European freedoms had seemed to rest, destroyed. Innocent people were persecuted for no reason than that they belonged to a racial minority. A whole generation of the young was taught violence, the absolute authority of power, and that lies were justified if they served a nationalist cause. There was something nightmarish about what was happening in Germany. Watching flagrant public injustice committed where there is no effective protest, is like a man's condition in a terrible dream where some catastrophe takes place in front of his eyes and he is unable to prevent it. All he can do is utter a shout, but this too is ineffective – unless it awakens him to the sanity of the daylight. But no shout awoke the world from Hitlerism during long years. Hundreds were shut into their separate nightmares.

The first of these events was the burning of the Reichstag. The real trial which followed was not that in which Goering shook his fist at Dimitrov, and the slobbering Van der Lubbe mumbled 'Yes-no', but the general election following the fire, in which the German people were condemned to Nazism. From this, there followed the arrest of members of the opposition parties, the burning of the books, the persecution of the Jews, 30th June 1934, and all those macabre events which most English Conservatives only noticed in September 1939.

Almost as terrible as the actions of the Nazis was the indifference of many people to these things, the lack of horror in the face of horror. This was more than a failure to read the signs of approaching war. It was a moral indifference among those not directly involved, although just such callousness had made Fascism possible among the Germans. Certain Germans, living in some square of a German city, could be reproached for not inquiring into the disappearance
188

of neighbours who were Jews or Communists. But this attitude was equally reprehensible in people of other nations who allowed individuals, and whole groups, and finally even nations, to be crushed.

Perhaps the worst of the 1930's was not that politicians attempted to compromise with Hitler: but that they did Hitler's work by blinding themselves, and others, to the forces with which they were compromising. Hitler did more than gain political victories in Europe. He also demoralized international politics. There came a day when the democratic statesmen who played politics with him, were forced to accept elections in Austria and the Saar, directed by Hitler as expressions of the will of the people; to recognize the Anschluss and the seizure of Czechoslovakia as voluntary corrections of European frontiers; and to deny, during the Spanish Civil War, that British ships were sunk by Italian submarines in the Mediterranean. These statesmen came to represent a cynicism which lacked the courage of Hitler's blackguardism. If it is pointed out that after all the democracies overthrew Hitler, I must reply that this was not until they had inherited and taken to themselves the worst of his plans – total war followed by a dictated peace.

The advances of Hitlerism were, during the 1930's, the background of my life and the lives described in this book, which is not concerned primarily with politics but with my experience of these events. I am not trying here to justify my attitudes: but to describe a feeling of outrage. The intellectuals who earned themselves the label 'anti-Fascist', and who were reproached often for their unwarranted intrusion into politics, were really in the position of Emilia in the last act of *Othello* when she cries: 'The truth must out', and denounces him who is probably most dear to her – Iago – in order to set right the fearful wrong into which the heads of the Venetian State have blundered. At this moment, Emilia is taking upon herself a political action: and Iago, of course, is the first to point this out and ask that she should be silenced.

Politics is an elastic term. In a settled state of society of the kind which my uncle admired, it is the concern of the experts. Then the non-politicians are political only in the sense that a member of the public, when he serves on a jury, is a fractional judge, with limited

189

powers of agreement or disagreement on the occasion of a trial. An election makes the voters a jury who say 'Yes' to the government whom they elect, 'No' to the party they reject, without the electors thereby becoming professional politicians. But in certain circumstances, whole classes of people, not in ordinary times political, may have a politically conscious role forced upon them. Thus, when Hitler passed laws depriving Jews of their rights as German citizens, Jewry became a single political cause, and every German Jew had to choose between being a political victim accessory to his own destruction, or a fighter.

Hitler forced politics on to non-political groups who suddenly became aware that they had interests in common. Not only the Jews, but also the intellectuals, because their position was directly attacked, and through sympathy with their colleagues who lived tormented under Fascism, acquired an intensity of vision and a fury in their non-political politics which the professional politicians did not share.

The intelligentsia also had more sinister reasons for understanding Hitler. These were the elements of pure destructiveness, of attraction to evil for its own sake, and of a search for spiritual damnation, which had been present in some European literature for the past century, and which were fulfilled in Nazi politics. European literature had diagnosed, without purging itself of, the evil of nihilism. In Hitlerism the nightmares of Dostoevsky's *The Possessed*, of Nietzsche and of Wagner, were made real. The cultured Europeans recognized in this political movement some of their own most hidden fantasies. Hatred of it was deeply involved with a sense of their own guilt. As though to demonstrate this to the utmost, certain writers in the occupied countries were actually to welcome Hitler as a destructive force which their art had prophesied.

In a curious way the crimes committed by the Fascists became my own personal life, vicariously lived. Every morning I searched the newspapers for the German news. If I read of a fall in the German markets, or of some act which seemed to indicate that a spirit of defiance still existed in Germany, or even of an arrest of an anti-Nazi, I felt an almost sobbing satisfaction. External things over which I had no control had usurped my own deepest personal life, so that my inner world became dependent on an outer one, and if that outer

190

one failed to provide me with its daily stimulus of crime and indigna-tion, I felt often a kind of emptiness. At the very worst there were moments when I felt that there was a conspiratorial relationship be-tween the evil passions of the Fascists – which I so profoundly under-stood – and my own anti-Fascist virulence. On a more superficial level, the existence of this vast immoral spiritual demonism in the world which was Fascism, dwarfed my own moral problems. How-ever bad I was, Fascism was worse; by being anti-Fascist, I created a rightness for myself besides which personal guilt seemed unim-portant.

In poetry I was confronted with the dilemma of stating a public emotion which had become a private one, and which yet never be-came completely my own inner experience because, as I have ex-plained, it invaded my personality rather than sprang out of it. Critics like Virginia Woolf, who reproached our generation for writ-ing too directly out of a sense of public duty, failed to see that public events had swamped our personal lives and usurped our personal experience. Yeats was perhaps the writer who best understood that public passion can 'make a stone of the heart'.

To write about Fascism was then to write about the experience which had usurped the place of more personal ones. Yet I tried to relate the public passion to my private life.

Although this attempt was a failure, I think I was probably right to enter deliberately into a confused situation, and reject the great simplifications of a deeply felt but impersonal public point of view. The truth of my own existence was that, in spite of everything, I did not plunge myself wholly in public affairs. Therefore a poetry which rejected private experience would have been untrue to me. Moreover, I dimly saw that the conflict between personal life and public causes must be carried forward into public life itself: it was my duty to express the complexity of an ambivalent situation. For our indivi-dualistic civilization to be reborn within the order of a new world, people must be complex as individuals, simple as social forces. They must recognize their public duties, accept sacrifices, recognize neces-sity: but at the same time they must insist on their individuality, their difficulties, their privacy, their irrationality. The simplifying struggle to achieve social justice and pacification of the world preoccupies

191

men today. But yesterday there was that complexity which made the Renaissance prolific, wonderful, rich, mysterious: and tomorrow there must be the miracle of a just civilization which is also capable of the complex folly of building a Venice.

The most ambitious – and perhaps the least successful – attempt I made to solve the problem of making such a statement was in a longish poem called *Vienna*, which I wrote in 1935. In part this expressed my indignation at the suppression of the Viennese Socialists by Dollfuss, Fey and Starhemberg: but in part also it was concerned with a love relationship. I meant to show that the two experiences were different, yet related. For both were intense, emotional and personal, although the one was public, the other private. The validity of the one was dependent on that of the other: for in a world where humanity was trampled on publicly, private affection was also undermined.

The poem fails because it does not fuse the two halves of a split situation, and attain a unity where the inner passion becomes inseparable from the outer one. Perhaps the world in which I was living was too terrible for this fusion to take place: the only people who attained it were the murderers and the murdered. Throughout these years I had always the sense of living on the circumference of a circle at whose centre I could never be. During the Reichstag trial I was in my flat in Maida Vale; when I read of 30th June 1934, I was sitting on the grassy bank of a road in the Wiener Wald at a place called Sulz-Stangau, waiting for a bus; the murder of Dollfuss was for me the waves of excitement which I felt in the crowds surging through the streets of Vienna. One day, when I was at Mlini, the little resort five miles from Dubrovnik, where I spent the spring of 1934, I climbed up the path from the pensionnat to the coastal road, and was almost run over by a large six-wheeled car, followed by four others of the same make. The man in the first car, who turned his head and stared at me so that I met his eyes, was Goering.

Somewhere I felt that there was a place which was at the very centre of this world, some terrible place like the core of a raging fire. Perhaps it was in a cell where some helpless old man was being beaten to death, perhaps it was in a café over some frontier where exiled leaders were plotting to return. If I could ever approach it, I felt it

192

would be the centre where the greatest evil of our time was under-stood and endured. But at this thought I was appalled, for it made me realize that the centre of our time was perhaps the violent, incom-municable death of an innocent victim.

*   *   *   *   *

Mlini was a little village on a stretch of the Adriatic coast, south of Dubrovnik, where there was a stony beach. The pension was a build-ing not unlike a stone farmhouse. In front of it was a terrace with chairs and tables under trees, where the guests ate outdoors. The view from the terrace, across the crisp and sparkling sea like a lake, was of a wooded island, one of the hundreds with which that part of the Adriatic is sprinkled. Beyond the terrace, jutting into the sea, was the little jetty where the steamer from Dubrovnik, on its way to and from Cavtat, stopped. Above the beach, to the north of the pension, there was an orchard on the hillside where I used often to write at a table under the trees: to the south, a walk through fields of flowers to a ruined castle falling into the sea, surrounded by its garden running into a wilderness.

While Jimmy and I were staying at the pension in the spring of 1934, Elizabeth, with her little daughter aged three and the child's nurse, an attractive Austrian girl, arrived for a few days' stay. The three of them looked charming, with the two women sitting on the terrace while the little girl played on the shore. Elizabeth's profile, as she looked out at the sea, reminded me of my mother in certain photographs taken at an age before I can remember her: black hair and eyes, a clear complexion slightly tanned but not expressionless with sunburn. In her appearance there was a look of her having suffered at some time. This was particularly noticeable in an un-expected tension of her mouth at certain moments which made me think that she must on some occasion in the past have shown remark-able determination.

During these few days when they were at Mlini, I simply watched Elizabeth. Dividing me from her was a curtain of wonder, which I knew at some time I would draw aside. I imagined her cool, clear, admirable life, unspoiled by pettiness, controlled and intelligent. But there was also that little scar of a suffering overcome, on her lips like the mark left by a seal in soft red wax.

She told me that she came from Vienna, where she was studying medicine and psychology. It so happened that Jimmy had at this time a 'grumbling' appendix, so I mentioned that we might visit Vienna for him to have an operation. She was sympathetic and full of practical plans for help. She would be glad for us to stay in her apartment, and through her contacts with the clinics of Vienna she would obtain a surgeon and a bed in a hospital for Jimmy, if these were necessary. We parted with the idea of meeting soon again. All she offered was generous and yet not thrust upon us. We had the greatest freedom either to accept her help or refuse it without ill feeling.

I learned that she was an American. This mystified and attracted me. Elizabeth came from Chicago, and later she told me in her laughing, expansive way that if I wanted to know where her wealth came from, I need only read Upton Sinclair's novel (I forget which one) dealing with the meat-packing factories of that city.

She had a kind of beauty which, when I had seen how different it really was from that of my mother, also seemed to me very American. It was a combination of the classicism of the Renaissance with the freedom of the New World. Certain American women recall portraits by Titian or Rubens – as do certain European ones – but whereas the Europeans are like remote descendants of the models for those paintings, the Americans have the freshness and newness of some dusty portrait from which the varnish has been removed, revealing the colours of the glowing flesh in their almost shocking brilliance. Elizabeth recalled a portrait of Leda by Leonardo. She had the same dark eyes, oval face, and smilingly attentive expression. Her hair framed her face, and if it had been plaited and braided into tresses would have had a snake-like sinuous quality, as in the drawings of Leda.

After Elizabeth's return to Vienna, we decided to go there in order that Jimmy might have the operation now strongly recommended by the doctor at Dubrovnik. We stayed at Elizabeth's apartment, which was oak-panelled, rather old-fashioned, near one of the great Vienna churches. We were alone there most of the day when she was studying.

At the age of twenty-nine – I now learned – she had been married twice, both her marriages having proved failures. Owing to the

194

break-down of her second marriage she had passed through a crisis in which she had turned to psychoanalysis. In a previous (to me almost unthinkable) stage of her history, she had been a student at Oxford, where she had studied the English Romantics.

She explained these things with her amused clarity, which seemed so objective and yet had something very feminine about it. Until she was 'analysed', she said, she had 'just felt guilty all day long', and when I asked her once whether it wasn't rather appalling to have had two marriages dissolved, she said, yes, it had certainly been painful, and she was really sorry for her most recent husband, but she guessed there was no reason why one shouldn't just go on trying with marriages until one succeeded.

One day I told her, rather as if projecting myself into one of her experiences (that of being psychoanalysed), that I was attracted by her. As an excuse (I felt there was need of this), I offered a psychological explanation – that when I first saw her, I had been reminded of the photographs of my mother when she was young. Elizabeth laughed and said: 'Well, that isn't at all a bad reason for falling in love. A great many men spend all their lives falling in love with an image of their mother.' She looked at me in her calm, clear, appraising way, which yet had something tense about it, the throbbing of her own childhood and past, something which after all I could console.

Elizabeth was very occupied with her work, her child, and her apartment. Throughout the day she underwent a whole series of transformations. In the morning, when she left for the University, she was the schoolgirl with a satchel of books; at luncheon, arranging and cooking a delicious meal, she was the mistress of her flat; with her daughter, she was the patient mother using all the up-to-date methods; and then, at evening, she was the lover.

A few miles from Vienna, in the Wiener Wald, she had a small wooden house called the Blockhaus. It was in a clearing of the forest, in a meadow. It had large windows, each of them a single pane of glass, against which the steeply rising field of grass and flowers pressed like a brighty-painted panel, on fine days of summer. This field was full of the throbbing, singing noise of cicadas. Lamplit at evening, seen from the outside, the Blockhaus glowed like the interior of a cedar box. Our life there was woven into the meadows and sur-

195

rounding woods, as the innumerable flowers were woven in the scented grass. There, often sleeping at night out of doors, we were like figures moving through a tapestry of our forest and our field.

From her varied experience, Elizabeth had learned to give herself wholly to whatever she was doing. One part of her busy life never infringed on another. When we discussed her work, the problems of her child's education, her difficulties in running her flat, the care and weight of these things never pressed upon the moment of our conversation. Though, on my side, I talked of things which did intrude: above all, of my relationship with Jimmy. It was unthinkable that I should abandon him; yet it remained like a leash which held me back, against which I was straining.

There is in modern love an awareness of the psychological motives involved which must be without parallel in past times, and which gives it, when it is complicated as ours was, the texture of catastrophe. When I said, 'I cannot abandon Jimmy,' we both knew that I meant at least three different things. Firstly there was what we called the 'objective situation' – Jimmy existed, I had got him where he was and I had definite responsibilities towards him. Secondly, my relationship was as strong as it had ever been with him, and if he needed me there was also a despairing sense in which I needed and clung to him. Thirdly, he symbolized a psychological factor within me: if there hadn't been a Jimmy there might well have been someone else; if there hadn't been someone else, there would have been a gaping need.

The counterpart of my relationship with Elizabeth was that with him. There were the visits to the hospital where he lay in a ward by the side of a crippled English boy, and opposite a man who was horribly dying. This brought out Jimmy's best qualities: cheerfulness, kindliness and resistance to depression, when he was directly confronted with a challenge. Then there was his convalescence when he and I went away for a few days to a place called Mariazell, where there was a Baroque church, centre of pilgrimages, in the middle of grassy mountains looking like the Bavarian Alps. All these days, I was feeling that Jimmy's illness, which had brought us to Vienna, was now keeping me from Elizabeth. Then there were the weekdays when, while Elizabeth was in the city, Jimmy and I would sometimes go alone to the Blockhaus. There were perhaps the hours of arrival when we felt a calm of reconciliation at being alone together: but they were followed by others when we had senseless and passionate rows, seemingly about nothing. These nearly always took the form of his criticizing me for 'gross inaccuracy' in something I had said (for example, when I said that one could buy tinned roast chicken), and my saying that his attitude in some particular instance was 'symbolic of our whole relationship'. We went on from there.

In past times people would, in such a situation, only have been aware of one or two of the factors, and they would not have been able to account for them all. They would have blamed circumstances which had created a situation where I had happened to meet Elizabeth just when, owing to his illness, I was most tied to Jimmy. What we faced was the knowledge that there might be a real inability on my part to choose; which was different from saying that circumstances made it impossible for me to do so. Our clarity gave Elizabeth's and my relationship an objective quality, as though even when we entered most fully and intimately into it, we still also regarded it as a 'situation', seen by both of us from the outside. Elizabeth certainly would not have me until I chose for myself. At the same time she understood, more than anyone ever had done, the nature of the difficulty. Something which we called my 'ambivalence' for ever kept unsleeping watch between us, like a sword. Though she understood so well, I was aware at moments of an outraged frustration on her side, something which reasonableness would not silence. I wondered sometimes whether our explanations, which made my 'psychology' responsible for everything, did not actually increase my sense of guilt, and whether I would not have felt less guilty if I had known fewer explanations for my behaviour and been able to attach more blame to accidental circumstances. For I think that the study of psychoanalysis has, for most people, increased their sense of guilt by widening their awareness of the part played in apparently fortuitous circumstances by the subconscious personality.

*   *   *   *   *

During the coming months I divided my time between London and Vienna, rather as, formerly, I had divided it between London and Berlin.

Meanwhile events in Austria were developing, and Elizabeth had added to her other rôles a political one. She put her flat and a good deal of her money at the disposal of a group of Austrian Socialists whom she herself joined. Part of this group moved across the Czech frontier and opened an office at Bratislava. Here they were able to print material which could then be smuggled back across the frontier. They also provided a centre for the care of political refugees.

Now when I went to stay with Elizabeth, I was sometimes present at meetings of the 'cell'. It consisted of half a dozen people who called themselves by Christian names not their own, such as Karl, Jo, Anna, Poldi. They had in common the kind of anonymity which casts a certain drabness over even the most eccentric, when they are bound together by exile, persecution and anxiety. They lived hunted lives. Despite their courage, they were exposed to a kind of corruption which was a result of their circumstances. There was rivalry between the committee at Bratislava and the comrades who remained in Austria, some of whom, later, refused to recognize the authority of an *émigré* committee. Elizabeth, in supplying funds to them, experienced the painful realization that people who will risk their lives to fight tyranny, can still be dishonest about money. Though these political victims were living a life which seemed to offer no rewards, nevertheless some of them fought for shadow positions in indefinitely postponed shadow governments.

Despite this additional work, Elizabeth did not lose her gift for throwing herself into our personal relationship whenever we were together. In the winter we went for a few days to the Blockhaus, where we ski-ed in the sloping fields and down the steep snowy paths through the woods. When, after some hours outside, we returned to the Blockhaus and, throwing off our outdoor clothes, cooked a meal on the oil-stove, there was something sparkling and joyous about our life, which seemed an inheritance from the past Vienna of horse-drawn sleighs with tinkling bells.

While Elizabeth was working at her medicine, I would often sit in her flat writing or reading. Then she would come in from the snowy streets, her face like cold marble under her fur cap, and when I kissed her it was as though my lips, warm from sitting indoors, were like fire against her cheeks.

198

Sometimes I would walk alone through the Vienna streets, along the Ring, or into the centre of the inner city, the Graben, with its ebullient monument of clouds in stone. Here there were the relics of a past magnificence, the roads of the Ring flanked with gardens, the palaces adorned with the Baroque statues in which the life of the spirit speaks a rhetorical language through elegant and worldly marble men, women, saints and angels. In no European town did the shabby contemporary life contrast so with the grandeur of the background of the past as in Vienna. The people in their suits and homburg hats or their leathery peasant costumes shifted like water at the very bottom of a tank against the exalted churches, palaces, monuments and galleries. To go to the Vienna Opera and see the weary audience like dwarfs against an ornate interior which demanded the parade of uniforms and splendid dresses, was to see the condition to which Vienna had fallen. It was in the countryside, at the swimming-pools, at the wine houses, when the new season's raw wine called Heuriger was being drunk, that the cheerful amiability, turning easily to lachrimose self-pity, of the Viennese temperament seemed suited to its surroundings. Perhaps, too, in the great working-class tenements – Goethehaus and Karl Marx Hof, built by the Socialists – one glimpsed a new Vienna, a people's city. But the old imperial Vienna was a gigantic carven shell of past pretences in a city where no one pretended any longer.

In describing my life with Elizabeth, I feel as though I were writing of a kind of lived poetry, which I re-live in the writing of it. At the time, perhaps just because it was so like poetry to me, I failed at any moment to lose myself completely in the life with her: although, so great was her understanding, that this not losing myself was something which we both shared. It was as though I were standing outside and watching experience even while I partook of it, taking it into myself instead of giving it back to her, in love for some future occasion. Moreover, in the actuality, there were always the things that came between us – above all, my 'ambivalence'. These are shed when I look back, but they were always there then. Whilst I admit this, I do not mean that the experience was 'literary'. It had its palpable consistent reality which we both understood and never forget. The things that made it poetry were perhaps those very ones which divided us, even in our moments of being most closely together.

I returned to London, with the intention of going back to Vienna in the spring. Shortly before my return I received a letter from Elizabeth saying that she was engaged to be married. In the course of her work with the Vienna Socialists she had met the man who – she was sure – could make her happy. She hoped nonetheless that I would come back to Vienna.

The letter was not entirely a surprise. It was obvious that the arrangement into which we had fallen, whereby I spent a few weeks in Vienna every six months, could not be satisfactory to either of us.

I did go back to Vienna. Elizabeth and her fiancé received me with a warmth, mingled on her part with a new and enduring affection, born of the confidence with which I had accepted her decision. We were aware that we had survived a relationship in which we might have been disappointed, and had discovered a new one within our separation. This to some extent compensated me for what I had lost, for part of our clarity was to realize that we were not made for one another. I did not satisfy her; and from my point of view, she was too clear, too decided, too much in possession of all the threads of her life, too confident in what she knew, too little mystified by what she did not know. For instance, to her religious belief was simply an encumbrance to clear thinking. I had a kind of piety of not judging what I did not understand, a reverence for the beliefs of others, and even a certain understanding of religious experience. I could not accept such a rationalist view.

The new depth and the enduring quality of our relationship was made possible by her fiancé Franz, who, as part of his love for her, loved me also.

Franz was an Austrian worker by origin and was now leader of the Socialist group which met at Elizabeth's flat. He had a lightness, sureness, energy and gaiety in contrast to the depressing quality of Jo, Karl, Anna and Poldi. Stocky and broad, round-headed, flat-nosed, light-haired, with clear blue eyes, smiling lips and a cleft chin, he looked like a peasant who had come to the town. Politically, he had three outstanding gifts: a real faith in socialism, interest in Marxist theory, and a love for political action and struggle. Franz had not lost an almost naïve interest in himself as a political phenomenon.

He was amazed to find himself – the peasant boy who had come to town – making speeches, writing pamphlets, and working underground. His experiences always appeared fresh to him, and the fact that he did not take his position for granted, meant that he understood the non-political politics of others. Franz was incapable of becoming a cog in a political machine, and he remained profoundly human.

He had a genuine respect for a non-realist approach to politics. In this he differed from most politicians, who respect only the political methods which they use themselves, and are suspicious of attitudes which neglect problems of action and power. He saw the political implications of ideas not directly concerned with political means, yet he did not draw the conclusion of many Marxists that because these ideas had political implications, those who held them should be directed by political activists. In fact he had a profound tolerance which made him actually respect means and ends different from his own.

In his personal life he observed the Quakerish discipline of the Austrian Socialists. He smoked and drank little, never exceeded the limits of a fixed monthly allowance for his personal needs. He had taken a vow of moderation.

At first I felt some uneasiness with him, but he and Elizabeth and I were determined to overcome this. We did so by talking of objective things. At this time I was writing a book called *Forward from Liberalism*, in which I set down my ideas about politics. We took the manuscript of this to the Blockhaus and spent a week-end discussing it.

* * * * *

In *Forward from Liberalism* I argued that Liberals must reconcile Communist social justice with their liberal regard for social freedom, and that they must accept the methods which it might be necessary to use in order to defeat Fascism.

In this book I did not succeed in stating the case in my own idiom of personal experience. Instead, I strayed into realms of historical analysis and political ratiocination, a task for which almost any university student of history was better equipped than I. I should have done better to try and state a moral case with the utmost simplicity, illustrating it with examples drawn from my own limited experience; or placing it perhaps, as I have placed similar problems

201

here, within the framework of an autobiography intended to be a projection of my personal existence. Or again, I might have treated it in images, using my poetic insight, and trying to make the reader (as Virginia Woolf had done in some of her essays defending a feminist point of view) visualize my own inner picture of the situation.

In the 1920's there had been a generation of American writers – Scott Fitzgerald, Ernest Hemingway, Malcolm Cowley, and some others – whom Gertrude Stein had called the Lost Generation. We anti-Fascist writers of what has been called the Pink Decade were not, in any obvious sense, a lost generation. But we were divided between our literary vocation and an urge to save the world from Fascism. We were the Divided Generation of Hamlets who found the world out of joint and failed to set it right.

The call we heard was by no means so absurd as it may sound to a later generation. For in those days Japan could still have been prevented from invading Manchuria, Hitler could have been thrown out of power at the time of the Anschluss or the invasion of the Rhineland, the Spanish Republic could have been saved. If any of these opportunities had been seized, there would have been no terrible totalitarian war followed by a totalitarian peace: the one thing required then was a conscience extending far beyond the existing circles of professional politicians in the democracies, to the people. This deeply awakened public conscience could have forced Britain, France, and perhaps even the United States, to take the stand necessary to prevent war.

The impulse to act was not mistaken. But the action we took may not have been of the right kind. It was, for the most part, the half-and-half action of people divided between their artistic and their public conscience, and unable to fuse the two. I now think that what I should have done was either throw myself entirely into political action; or, refusing to waste my energies on half-politics, made within my solitary creative work an agonized, violent, bitter statement of the anti-Fascist passion.

The Spanish Civil War offered an opportunity for several people to adopt the first alternative. Of the English, Ralph Fox, Christopher Caudwell, Julian Bell, John Cornford, Tom Wintringham, Humphrey Slater and a few other writers joined the International Brigade. Most of them were killed fighting in Spain. Wintringham and Slater, the two who survived, were trained soldiers, which seems to indicate that the rôle of the others was to be martyrs. This martyrdom was perhaps the greatest contribution made by creative writers in this decade to the spiritual life of Europe.

But Wordsworth has spoken for those who in a parallel situation – at the beginning of the French Revolution – felt that their duty was to survive and bear witness:

> Well might my wishes be intense, my thoughts
> Strong and perturbed, not doubting at that time
> But that the virtue of one paramount mind
> Would have abashed those impious crests – have quelled
> Outrage and bloody power, and – in despite
> Of what the People long had been and were
> Through ignorance and false teaching, sadder proof
> Of immaturity, and – in the teeth
> Of desperate opposition from without –
> Have cleared a passage for just government,
> And left a solid birthright to the State,
> Redeemed, according to example given
> By ancient Lawgivers.
>   In this frame of mind,
> Dragged by a chain of harsh necessity,
> So seemed it, – now I thankfully acknowledge,
> Forced by the gracious providence of Heaven, –
> To England I returned, else (though assured
> That I both was and must be of small weight,
> No better than a landsman on the deck
> Of a ship struggling with a hideous storm)
> Doubtless, I should have then made common cause
> With some who perished; haply, perished too,
> A poor mistaken and bewildered offering, –
> Should to the breast of Nature have gone back,
> With all my resolutions, all my hopes,
> A Poet only to myself, to Men
> Useless, and even, beloved Friend! a soul
> To thee unknown!'

Those who stayed, did not put the whole energy of their feeling into what they wrote. They tried too often to direct their talents into the channels of a political cause which was too exigent, when what was needed was individual passion which could embody the time in personal experience. These writers of the Divided Generation first turned their attention to the situation, and then shifted it to the problem of political means. What was needed was a Dostoevsky, submerging himself in the spiritual blood and mire of his time, or a Voltaire who, though holding a revolutionary point of view, ruthlessly satirized both sides.

*   *   *   *   *

When I returned from Vienna to London in the autumn of 1936 my personal life seemed a failure. I decided that I must separate from Jimmy. Accordingly, I moved from Maida Vale, and took a flat in Hammersmith, where I lived alone. Jimmy meanwhile was installed in Battersea independently of me. He started looking for a job.

Forward from Liberalism had been chosen by the Left Book Club as their Book of the Month, and for this I received a cheque for £300, most of which I spent on modernizing my high-up studio flat, looking towards the river across a view of many roofs. At one end of the living-room I had a very long desk built of inlaid wood, with an ebony black top. I bought three-plywood chairs and tables like those I had seen in Joachim's flat in Hamburg. I had copper-bowl lamps which threw indirect light up at the ceiling, and lamps of tubular ground glass which also resembled Joachim's.

Shortly after this I was asked to speak for an Aid to Spain meeting in Oxford. At a luncheon party on the same day, I sat next to a girl who had an oval, child-like face, under fair hair cut almost to an Eton crop. She had nearly perfect classical features, and very brightly shining eyes, with which she gazed at me with a kind of cool childishness. Inez was a member of the Spanish Aid Committee. She told me that she was a Spanish scholar and that she had spent the summer in Spain, where (as I learned later) she had been governess to the children of rich Spanish reactionaries. She had managed to combine this function with a love affair with a Spanish painter (who now, she feared, was on Franco's side). At Oxford she was studying the poetry
204

of Gongora which she talked about in a drily brilliant way, like a very clever small girl reciting her lesson. Wogan Philipps, who was at the luncheon, congratulated me on my neighbour's brilliant eyes. After I had made my speech in the evening, I invited Inez to come to the house-warming party which I was giving at Hammersmith a few days later.

Almost the first thing Inez told me when she entered my flat was that she hated modern lighting. Instead of thinking it rude of her to say this, I was puzzled and attracted, thinking that she was outspoken and honest. Often later, when we were married, I was embarrassed and even annoyed by what seemed her rudeness when we were with friends, and then when we were alone together again I suddenly felt a rush of affection for her honesty and shame for my own embarrassment. Her looks made Inez the success of my party, and two young men had a violent quarrel at our supper (in the kitchen) as to which should sit next to her. I asked her to luncheon next day at the Café Royal, and later in the afternoon I proposed to her.

It is difficult at this distance of time to understand why I did this. I certainly felt strongly attracted and this made me suspect that if I did not marry her quickly someone else would. I hated living alone, and was in a state of reaction after the ending of my love affair with Elizabeth. But these in themselves seem inadequate reasons for getting married. I argued that I was now twenty-seven, and since I had never before proposed to anyone else, I must have some specially strong motive for doing so now. My lack of previous impulse could be used as evidence that now I was not acting on impulse. But, of course, beneath this fallacious and superficial ratiocination was my despairing knowledge that if I did not act on impulse I decided nothing. So that action for me consisted of seizing on to impulses without considering the results, and letting them carry me whither they would. The words I had written in my diary in Hamburg when I was twenty still remained true: 'I have no character or will-power outside my work.' Unless I forced myself to do things, I simply did what other people asked me to. Perhaps, though, I was forced to act because I had reached that stage where work is not enough to fill the emptiness of living alone, friends had failed, and therefore mar riage seemed the only solution.

Inez, on her side, was not really more serious than I about getting married. We were both attached to the idea of marrying one another, and we both saw marriage as a solution of temporary problems. She, just as much as I, had a relationship to get over. Our marriage seemed to her in many ways a delightful prospect. The fact that neither of us approached it seriously could even be made to appear one of its attractions, giving us in our minds a kind of reserve of freedom. Our engagement, like most engagements, brought with it a certain prestige to the woman's side, especially as Inez was surrounded by friends at Oxford who knew about my work. Therefore it soon seemed to me that it would be better even for our marriage to collapse in a dim future than to break off our engagement now.

All the same, this way of looking at things filled me with misgiving. Just before we were married, Inez and I went to stay with Rosamond and Wogan Philipps at Ipsden. One afternoon I walked away from the house and through the countryside, alone. I went uphill along a road with little coppices of beech trees on either side. It was a grey autumnal day and beyond the blackness of the boughs, blotting out the red and golden leaves, there were sodden fields of clay and grass. A damp wind blew and it seemed to me as if the whole day had turned black. It is difficult to describe moods of intense depression, because they are, in their way, revelations, and they pass away when what they have revealed (overwhelmingly true as it seemed then) has vanished, been refuted by a different mood, and cannot be recalled. All I can remember is that I felt my life to be revealed as intolerable, and that this seemed a fixed, immutable, rock-like state of affairs, only hidden from me by a mist of distractions and delusions. Blackness and desolation seemed the truth and all else an evasion and escape. My day-to-day activities seemed a process of flight from an awareness of horror: and I despised myself profoundly for ever being happy. My marriage now seemed like a prison sentence. Yet these feelings were so strong that their very powerfulness made them seem incommunicable to Inez. I did not know her well enough to reveal my doubts about the wisdom of our marriage.

Within three weeks of our engagement, and without ever having had a serious conversation about our future, we were married at a Register Office. After the abrupt little ceremony we drove in a hired
206

car to my grandmother's flat. Inez wore a dress which was the colour of crushed strawberries. She had a bunch of flowers fastened to it at the neck. When we were alone in the car, turning to me, she laughed and exclaimed: 'Oh, I am so happy!' I kissed her, and this moment was like an enormous load suddenly lifted from my mind. For the first time I saw her radiant, and revealed in a moment of spontaneity, where her whole being seemed reborn in the words she had just spoken. At the same time, I did not completely share this exquisite moment with her. I did not give her back even the joy she had made me feel. Part of my mind stood aside and, as it were, recorded the moment without letting her know how much it meant to me.

The wedding party at my grandmother's flat was absurd, though not much more so than most wedding parties, I dare say. It consisted of my oldest relatives and some of my youngest friends. Amongst the friends were Auden and Isherwood, and some rather revolutionary new acquaintances. My Uncle Alfred looked at Auden for some time and then turned away, murmuring: 'A remarkably self-possessed young man.'

Amongst the wedding presents were a few toast racks, silver trays, and so forth. Seized with a sudden impulse of pity for those amongst my friends who were paupers, I thrust these upon them as they left. In the middle of the wedding party, a special messenger arrived with proofs of a magazine article for me to correct. I went into a room alone and looked over these, not without a sense of self-importance and also a comforting feeling that I was not sacrificing my daily tasks even on my wedding day.

Now Inez and I were married, we began to know one another. We had certain tastes in common, chief of which perhaps was a passion for music. Her taste, though, was somewhat more austere than mine, her favourite work being Bach's Goldberg Variations. We joined in our admiration for *Don Giovanni*.

She had been educated in convents in Portugal, France and England. A result of this education was a passionate hatred of Catholicism, especially when it was incarnated in nuns. She told me that at school what she had feared most was the sermons on eternity. After having thought deeply about the prospect of living for ever, she decided that to her an everlasting existence even in heaven would be

207

hell. She went to the Mother Superior and begged, as a special favour, that she might be let off having to live for eternity.

Her mother, who was Irish or Anglo-Irish, kept a boarding-house near Victoria. This was the scene of endless disasters: burst pipes, falling ceilings, headaches, pregnancies, priests, white faces, drunken lodgers, etc. It was like something in Balzac, and encouraged Inez to write novels: for in its way it was a literary heirloom. My mother-in-law, who was a persecuted, innocent woman, suffered much from her two sisters, one a raffish, genial but unfortunate character, the other a streamlined follower of the fortunes of decayed gentility. The latter aunt had been, during Inez's childhood, the companion to a duchess. Inez herself, during her vacations from convents in France, Portugal and Roehampton, had been smartened up, threatened, inhibited, and taken to tea with the duchess. This explained her rather hostile social manner.

Inez had a partly laughing, partly pitying, slightly patronizing attitude towards her mother on the surface, which concealed a real warmth and tenderness underneath. One night she woke up sobbing bitterly. She had dreamt of an actual incident in her childhood when her mother had eaten nothing for a day in order to buy her a box of water-colours.

At Hammersmith we had a dwarfish, hunchback 'daily' called Irene (or was it Flossie?). Irene (or Flossie) had the odd idiosyncrasy of twisting the silver when she cleaned it into shapes almost as distorted as herself. Despite her titanic strength she was not particularly clean. Yet Inez had a deep sympathy for her. When she talked about Irene-Flossie, she used sometimes to laugh until she cried (and perhaps the point where laughter turns into tears is one of deep tenderness). When at last we sacked this girl, Inez was very distressed, and afterwards the sight of one particular twisted silver fork always brought tears to her eyes.

It is difficult to define exactly the emotion which existed between us. But, in the sense in which the term is used nowadays, I think it would be true to say that we 'adored' one another. Usually I used to get up before she did. Then I would go into the kitchen, make our breakfast, go back into the bedroom and call her. When she came into the room with her eyes scarcely open, and something about her

208

which was a mixture of a cat and a ballet dancer, I was enchanted. She had a touch of absurdity which I find a gracious thing in people. Thus when she worked at Gongora or her novel, she always frowned heavily, licked her pencil a great deal, stuck her tongue out of the side of her mouth. Once, when we were out walking, I noticed that she made her eyes so shiny by dint of deliberately shutting them until they were filled with tears which stayed and did not quite flow. I was not disillusioned, I was charmed by this discovery.

I could sympathize with her fears and even adopt a protective and paternal attitude towards her. It is quite obvious that, just as Elizabeth had been a 'mother figure' to me, so I was a 'father figure' to Inez. She had actually never seen her father, who died before she was born, but curiously enough her mother often remarked that I resembled him. There is something comforting in the thought that our marriage represented a kind of father-daughter phase in her life, because that means it was a constructive phase in her development, as it was in mine. So it was not wasted for either of us.

My friends were sometimes critical of her aggressiveness, but I soon discovered that it arose from a sense of fear, a kind of panic that her inner life was arid. This knowledge opened up to me a whole secret world in her, and where other people sometimes thought her dry and hard, I saw the reverse, the truth that she was responsive and gentle. At the same time there was always the possibility of her directing against me the aggressiveness which was her habitual attitude towards the world. For the world was still, I suppose for her, to some extent the convent. She justified this harshness by saying that she thought 'any amount of mental cruelty was quite all right'. What she could not bear was the idea of physical cruelty. She hated the Fascists because of their violence.

Although up to a certain point I protected her, I failed at the same time, because I also provided occasions for future fears. For one thing, I inhabited a mental world which terrified her. Our imaginations were incompatible. I had a longing for eternity as great as was her fear of it. I was constantly preoccupied with the idea of judgment; for on a certain level of my mind it seemed impossible not to believe that everything we do is judged, and that life is a kind of sum which has meaning because good is related to bad, and there is an answer.

My mind appeared to be a vehicle for a thought which existed independently of my own reasoning. This was that at some stage of our eternal and personal existence, we become aware of our significance in other lives, measured in terms of happiness and unhappiness, good and evil. We become conscious, too, of the moral condition at which we have arrived inwardly as a result of fulfilment or failure in our vocation. It was unbearable to me to think that people could do great good or great evil, without ever being completely aware, even for a moment – a self-awareness – of what they had become as a result of what they had done. That a man like Hitler should be a blind force, even happily deceived into thinking that he was doing good, was intolerable to me, and I could not bear to think that he would never become conscious of the unity of his own being with the evil he had produced.

So I had a thirst for moral knowledge, combined with a perpetual fear of the moral sum with which I myself would be one day confronted. Yet in the end I wanted to know the answer of good and evil. What was unbearable was to think that there is no moral awakening, that we creep from moment to moment, deceiving ourselves, sometimes guilty and remorseful, sometimes happy, but never knowing the answer, never seeing things as a whole. This was precisely the kind of search which Inez regarded as unnecessary and cruel.

Nevertheless our life was by no means unhappy together. There were many things we loved in one another. Above all, we saw each other's goodness, and little that was evil. There was fear, but never any hatred between us.

*   *   *   *   *

In the winter of 1936 I was again taken up with politics. Soon after the publication of *Forward from Liberalism*, Harry Pollitt, the secretary of the British Communist Party, wrote asking me to come and see him. I went to the offices of the Party near Charing Cross Road. Mr. Pollitt shook me warmly by the hand. There was something paternal in his friendly twinkling manner. He said my book had interested him, particularly because of the different paths by which we had been led towards Communism. My approach, he said, was intellectual, whereas he had become a Communist because he was a member of the working class. As a boy he had watched his mother, who had worked in a mill, die, a victim of the capitalist system. I did not believe in hatred: but he, as a proletarian, regarded hatred of capitalist injustice as a weapon of the working class.

He took me to task because I had written about the Moscow trials, that I was not convinced of the guilt of the accused. He seemed to think that they were extremely lucky to have had such nice trials. Then, coming to business, he went on to say that though he knew we disagreed about certain matters, we agreed, didn't we, over Spain? I said that I wished to help the Spanish Republican cause in any way possible to me. In that case, he had a proposition to make. This was that I should support the Communists in their effort to help the Spanish Republic by joining their Party. He, for his part, would be prepared to accept my disagreement on certain points. In fact, he was willing for me to write an article, in which I put my point of view, to appear in the *Daily Worker* at the time when I joined.

I accepted this proposal, and Pollitt at once gave me a membership card, telling me that the Party Cell in Hammersmith would get in touch with me. He then said that he would like me to go to Spain. I said that I would be willing to go, but to his suggestion that I should join the International Brigade, I replied that I could not see what qualifications I had as a soldier. However, if there was any capacity in which I could be useful, I should be glad to go.

A few days later my article was published in the *Daily Worker*. But the Hammersmith cell never got in touch with me, and apart from my original subscription I never paid or was asked to pay any Party dues. Later I heard that several influential Communists had been indignant at my article and also at the terms on which I had been admitted into the Party.

Somehow I had expected that when I joined the Party I would soon become endowed with that blessed sense of being right about everything which most Communists seemed to feel. But this did not happen. The Communists whom I met mystified me now that I was one of them, even more than they had done before. I could understand what they meant when they said, for example, that there was no such

211

thing as a subjective point of view and that every statement was conditioned by the class interest of whomever made it. Therefore, if one was struck by facts and opinions which did not accord with the Communist theory, this in no way indicated that these ideas had objective reality, but merely that one had a bourgeois mentality oneself. But what amazed me was to find that Communism could not only control a party member's theory and behaviour, but also his awareness of actuality. Indeed, I have never ceased to be astonished by the extent to which Communists are indifferent to awkward facts. For example, one day I asked Chalmers what he thought of the most recent Moscow trials in which Yagoda, who had been largely responsible for incriminating the victims of the previous purge, had himself been sentenced to death. Chalmers looked up, with his bright glance like a bird-watcher's, and said: 'What trials? I've given up thinking about such things ages ago.'

What he really meant, I suppose, was that having chosen to be a Communist by an act of will, he now admitted no point of view which was inconvenient to the Party. The dictatorship of the proletariat did not pretend to be bourgeois justice. Stalin had only to decide that someone was an enemy for him to become one. To criticize (except within the Party) what the Party did was to put oneself on 'the wrong side of history'.

Jimmy Younger became a Communist shortly after I did. His conversion seemed more satisfactory than my own, and now, when we met, he often criticized me for having a 'bourgeois attitude'. Quite suddenly, he applied in London to join the International Brigade and announced his intention of going to fight in Spain. This decision confronted me with the consequences of my own actions. Without my influence he would never have become a Communist, and unless I had decided to live apart from him, and had then married, he would certainly not have joined the Brigade. At the same time, I had put myself in a position where I could not prevent him from making what I was sure was a mistaken decision. Having influenced him in one direction which led to an error, I had lost the power to influence him in another. I could only hope that he would either change his mind before it was too late, or else not repent of his decision when he got to Spain.

212

In a very short time he was in Spain. His first letters were cheerful. He had met a soldier called Bert, who had been in the Army at the same time as himself. Bert had become the 'democratically elected' head of a platoon of his fellow Brigaders. The journey to Brigade headquarters at Albacete had had its surprises: for instance, some of the recruits turned out to be a gang of Glasgow razor-slashers. They carried razors in their caps: 'They could throw a piece of orange peel in the air, spit, and hit it. They drank heavily, passed out, and then drank again.' However, they were only ten out of the fifty men with whom he travelled. The others had come out to Spain from idealism.

At the frontier, near Perpignan, they were received by Spanish Republicans with clenched fists uplifted in welcome. At Barcelona they marched through the streets, but little attention was paid to them. As soon as they arrived at Albacete they met with the leaders of the Brigade: Wintringham, Springhall, Kerrigan, Macartney – leather jackets, berets, salutes and smiles.

They were trained at Madrigueras, about ten miles outside Albacete. 'A certain amount of training and a great deal of boredom. Uniforms by this time, but no real arms. Outbreaks of unrest in the village among the troops, the Scotsmen being the worst offenders, and —— began a prison, a real one with armed guards, and cells which were none too savoury. On account of refusing to obey an order with which I didn't agree, I was put in it for a while, was warned that I was not in a militia, but in a real army where orders had to be obeyed first and talked about afterwards. Profound disillusionment No. 1. I fell out with the Communist Party here, and in my relationship with them a rot set in which affected much of what happened later. Briefly, I think the reason was that I had no beliefs at all, or none that would stand up to boredom.'*

His first experience of fighting completed Jimmy's disillusionment: 'The Battle of Jarama, on 12th February 1937, was one of the toughest of the whole Civil War. The Moors and the International Brigade clashed head-on in the hills. It was slaughter. At the end of the first day my Battalion, the Saklatvala, 400 strong to start with, was reduced to less than 100. I could hear the wounded moaning and calling to us as they lay between the lines. At the end of a week I

* The quotations here are from notes given to me by Jimmy.

knew the meaning of war. I can still see the blood and the dead faces; worse still, the expression in the eyes of the dying. I felt no anti-Fascist anger, but only overwhelming pity.'

The greatest distress of my life during this decade began when I read his letter telling me of this. Someone I loved had gone into this war as a result of my influence and of my having abandoned him. A problem which should have been solved by our gradually becoming independent of one another, might well be solved now by his death. Nor would he be killed for a cause in which he essentially believed, since he had in fact volunteered for personal and not for public reasons.

Shortly after Jimmy's departure for Spain, and a few days after my joining the Communist Party, the *Daily Worker* telephoned and asked me to report on the case of a Russian ship which had been sunk by the Italians in the Mediterranean. The crew of the *Comsomol* had simply disappeared and the Russian Embassy was anxious to know what had happened to it. This was the real reason I was asked to go and report – a request which both disturbed and astonished me. It raised the question whether to supply such information would be spying. However, it certainly did not involve betraying my country, nor obtaining military secrets, nor indeed anything outside the run of ordinary journalism. All the same I had a scruple about being paid: so I insisted that I should receive no more than my expenses. I also asked that my friend Cuthbert Worsley should be allowed to accompany me on the trip.

In my agonized state of mind, I was glad of the diversion which this rather absurd trip provided. Worsley and I flew to Marseilles, and then, on the following day, to Barcelona and Alicante. At dawn we passed over the Pyrenees, and then with the gathering light over the Costa Brava of Catalonia. In the half-dark, white clouds below our wings looked like feathers pressed against the flat-steel sea thousands of feet below. At the airport of Barcelona I looked for signs of civil war: but except that there were a good many raffish-looking police about, and that the air crew who ran to the aeroplane had a carefree untidy appearance, I noticed nothing. As we flew on from Barcelona to Alicante, I strained my eyes for some sign of gunfire or of ruins. The outspread map of a country torn by war seems to the imagination like a mutilated corpse, but under the bright sunlight the

214

mountainous landscape had an appearance of incorruptible morning peace. It suggested nothing more war-like than the creaking of a wooden axle, as a wagon moved among the wintry vineyards.

Pursuing our inquiries, we went to Gibraltar, Tangier and Oran, and from Gibraltar we tried to get to Cadiz, but were turned back at the frontier by Franco's guards.

I had no idea how to look for the crew of a sunk ship, so I simply interviewed people who seemed likely to be informed, revealing to them the purpose of my mission. These were officials, journalists, and the local Communists. Rather to my surprise, the *Comsomol* was a *cause célèbre*, and nearly everyone we spoke to had an opinion about it. We analysed the opinions which we had collected, and, on this basis, decided that the crew was probably interned at Cadiz, but of course we had no definitive proof of this. The most mysterious feature of our trip was that our supposition was confirmed by some-one who inquired at the Italian Consulate in Cadiz, an obvious step which could easily have been taken without our leaving London.

Our journey on the fringes of the Spanish war provided us with some vivid impressions of the alignment of interests and classes over Spain. Everywhere the British officials were in sympathy with Franco. The British members of the Calpe Fox Hunt (which continued to function in Franco territory throughout the Civil War) repeated atrocity stories about the Republicans told them by aristocratic Spanish members from over the frontier, but did not mention any stories of Franco atrocities. The refugees who came into Gibraltar for British aid were Francoists, not Republicans. Nevertheless, the Gibraltese, and the Spanish workers who came every day from La Linea into Gibraltar, queued up at the newspaper kiosks to buy the Republican newspapers. A retired British official put the position to me with unconscious irony when he said: 'People at home don't understand that the Spanish Republicans aren't democratic in our sense of the word. They represent what ninety per cent of the Spanish people want. Go into the streets and ask the first Spanish worker you meet whom he supports – and he'll tell you the Republicans. Now that isn't our British idea of democracy.'

In Tangier, Worsley and I decided that we should consult Prieto del Rio, who represented the Republican Government in the commission administering the International Zone. The taxi driver immediately drove us to the Central Post Office, Franco's headquarters. In doing this he was following the usual procedure, for although the Spanish Republic was the recognized government of Spain, the British, Italian, Belgian and French officials treated Franco's representative as the *de facto* minister. When Worsley and I went to a cocktail party given at the residence of the British Minister, the conversation was all about 'poor old Prieto del Rio, such a nice chap', with whom they commiserated for having made the incredible mistake of remaining loyal to the Red Spanish Government.

But Prieto del Rio, who lived an isolated life in his residence, invited us to attend a public meeting held in support of the Spanish Republic. This vast meeting of the poor, the sick, the maimed and the blind – their upturned faces illumined by a smile of hope – seemed like a scene in the New Testament – like the crowds listening to the gospel. At Oran the Communists at their little café near the port were living in decency and order, which contrasted with the life around them like the future with the past. This civilization on the fringe of the Spanish War was a kind of margin, a chart in which the conflicting currents of opinion were registered like pulsations of energy made visible on a screen. The conflict was between a small, ferocious, reactionary, clinging class, and an awakening, ignorant, combative proletariat, who looked to the Spanish Republic as the realization of their aspirations.

An event bordering on absurdity will show how my mind was preoccupied all this time with Jimmy. Worsley and I had gone for a day's excursion to Marrakesh. We took a horse-cab and drove outside the city. At a certain moment we were stopped on the road and I found myself staring at a donkey standing stock-still in front of us. The animal stood like a trestle bench, submitting to the great weight of its burden. As it looked patiently ahead it seemed to be carrying the weight of the whole day. The blueness of the sky, the stoniness of the road and the sandiness of the desert all seemed pivoted upon the mild uncomprehending beast, which could no longer move forward. Suddenly I realized that tears were streaming down my face. Then searching for a reason, I discerned something in the donkey's appearance which reminded me of Jimmy! Jimmy had a flat brow beneath thick,

216

wiry, reddish hair which stood up in a brush-like way. Sometimes his eyes had an expression of unflickering patience under the loads of ideas, of music, of literature, of politics, which I forced on to him. His nose had a squarish base, and his mouth turned upwards at the corners in a way which recalled some patient animal.

Yet to some extent the Moroccan part of this journey was an escape from these preoccupations. There were moments when I felt myself absorbed completely into the atmosphere of, say, the narrow streets, between houses whose walls seemed all one wall, of Tangier. There was the feeling in all these Moroccan cities of being in a maze, enclosing behind grills, in hidden darknesses, a timeless Arabian minotaur. I was astonished by the heat and fury of Marrakesh, like a fortress built of granite and mud; and depressed by the contrast between the tidied-up native quarter of Casablanca, like the model 'native village' in an Empire exhibition and the flashy modern French quarter. Then there were the Arabs, turbaned and blanketed, wrapped away as though in a dark unspeakable hatred against every European. Every town was a bazaar to which natives of a dozen different ancient races trailed across the desert and rugged countryside.

On our return journey we stayed at Barcelona for two or three nights. As we came into the town from the airport, I saw for the first time a sight with which later I was to grow very familiar: strips of paper stuck cross-wise across window-panes. I did not understand that the purpose of these was to prevent the glass splintering in case of air raids: and it is a comment on my mood that I took them to be some kind of sign with a political significance, so that they excited me with a feeling of Republican ardour. In the main avenues of Barcelona, the central square and the Ramblas, proclamations and great posters covered the buildings which had been taken over by political parties. These vast portraits of political leaders, and slogans stuck up everywhere, dwarfed the city itself, and made it seem as if it were listening for some enormous announcement to come from the height of the sky. It was as though some proletarian Gulliver had attached labels to his Lilliput, announcing the liquidation of the bourgeois Lilliputians and his intention to build a new city for a race of Gullivers. The people had taken over the streets, and walked about them in wandering crowds like heirs examining

217

an inheritance which had suddenly fallen to them. The bookstalls in the Ramblas were stacked with charmingly printed cheap editions of the classics of several literatures, beginning with Homer, in Catalan.

One evening, when I was in the main square, I heard a rather languid English voice broadcasting from loudspeakers attached to the eighth-storey windows of a building above me. Listening hard, I suddenly recognized it as that of the poet David Gascoyne.

In order to obtain my clearance to leave Barcelona I had to go to an office run by the British Communists. An officious man, tall and lean, with protruding ears, asked me my name. 'Prove that you are Stephen Spender!' he said. I showed him my passport. On seeing this he gave a bitter laugh: 'If you knew how many people come into this office and show passports!' I protested that the passport was genuine, but this he would not believe. Then I remembered the article I had written in the *Daily Worker*, where it had appeared with my photograph. When he had discovered the article in his file of *Daily Workers* even he could not pretend I was someone else. But I was left wondering what happened to people who had no better evidence than passports with which to prove their identity.

Our two days in Barcelona were enough to make Worsley and myself realize we wished, as soon as possible, to return to Spain. Within a few weeks he had joined an ambulance unit, where later he looked after the sick and wounded in the retreat from Malaga.

Shortly after my return to London I received a letter from a Señor Thomas, who described himself as head of the Broadcasting Station of the Socialist Party in Valencia. He offered me a post as head of English broadcasting in his station. I wrote at once accepting.

Wogan Philipps was driving with an ambulance unit to Albacete, and he suggested that I should accompany him as far as Valencia. We met at Barcelona.

Crossing the Spanish frontier from France, I spent a day in Port-Bou, alone. This was a charming little port, with two headlands like green arms stretched into the sea and almost embracing, but leaving a little gap between, which was the harbour mouth. Port-Bou had been bombed, though the quay was intact. Having nothing to do while waiting for my connection to Barcelona, I sat at a table in front

218

of the quayside café, reading the newspapers I had brought from France. A lorry full of Republican soldiers in their rather dirty uniforms stopped in front of me. They looked down at my newspaper with all their smiling flag-like faces like one face, and one soldier shouted: 'What do they say of our struggle over the frontier?' I smiled some reply, and the lorry roared away bearing its cargo of uplifted clenched fists.

Then firing practice began from headland to headland across the harbour, bullets flecking the sea to white foam. The whole town became agitated, with children shouting and dogs barking. An old man, running along the road, jogged past me with a senselessly elated smile on his face. 'Pom-pom-pom,' he called out in blissful imitation of the firing.

I got to Barcelona and found Wogan. The next day, before starting on our journey, we had to go to some offices of the militia, where we were given two soldiers as guides. Rather to our surprise, they announced that they would take us inland to Valencia through Catalonia, and not along the coastal road. We drove along roads winding through mountainous scenery, full of fertile shut-in valleys, not open and parched and massive like central Spain. Suddenly we found that we had been misled. A sign of *Al Frente* showed that we were driving towards the front and into Franco's lines. We turned back towards the coast, which we reached at Tarragona, a sprawling city with a Roman amphitheatre and many other remains which had been a huge centre of Mediterranean culture in Roman times. At night, the coastal road lay white in the moon. When we stopped for a few minutes, we heard the waters below us, whispering in many bays and inlets, and the heavy rustling of eucalyptus leaves above. Beyond the line of trees the mountains were transparent outlines in the dark.

We had with us, besides Wogan, two drivers, George Green and another whom I remember only as Henry. George Green was firm and stolid, with bristly fair hair, brick-red complexion and spectacles, through which he looked out at the world with unwavering eyes. Behind the glasses and behind the blueness of his eyes a watchful, patient humorousness seemed waiting. Henry was lithe and wiry, a loquacious active type, for ever making wisecracks. George told me that he had been a 'cellist in the Lyons Corner House in Tottenham

Court Road. He gave me his reasons for coming to Spain in the following story – a monument to the memory of George Green. 'I've only cried three times since I was grown up,' he said. 'The first time was when I went to the British Empire Exhibition and at the end of the Searchlight Tattoo I heard the whole crowd stand up and sing ''Land of Hope and Glory''. I cried then to think how they'd been fooled. The second time was in the orchestra when, for once, we played the Overture to the *Marriage of Figaro*, instead of all the usual slush. The third time was yesterday in Barcelona, when I went to a meeting of the People's Front and heard the crowd sing the International. I cried for joy that time.'

We spent the night at the coastal town of Tortosa. At dawn we were woken by the rattling of hundreds of carts through the streets. The whole population slept in the hills for fear of air raids, only returning at daybreak.

As we drove, Wogan talked of difficulties and problems which were complications of his personal life. We came to a military hospital run by a well-known English doctor. After lunching there we went outdoors, and there was a Fascist aeroplane overhead, which circled several times over the hospital. I felt a deep hypnotic fear, as though the eyes in the aeroplane were a stiletto pointed at my heart. Nurses and a medical student who was a friend of ours told us of quarrels among the staff, despite the wonderful work that was being done. So (I thought, as we drove on) it was only a few people, like George Green, who came to Spain with undivided hearts. As we approached Valencia there were orange groves in which the ungathered oranges lay under the trees in golden pools.

On the morning after our arrival at Valencia, I went to the address given me as that of the Socialist Broadcasting Station. I was received by a secretary who asked me what I wanted. I said that I wished to speak to Señor Thomas. She asked me why? I explained that I had come to give English broadcasts from this station. She said she knew nothing about this. I asked if I might see Señor Thomas. She said that he was busy. Fortunately, I had with me the letter I had been sent. I produced this. The secretary left the room and returning a moment later said that Señor Thomas would see me. Señor Thomas asked me how much money I wanted. Surprised, I said that I was prepared to work for nothing if he would tell me when to begin. At this he brusquely said that there was no longer a position open to me. The interview was at an end. I learned later that the Socialist station had been abolished with the unification of political parties.

There was now no reason for me to stay in Valencia. Wogan had not left for Albacete so I decided to go with him. I could see Jimmy.

Albacete was a barracks-like town in a dull plain. It was as unlike my idea of picturesque Spain as any town could be. Around a wide central square, like a parade ground, there were some streets of tall characterless houses, containing a few shops, restaurants and cafés. The whole of Albacete smelled of olive oil frying.

It was impossible to find Jimmy. After wandering through the cardboard-coloured depressing streets, I went into a café which was like a place in Soho. Members of the International Brigade sat at tables, talking, or playing chess or cards. I went up to a group who were English and asked whether they knew the whereabouts of Jimmy Younger, and of his friends, whom I named. They said there was another café where this group always met at six.

Jimmy was there. He looked fit and bronzed and young in his uniform. We went out into the square outside the café and then I realized that this physical fitness concealed an extreme nervousness. As soon as we were outside he said with great vehemence: 'You must get me out of here!' He went on to explain that he had changed all his ideas. He had come to Spain on an impulse, but now he knew that he did not want to die for the Republic. Above everything he had discovered that he hated war. Now he was a pacifist. He wanted to go back to England and be an 'ordinary chap'. He would like to have a job in a factory or bottle-washing . . . anything, so long as he left Spain.

I said that I might ask for him to be transferred to some non-combatant position in the Brigade, but not for him to leave Spain. Having joined the Brigade he could not return to England. To return would make others wish to do the same. On the other hand, I thought that if he was ready to accept the humiliation of staying on without fighting, and was willing to work in some office, he would not be doing the Republic a disservice.

Finally I persuaded him to accept this point of view.

221

On the following day I went to see Peter Kerrigan and Springhall, the English political commissars. Kerrigan was tall, with grey hair: in his thin handsome face austerity was combined with a faintly flickering humour. He spoke with a Glasgow accent. I had never heard the 'u'-sound in words like 'you' so drawn out. To hear Kerrigan say 'you' was like hearing the silver trumpet of an accusing angel.

Springhall was thick-necked, tough and friendly. Kerrigan said he would like me to go to the front, and I gladly agreed to do this. I asked about Jimmy Younger. He said he was troubled about this case. He pointed out to me that they had several sick and ill-adjusted members of the Brigade: and though he did not think Jimmy was any use at fighting, they were also faced with the problems of discipline and morale. If they let all the sick and dispirited leave Spain, then others might want to return as well. It was difficult to withdraw one man without discouraging the rest. I said that I quite understood this and that I did not think Jimmy should be withdrawn. But I pointed out that he was sick and therefore it seemed reasonable that he should be given non-combatant duties. 'All right,' said Kerrigan. 'We'll keep him here, but I promise he won't have to fight.'

This seemed to me a just solution. I was convinced that it would be wrong to repatriate Jimmy and that whatever he felt, I should not ask for this.

After having told Jimmy what had been decided, I went to the front near Madrid. Divisional headquarters here occupied a white farmhouse in a valley, and from this a road led up to a ridge looking over rolling grassland with olive trees, beyond which there were more hills. On the ridge there was the single line of trenches held by the Brigade. Opposite, at the further extremity of the plain, was Franco's line, held here by Arab troops.

It was a quiet day in the fighting, but as we walked up to the trenches some bullets spat round us like shrieking starlings among the olive trees. An Indian writer was, like myself, also visiting the front. Captain Nathan and a boy M—— accompanied us. M—— explained that the bullets we heard were the ones we could not be killed by. When we got up to the ridge we saw corpses lying in No Man's Land like ungathered waxy fruit. It was all like something I had dreamed long ago, and as we walked I remember thinking how certain things, such as the Alps, have been exactly as I imagined them. Here, in the front line on this quiet day, I had the peculiar sense of living in a special kind of time, unrelated to the clocks of time outside. It was a time in which, when there was a lull, the minutes seemed held back and did not move forward: when there was a battle, the hands were suddenly put forward.

We walked along the trenches. The soldiers who were there treated us with a solicitousness which made me feel ashamed. 'We make a point of not allowing our front-line visitors to be killed,' said Nathan, who was an elegant, cane-swaggering, likeable type of adventurous Jew. He told me to stoop, because I was tall, and the fire from the trenches opposite was focusing on our little group as we walked along. The Indian writer, who was very short, took the order to apply to himself, and stooped also, which made us look absurd. So there we went, two caricature figures, he five feet high and bent almost double, I six feet three, and stooping. Suddenly the Indian looked round from his bent posture and turned his face up to mine: 'I can see death's great question-mark hovering between the trenches!' he said in a hoarse whisper. This was the only occasion in my life in which a lapse from dialectical materialism has irritated me.

We came to a machine-gun emplacement, and the gunner in charge of it insisted that I should fire a few shots into the Moorish lines. I did this, positively praying that I might not by any chance hit an Arab. Suddenly the front seemed to me like a love relationship between the two sides, locked here in their opposite trenches, committed to one another unto death, unable to separate, and for a visitor to intervene in their deathly orgasm seemed a terrible frivolity.

We walked back to headquarters for luncheon. As we did so, M——, aged eighteen, born of a Liberal family, told me how he had run away from school because he identified the Spanish Republic with the cause of Liberalism. But now he found that the Brigade was run by Communists, for whom he had no sympathy. I pointed out that, although this was true, the Republic remained a Liberal cause. 'But I don't know about that. All I see are the Communist bosses of the Brigade,' he protested. I said: 'You are under age. Shall I try to get you out of here?' 'No,' he answered. 'My life is to walk up to

223

the ridge here every day until I am killed.' He was killed, though on a different front, six weeks later.

After luncheon I talked with some members of the Brigade who had collected at the little farmhouse behind the lines which was their H.Q. One of them asked me: 'Are we spoken of in England?' At this the rest fell silent and watched me eagerly as I answered that there were meetings and demonstrations on their behalf. Someone said: 'Didn't you have a secretary who was a member of the Brigade —a chap called Jimmy Younger?' 'He left us,' another one remarked, and they fell silent. I saw all their eyes.

Nathan asked me to stay for three or four days – perhaps a week – with them at the front, but I refused, saying I was expected at Madrid. The fact is that I was frightened and wanted to get away as soon as possible.

The next day I went to Madrid. This was the centre of the Spanish war as nowhere else. The population seemed to be a people's army, and not just a dazed, wondering throng, as in Barcelona.

Together with the Indian writer who was at the front with me, and Denis Campkin, a journalist and friend of Inez, I stayed at the Casa de la Cultura. This was a grandiose palace which had been taken over for the use of '*los intellectuales*'. It was luxurious in a stuffy way, hung with dark brown paintings and purple velvet curtains. The butler and other servants of the aristocratic owners of the house looked after us, and we were told that none of the original arrangements of the house had been interfered with. The bowing, respectful, taciturn servants, waiting on their unexpected visitors, who were asked never even to move a piece of furniture, gave a silent demonstration of the ironic pride on both sides of the Spanish Civil War.

At the Casa de la Cultura, I met research workers who, taking advantage of the occupation of the palaces in Madrid, were cataloguing the private art collections. They told me they had made several discoveries, among them two El Grecos. They took me to churches and showed me how the structure had been strengthened against the bombardments. In one church the floor of the vault was covered with images removed from buildings where they were exposed to danger. This army of stone and painted wooden virgins, saints, angels and cherubs, was known as 'the fifth column of the blessed'.

It was only some months later that I went to the University City Front of Madrid on the outskirts of the city, but it seems better to describe it here. The Fascists, driven from Madrid, held on to some of the University buildings. Others were held by Republican troops.

I went into a building where sandbags were piled half-way up the windows. Above the level of these, bullets from the Fascist-occupied building opposite occasionally sprayed into the room.

The Republican soldiers, finding themselves in the University, were learning to read and write. Alphabets and charts were spread out on the walls so that the whole place looked like a school for children who were dressed as soldiers, playing at war.

I went into a lecture room with tiers of seats descending to the well of the lecturer's platform. Without reflecting, I walked down towards this. A guard shouted to me to come back at once. Then I noticed, stretched out on the floor under the blackboard, a corpse. This floor was in the direct line of fire from a window opening at the end of the room.

In March 1937 Madrid was extremely cold. At the Casa de la Cultura we spent most mornings in our beds, crouched down under our purple velvet bed-covers. Then we got up and went to a café, where the crowds of people wearing their greatcoats, seated at tables and sipping a little atrocious cognac (coffee was unobtainable), slightly raised the temperature. Then we went to the hotel where the journalists lunched.

One of these journalists, who worked for a great Liberal newspaper, had previously been a correspondent on Franco's side. One day I asked him to explain the difference he found between the two sides in the Civil War. 'None,' he answered. 'What do you mean? Is there the same enthusiasm on Franco's side?' 'Yes.' 'But isn't it just the ruling classes who are pleased?' 'There's only one difference which I noticed. There they salute by raising their hands like this' (he imitated the Fascist salute), 'and here they clench their fists like this' (he imitated ours).

I could not angrily dismiss this answer as I did when people talked of the atrocities committed by the Reds. But I clung to my Republican faith that our minority of genuine supporters had more justice on their side than the minority of Falangists. Nor could I dismiss from my mind the impression made by the meeting of the Popular Front at Tangier.

The question of atrocities was more deeply disturbing. Denis Campkin, who had great scrupulousness in these matters, pointed out that whilst we grew indignant at the shelling of refugees from cities captured by Franco, we said nothing of similar actions committed by the Republicans. Our indignation at the death of a child killed in an air raid was deeply suspect unless we were opposed to all air raids. Unless we spoke out against the murder of children by both sides, were we really not utilizing as propaganda the horror and sympathy we imagined ourselves to feel?

I told myself that the Republicans were not responsible to the same extent as the Fascists for atrocities, since Republican violence was the result of the ignorance of the Spanish peasants and workers; and this was the fault of the aristocrats. In any case, more atrocities were committed by the Fascists than the Republicans.

But despite these arguments, I was sure above all only of one thing: that one must be honest. If we knew of atrocities committed by the Republicans we must admit to them. Here, of course, I found myself disagreeing with the Communists.

One day, when I was lunching with the journalists, there was a report that the Fascists had made a great advance of several miles near Madrid. It was expected that Madrid would fall into their hands within a matter of hours. A head of the Press Bureau at Madrid was one of the Socialist group I had known in Vienna with Elizabeth. On the day of the Fascist advance I asked her how the Spanish Republican soldiers had done. '*Sie läuften wie Hasen!*' was her answer – they ran like hares! But the next day the Republicans – aided by the International Brigade – counter-attacked and threw the Fascists back thirty miles. This was the battle of Guadalajara: surprising as one of those battles in the Peninsular War in which the Spanish popular forces astonished first by their cowardice and then by their bravery.

Afterwards, on my way back to Valencia, I returned to Albacete. As soon as I arrived I went to the café where Jimmy and his friends met. There I learned that, during my absence, Jimmy had deserted. He and a friend had gone to Valencia, remained in hiding there a few days, and finally been captured. His notes go on: 'We met Miss

X who was sympathetic and said she would help us get away. She knew, she said, the captain of a boat which was collecting oranges and bringing her pesetas, illegally. After nearly a week we were told by B—— that she had the whole thing arranged. We should go to a certain café where the captain and Miss X would meet us. The captain would then take us on to the boat as his crew. We went to the café and waited. Instead of Miss X came the police. She had betrayed us, B—— told me later. She was a member of the Communist Party. We were put into prison at Valencia for a few days. A very dirty cell, very small, in which there were some men of mixed nationality who had been there for weeks or perhaps months. They were filthy and half-starved. Two did not speak at all but lay on a heap of straw under their blankets. The food was mainly beans and thin soup, and coffee which tasted like liquorice. In the corner a bucket which stank more and more. No daylight, not much air. The cell seemed to be below the ground.

'Then there came an armed soldier who took us to the station and put us on the train to Albacete. He was French. In Albacete we were put in the prison in the barracks. A visit from Kerrigan showed that he was surprised that we had deserted because he was really going to give us jobs . . . . We were questioned by a Polish officer, a young intellectual, who thought we were spies and went to Valencia to contact other spies. I lied about the people I met there. Later the sentence. Two months in a camp of correction. The interview with the Polish officer was the trial.'

At the time of the battle of Guadalajara there was a sudden call on the Brigade. Everyone available had been sent to the front. In the crisis Kerrigan forgot his promise to me, with the result that Jimmy was ordered to the fighting.

Kerrigan was still at the front. There was nothing for me to do but return to Valencia.

I got up at 4 a.m., as Jimmy had done a few days previously, to catch the train. But it did not leave until about eleven, being six hours late. I stood waiting on the platform in the cold darkness, without impatience: I hardly cared whether it came or not. Men going on leave, some of them with wounded limbs in plaster extended in front of them like very thick hockey-sticks, were gradually revealed by the

227

early, milky-white light which shone on the rails. Many of them were French. They hailed one another in guttural vinous Mediterranean dialect. As they shuffled about the platform they seemed, with their stiffly extended limbs and hulking bodies, calling, whistling, urinating, expectorating, like tugs nosing round quayside waters, with hootings and sluicings of bilge water.

In broad daylight the train arrived. I stared out of the carriage window, in a state of mind when fatigue seems to open a door upon a further awakening, on an involuntary awareness of the darkest movements of thought within the mind. Lines suddenly ran into my mind, as though gliding with the movement of the train:

> Clean silence drops at night when a little walk
> Divides the sleeping armies, each
> Huddled in linen woven by remote hands.
> When the machines are stilled, a common suffering
> Whitens the air with breath and makes both one
> As though these enemies slept in each other's arms.

Sitting opposite me in the train was a young Scotsman with a stern and virginal expression, like a hard young pretty girl. We started talking about the problem of the sick and the deserters. 'Why, when five hundred of our bravest chaps have been killed, should they get away?' he asked. I could not answer, for he was quite right: the dead call for more dead, and if the brave have spent themselves how can one justify hoarding the weak? Yet I could not give up a life which might be saved, and which was of no value in this war, in order to satisfy a state of mind with which I sympathized.

For several months after this my life was dominated by my concern with Jimmy's problems. A good deal of my activity was connected with trying to help him, though very little could be done.

This was a turning point in my affairs. It was the first time I had acted without hesitation and without being obsessed by the need to justify my actions. I was simply determined to do everything in my power to prevent him dying in Spain. Apart from this, I saw of course that there was a moral problem. Ought I to save him? Many people would say no. In going to Spain, he had taken a decisive step which I should perhaps have regarded as irretrievable. It is true that he had personal reasons for going, and perhaps true that I bore the responsibility for these: yet many other volunteers went for personal reasons: and perhaps a good many parents, friends and lovers felt guilty for many who had gone. When Jimmy went to Spain he was struck by the fact that ten of his fifty comrades were members of a razor-slashing gang. With a little more insight, he might have discovered that ten others were there for personal reasons. The clash of arguments going on in my mind did not make any difference to my determination to save him.

*   *   *   *   *

Valencia had a far more normal appearance than Madrid. Only on nights when there was a full moon like brilliant floodlighting exposing walls of bone-coloured palaces to the meticulous observing instruments of bombers, did it seem a city haunted by war. The heads of the Republican Government were here and the Press Bureau and a certain social life connected with these. I lived in the Victoria Hotel, which was the journalists' headquarters, and I wrote one or two articles, and met many people. Denis Campkin was there, and as he spoke excellent Spanish, he introduced me to Spanish poets who were his friends.

One of the writers to arrive at the Press office was Ernest Hemingway, a black-haired, bushy-moustached, hairy-handed giant, who did not belie the impression one might have of his appearance from his novels. In his behaviour he seemed at first to be acting the part of a Hemingway hero.

I wondered how this man, whose art concealed under its apparent huskiness a deliberation and delicacy like Turgenev, could show so little of his inner sensibility in his outward behaviour. But one afternoon, when he and I were walking through the streets of Valencia, I caught a glimpse of the æsthetic Hemingway, whose presence I suspected. I had happened to mention that I had no books in Valencia and that the bookshops were empty of all but Spanish and a little French literature. In one bookshop, I went on, I had seen a novel which I had never read, Stendhal's *La Chartreuse de Parme*, and I did not know whether to buy it. Hemingway said that he thought the account, at the beginning, of the hero, Fabrice, wandering lost in the middle of the Battle of Waterloo, with which *La Chartreuse* opens is perhaps the best, though the most apparently casual, description of war in literature. For war is often really like that, a boy lost in the middle of an action, not knowing which side will win, hardly knowing that a battle is going on. He warmed to the theme of Stendhal, and soon I realized that he had that kind of literary sensibility which the professional critic, or the don, nearly always lacks. He saw literature not just as 'good writing', but as the unceasing inter-relationship of the words on the page with the life within and beyond them – the battle, the landscape or the love affair. For him writing was a kind of wrestling of the writer armed with a pen, as a huntsman with his spear, with his living material. I mentioned the battle scenes in Shakespeare. 'Why do you talk to me about Shakespeare?' he asked with annoyance. 'Don't you realize I don't read books?' and he changed the conversation to – was it boxing? Shortly after this he was saying that his chief purpose in coming to Spain was to discover whether he had lost his nerve under conditions of warfare which had developed since Caporetto. By now we had reached a *taverna* on the shore. We went in and found some gipsy players. Hemingway seized a guitar and started singing Spanish songs. He had become the Hemingway character again.

He told me often that I was 'too squeamish', by which, I suppose, he meant 'yeller'. Yet on one occasion he came down heavily on my side. K——, on sick leave from the Brigade, used to hobble around the cafés where the journalists met, leaning on a stick. Whenever there were arguments about Communism this man attacked me viciously, and most people knew that his motive was to draw attention to the fact that my name was linked with that of Jimmy. As K—— was believed by all the journalists to be a hero, these attacks were humiliating. After a particularly acrimonious discussion, Hemingway took me aside and said: 'Stephen, don't you worry about K——. I know his type. He's just a malingerer. He's yeller.' He then gave me an outline of K——'s story, which became, in the telling, such excellent Hemingway that I begged him to write it. He said: 'I give the idea to you. Why don't you write it?' And from that we went on to make a compact that we would both write the same story. Of course, neither of us did so, and now I forget what it was. All I remember is the curious fact of receiving Heming-way's support in a situation where I should never have expected it. For I had to accept the humiliation of knowing that I was not on the side of the heroes. This was a difficult attitude to maintain, because as my experience of Spain deepened I found myself more and more appreciative of the difficulties of the people, like Kerrigan and Springhall, who were strong, even whilst I wrote often in defence of the weak.

In Valencia I met the poet Manuel Altolaguirre, who became one of my best friends in Spain. The great lady who was known to all the Press correspondents as 'Constanza', head of the Press Bureau, and her husband, Hidalgo de Cisneros, Commander of the Republican Air Force, invited me to meet him one day. Hidalgo de Cisneros was a lean, tall, handsome quixotic figure, dressed in blue dungarees. Before luncheon we stood talking at the bar of the hotel, in front of a map of Spain. Suddenly he pointed to a place amongst the Asturian mountains, printed almost black, and said: 'Even if they defeat us, we shall go on fighting *there!*'

Their cousin was Manuel Altolaguirre. He asked me how I had spent the morning, and I told him that I had been hunting through the bookshops for a Shakespeare. 'Oh,' he said, 'I have an edition of Shakespeare at home, I would like to show it to you.' He went away and came back twenty minutes later, with his broad, good-natured face perspiring. He was carrying the eleven volumes of Samuel Johnson's edition of Shakespeare, published by Bell in 1786. He insisted on presenting these to me. When I tried to refuse he pointed out that the first volume was already inscribed with words which I am still proud to read: '*A mi querido camarada Spender con profonda gratituda por su visita a España.*'

This luncheon in the dining-room of the hotel among all the jour-nalists had that absoluteness of certain experiences in Spain which sometimes bore me completely away, as it seemed, from all previous associations into hours and days which were entirely Spanish. As when, hitch-hiking to Madrid, I got into the back of a lorry which contained twelve Spanish soldiers, and, having some chocolate, I gave a bar to the soldier next to me who, making a mental calcula-tion, immediately divided it into six exactly equal portions, giving one to each of his comrades. Throughout the night we lay on the floor of the lorry, waiting for the pot-holes in the road to send sledge-hammer blows up our spines as the back wheels went over them. Each such blow produced a loud cheer from the soldiers, and somehow they completely wrapped me, as though with their cloaks, into their world. Most of them were unshaven peasants, but there was a gay and elegant young officer whose smile belonged to another century. Or the day when I sat in the front of a lorry with a driver and his mate, one or the other of whom at intervals of an hour or so simply exclaimed in a loud voice: '*A Tarragon*'! referring to some joke of which I knew nothing, which sent them into fits of laughter. Or nights when it was freezing cold, sitting in a car and going to Madrid through villages which, as we approached the capital, seemed to share the life of the city with increasing intensity. Or, at inns, the meals consisting of elaborate rice dishes, or of cuts of meat, or chops thrown into an open charcoal fire. There was always in all this the sense of living so dramatically within the moment that everything else was forgotten and therefore one was transfixed within a feeling of something uniquely Spanish.

Now when Manuel and his cousins started talking, they invoked at once a world of gaiety and harshness which was completely strange to me. Someone said: 'Congratulations on the death of all your reactionary relatives in Malaga, Manuel!' Manuel laughed and replied: 'But now they are dead, I begin to feel a little sentimental about them.' 'Impossible. They were the most terrible Fascists and reactionaries.' 'There is something almost feminine about Manuel,' said Cisneros, 'that he regrets them.' 'But some of them did amusing things.' 'What?' 'For example, I had an uncle who died of a broken heart because he could not breed a green-eyed bull.' 'Well, he bred you. That was more astonishing.' 'He died of a broken heart, that shows a great sensibility. There was another relation from Malaga who got out of his carriage to follow a partridge, and spent three days walking after it in the hills.' 'Oh, but all the amusing ones lived in the eighteenth century!' 'Did I tell you about the funeral of my uncle, the general? He was a very important general, and when he died all the aristocracy of Malaga attended the funeral. The body was laid out in the coffin, and the family stood round it in the main room of my uncle's house. My aunt was kneeling in front of the coffin. She was dressed in swaddling clothes like a huge baby, only they were black. The first thing that happened was, when she stood up, an awful hush, perceptible even in a completely silent room. Then when she moved away from where she had been kneeling, her bloomers were observed, left as though still kneeling, in the place where she had been. Naturally my eyes remained downcast, as we none of us dared to look at one another. The next thing I noticed was a procession of all the ants of Malaga coming in at one corner of the room, crossing the floor, climbing up one corner of the table, then entering one corner of my uncle's coffin and emerging at the opposite corner at the far end of the coffin, then climbing down the corner of the table, then crossing the floor and leaving the room at the corner opposite where it had entered, each ant carrying in its little jaws a tiny portion of my uncle.'

*   *   *   *   *

One day, when I was sitting in the lounge of the hotel, an Englishman, who explained that he was a member of the staff of the British Embassy, inquired whether I was a friend of Jimmy Younger. He explained he had tried to help Jimmy get out of Spain. Since the International Brigade was an illegal organization it was difficult for the Embassy to help Brigaders who wished to be repatriated; for they had, in effect, renounced their rights as British citizens. Nevertheless the staff did what they could to help, though taking into account the wishes of the Spanish Government. Recently the Government had protested against the aid that was given to deserters, so the position had become more difficult. But this case worried him. He could not get the expression in Jimmy Younger's eyes out of his mind. Did I think that Jimmy would be shot? This was extremely unlikely, I answered. More probably he would be sent to a prison camp. I emphasized that nothing should be done to prevent this: my sole preoccupation was to see that when he was released he did eventually get home. For he would not be of any further use in Spain, having served his sentence. The Embassy representative asked me if there was anything to be pointed out to the Government in Jimmy's favour. I said that it might be taken into account that he had a duodenal

233

ulcer. My new friend said that he would get into touch with Del Vayo, the Spanish Foreign Minister, and see what could be done.

Meanwhile, Altolaguirre and Cisneros had arranged for me to have an interview with Del Vayo.

Del Vayo had an intelligent open face of a rather North American type, with a grave expression which could easily become a beaming one. As soon as I had sat down he asked: 'Can you explain to me the foreign policy of your country?' I hesitated, and he went on: 'I am not just talking propaganda to you when I say that the Spanish Republic is the best defence of British interests in the Mediterranean. We have every evidence that the attack of Germany and Italy is, above all, an attack on the British Empire. The British Government must know this. And yet they allow us to be destroyed.'

I said that when I returned home I would try to get an opinion about British foreign policy from Mr. Eden, by means of Harold Nicolson. (I did so, and was told that the British Government were aware of the dangers involved, but hoped that if they did nothing the situation would change in some way which would prove favourable to them.) But to return to my interview with Del Vayo. He explained to me the bad effects on morale of letting the volunteers who had come to Spain go away as they wished. I said that I understood this perfectly and wished only to be sure that eventually Jimmy Younger would be released. Del Vayo said that it would be best for him to serve a sentence, but he would guarantee that, having done this, he would be free to leave Spain.

A few days later Hidalgo de Cisneros, who was driving to Albacete, took Altolaguirre (who had decided to accompany me) and me with him. We stopped in the middle of the journey because Altolaguirre felt car-sick. We got out and walked up and down the road beyond which there was a valley of maize and corn, and then the mountains. When we arrived at the hotel, I suddenly felt overwhelmingly depressed and I lay down on my bed. Altolaguirre, who had lain down also on his bed, took off one or two jackets and a shirt. He seemed to have layers of clothes, as an onion does skins. He said: 'I know what is the matter with you. You are worried about your friend. But it is perfectly simple. All we do is to persuade some important member of one of the political parties to

234

lend us an official and a car. Then we drive to the prison and show a paper to say that we need the prisoner. He will then be handed over to us and we shall drive away again. It is quite easy. This happens all the time in Spain.' I smiled and explained that I could not act in this way. 'Let us go and see Cisneros,' he said. We got up and went into the street. We walked for about three-quarters of an hour, going round and round in circles. Just as I was wondering how it was possible that the headquarters of Cisneros could be so far from the Central Square, Altolaguirre asked: 'Where are we going?' I explained that I thought he was leading me. 'But I do not know where it is,' he said. 'I thought you were taking me. Never mind, we can ask here.' We went into a *taverna*, and immediately were in that impassioned Spanish atmosphere which everywhere was like doors leading into rhetoric and absurdity and violence and song. A dwarfish, fanatical man was making a magnificent speech about liberty. He seized hold of Altolaguirre by the coat. Altolaguirre smiled and they started telling stories.

The next morning I went to the British Battalion's headquarters. Kerrigan, who was seated in the main office, looked up at me when I came in with a severe judicial expression, and said: 'We have to talk to you.' Springhall and another commissar appeared, and they sat in front of me in an accusing little group.

'Yew-ew hav bin commew-ewnnicetting with the Kluss Ennimey,' said Kerrigan, like an angel blowing an accusing Last Trump.

'What do you mean?'

'I mean this.' He showed me a telegram from Del Vayo, requesting all information regarding the prisoner Jimmy Younger, held *incommunicado*.

'But Del Vayo is the foreign minister of the Republic.'

They looked at one another and smiled ironically. Then one of them said: 'You have been in contuct with the British Embassy. That is the Kluss Enemy.'

I explained the conversation which I had had at the hotel with the British representative. I pointed out that all I had said was that Jimmy would not be shot and that he was sick.

One of them said: 'Wouldn't the British Foreign Office just love to publish a pamphlet stating that the International Brigade held British citizens in Spain against their will, quoting the poet Stephen Spender as their witness?'

'All I said was that Younger wouldn't be shot.'

Suddenly this scene struck me as utterly absurd, and I went on: 'Even Saint Paul, when he was an enemy of the Roman Empire, pleaded *Civis Romanus sum* when he was on trial. Surely a British citizen supporting the Spanish Republic has the right to claim protection of the British Embassy?'

They all burst out laughing. By an extraordinary chance, Saint Paul had gone straight to their Presbyterian hearts. Perhaps, too, they had really been afraid that I had given away some secret, and now they saw that I was innocent. The next thing that Kerrigan said was in a much more friendly voice: 'Loo-oo-ook here: this matter is no longer in our hunds. But we can arrange for you to see the comrades who will be Younger's judges. They are not the British.'

He telephoned and arranged that I should dine with the judges at their house.

In my memory the rest of this day has a dream-like quality. I forget how I got to the house, which was, I think, on the outskirts of Albacete where a kind of boulevard confronts the plain. I took my hosts to be Jugo-Slavs: Younger, in the notes from which I have quoted, speaks of his judge as a young Polish intellectual: perhaps he is right, or perhaps they were Russians. The Russian members of the Brigade were kept apart from everyone else, and probably if I had visited them I would not have been told if they were Russians.

The three judges provided me with a dinner which consisted of some very well-cooked fish, I seem to remember. It tasted in my mouth like food on the tongue of a terrified child. When I began to eat, I suddenly had the same experience as I have described when I saw the donkey at Marrakesh: I was overcome by despair. One of my hosts said gently: 'Why are you so distressed, comrade?' I explained that it was on account of my friend. 'What do you think we shall do to him?' 'I suppose that you will send him to some prison camp.' 'Why does that worry you?' This I could not answer. 'Well, yes, that is what we shall do. But we are always happy when our friends are sent to the camps. It is so good for their education.'

236

'The camp,' Jimmy Younger's notes continue, 'was about ten miles outside Albacete. It resembled a rather prosperous farmstead, isolated, dusty, windswept, and dry. Additional buildings had been built, and about two hundred men from the Brigade were housed there. They were mainly French. I got well at this camp and developed a desire to please. I did co-operate eventually. I hoped that it would be quite clear to those responsible for my being there that as a fighting soldier I was hopeless, but that I might do useful work behind the lines. There was new hope.

'At the end of two months nine of us were put into a lorry. We thought we were going to freedom, but it was back into the prison in Albacete. All nine, representative of different European nationalities, were put into one tiny cell. The air was thick with the stench at night, and with discontent by day. No explanation was given. Messages to the Political Commissars outside and the Prison Governor were ignored. After a week John and I were seen by P——. He saw us one at a time in the office of the prison. He still could not give any reason for our having been sent back to prison, but I did find out that the camp had been cleared of prisoners and closed down. What happened to the other prisoners, I don't know. I asked P—— about friend in England and Spain with whom I had lost touch, but he gave vague answers. I asked him when Pollitt was coming out, because I wanted to see him. He was even more vague about this. He went away, promising us nothing, but saying he would do his best for us.

'Existence in the cell became more and more intolerable. The nights were worse than the days. In addition to the smell, the lice, the obscenities, snores, mutterings, were the strange sounds in the passageways and coming from other cells. Every night prisoners seemed to be called and made to dress to be taken away. In the lavatories I met people who saw this happen. They didn't know where the men had been taken. Imagine the rumours and the fears. They had been shot: sent to the front: released: taken to the frontier and sent home: anything you like to think of. A large Polish anarchist let his protests be known by kicking on the cell door and shouting for the Governor: ''Copick, you low type, get f—— by the Pope, and sh—— in the milk of your mother. Let us out.'' If no one answered

237

he shouted: "*Cabinet.*" This brought the guards, who escorted him there and back. But he never saw Copick.

'P—— came back. He told me that I was going to be released . . . on condition that I should return to the front.

'I was genuinely more frightened of these people who were controlling me than even of having to fight again. My worst fear was that being sent to the front was the easiest way of killing me off. Someone detailed off to do the job during some battle, and it wouldn't be noticed. This, according to the other prisoners, was the favourite way of getting rid of undesirables. I made a bargain with P——. I asked for one week of freedom in Albacete, during which I would see the Medical Officer. If fit, I would go back to the front. I knew I was ill. There was an almost continual pain in my stomach. Release came. Then the medical. An ulcer was diagnosed. I was recommended duties behind the line, on a milk diet. When I took the card to P——, he practically accused me of cheating and faking.

'Later I made discoveries which explained some of what had happened. An informer in the camp had gone to the Commander and told him I was a Trotskyist who planned a rising the first of May. The others were my confederates. Hence the transfer to prison.'

After more pressure, Younger and few of his companions were sent home.

* * * * *

My next visit to Spain was in the summer of 1937, when I was a delegate at the Writers' Congress held in Madrid, then being shelled. For this visit the Foreign Office refused to grant me a visa, so I had to go without one. A forged passport, for the purpose of crossing the Spanish frontier, was obtained for me by André Malraux. During most of the journey from the frontier to Madrid, I journeyed with him and Claude Aveline. My passport, consisting of a single sheet of paper, described me as a Spanish citizen, called Ramos Ramos – a name which seemed to involve a minimum of invention. Malraux amused himself by explaining at the frontier that I was a very special kind of Spaniard, tall and with fair hair and blue eyes, speaking a dialect indistinguishable from English, and coming from a remote northern mountain district.

The delegates to the Congress drove in a fleet of cars from the Spanish frontier to Barcelona, Valencia and Madrid. Everywhere we were banqueted, everywhere received with the same enthusiasm and generosity of a people who appeared to have a touching faith that the presence of '*los intellectuales*' strengthened their resistance.

The outstanding figure of the Congress was undoubtedly André Malraux. In 1937 he had an air of a battered youth, with face jutting pallidly over his intently crouching body as he looked at his audience. He wore a tweed suit into whose trouser pockets he thrust his hands. The Congress was dominated by his nervous sniff and tic. One day in Madrid, Hemingway, wistfully looking in Malraux's direction, said: 'I wonder what Malraux did to get that tic? It must have been at well over ten thousand feet.'

My French at this time was far from good, but in the course of several days of listening to Malraux's conversation and watching him, I formed certain impressions.

The purpose of his life of adventure mingled with artistic creation was to write out of a personal legend and an environment of activity. His politics were those of a Liberal individualist, but as a result of his immense self-confidence he had a certain impatience with the ineffectiveness of others. Malraux told me that he had always insisted on Liberal justice in the Malraux Squadron of the Republican Air Force, and he had refused to allow the Communists to interfere with him. *Il faut agir* was for him the secret of his novels as well as his politics. He renounced a static background and wrote out of a life of travel, movement, war, politics.

One day he told me that poetry was superannuated as a great art. It was only – he argued – in an environment where a few simple objects could be immediately apprehended as spiritual symbols, that it could be a major art. The forest, the lion, the crown, the cross: when the actual, lived reality of these was invested with inner significance which men immediately recognized, then the poet could make use in his poetry of these clearly recognizable symbols of a lived poetry of sacraments, figureheads and beliefs, within the world. But in our day of many inventions rapidly superseding one another, the most powerful poetic symbols of the past had been driven out by symbols derived from machinery, which had an overwhelming

239

and disturbing force, but lacked the transparent, spiritual meaning of the symbols which had been superseded. Moreover, the phenomena of industrial civilization symbolized totally different things for different people, so that the modern poet was not only preoccupied with his own poetic vision but also with establishing the validity of his symbols. Hence poetry inevitably became over-complicated and obscure, because it was trying at the same time to make statements and establish the terms for making them. But the task of characterizing the individuality of people and their environment, was really that of the novelist and not of the poet at all.

Here I have allowed myself to reconstruct an argument from a few remarks thrown out by Malraux in the middle of journeys across mountainous country on hot summer days, in a language which I understood very imperfectly. Moreover, I have been interpreting his remarks to myself ever since I heard them, thirteen years ago, so what I have written may be remote from what he said then or thinks now. However, these considerations were put into my mind by meeting Malraux, so perhaps I may be excused for attributing an argument to him which has its place in this book, even if the attribution is largely erroneous.

Malraux was the most brilliant and dynamic conversationalist I had met. He made an art of exposition. He could take ideas, express them as images, and set them before the mind's eye. When he was talking of poetry, he placed the poet in a past environment surrounded by living objects which were also universally accepted symbols. Then, as it were, with a conversational hand, he set him against the background of modern industrial society.

The public purpose of the Congress was to discuss the attitude of the Intellectuals of the World to the Spanish war. But there was also a hidden theme constantly discussed in private and almost as often dragged on to the open platform. This was: the Stalinists versus André Gide. For Gide had just published his famous *Retour de l'U.R.S.S.* in which he had made a detached and critical account of his impressions of a tour of Russia, where he had been the honoured and flattered guest of the Soviet Government. Far more sensational than the book itself was the fury with which it was received by Communists. Gide who, only a few weeks previously, had been hailed in

240

the Communist Press as the greatest living French writer come to salute the Workers' Republic, became overnight a 'Fascist monster', 'a self-confessed decadent bourgeois', and worse. The Writers' Congress was divided over the issue of Gide.

The Russian delegates confined themselves in their speeches to praising the rôle of Russia in the Popular Front, and denouncing Trotsky and Gide. Michael Koltzov, the crack correspondent of *Pravda*, excelled in improvising parodies of Gide's *Retour de l'U.R.S.S.* However this did not save him from disappearing on his return to Russia.

The Congress served the purpose of showing that there were intellectuals from many countries who went to shelled Madrid in order to show their opposition to Fascism. Moreover, it enabled writers from abroad to become acquainted with the varied, fantastic, paradoxical, subtle, and yet passionately simple Spanish poets and writers: men like the grandiose and rhetorical Rafael Alberti, a kind of Baroque Communist, the paradoxical and sensitive José Bergamin, follower of Unamuno, with a mind at once whimsical and definite, a little like that of E. M. Forster, or the poet Machado, absorbed in his world of pure poetic values, recalling Walter de la Mare, or perhaps the most astonishing of all – the young soldier-poet of Madrid, Miguel Hernandez, by origin a peasant and shepherd from the village of Oricuela. (There was a legend that Miguel Hernandez had been taught to read and write by a priest who met him in the hills, and educated him on examples of sixteenth- and seventeenth-century writing. So that his own passionate and ecstatic poetry produced a reaction against the prevailing modernism, when he came to Madrid in 1934, and began to publish in *Cruz y Raya*.)

The Congress, with all its good qualities, had something about it of a Spoiled Children's Party, something which brought out the worst in many delegates.

This circus of intellectuals, treated like princes or ministers, carried for hundreds of miles through beautiful scenery and war-torn towns, to the sound of cheering voices, amid broken hearts, riding in Rolls-Royces, banqueted, fêted, sung and danced to, photographed and drawn, had something grotesque about it. Occasionally we were confronted with some incident which seemed a reproach, a mockery, emerging with a sharp edge from the reality which had been so carefully disguised for us. One such occurred at a little town called Minglanilla, on the single road connecting Valencia with three-quarters-surrounded Madrid. Here we were as usual banqueted, eating *arroz a la valenciana*, followed by sweets, and washed down with excellent wine. The meal was (as nearly always happened) delayed. Waiting for it, we stood on the balcony of the town hall while the children of Minglanilla danced and sang to us in the brilliant sunlight of the square below. Suddenly Señora Paz, the beautiful wife of an equally beautiful young man, the poet Octavio Paz, burst into hysterical weeping. This was a moment of realization. There was another one, for me, after the meal. We had all walked out of the banqueting room into the square, when a peasant woman seized my arm and said imploringly: 'Sir, can you stop the *pájaros negros* machine-gunning our husbands as they work in the fields?' By the 'black birds' she meant the Fascist aeroplanes. Somehow the villagers of Minglanilla thought that the Congress of Intellectuals was a visitation which would save them. The same peasant woman invited the Chilean poet Pablo Neruda and myself to her house, where she showed us photographs of her two sons, both of them fighting at the front. Then she took from a cupboard some sausages and pressed these on us, insisting that we would most certainly need them on the journey. We accepted them in order not to offend her, for she was convinced that we would go hungry.

When we got to Madrid, André Chamson, secretary of the French delegation, behaved oddly. One evening, after a banquet followed by the singing of Flamenco songs and a ballad on the subject of Franco, written and recited by Rafael Alberti, one of the Spanish delegates jumped on to a table and shouted that Madrid was being shelled. The meeting was dispersed. Claud Cockburn, correspondent of the *Daily Worker*, Edgell Rickword, the poet, Réné Blech, a French Communist writer, and myself walked to the Puerta del Sol and watched the upper storeys of the Ministry of the Interior blazing where a shell had struck them. The next morning Chamson announced that he and Julien Benda, the author of *Le Trahison des Clercs*, must leave Madrid at once. For if by any chance either of them were killed, France could not choose but declare war on Franco, and this action would lead to world war. Chamson refused to accept the responsibility for such a catastrophe. There was something serious and impressive about Chamson's fanatical self-importance which contrasted with the tourist spirit of some of the delegates. Each morning when I saw him I would ask: 'How are you today?' to which he invariably replied: 'Mal, *mal*, MAL!' 'Why?' 'Because I am the only one here who *feels* all this. *Moi, moi, je suis responsable. C'est le devoir d'un écrivain d'être tourmenté.* The others are irresponsible, light-hearted, they do not feel.'

Speeches, champagne, food, receptions, hotel rooms, were a thick hedge dividing us from reality. A kind of hysterical conceitedness seized certain delegates. An English Communist novelist, who had some connection with the Republican Army, gave the English delegates a lecture on its organization. 'The Republican Army is full of anomalies,' he began. 'For example, take my uniform. You will notice that I am dressed as a private, but really I have a rank corresponding to that of general.' He was a nice, sincere, simple and genuinely cultivated man, interesting when describing his working-class youth, or when speaking of the craftsmanship in Catalan ironwork. His public activities revealed a less sympathetic side of his nature. One day he told me that, in his rôle of political commissar, he had been asked to decide the fortunes of a member of the Brigade who was a coward. He had had a long talk with the young man and persuaded him that he should go back into the fighting. Secretly he had arranged that he should be sent to a place where he was certain to be killed. 'I have just had a message to say that he is dead,' he said rather pompously. 'Of course, I am a little upset, but the matter does not weigh on my conscience. For I know that I did right.' There was a pause. Then, looking at me he added: 'I am telling you this because there is a moral for you in the story.' What made this more frivolous (though really, of course, much better) was that I did not think that he had the authority to make such a decision. His telling was the showing off of a literary man who had tasted a little power.

I observed my own behaviour with as much cynicism as I did that of others. I was secretly offended when I was not called upon to speak (though presumably I had nothing to say since I remember scarcely a word of any public utterances by myself or any other member of

243

the Congress). Sometimes, when I was sitting in a conference hall, I saw a camera pointed in my direction, or an artist, with pencil poised above drawing block, looking towards me. Then, hating myself, I kept very still, until I noticed that the photographer or artist was really concerned with Malraux or Neruda or Alberti who happened to be sitting nearby.

At a banquet in Valencia I sat next to the correspondent of a Communist newspaper. He was a brilliant and entertaining young man whose amusing anecdotes and gentlemanly manner I always enjoyed. He was of good family and his particular aristocratic eccentricity consisted of his not being a gentleman when he was writing for the workers. (In this, I suspect, he may have shown his secret contempt for them.) He said that he had read an article which I had published in the *New Statesman*. In this I had drawn attention to the fact that the International Brigade was Communist controlled, and – thinking of boys like the unfortunate M——, – I had argued that this should be made clear to volunteers before they joined. The correspondent agreed that the facts in my article were true, but he said that nonetheless I should not have written them. I should consider not the facts but the result which might follow from writing them. The truth, he went on to argue, lay in the cause itself and whatever went to promote it. Apparently, truth, like freedom, lay in the recognition of necessity.

When I was not driving with Malraux and Aveline, I usually preferred sitting next to the Spanish drivers to riding in the rather austere company of the British delegation. One of these was the poet Edgell Rickword, with his air of being a retired cricketer who had once played for a side captained by Rimbaud. He was sympathetic on account of the poetry he had once written, and because of the dignified and almost unbroken silence he had preserved since joining the Party. There were also a Communist lady writer, and her friend, a lady poet. The Communist lady writer looked like, and behaved like, a vicar's wife presiding over a tea party given on a vicarage lawn as large as the whole of Republican Spain. Her extensory smiling mouth and her secretly superior eyes under her shovel hat made her graciously forbidding. She insisted – rather cruelly, I thought – on calling everyone 'comrade', and to me her sentences usually began,

'Wouldn't it be less selfish, comrade', which she followed by recommending some course of action highly convenient from her point of view.

On our way from Barcelona to the French frontier, the Catalan driver happened to mention to me that during the liquidation of the Poum (the Trotskyist Party) in Barcelona he had shot six people in cold blood. He did not attempt to justify himself. In fact, he spoke of the episode as fun. (Another discovery I made, through being with the drivers, was that the Catalan drivers referred to the Valencians as Fascists, and could not be at all persuaded to go on to Madrid, whilst the drivers from Madrid referred to the Valencians as Fascists and of course almost everyone who was not himself a Catalan called the Catalans Fascists.)

I experienced the most striking example of the rather brutal separatist spirit in Barcelona.

Here there was a huge meeting addressed by the delegates. Each speech lasted a few minutes and was translated into Catalan by a translator who seemed able to convey the gist of it in six words. (An absurd feature of this meeting was that an orchestra played the national anthem of each delegate before he spoke. So that when I got up it burst into God Save the King whilst the audience rose to their feet with clenched fists.) In my speech I praised the Catalans for their enterprise in translating the classics into Catalan and making them available to the people in beautifully printed cheap editions. This seems harmless enough, but the results were perceptible. The non-Catalan Spanish delegates were furious and showed me that they were. Bergamin, who was amused, always greeted me with the words '*Visca Cataluña!*' after this. The Catalan intellectuals sent a small deputation to tell me that I was one of the few foreigners who had appreciated their cultural efforts. They invited me to tea on the day following the meeting, and the poet Rafael Alberti accompanied me. As soon as we had arrived he launched into a diatribe against the Catalans, criticizing their failure to take sufficient part in the war and ending by asserting roundly that if they did no better the Republic, 'after the victory', would know how to deal with them.

When we had left Spain, and were sunning ourselves on the quay of the little town of Port-Bou just across the frontier, the Communist

245

lady novelist, half-closing her eyes, said reminiscently: 'And what is so nice is that we didn't see or hear of a single act of violence on the Republican side.' This was too much, and I recounted the cheerful confession of the Catalan driver. The lady and her friend turned from me in a pained way. Then the lady novelist remarked to the poetess: 'Isn't it strange that now, for the first time after all these long, long days, I feel just a little bit tired?' Her friend replied: 'That's because all this time, comrade darling, you haven't had a single moment in which you have been thinking of yourself. Now that there's no need for you to be so unselfish any longer, you are able to realize how tired you feel, that's all.' 'Ah, how intuitive of you. That must be it.' 'You see, darling, The Other Comrades Don't Need You For A Little While, so you should try to relax.'

The presence of Altolaguirre during the Writer's Congress was a relief. He was a little affected, like nearly everyone, by the prevailing hysteria, but in a way which I found sympathetic. One day, when Rafael Alberti was declaiming one of his social realist ballads, I asked Altolaguirre whether he cared for the poem. 'No,' was the reply. 'Why not?' 'Because I, I, I, I, should be reciting!' he answered passionately, striking his chest.

When we got to Barcelona it was arranged that a few of the Spanish delegates should go on to Paris with us in order to speak at a meeting. Altolaguirre, whose wife and daughter were in France, applied to go. He was interviewed, with other applicants, by officials. All the other writers said that they hated to leave Spain, but felt that they would serve the cause best by tearing themselves away from the Republic for a few days and speaking in Paris. When Altolaguirre was asked his reasons for going, he said: 'Because my wife Concha and my daughter Paloma are in France.' He was refused permission. Later a few of his friends asked him, after a meeting of the Congress: 'Why did you tell them about your wife and child?' 'Because it is true. They are in France,' he replied. 'Yes, but why couldn't you have invented some more patriotic reason for leaving the country?' 'No! No! No!' he exclaimed violently, and walked away from them. They explained apologetically to me that really Manolo was very childish.

We were provided with a luxury train, consisting entirely of sleeping cars, from Port-Bou to Paris. The French organiser, who favoured me, had put me into a Wagon Lit. While I was standing in it, I heard some of the other delegates screaming and banging with their fists against the sides of carriages. Although they were indeed tired, this scene of distinguished intellectuals who had just been on a luxury tour of a war-shattered country, screaming to get into their sleeping cars, has lingered in my memory. For a moment I almost gave up my own place, but on second thoughts I decided not to make any such gesture. Yet it is characteristic that on this satiric occasion I should have been an object of satire to myself as I stood in my compartment. I wondered whether the Canterbury pilgrims behaved in this way. The delegates had undergone risks to show their sympathy for the Republican cause: and yet somehow the tone of the Congress had been inappropriate. It may be that it is sometimes better to do inappropriate and perhaps grotesque things, and even expose oneself to self-contempt, than to do nothing at all (my visit to the Madrid front was an example of grotesque action after all worth doing). But a deep dissatisfaction was the strongest experience I gained from the Writers' Congress.

*   *   *   *   *

After this I returned to England and did not visit Spain again. For the rest of the summer Inez and I took a small house near the Kentish coast. Here Auden visited us and wrote his rather callous ballad, *Miss Gee*. He and I talked of the Congress and the Gide case. His attitude was perfectly clear. He stated emphatically that political exigence was never a justification for lies. I had the impression that he was less drawn to Communism than his contemporaries. He had offered his services in Spain as a stretcher bearer in an ambulance unit. Yet he returned home after a very short visit of which he never spoke. But as a result of this visit he wrote the best poetic statement in English of the Republican case – the poem *Spain*. He had a firmer grasp of Marxist ideology, and more capacity to put this into good verse, than many writers who were closer to Communism. This led to the legend that he went through a Communist phase. But his poem, *A Communist to Others*, is an exercise in entering into a point of view not his own. It is his summing up of conversations with Communists rather like the ones I used to have with Chalmers in Berlin.

In the autumn of 1937 I was ill and had to have an operation. For my convalescence we went to Salcombe in Devonshire, a town where we went, year after year, when we were children, for boating and fishing summer holidays. The town, situated at the end of the harbour, inaccessible to large ships on account of the sandy bar across the harbour mouth, is sheltered by little hills, and the most tropical plants grow here as nowhere else in England. Five or six creeks spread out beyond the palm of the harbour like the fingers of a hand, and combes covered with dwarf oak trees reach down to the water's edge, where their spread boughs cover it like umbrellas.

Here we used to walk to the rugged Bolt Head, or inland towards Kingsbridge. But we did not escape from the haunting Spanish war.

There was, in the hotel where we were staying, a businessman and his wife. The man, with a black 'walrus' moustache adorning a purple, scraggy face, and wearing loud check tweeds, was a caricature of himself. His wife was usually occupied in sitting close beside him, knitting placidly, a tolerant expression on her face.

One afternoon we went for a fishing expedition with these two. The man committed every absurdity possible to an amateur fisherman, including catching his tweed cap (which had fallen into the sea) with his hook and imagining that it was a fish. He told us that his business was in the line of trucks and lorries. He asked me what I did, and I told him something of my journalistic experiences in Spain. At the end of the afternoon, as we were drawing to the side of the quay, he said in his absurd, wheedling voice, which made an insult sound as if he were begging a favour: 'It may interest you to know that in my business we've just received an order from Spain for a new type of caterpillar trucks. And those trucks will carry heavy guns which will' (and here, while scrambling clownishly out of the boat, he made a sawing gesture with his hand in the air), 'smash your friends in Madrid to pieces!' He ended, like a farcical villain, gnashing his teeth.

248

This meeting reminded me of the forces behind Fascism. I felt restless and wanted to go back to London at once.

When we returned to London, I was once more taken up with the Popular Front movement, not now in the sunlit and tragic arena of Spain, but amongst the rain falling in streets black as enamel, shop windows at foggy dusk with garish lights like tinsel stars, and queues waiting for buses and trams. I belonged to several different groups of organizations which often met in rooms above cafés near the Charing Cross Road; and I was one of the six directors of the Group Theatre, whose able producer, Rupert Doone, brought on to the London stage the verse plays of Auden and Isherwood, and my own *Trial of a Judge*.

One subject constantly discussed at all these writers' meetings was whether there was a necessary connection between politics and literature. I myself believed that within modern conditions there is such a connection: that is to say, that sensitive minds must be conscious, in one way or another, of the general political fate in which almost everyone today is involved. I used the word 'political' in a very wide sense, to cover a fatality which I felt to be overtaking our civilization and which influenced our modern writing more explicitly than was generally realized. Or, to put this in another way, a kind of literary material which our predecessors had not thought of as political had obvious political implications for us today: for example, there had always been in Henry James's novels a sense of the social decay of Europe. The peculiarity of the 1930's was not that the subject of a civilization in decline was new, but that the hope of saving or transforming it had arisen, combined with the positive necessity of withstanding tyrannies.

The sense of political doom, pending in unemployment, Fascism, and the overwhelming threat of war, was by now so universal that even to ignore these things was in itself a political attitude. Just as the pacifist is political in refusing to participate in war, so the writer who refuses to recognize the political nature of our age must to some extent be refusing to deal with an experience in which he himself is involved. But why should he not refuse? No reason, except that the consciousness of excluded events would probably affect the scale of his writing. A pastoral poem in 1936 was not just a pastoral

249

poem: it was also a non-political poem. A poem that rejected the modern consciousness of politics as a universal fate.

I was 'political' not just because I was involved, but in feeling I must choose to defend a good cause against a bad one. Auden remarked to me at the end of the war that he was political in the 1930's just because he thought something could and should be done. On the other hand, I never felt that the writers who did not feel this obligation were wrong. They might be concerned with values beyond action which, after all, alone justify action and therefore must not be allowed to lapse. Or they might be witnesses of a fatalism and despair which were equally important truths for the human soul as the '*il faut agir*' of André Malraux. Politics of a rather direct kind had become my experience, but I defended those who had other attitudes.

Thus the speeches of those who tried to connect writing with political tasks always left me uneasy. When speakers said that those of us who wished to write about themes which offered social hope should learn to speak to the ordinary people and abandon an esoteric style, I could see the force of this. But when they went on to condemn other writers as escapist because they did not choose subjects which could be easily identified with the 'struggle', I could not agree. For the social 'struggle' itself – if it were worth anything – must aim at making generally accessible those very values which were labelled 'escapist' simply because they were not concerned with the immediate 'struggle'. I felt particularly opposed to men of lesser talent, like the critic who, on the death of Virginia Woolf, wrote condemning most contemporary writers for having 'consistently rejected history'. He added that 'she herself, the outstanding prose writer of the English twilight of individual subconsciousness, had accepted the judgment of history and taken the logical step' (by which he meant her suicide), and went on to dismiss Kafka, Proust, Joyce, Yeats, Eliot, Lawrence and others because their political attitudes were not 'correct'. I felt that there was something disastrously wrong with the political conception which could so mechanically condemn the complex expressions of complex individual genius. An impertinent and even impious principle was involved in invoking a theoretical Communism or Socialism to refute such *temoignage*. Individual experience could only

250

be refuted by profounder, more intelligent, acuter, more sensitive, and better expressed, individual experience.

*   *   *   *   *

Even more than their attacks on living writers, I resented the profoundly hypocritical attitude of Communist critics towards the past. They patronized Dante, Shakespeare, Goethe, Balzac, Blake, and anyone else whom they cared to discuss, by arguing that their works epitomized in mythological form the economic and social aims of their eras, and were justified in so far as they were adapted to the historically materialist aims of their time. In this way they avoided being confronted with the awkward fact that most of these writers held views utterly incompatible with Stalinist Communism, in any conceivable time or place within the whole of history and the whole universe. When they lectured unctuously about our 'cultural heritage' they meant wealth which they proposed to debase and squander, inherited from ancestors whom they would have regarded as their worst enemies in their own lifetimes. But the Communists were under no constraint to pass sentences on these writers as deviationists, since they were dead already, so they made them ex-officio Marxist saints, in the same way as they canonized the poet Garcia Lorca, who had been obligingly assassinated by the Francoists, and whom they would have attacked as a Catholic reactionary, had he survived.

To me it seemed important to emphasize that for Dante, Blake and the others, God existed in exactly as real a sense as Karl Marx for Harry Pollitt. Posthumously to provide poets with the alibi that they were not on the historic scene at the time of Karl Marx so could not be accessory to anti-Marxist activities, in fact must have been 'historically correct' within the context of their times – was a worse slander against truth than sending them to Siberia, had they been alive.

Not to accept that in the past beliefs were just as real as our own beliefs appear to us today is to imprison ourselves within our own contemporary attitudes, and to permit only a dim reflection of ourselves, instead of a light of others better than us, to reach us from past times. The consequence of such an attitude towards the past

251

is to turn the thought of this living generation into a prison of attitudes and rules dictated by 'historic necessity' and not only dominating our own thought, but also projected into the past.

The uneasiness I felt in these meetings of 'writers' groups' was
really the same as I had felt on my personal contacts with some of
the delegates of the Writers' Congress in Madrid. Social criticism
had taken the place of scrupulous self-criticism. Of course, in order
to be a good citizen one had to have certain socially useful qualities:
industry, hatred, perhaps purity (Lenin had said something on this
subject), abstemiousness – in a word those which made for the utmost devotion to the cause. One did not need charity, pity, tolerance,
humility, truth, personal loyalty. The idea for the novel which Chalmers had once sketched when we walked through Berlin, near the
Gedaechtniskirche – a novel in which the virtuous and sympathetic
characters would be capitalists and the unpleasant ones Communists, but which would show that nevertheless the Communists
were 'right' because they were 'on the side of history' – seemed now
a parable of our time: a parable, though, whose moral I took in the
sense opposite to that intended by Chalmers. I began to realize what
I had always known in my heart: that there is no 'historic
correctness' which achieves good independently and in spite of
the moral qualities of those who support the cause. Unless the
cause is maintained by an effective number of those who are as
scrupulous in their personal behaviour, judged by personal standards
of loyalty and honesty and affection, as by their outer devotion to
it, violence, hatred and lies which are too easily justified by an
external cause, become the personal attributes of its supporters.
Those who represented 'exigency', and had their minds fixed on
the means whereby to achieve their aims, always had reasons for
silencing those who saw more than one point of view. But this unification of all points of view into one Party Line was really the
exercise of a dead hand on the most living, original, spontaneous
and varied forces in politics and culture. Everywhere the men of
talent who, through good will, had been brought to Communism
were silent unless, indeed, they became mechanical voices, mega-
phones, like the Russian writers whom I had met in Spain. Because
Communists supported means which mocked at charity and scrupu-

252

lousness, qualities outrageous to the individual human life dominated the public scene.

* * * * *

Since I left Oxford I had hardly seen Tristan, the distressed, gently teasing, affectionate companion of my last year there, whose pale face, bleary eyes and pathetic expression reminded me often of Blake's lines about the lamb: 'Come and lick / My white neck.'

But occasionally I heard news of him. He had turned from a lamb into a tiger. After leaving Oxford, he had joined the Communist Party, as his four brothers also had done. He had gone to America and taken part in some strike-breaking riot, about which he wrote an article in a weekly periodical. He had interrupted a trial of anti-Nazis in Germany by getting up in court and protesting.

In London one evening, in the autumn of 1937, I happened to see a poster announcing that Tristan would speak at a meeting of the Young Communist League. Or rather, it was not 'Tristan ——' but 'Bill ——' who was announced because, for the purposes of his Party work, he had changed his Christian name. The hall, when I arrived, was rather empty. Bill-Tristan's speech was preceded by that of another youth leader who spoke in the accusing Glasgow accent, which had not lost its power to terrify me. Then Tristan got up. He began his speech in a unique way (I thought) by attacking his audience for not being twice its size. It was disgraceful, he said, that there were not more of us. How could we expect to help Spain if we did not at least double our numbers? And we called ourselves youth, etc. etc. We shifted uncomfortably in our seats, trying to look larger, but no one achieved the miracle of duplicating himself.

This new, fiery Tristan, whom I had never seen before – Bill, in fact – now relented a little. He said he would read us a letter which would entertain us: it was so typical of wet, wishy-washy, Liberal, Oxonian writing. So, as light relief, he read a letter written in the style of an Oxford moral philosopher. The writer said that he had carefully weighed the moral issues involved in the Spanish conflict and, as far as he could see, good was overwhelmingly on the side of the Republic. He therefore enclosed a cheque for the largest sum he could afford, which he wished to give to the Republican cause. Bill-Tristan's audience showed good sense in not splitting their sides with laughter over this dignified letter. Afterwards, when I went back-stage to greet Tristan, he said: 'Who do you think wrote that letter?' I said nothing, and he answered himself: 'My father.'

I next heard of Tristan-Bill at the time of the German-Soviet Pact. My friend, Philip Toynbee (who was a neighbour of Tristan's family at Oxford), had written a letter to the *New Statesman*, raising the question of what attitude Communists should now adopt, on the assumption that they no longer supported Soviet foreign policy. Going home that week-end, he found himself seated next to Tristan in the train. 'Hullo, Tristan!' he said. There was no reply, so he repeated the question a little louder. 'I do not know you,' Tristan said with an expressionless face.

This transformation of Tristan into Bill is an example of the sacrifice of personal qualities to political exigency in one individual. Tristan-Bill was consistent and courageous and his behaviour certainly shows no lack of integrity. But it does show a complete disregard for all personal feelings. He could reply that personal loyalty is a bourgeois conception anyway. Yet there is surely a flaw in such thinking. For it assumes that one can renounce the private qualities of one's own personality, and become an entirely public function. But this cannot really happen, for one cannot escape from having an inner self: and the qualities which may seem publicly good become bad personal ones. Something happens to the inner personality, something worse even than Tristan's becoming gloomy and fanatical. The worst private qualities (shown already in Tristan's enviousness at Oxford) become invested in the politically correct public ones. But in the long run they taint the public personality with qualities which would be condemned in individuals.

*   *   *   *   *

After my return from Spain I reacted from the attempt to achieve Communist self-righteousness towards an extreme preoccupation with the problems of self. I wrote poems in which I took as my theme the sense of being isolated within my personal existence: but
254

I tried to state the condition of the isolated self as the universal condition of all existence.

For a time I even made the experiment of being psychoanalysed. This, like Marxism, was disappointing in that it did not resolve the problems for which I sought a solution. It seemed that I had to work out these things for myself within myself and could not look for any external aid to work the change. But it extended my knowledge of the material made up of personal memories, with which I was now concerned.

Another interest which I rediscovered at this time was in painting. At one time, painting had preoccupied me almost as much as writing. At school I prayed for rainy afternoons in order that I might spend them working at still lives and portraits. I never painted out of my imagination, because it seemed to me that to arrive at a stage where I might do so, I must first learn to represent figures and objects convincingly. I must be able to imitate before I could paint my dreams.

Now it occurred to me that, at the age of twenty-nine, I might still become a poet and painter, as others had done. I envied the painter's life – the way in which he is surrounded by the material of his art. A writer does not have a visible palette of words laid out before him into which he dips his pen, mixes them and lays them on the page. The painter can immerse himself in his work more than a writer, because painting is largely a craft, a sensuous activity with tangible material, whereas writing is largely cerebral.

So I bought canvases, brushes and paints and started working by myself. I painted the milky blue and plum-coloured roofs which we saw from our Hammersmith window. Just then, William Coldstream, Victor Pasmore, Claud Rogers and Graham Bell started an art school in a room situated in the Euston Road (hence they were known as 'the Euston Road Group'). I studied here for a time. This experience of painting brought home to me two lessons. One was that it is possible entirely to lack talent in an art where one believes oneself to have creative feeling. Banal as this may seem, it is difficult to realize that one can *think* a picture which one will never be able to paint. Even today I find myself thinking that if I had my materials I could paint some picture which is real in my mind's eye. The other, and much more significant lesson, was that the art in which one may hope

255

to excel is that in which one can take immense pains over detail. When I tried to paint, detail always maddened me. When I write prose, I am impatient with that side of writing which consists in balancing a sentence, choosing the exact word, writing grammatically even. Only in poetry do I delight in writing and rewriting, making numerous versions of a single poem, leaving a sketch for several years and then taking it up and working on it. This may involve much wasted effort, but perhaps it shows an artist that he has found his right medium.

I see now that these apparently disconnected activities, of being psychoanalysed and painting, did in fact have a secret connection, a kind of complicity even. Strangely enough they were both attendants on the breaking up of my first marriage. They did not cause it, but they made it more bearable.

There may seem to be little connection between psychoanalysis and my desire to be a painter. But whilst, on the one hand, I wished to plunge deep into the sources of childhood and accept myself, on the other I wished to attach myself to outward things. That summer I looked and looked as I had not done for years at the green of the chestnut trees and the ochre of walls, broken by patches of blue and cold grey. I was fascinated by the contrast between opaque surfaces of light, where sunlight is clotted on leaves or flesh, and the transparent darkness of shadows like brown and green glass pools, through whose coldness I could look deeply on to still darker shadows like rocks – the foundations and anchors of the opaque surfaces of light flying like kites in the sun.

We had moved from Hammersmith to Bloomsbury. Near our flat, beyond the Foundling Hospital, there was a curious old graveyard, now a public garden. It was at the back of a church and situated between angles of houses like elbows. Some of the gravestones had been taken up and replaced against a high wall, making a kind of egg and cup, or spade-shaped, moulding along its base. Here there were benches where certain old pensioners, dressed in their blue uniforms, would often sit. The sunbright blue of their clothes and the rose-pink of their faces seemed like the inset glow of stained glass against the dark cold shadow of the wall. Here I came every day, plunging my eyes into these colours which could absorb the

256

sense of something fatal in my life. For this blue and rose had the depth of a self-portrait of Rembrandt with its patches of opaque and transparent colour.

*   *   *   *   *

It seems to me now that the end of my first marriage was the breaking of something which had never been completely joined. But in 1939 things did not appear in this light. My marriage, whatever its defects, seemed to me the centre of my life and absolutely irreplaceable. I can see now that Inez and I had not created a complete relationship: but we had everything except one. That is to say, we respected, we adored, we even loved one another, though the love was not of a kind which made us feel as though we were always one person. We were never completely together, and this made separation the more despairing.

We did achieve a certain kind of life when we were alone together, but this was of a play-acting, almost childish kind. In this way we warded off a dangerous confrontation of our real personalities.

However, we treated one another's work with seriousness. Although I could never enter very deeply into Inez's scholarship, I was almost as interested in the novel she was writing as in what I wrote myself. She, on her side, surprised me when my *Trial of a Judge* was produced by knowing long passages of it by heart.

Thus our life was given happiness by our delight in certain aspects of one another. Sometimes, when I came home, I paused in front of our house in the evening, and the feeling that she was in the flat upstairs was one of intoxicating wonder. As though, high up above the street, we had a nest of nests, a magic box, where the way she walked across the room remained always a vivid enchantment to me. I felt the joy and miracle of another life more precious than my own.

Soon after my return from Spain we bought a house at Lavenham in Suffolk which we shared with my brother Humphrey and his wife Margaret Spender.

My sister-in-law, Margaret, was one of the most vital people I have ever known. She entered into the project of arranging our Lavenham house with enthusiasm, combined with her skill as a trained architect. The strange fusion of the determined and independent with an extreme gentleness and sympathy, which was her character, showed in her features. She seemed square and brusque and wild with her strong, rather bony face and her fine figure, until one noticed the changefulness of expression in her deep-set eyes, which were sometimes quite light with gaiety, sometimes mournful with sympathy, and sometimes so affected with a kind of inspired interest and enthusiasm for some project, that their shining look was loveable and almost absurd. Perhaps she hoarded a secret throughout her short life: which was that she was not so strong as she seemed. She was one of those who may truly be said to have burned themselves out with their passionate love for others and for life itself. In the Suffolk countryside of little hills providing many little views of fields enclosed by cushion-like hedges Inez and I spent some of the happiest months of our marriage. Other happy occasions were our visits to Paris: for France brought out something carefree and spontaneous in Inez which seemed crushed and self-conscious in London.

However, throughout the whole duration of our marriage I was obsessed as I have never been before or since: by hatred of Fascism, by the Spanish war, by the anxiety on Jimmy's account. All these things Inez understood, was patient about and sympathized with But she was not reassured when she needed reassurance.

She was afraid, and I was not able to prevent this. Sometimes, involuntarily I caused her suffering by confronting her with my own nightmares. Shortly before the war, the German poet Ernst Toller came to see me. He had some scheme which he wanted to discuss, about an appeal through high functionaries to the conscience of the world on behalf of the Spanish Republicans. He had a whole suitcase full of documents about this, and he was tremendously excited and full of his own importance, telling me that he had been received by President Roosevelt and by the Archbishop of Canterbury. Toller invited Inez and me to dine with him one night at the Gargoyle Club. He had ideas of himself as a gallant, so all through dinner he was markedly attentive to Inez. Indeed there was something fascinating about him with his large brown eyes like a doe's, and his pale skin like an American Indian's. At the end of dinner, Toller, rather surprisingly, fished a silver brooch out of his pocket and presented it to Inez.

A few days later Toller hanged himself. I read this in the news-papers and was deeply shocked. When I told Inez, her face became distorted with anger as I had never seen it before, for she did not as a rule dramatize things. She turned on me furiously: 'You understand *why* he committed suicide. You *would* know someone capable of do-ing such a thing. That's what I can't bear about you,' and she threw the brooch which Toller had given her, across the room.

Sometimes, when we were in a playful mood, she would say to me, quite lightly: 'I love you and shall love you always, but I might leave you.' In the middle of our affection which enclosed a remark of this kind in a shining envelope, I could say in a tone of voice which echoed hers: 'For how long?' 'Oh, perhaps for three years!' 'Would you come back?' 'Oh yes, I would always come back.' Such a conversa-tion did not alarm me, even if there was a certain level on which I knew it to be serious, for this level was a place where such an idea was not frightening. Her words were like my seeing a city outlined in lights from a ship on which I was far out at sea. Every detail was outlined by starry light and yet the beautiful and calm vision seemed quite unrelated to the harsh realities which would confront me when I arrived at this place in broad daylight.

So that when I realized that Inez was in love, I was in the same position as I had been when Elizabeth had written to me announcing her marriage, or when Jimmy Younger had decided to go to Spain. To protest would have been demanding loyalty of a kind different from that which I gave. I was jealous and I made scenes, but I did not demand that she should act against her inclination. To be certain that I could make her happier than anyone else would be the basis of confidence, and I did not have this certainty. Perhaps, quite be-yond all this, I had a much deeper confidence within the lack of it: a confidence that if the love was real it might change in nature, but I could not lose it. It would go on existing beyond the vows which we had made so unreflectingly in the Register Office. The relationship in which I could excel found its justification in accepting what we were and recognizing what we were not or could not be. It was based on a faith that people have to be free to make mistakes and then to rectify them.

All the same, I was extremely jealous. As Inez was frightened, she

259

did not behave in a way which would strengthen my confidence, and there were hours when I simply became a prey to the most stupefying anger and jealousy. Instead, as with Elizabeth, of my seeing the necessity of the decision, I felt cast out, and I contrasted the perfect happiness which someone I loved could enjoy with another, with my own wretchedness. This may seem to contradict what I have said in the previous paragraph, but such situations are full of contradictions. There were curious inconsistencies in my attitude towards her other relationship. One day, when I noticed that Inez had forgotten for a week to post a letter to my rival, instead of being pleased I was deeply shocked.

We separated in the early summer of 1939. The separation was at first like the accounts I have read in books of the madness experienced by addicts when they are disintoxicated of some habit-forming drug. Each day seemed an interminable withholding of that commonplace and even vulgar miracle by which one, by the mere act of walking in at the door of a room, can grant another the whole happiness of living. What added to my perplexity was that when we did meet, we still understood one another well and did not quarrel. . . . At this time I formed that involuntary and rather terrible vow which governs behaviour afterwards, that I would never be in a position whereby I would suffer in this way again.

Meanwhile, a far worse disaster than mine threatened the family life of my brother. My sister-in-law, Margaret, was diagnosed as having an incurable disease.

Our Lavenham house, where I was now staying with Humphrey and Margaret, was an Elizabethan house on to which a Georgian front had been built in the eighteenth century. At the back was a small Elizabethan courtyard, in the centre of which was a fig tree. One night in August 1939 we were woken by a great crash. The fig tree had fallen to the ground.

Margaret was my confidante throughout these months. She showed now a courage and hope which seemed the final development of a line throughout her fearless and happy life which even illness could not break. When she was so wasted, as she lay curled up in her bed, that her bones seemed like knives cutting through her parched flesh, her eyes still shone with confidence. She said to me one day: 'As I lie here in bed, I think of the holiday we'll take when I'm better. We'll go to Cornwall next summer and sit all day on the beach by the sea.' So vivid was her expression when she said these words that I seemed to see the days of bright sea-light like wave-worn beads of rounded blue glass, strung on a chain of golden sand. Answering from my own distress, and from an optimism as deluded as her own, I said: 'By then Inez will have come back. For I intend to go to Rome for three months and then to Paris, to study French and Italian literature. If I lead a calm and independent life, she'll want to be with me at those places.' And remembering her words about always coming back, I even thought that there might be some reverse arrangement to that of the past year when she had spent her holidays with my rival, and that it would be with me that she would enjoy breaks from domesticity. Margaret touched my forehead with her skeleton-like hand, and at that moment I realized as I identified my misfortune with hers the egotism of my demand for sympathy and of my claim to be unhappy.

I am astonished that there are people who boast of being egotists, because actually the consciousness of egotism is like a sour taste on the tongue. Now Margaret's gesture, which spoke of her far more serious unhappiness, brought back to me the truth of various remarks which had been scattered throughout the years, all pointing to the thought that unhappiness is a condition which few people have the right to claim. I remembered Auden's remark when we were at Oxford that if I were in love, had good health and sufficient money, I ought to consider myself happy.

*　　*　　*　　*　　*

The background to these personal events was the victory of Franco in the Spanish Civil War, the Munich settlement, and the occupation of Czechoslovakia. Of these, the fall of the Spanish Republic symbolized the end of an epoch. The other events were the beginning of a new one – the beginning of the war.

The epoch ended with the collapse of the hope that the intervention by certain groups, and even by individuals, could decide the fate of the first half of the twentieth century. For the words 'intervention', and its counter, 'non-intervention', are better keys to the under-

261

standing of this phase even than 'Republican', 'Red', 'Fascist', and the rest. It was a period of intervention by Germany, Italy and Russia, exercising their strength within limits against which the volunteer International Brigade and even the acts of individuals were measurable. If the Liberal forces could have been more effective, these limits would not have been exceeded and there would have been no war.

With the fall of the Republic, followed quickly by Munich, this phase ended. The last shot fired by the Men of Good Will was the gallant little speech by Duff Cooper when he resigned after Munich. He was a recruit who might have done more good if he had arrived earlier on the scene.

After this the emotions and the arguments used by the anti-Fascists were taken over by the democratic governments in their war against Hitler. Journalists sometimes complained in the Press that the anti-Fascist writers who had shown such zeal in 1936 and 1937 seemed perversely uninterested, now that the action against Hitlerism for which they had been clamouring, was really taking place. But the fact was that the anti-Fascist battle had been lost. For it was a battle against totalitarian war, which could have made the war unnecessary. The war certainly produced its heroes: pre-eminently the fighter pilots who won the Battle of Britain. But their flame-like resurgence of a quality flowering throughout English history was something different from the individualistic anti-Fascism of the 1930's.

I had last seen Manuel Altolaguirre at the Writers' Congress in Madrid. During one of our journeys from Valencia to Barcelona, I noticed that he had no suitcase, only a little briefcase. When we stopped at some village, he opened the briefcase, which contained two volumes of my poems and nothing else. 'Will you inscribe these for me?' he asked. 'I had great difficulty in getting them.' When I had done so, I inquired: 'But where is your other luggage?' 'I have almost nothing else.' 'Why?' 'I lost everything except my dress-clothes, a top hat, and what I have on, in an air raid.' 'But why haven't you ever told me you were in an air raid?' He laughed: 'As a matter of fact I've told no one. I was so ashamed.' 'What happened?' 'Above the window of my room there was a gable. One day, I was looking out of the window of my room when the stucco pigeon

262

on this gable suddenly circled in front of the window, uttering a loud coo. Then everything in the room was destroyed. I was not hurt. That is all.' 'What did you do then?' 'Ah, that is why I have been too ashamed to tell about the air raid. Immediately afterwards I remembered that the Casa de la Cultura had a fund for providing aid to war-damaged intellectuals. Thinking that I now qualified as one, I set out at once for their offices. I must explain though that just below my room there had lived another poet with his wife and ten children. When I arrived at the office this poet and his wife and his ten children were all there, seated on twelve chairs. Each of them, from the father and mother to the youngest little child, aged three, had a leg or an arm or a hand or a head done up in bandages. I felt so ashamed that I just crept away. And that is why you are the first person I have ever told of this.'

At the time of the fall of Spain, I heard that Altolaguirre was one of the great crowd of refugees who poured over the Spanish frontier. In order to carry the clothes which he still possessed, he wore the dress-suit, which had survived the air raid, over his other clothes, and he wore also the top hat. He was passenger in a car, but soon he gave his seat up to some old woman and walked with the crowd across the frontier. When they arrived at the refugee camp, the peasants seeing this strange, burly figure, wearing such clothes became indignant, and surrounded him, shouting 'Aristocrat!' and 'Fascist!' Suddenly Altolaguirre flew into a mad rage, tore off all his clothes and threw them to the ground. He was taken to hospital naked.

This story, told as I have heard it, I quote because somehow it seems to symbolize the end of an individualistic epoch.

*   *   *   *   *

From my Journal, London, September 1939

'I feel as though I could not write again. Words seem to break in my mind like sticks when I put them down on paper. I cannot see how to spell some of them. Sentences are covered with leaves, and I really cannot see the line of the branch that carries the green meanings. . . .

'I must put out my hands and grasp the handfuls of facts. How extraordinary they are! The aluminium balloons seem nailed into the sky like those bolts which hold together the irradiating struts between the wings of a biplane. The streets become more and more deserted, and the West End is full of shops to let. Sandbags are laid above the glass pavements over basements along the sidewalk. Last night during the blackout there was a tremendous thunderstorm. We stood at the bottom of Regent Street in the downpour, the pitch blackness broken intermittently by flashes of sheet lightning which lit up Piccadilly Circus like broad daylight.

'The best thing is to write anything, anything that comes into my mind, until there is a calm and creative day. It is essential to be patient and to remember that nothing one feels is the last word . . . If Toller had waited he would be one of the few people happy about the war today. . . .'

Ten years after the war Germany was full of peace. It dripped with peace, we swam in peace, no one knew what to do with all the German peace. They built houses with flat roofs, they sunbathed, they walked with linked hands under the lime trees, they lay together in the pine forest, they talked about French art. Above all, everything was new and everyone was young. They liked the English very much, and they were sorry about the war. They talked about the terrible time they had during the Inflation.

This was in Hamburg. I used to bathe, and I went to parties of young people which were like moving in the atmosphere of a Blue Period Picasso. Everyone was beautiful, and gentle, and poor; no one was smart. On summer evenings they danced in the half-light, and when they were tired of dancing they lay down in the forest, or on the beach, or on mattresses, or on the bare floor. They laughed a great deal, smiling with their innocent eyes, and showing well-shaped, not very strong, teeth. Sometimes they let one down, sometimes the poorer ones stole, but there was no Sin, like there is in this kind of life in Paris or in London.

I could not dance. I could not speak German. I stood rather outside it all. I think now of the sad refugees who were the exquisite, confident students of the days of the Weimar Republic. Perhaps it was all fictitious, but now, in letting the mirage fade from my mind, I get very near to the truth: for everything in Germany tends towards the fictitious. There was the War, then there was the Inflation,

264

then there was New Architecture and the Republic, then there was the Crisis, then there was Hitler. Every German can explain himself as *What I Have Been Through.*

This passive attitude towards life, the tendency to consider oneself a product of circumstances and environment beyond one's control, gives the connection between the breakdown of external standards and the private values of a people. . . .

In the afternoon I got a taxi to Waterloo before going into the country. We were stopped near Southampton Row by five Frenchmen carrying a flag and singing the Marseillaise. The taximan said to me: 'They won't be doing that for long.'

Peter Watson travelled from Paris to Calais a few days ago in a troop train. The compartment was crowded with soldiers. They sat all the way in absolute silence, no one saying a word.

Some readers may notice that the account of my relations with the Communist Party here is not identical with that contained in The God that Failed, *a Symposium in which Arthur Koestler, Ignazio Silone, Andrè Gide, Louis Fischer, Richard Wright and myself, expressed our disavowals of Communism. The reason for what may seem discrepancies, is that when I wrote the essay, I was also writing this book: I therefore wished as far as possible to avoid covering the same ground. The two accounts of my relations with the Communists are intended to be complementary to each other, and readers who are interested in knowing more of the matter, and who have not already read my essay there, may find further material in* The God that Failed.

V

IN the autumn of 1942 I joined the Cricklewood, London, Branch of the Auxiliary (soon to be called the National) Fire Service. I had a certain difficulty in joining, as I had been rejected twice when applying before my call-up, at which I was declared unfit for heavy duties. However, I persuaded the doctors who examined me to transfer me from a 'C' to a 'B' classification.

The training, as in most war-time services, put the men who took part in it back to school. They wore dungarees like rompers, were made to obey humiliating and often ridiculous orders given to them by officers whom they sometimes considered to be their inferiors, and were robbed of the little dignity which they had attained in civilian life.

On the whole, the workers, more than the public-school boys, found this aspect of fire training humiliating. To the 'toff' his temporary war-time personality seemed added to his peace-time picture of himself. But to the worker who was a van or taxi driver, bricklayer or builder, the Fire Service was too close to his peace-time existence for it not to appear at times simply a change for the worse. Thus it was the workers and artisans who were most insistent on calling one another 'Mr.' to retain some outward sign of a peace-time gentility, and who boasted most frequently of the good positions which they held before the war.

It was humiliating to see these middle-aged men, who had developed a few unchallenged eccentricities, shaken about like dice in the asphalted schoolyards of the Training Centre at Parsons Green. Being new to the job, they had not as yet had time to develop a personal world of relationships within this impersonal one of drills and exercises. What held them together was their completely serious acceptance of the necessity of their work. At the back of their minds was a picture of the air raids in which they would have to put out fires. The thought of the air raid and the fires was like a string running through the burly, crooked, fat, thin, tall, short, morose, garrulous, taciturn, dull and amusing men, threading them together.

The idea that buildings would be knocked down by high explosives was as familiar and even normal to them as that they should be put up. It was all part of 'the job'. By comparison with 'the job', 'the cause' appeared to them abstract and theoretical; they thought of the Nazis as normally occupied and 'on the job' as they were themselves. 'That's his job,' was their attitude to a Nazi bomber dropping an incendiary bomb; 'and this is ours,' as they put it out. 'I suppose they have to obey orders the same as we have,' 'It's all in the day's work,' expressed their ideology. This functional view could get to a pitch where the war no longer seemed a conflict between Germany and Britain, but simply an inter-relationship of jobs within a system. A bombing pilot whom I met in a train when I was in fireman's uniform said: 'When we're dropping our bombs, I always feel sorry for you chaps who have to put out the fires down there. You have the worst job of all.' One day, one of my fellow firemen said: 'You've been to Germany, haven't you? What are they like?' While I hesitated, he answered his own question: 'I suppose they're just the same as what we are, hating it all and having to do it.'

To me, the idea of air raids and destruction was never quite real. The lectures at the Training Centre on different types of bombs were like lectures on Hell, or on the perversion of the human will. At the end of a lecture on the effect of gases (for we had to distinguish between those which smelt like pear-drops, carnations and sickly-scented hay), I hid for half an hour in a telephone box, overwhelmed by the vision of human beings asphyxiating one another in poisonous over-sweet scents. But I respected the more realistic minds which could grasp the situations with which they would have to deal without looking beyond or to the side of them.

At the Training Centre we used to have a break every morning at eleven o'clock. Then all the firemen ran for cups of tea to a little shop just down the road from the school.

Our blue dungarees smoothed out the excrescences of middle-age, reducing all our bodies to a childish-looking uniformity. Above the dungarees our heads jutted out, with obese or bony chins, red noses, bristles, lines. As we ran we shouted, behaving like caricatures of some terrible adolescence. Looking at any one of us you would think: 'That's how he'll look when he's middle-aged' – and then realize that he *was* middle-aged.

One morning the tea shop was so crowded that I gave up the idea of 'elevenses', and walked across the road to join a group of men who were standing in front of a shop window.

I noticed then that the window was that of an undertaker's shop. Crosses and columns, made not of stone but of a substitute, moulded and painted grey or pale green, were displayed all over the floor. The graves were like bath-tubs filled with artificial gravel, with a cross at the end where the taps would be, and an oblong surround.

One man was looking intently through the window at one of these objects, which seemed to have taken his fancy.

'I wonder how much one of them would cost?' he asked, as though to himself.

No one took the slightest notice of him. My fellow firemen had a way of not answering certain remarks. They responded with a tolerant silence, as though handing the question back like a returned letter.

'I wonder how much one of them would cost?' the man repeated. I looked at him, trying to express a polite interest.

'Do you think you could buy one on instalments?'

Still no one replied. Then a man said, addressing no one in particular: 'What do you think we'll have after this? Scaling ladder? Escapes?'

Another man drew himself up stiffly and yelled: '*Taut sheet!*' This was a jocose, self-reassuring reference to the most intimidating of our exercises, when we had to jump off a roof into a sheet held out flat about four feet from the ground, by men below.

'I'd 've liked to have bought one of those for my missus.'

'I hope we have a lecture indoors. It's bleeding cold.'

'My old lady would've liked to be buried in one of those.'

'Time! It's 12 o'clock!' They all started running back towards the school. I was left standing by the man at the window.

'All the same, it doesn't make no difference. We never found the body,' he said, turning away. Then he looked back again: 'I do wonder how much they cost.'

'We'll be late. We'd better get back,' I said, and started running away from him towards the others.

*   *   *   *   *

After training I was attached to a sub-station in Cricklewood. This consisted of four army huts: one, a recreation room; one, the bunk-house for sleeping; one, the kitchen and mess-room; the fourth, a wash-room and lavatory. There was also a garage for the fire-fighting cars and 'appliances'.

Our day fell into a simple routine. We got up at 7.30; breakfasted at 8; cleaned the huts out from 8.30 till 9.45; went on parade at 10; drilled from 10.15 to 11; did more cleaning until 1. After that there were special duties for each of us, washing up dishes, guards, etc. Each in turn was allowed two hours escape from the station in the course of the afternoon on what was called 'short leave'. Then it was possible to gaze into the shop windows of Cricklewood.

At one end of the recreation room there was a snooker table; at the other a wireless. The B.B.C. Light Programme and the clicking of snooker balls were the warp and woof upon which for forty-eight hours out of every seventy-two, during the months when there were no fires, the patterns of my fire brigade experiences were woven.

Before I joined the Fire Service one of my fears was that it would be like school or even Oxford, and that I should be made to feel self-conscious at every point where I was not exactly like the others. But I found my mates tolerant. They regarded eccentricity not as a challenge to their own self-esteem, but as the result of circumstances. Living in a world where they were constantly brought into close contact with their own and their neighbour's misfortunes, they attributed all unusual characteristics to some material cause, such as being dropped when one was a baby, or falling off a ladder, or a nagging wife, or having done time in prison. All these things demanded sym-

269

pathy and needed to be tactfully passed over, like the remarks of the fireman who had looked into the window of the undertaker's. Poetry they thought of as a hobby which perhaps brought in a little money, like winning newspaper competitions. The only eccentricity they resented was the ambition to be an officer.

I had a bad moment when someone brought a copy of a magazine to the station in which there was a poem of mine. He showed it to the other men, and they asked me to read it aloud. This request aroused such interest that someone even went so far as to switch off the Light Programme (which, apart from this, was only switched off if it happened to be playing classical music), and although snooker did not stop, those who were not playing gathered round. Feeling rather as I had done on the occasion when I read Blake to the undergraduates who had come to break up my room at Oxford, I simply read the poem out. To my surprise no one sneered. Someone said: 'When you read we can understand it, because you read without stopping between the lines. But when we read it to ourselves we can't understand, because at school we were taught to make a pause at the end of each line.'

There was a man with an inspired expression who used to leave religious tracts on our beds. He disapproved of the other firemen because they swore. He thought they were immoral. One day I asked one of them what they thought of him: 'Oh, he has his hobby, just like you have yours,' was the reply.

Living together in this one recreation room for forty-eight hours on end out of every seventy-two, our lives became like a documentary play, in which each of us played a rôle allotted to him. And yet no one was consciously acting. It just happened that the sub-station brought out the warmth, good nature and humour of the men. It created a character for each of us, based largely on what we really were. This character, which might have been unsympathetic in other circumstances, was made sociable by our tolerance of each other.

The leading personalities were those who had been longest at the station, for legends of their actions in fires had grown around them. Probably there is some foundation in reality for the many metaphors about fire: 'being proved by fire', 'tests of fire', etc. For those men who had been through the worst of the Blitz seemed to have been

270

purged in some way, and reborn into the camaraderie of the sub-station.

There was a man called 'Grannie' who was always grousing in a tone of voice which the others imitated, and frequently became fussed, though I never heard of him losing his temper. He had the reputation of getting lost on fires, and of wandering around in the dark. Once he was noticed by a crew from the sub-station far away up the road where they were working a job, a mad figure, like Edgar on the Heath, dancing about in the dark. This was Grannie, who, wandering away, had been partially electrocuted by a fallen cable. Another time when he had disappeared, he was discovered lost in a basement.

The most striking personality of the station was Bill, a huge, un-gainly Cockney, a primitive giant, with enormous limbs. He had a face with enlarged formless features, a lovely smile and keenly atten-tive eyes. He used to go around the station roaring at anyone he met: 'You worry too much, that's what's wrong with you!'

The climax of the spirit of the sub-station was an event which took place just before my arrival. This was the marriage of Bill to his girl, Flo; and many photographs of the smiling pair standing under an arch of axes formed by our four crews gave an idea of its glory. The marriage was recent enough for Bill to get plenty of teasing: 'How d'yer like being married, Bill? Find it wears yer out a bit?' 'Oh no, we goes quite gently, gently: twice a day, that's all.'

Before the war Bill had been a truck driver. He got a severe internal injury after lifting some heavy object. During the war he developed gastritis, which was an after-effect of this injury, and he nearly died. Very seriously, with great gestures of his heavy hands and an inspired expression of his eyes, he would explain how he had lain on his bed in the hospital ward and felt his soul leave his body. It hovered about the ceiling, floated to a corner of the room, and then returned to his body again.

The other men loved Bill, but felt he needed a bit of explaining with suitable clichés such as that he was a 'rough diamond' who had a 'heart of gold'. What they tried to cover over was a coarseness of an almost animal kind. One day I went into the wash-room to dis-cover him furiously tying a bandage round an unmentionable part of

271

his body. He roared at me: 'She wears a bandage round her now. Why the hell shouldn't I?' and he stumbled out of the room.

Cooky and Locke worked mostly in the kitchen. Pasty-faced little men, both of them with tooth-brush moustaches, they were like as two peas. Always cracking jokes together, they seemed to take no notice of anyone else. They, with another man, called Buckfast, were the leading spirits at the Christmas party which took place soon after my arrival. At Christmas they suddenly became electricians as well as cooks; wiring up the recreation room until they had fixed dozens of little bulbs like sprays, emerging from clusters of paper hangings.

Sometimes Cooky and Locke reminded me of the Assistants in Kafka's novel, *The Castle*. They were inseparably facetious, useful, yet always making everything seem trivial. One evening we all went to a dance at the largest fire station in the neighbourhood – Willesden Central. Cooky and Locke slipped away in the middle of the dance. To absent themselves was against the rules, because even at a dance we might have a call to go to a fire. They tripped out on tip-toe past the sub-officer in charge. Then outside, in the moonlight, their hands on their lips, twirling round one another, they indicated with little nods and signs that they thought they had been seen by the Sub. Arm-in-arm, they tripped back into the garage, saw that the Sub was no longer there, and slipped out again into the darkness.

About two hours later they reappeared at the dance, looking less pasty-faced than usual. Their eyes were shining. When they looked at one another, their vain, yet by no means immodest little faces, were like mirrors for each other's smiles. Seeing me, they became more Kafkaish than ever. One was on each side of me, Cooky saying: 'Oh, is it Mr. Spender, Spender and Spender, whom we have the pleasure of addressing?' Locke rebuked him: 'No, you mean Mr. Marks and Spender, surely?' Then they twirled away, retreating backwards, each with a girl on his arm. But their girls seemed to look as exactly alike as Cooky and Locke did.

During the Willesden dance, I talked a lot to Leading Fireman Abrahams. He was gravely concerned, as always, with what was best for everyone. He was a very orthodox Jew. One night at the sub-station, I woke up to see him at the edge of his bed, praying. He brought special food to the station in a Pyrex dish, which he cooked

272

on the gas stove. The men said that his father was a Rabbi. This may have been true, but it may also have been one of those myths they constantly invented in order to surround our lives with reassuring materialist fables, such as that one of the cooks at a nearby fire station had been a chef at the Savoy, or that at the Training Centre you had to carry a man down five storeys on a ladder, or that 'In Russia it's so cold that when you do a pee, you can break it off in sticks.'

When Leading Fireman Abrahams heard that I was going to be transferred to a station where I could do more of my own work than in our recreation room of snooker and the Light Programme, he smiled in his seriously considerate way and asked: 'What's your work?' 'Poetry.' 'I'm very glad, that will be much better for you, I suppose. I only wish that I had a chance to get on with some of my work, too.' 'What's yours?' 'Property.'

Abe had glossy black curly hair, almost black eyes, a slightly wrinkled forehead. He wore thick spectacles. His face was a generalization of the Jewish, without being Jewish in any striking particular: not idealistic, nor vulgar, nor Oriental, nor masochistic, nor spiritual. The quality it most expressed was a kind of realistic gentleness. He was good at leading men, because he never did so in an egotistic or exhibitionistic way. He treated each man as an individual. Now he told me in his quiet, firm voice that he thought no one else at the sub-station could get on with a crew as well as he. But he was naïvely concerned with the question of his own promotion and would discuss it eagerly, little realizing that this one weakness entirely lost him the sympathy of the men.

One man, Ned, had a secret cause of shame. He could not read or write. For this reason, he was never asked to keep the log. Ned had an energetic face full of expression, particularly in the large brown eyes and the mouth like a tense bow. Because of his illiteracy he was the only man in the station who told the truth about his fire-fighting experiences. The others had almost completely substituted descriptions which they read in the newspapers or heard on the wireless for their own impressions. 'Cor mate, at the docks it was a bleeding inferno,' or 'Just then Jerry let hell loose on us,' were the formulæ into which experiences such as wading through streams of molten

273

sugar, or being stung by a storm of sparks from burning pepper, or inundated with boiling tea at the dock fires, had been reduced. But Ned had read no accounts of his experiences and so he could describe them vividly.

The vainest man in the station was Fadden. He was always talking about his achievements at billiards, dancing, fighting fires. Self-conceit was sculptured in his face and even in his posture. He held his head up at a cocky angle, puffed up his chest like a pigeon, and stuck out his behind. His arms were held with the elbows projecting beyond the small of his back, in a caricature of a guardsman at attention. His nostrils were for ever arched in a smile of blissful self-contentment. All the same, Fad had a battered and spattered appearance, like a wooden soldier dropped in the gutter and covered in sawdust. He wore elaborate belts with many medals fastened on to them, and his trousers had dozens of extra buttons sewn on, so that if his braces burst with pride (as often happened) he could easily attach their ends to other buttons. The men delighted in puncturing his harmless conceit, which provided the station with its best comedy.

One day Fadden returned to the station after short leave, swelling with pride because he had bought a dog-fish, which was covered with spots. He was as pleased as if he had caught it, and he kept it for two days in the food safe in order to show it to us from time to time. Then it began to stink, so he asked Cooky to prepare it for supper.

Protesting violently, Cooky took it into the kitchen. Then, while we were having supper, he came into the room, and called: 'Fadden, put on yer f—— spurs, and come and fetch yer b—— fish!' Fadden went pale and started sweating with anxiety. 'D'yer really think it's dingerous?' he asked in his strong Cockney: ''Ad I better not eat it?' 'Don't eat it, Fad,' several firemen shouted out, 'it stinks the bleeding place out.' 'Cor blimey,' said Fadden, 'it cost me one and six at the market. What a bleeding wiste.' 'Orl right then, eat it. It's your funeral, not ours.' 'Orl roight, I will. 'Ow d'yer think it looks? D'yer think it looks good?' 'Looks good? Whoi it looks as if it's caught measles. It's covered with bleeding spots.' 'Well, that kind of fish's got them spots.' Fadden hitched up his trousers, smiled with a return of his old self-confidence, and sat down to his fish. Then he went pale again. 'Cor, it do smell,' he said, 'no mistiking it.' 'Tell yer what,'
274

someone said. 'Go and get the cat. Cats always know. If a fish ain't good they won't touch it. Go and get Nigger.' Nigger was fetched. Everyone watched while Nigger sniffed at the fish and then turned away. Fadden was disgusted and took the fish out to the dustbin. The others experienced a sense of deep atavistic exaltation that the cat had shown its powers of divination.

'Togger' was a large, beefy and horsey man who always came to the station on his leave days wearing loud check tweeds. He was boozy, sentimental and generous. He addressed everyone as 'old boy' in an exaggerated county accent, and was helpful to the point where aid risked becoming officious. His life was centred round his bull-dog, who also was the occasion of his main grievance. This was his discovery that the only flat where he could keep his dog was let by a landlord who stole everything from him, including his trousers.

Our chief comedian was Buckfast, a 'little Titch' type of Cockney. Everything about him suggested a 'thumbs up' attitude, including the way his bottom stuck out (in this respect he formed a kind of choric symmetry with Busby). He had the white-faced Cockney pathos; and the bunk room shook at night with his coughing.

All these men, and a few others, were in charge of the sub-officer, Alfie, aged sixty-five. I never saw Alfie without his having a panicked, hustled look on his sad fat face, which should have been so round and jolly. There is something particularly distressing about a flustered fat man. Alfie lived in unceasing terror of getting into trouble with his younger, more efficient, jumped-up superiors, who had been promoted since the war, and were for ever introducing new rules into the Service. Alfie referred to his immediate superior, the Divisional Officer at Willesden, as ''Im'. 'If 'E comes along, boys, we'll all be for it,' he told us every morning at parade after breakfast.

Having been an ordinary fireman for forty years, poor Alfie could not get used to giving, and not just taking, orders. In his embarrassment, either he treated us as men in positions equal to his own, asking us to do things which he secretly would have preferred to do himself, or else he groused at us, fortifying his will with occasional invocations of ''Im'. 'It isn't me who's asking you to do this. I wouldn't, mite. It's nothing ter do with me. It's orders come down from 'Im. If you don't get on with it, it's me what'll get the blime. So 'urry up and get on with it, do.' 'Now one of you fellows didn't report this afternoon. They'll come down on yer for that. Follow my advice and do what I say, otherwise you'll find yerself on a charge, sooner or later. And please to treat me with a little respect when I tells yer to do something. Not so much of the ''Alfie this'' and the ''Alfie that'', either. . . . If you must call me something, call me Sub.' 'Not so much of the Alfie,' became a joke with us.

The old hands resented Alfie. They lived in a narrow world bounded by Divisional Headquarters at Willesden, and they therefore took him seriously, when to me he seemed merely pathetic. They said that he was 'two-faced' and up to a point this was certainly true. He showed it in his attitude to ''Im', who would certainly not have cared to be spoken of as Alfie spoke. In the station Alfie sometimes complained about one man to another one. Also, he could be disagreeable. But it struck me as particularly unfair that the men resented his 'putting the bells down' during the night or when we were at meals. 'That's just the sort of thing the old sod would do,' they grumbled, with real vindictiveness, as we rushed to our posts. Their resentment seemed to me as profoundly irresponsible as their dislike of Abrahams because he wished for promotion. Surely, I sometimes protested, the whole point of an alarm exercise was that it should not be at a time to suit everyone's convenience. Poor Alfie, situated between the devil of ''Im' and the deep sea of us, would certainly have been 'for it' from Divisional Headquarters if he had only put the bells down when we were already dressed for parade.

Sometimes men were really rude to Alfie. The oldest man in the sub-station, apart from himself, was Pop, a wavering, slightly sinister old boy who wore a row of medal ribbons supposedly from the last war. Old Pop was distrusted, though tolerated, and played little part in the life of the station. One evening Alfie rebuked him for being in the kitchen eating sausages when he should have been on guard. Instead of getting up and going on duty, Old Pop started shouting: 'I'm not taking orders from you, Alfie, nor from anyone else round here. I've been on guards in my time which would teach you something. There isn't any guard here compared with what I'm accustomed to.' Alfie went very red and looked old and helpless. He just

276

made flapping gestures with his arms as though they were fins, and said nothing.

Alfie could never rest. He was always on the go and did the most menial occupations. All the morning he fussed around the recreation room, armed with dust-pan and broom, sweeping out the corners and the large areas under the bunks which we had neglected. As often as not he would grumble because we hadn't swept there already. This was part of Alfie bitterly resented 'two-facedness'. No one liked an officer who demeaned himself. The men pointed out that if he did so it was partly in order to spy out our negligencies, and partly because his nature was so menial that he was unhappy without dust-pan and brush.

The climax of my weeks at the sub-station was the Christmas party. Buckfast worked like a gnome, darting about the recreation room, adorning the walls with cardboard trellises, and the ceiling with spokes of wrinkly paper meeting in hubs of rosettes. The windows were covered over with dark-blue paper – colour of night – on to which silver stars and a golden sun and yellow horned moon were stuck. The frames were draped with bright-orange paper curtains. Being by profession a signwriter, Buckfast concentrated the whole of his talent on producing a sign of signs, A MERRY CHRISTMAS FOR ALL, in flourishing letters surrounded by bright silver serifs. Unfortunately after this effort he sprained his leg, and only managed to hobble into the station for the Christmas party.

For nearly two weeks, daylight was shut out of the recreation room, and we stumbled about in the dim light of purple, red and orange fairy bulbs, fixed by Cooky and Locke, to the accompaniment of hammering, louder even than snooker and the Light Programme. A bar, also stuck over with frills of coloured paper, was being erected at one end of the room. The stove was moved from one end of the room to the other, painted an aluminium colour, and a spotlight was fixed near it.

When all had been completed, I realized that the recreation room was now a classic example of something which the writers of the Left had spent so much time discussing during the 1930's: proletarian art, folk art even. This room, with its tawdry paper streamers, its festoons of coloured bulbs looking like bunches of bilious grapes, its papered-over windows pasted with artificial moon and stars, its ugly stove transformed into a gleaming silver object, above all its impassioned heat, daylightlessness and airlessness, was the expression of a will to create a womb of flesh-coloured crinkly paper. It could have been moved piece by piece and erected in a museum, as a perfect specimen of the people's taste in 1942.

The proceeds of a station sweepstake, amounting to forty or fifty pounds, were spent on food and drink for Christmas and Boxing Day. We bought two turkeys and made thirty-four Christmas puddings, enough not only for both parties, but for each man to have a pudding to take home.

The Christmas party started at three in the afternoon and continued till midnight. Several groups of wives, sisters and aunts arrived in the afternoon and left early, though there were hiatuses with no guest present at this non-stop party.

Conviviality began seriously at about eight in the evening, though at first it was very slow. The guests sat in rows on chairs at each side of the room. They ate sandwiches in silence, unbroken except for munching noises. By about ten, things had warmed up a little, owing to titanic efforts by Bill, who led a dance in which everyone trooped in single file around the room. Then two or three guests sang sentimental songs. Then Fadden and a man called Ginger sang selections from their repertoire of those amorphous, tuneless, grating and sawing songs which we have all heard street singers sing at corners and against railings through our childhoods. Ned then broke into a wild and violent step dance. Finally, Alfie was persuaded to do a *pas à deux* with Ned.

The party ended with speeches from Alfie and the Leading Firemen. Alfie began: 'I've got a fine lot of boys, a finer lot you won't see nowhere. I'd tell that to 'Im, honest I would. I'm proud of them. Honest, I am . . .' At this point he was interrupted with cries of 'Tell us the old, old story.'

A leading fireman made a sententious speech on the lines of: now you've enjoyed yourselves: tomorrow we get on with the job.

After this there were many more speeches about 'the job'. The evening ended with Fadden and Ginger having a row because each wanted to sing.

*   *   *   *   *

I was moved to a station at Maresfield Gardens in Hampstead. As I now lived next door to the station it was often possible to escape home. Thus I got more of my work done than at the sub-station. This station was distinguished by the presence of several remarkable men: amongst them William Sansom, the writer, who had arranged for me to be transferred there; Fernando Henriques, a Jamaican of vitality and considerable intelligence; and one or two musicians from London orchestras. The officer-in-charge was, like many London firemen, an old sea-dog, both bluff and sly, giving the impression of roaring round the station all day long, but really exercising a good deal of diplomacy. He treated me with tolerance.

But agreeable as was the atmosphere of Maresfield Gardens, it was cliquey, and there was little spirit of unity in the station. I never enjoyed any place in the Fire Service so much as Cricklewood. In fact, I now think that chance had created there a kind of existence which had parallels with the ideal uncelibate monastic life Rabelais dreamed of in his account of the Abbey of Thélème. Under the rule of Alfie, we can scarcely be said to have lived under orders, so we were almost like the Thélèmites, of whom Rabelais wrote: 'In all their rule, and strictest tie of their order, there was but this one clause to be observed, DO WHAT THOU WILT.' And though we were not nobly born, we observed a natural restraint and discipline, which grew from our loyalty to one another, and illustrated Rabelais's faith that those who are 'conversant in honest companies, have naturally an instinct and spurre that prompteth them unto virtuous actions, and withdraws them from vice'.

In April 1941 I had married Natasha Litvin, the pianist. We had met earlier in the war, at the time of the Blitz. After our marriage we enjoyed a few weeks of quiet before my call-up, in the house of friends at Wittersham in Kent. Here, both of us working, we got to understand one another and laid the foundations of our marriage. When we were first married, I suffered from an exacerbated sense of guilt arising from the break-down of the relationships I have described in these pages. I was for ever attaching blame either to others or myself for what I regarded as failures. One day, Natasha said to me: 'From now on there is no question of blame. There is only us,' and this was the faith, the research for a unity which was ourselves belonging to one another, on which our marriage was founded.

While I was at the sub-station, and at the Training Centre, we lived in the Cricklewood house where Bertha and Ella had retired after Ella's marriage. Natasha's piano almost filled the living-room, and my books and papers flooded the rest of the tiny house. Bertha and Ella looked after us with the same devotion as they had shown my family at Frognal. This was a strange return to childhood in such different circumstances after many years. Coming home from the Training Centre, where sometimes, as when I had to study the effects of poison gas, I was much distressed, was almost like returning from schools where I had been miserable twenty years previously. Much of Berthella's furniture had been our own at Frognal, for we had given them enough things for the furnishing of their little home. So the small house at Cricklewood, which was almost next door to the great Rolls-Royce factory, seemed like a raft bearing a few belongings from the shipwreck of our world.

Berthella were changed also. Bertha was quiet and much milder. Only in flashes did she become 'the old Bertha'.

Ella was the same patient, gentle person as before, seeming to carry the burdens of others as she went quietly about her tasks, mistress of her own house. But she carried a new and worse burden than any of the previous ones: the consciousness of the fatal heart ailment from which she could not recover.

Ella was a miracle of a kind in which few sophisticated people today appear to believe: she was a really good person. Dickens and Balzac describe such unaccountably good and pure characters: with the result that modern critics, versed more in psychological theory than experience of life, blame them for inventing impossible human beings. They are charged with describing perfection instead of analysing the conflicts which make a 'character' convincing. Yet in Ella there appeared to be no conflict. In the twenty years I knew her, I never heard her make a spiteful remark, or fail in any sacrifice demanded of her. Nor did she draw attention to her own virtues or expect any reward. If she ever showed resentment it was only of real injuries done, for she had the courage to show her mind.

True goodness is based on abnegation and that is why today, when repression is often spoken of as though it were worse than the passion repressed, we resent the idea that there are people who are simply good. We are probably right to suspect that people who gain fame by their virtues satisfy a secret lust for power. Yet meek, humble, obscure goodness, based on renunciation, and obtaining little or no recognition or reward, cannot be explained away like this. Ella was one of the meek. Her faults – that she was narrow in her views, and that sometimes her appeals to my better nature took the form of her asking, 'Would you like Sir John Stavridi* to see you doing that, sugar?' – were the defects of her virtues.

At Berthella's we had a Christmas luncheon which was a family reunion, toasted by Frank, Ella's postman husband. My brother Michael was there in the uniform of Flight Lieutenant in the R.A.F. He was an expert in using a machine which, by a method of projecting images, transformed photographs taken from the air into maps which were used for bombing. Humphrey and Christine were there, too. He was in the Army – acting at this time as a photographer – and Christine, who had become a Roman Catholic, was in some Ministry. Everyone conformed to type. The war was especially difficult for Michael, because his insights into the utter incompetence of his superiors got him into situations in which he was for ever being demoted or promoted, so that his war was like a game of Snakes and Ladders, and I never knew whether he was at the top of an official ladder on account of his outstanding efficiency, or had been thrown to the bottom for his impertinence. Humphrey was always having the bad luck implicit in the tame existence of a younger brother. Sent to photograph Miss Ellen Wilkinson on a demonstration of a new glider, the glider fell down, and Miss Wilkinson and he were injured. Returning on a routine air trip from Germany at the end of the war, he got caught in a thick English fog, and after circling round for hours, landed on a beam when all but the last drop of petrol was exhausted. Christine was always in an official muddle. As for me, the air raids on London stopped in the same week that I joined the Fire Service, and the first buzz bomb fell in 1944, two hours after I had left it.

For Michael the war was a terrible justification of his lifelong horror at inefficiency. He saw effort wasted, actions bungled, lives

* My Godfather.

281

thrown away. In his own work he was shocked by the way in which businessmen, selling material to the R.A.F., obtained high-ranking positions from which they interfered with technicians and those who fought. Michael had a feeling almost of reverence for the pilots who made photographs of the German defences for him, and he had an almost superstitious awe of aeroplanes, 'machines so delicate that they can't help behaving oddly'. Just as he respected the beliefs of Tibetan monks whom he had met on the Everest expedition or of the Eskimo in Greenland, so he was fascinated by the belief of certain pilots in 'gremlins'.

Michael saw beyond the waste and incompetence of administration to the folly of bombing which became progressively more and more a destruction of the basis of the post-war world. Bending over his photographs which showed the immense damage done to Europe by the policy called 'saturation bombing', he saw that the methods of war could lead to the end of European civilization. 'The bombing of Hamburg,' he said in his embarrassed, stifled voice, 'cannot be justi-fied as necessary to the victory. It's the destruction, not just of Germany, but of an essential part of Europe.'

Michael died in an aeroplane accident just after the war. He was buried at München-Gladbach.

My grandmother, at her immense age (she is a year older than Bernard Shaw) was evacuated to an hotel near Oxford, where, on a greatly reduced scale, she lived much the same life as in London, often cleaning out her own room, and in winter distressing everyone by her unwillingness to have a fire. Once, on a bitterly cold winter's day I went to visit her. She was at the bus stop waiting for me in the snow, when I arrived. We walked to the hotel, but turned back when we had got there, to spend half an hour fruitlessly searching in the snow by the path on which we had come, for one of her mittens, which she had let fall. Arrived in her unheated room, she surprised me by inquiring whether I would like a cup of tea. 'Oh, I'm so glad,' she said to my eager assent, 'I was afraid it would be wasted. You see it was brought to me early this morning and I couldn't drink it.' She reached to a cupboard in which a cup of almost frozen tea was waiting, and asked me whether I would also care for a bun. Cautious now, I replied that I was not hungry.

Then she started talking about the Schusters, asserting indignantly that one of my cousins, who had given me some information, was totally mistaken. Her revelations were like a pure stream of family truth which she alone knew, and I thought how her life led back into fountain-heads and origins far purer than my feckless, dispersed and rather dissipated generation, with our special brand of self-complacency, based on our pride that we had liberated ourselves from many past prejudices and inhibitions. I remembered now how, when I was nine, I had been taken to see my great-grandfather, Sir Hermann Weber, who had come from the Rhineland when he was a youth, in order to live in the land of Shakespeare's tongue. He had a serene, clear, smiling and gracious expression, and he showed me his collection of Greek coins – barley and Minervas embossed on thick, roughed rounds of gold – beautiful objects, some of them now in the Hermann Weber Collection in the British Museum. Then he gave me a shining, new-minted half-crown piece. On November the eleventh, 1918, Armistice Day, he returned home from the five-mile walk which he took every morning, and died peacefully, on that day of peace, sitting in his chair. There seemed something strangely fitting about this death, which, as it were, coincided with the striking of the hour which ended an epoch, as though that older generation of purity and faith of my ancestors, embodied in him, turned quietly to their graves, away from the disintegration of the years which followed. And now I looked back to it as to a crystal stream, and with a sense of pure loss.

*   *   *   *   *

Often, during an air raid on London in 1940, I would hear a bomber diving downwards with a roar, as though its trajectory described a valley in the mountain-high air inhabited by aircraft. Then I would reassure myself by imagining that, in the whole area of the county of London, there were no more houses, but that the bomber was gyring and diving over an empty plain covered in darkness. This picture was both reassuring and exact: for it fixed my attention on my own smallness as a target compared with the immensity of London. And this was the reality. Only my fears were exposed.

If I thought of London as the London of my mind, and not as a geographical expanse, I only imagined places I knew and whose names occurred to me: Oxford Street, Piccadilly, St. Paul's, Liverpool Street, Kensington, Paddington, Maida Vale, Hampstead, and so forth. And even these places were represented in my mind only by the names of a few familiar features, churches, streets and squares, and not by all the other streets and the innumerable buildings which I did not know.

Although the raids stopped, or happened only at rare intervals, this picture of the aeroplane over the huge plain with the people concealed in crevices, can be enlarged to a vision of the new phase of domination and threat by machine-power politics, which the world had now entered and which did not end with the peace. The aeroplane filled ever-widening circles in the minds of people beneath it; but the pilot and even the officers who commanded him at bases, their masters in governments and the vanquished and victors of the war, were diminished, until it seemed that they no longer had wills of their own, but were automata controlled by the mechanism of war.

It was a sign of this submission of human beings to the mechanical forces they had called into being and put into motion against one another that I was no longer interested in the personality of Hitler, since, having begun the war, he had not the power to make it stop.

Everyone had shrunk in his own mind as well as in the minds of his fellow-beings, because his attention was diverted to events dwarfing individuals. These events could only lead to more battles and a victory catastrophic for the winning, as for the losing side. Personal misfortunes seemed of minor importance compared with the universal nature of the disaster overtaking civilization. So that in the summer of 1940, when invasion seemed imminent, a friend could say to me: 'Within six weeks from now, if I blow out my brains and they spatter all over the carpet, in my own home and with my family in the room, no one will think it worth noticing.'

We lived in a trance-like condition in which, from our fixed positions in our island-fortress-prison, we witnessed, as in a dream, not only armies, but whole populations controlled by the magnetic force of power. Even in the minds of those who knew them well, France and other continental countries had become mental concepts only, areas in our minds where incredible things happened; there, puppet

284

dictators transmitted orders received from Germany, and Germany, a vast arsenal of mechanical power, added to its resources the industries of other nations and the slave labour of their peoples. Even today, *France under the Occupation* remains to me an idea only, to which I can attach little reality, a hallucinated vision of folly, betrayal, and despairing courage. So that, if some French friend begins to speak of his life during those years, I stare at him as though expecting to see him change into a different person.

During these months, a most poignant event, the suicide of Virginia Woolf, was observed by me as through a thick pane of glass, seen very clearly, but all sound shut out: the personal tragedy seen through the vast transparent impersonal one.

For the time being, the only hope was that the current of power should be reversed and turned back on those who had first employed it: that the pendulum of the bombers, swinging over us, should swing back again over Germany. Yet to admit this was an admission of spiritual defeat: for it was to say that hope lay in power, in opposing despair with despair. We said this, with the result that we are still saying it. All this has implied the surrender of the only true hope for civilization – the conviction of the individual that his inner life can affect outward events and that, whether or not he does so, he is responsible for them.

From now on, the fate of individuals was more and more controlled by a public fate which itself seemed beyond control. For control implies not merely putting a machinery into motion, but also being able to make it stop: modern war is a machine easy to make start, but it can only be stopped at the moment when it has destroyed or been destroyed by another war machine. Control means being able to relate a programme of action to the results of that action. Now we had arrived at a stage when a large part of the resources of great nations were poured into programmes of which no one could foresee the results. All this was only leading to subsequent plans for making atomic and hydrogen bombs to defend East against West or West against East in a meaningless struggle between potential ashes to gain a world of ashes. For, in the course of the struggle, the vast 'machinery of production', together with its capitalist or proletarian owners, and all the sacred theories of whichever class, would be as

285

outmoded as its own ruins, like the civilization and theories of Babylonian astrologers.

That part of living which was devoted to spiritual and personal values, became a marginal activity in society, and for individuals a side-line, unless they happened to be old, sick, or socially unreliable. The most serious result was the effect on the minds of individuals, particularly the young, who found themselves in a world where no action of theirs, and nothing they created or thought, could alter the course of events. Here, though, on the level of thought and spiritual life, was the real challenge. For it is intolerable that men who, with their minds, have invented machines of destruction, and in their policies made themselves the half-slaves of these machines, should not be able to unthink what is a product of their intellects.

*   *   *   *   *

Within this situation of a world hypnotized by power, there were, none the less, two movements which expressed a faith in human values.

Firstly, there was a revival of interest in the arts. This arose spontaneously and simply, because people felt that music, the ballet, poetry and painting were concerned with a seriousness of living and dying with which they themselves had suddenly been confronted. The audiences at the midday concerts of the National Gallery, or at the recitals of music and ballet in provincial towns and at factories, sat with a rapt attention as though they were listening for some message from the artist, who, though perhaps he had lived in other times, was close to the same realities as themselves – and to the pressing need to affirm faith and joy within them. There was something deeply touching about this interest in the arts; it was one of the few things which can still make me regret the war.

The affirmation of these timeless qualities was the only answer of human personality to war. In a word, it was – survival. It answered that side of humanity which had produced the war with the indestructability of this other side – human love.

Lest it be objected that war is infinitely destructive and human love infinitely destructible, I repeat what I have said before: the inner life of man must create his outward circumstances. Perverted love, in the

286

form of nationalism, or class solidarity (what is called 'Communist love'), produce the forces of destruction in our time. Although we should support every outward movement for attaining peace and social improvement, it is only within the inner life that man can will himself to be a coherent whole and not a part set against another part.

One day, at a midday concert in the National Gallery, I listened to the playing of an early Beethoven Quartet (Opus 18, No. 1, I think). In the middle of the minuet there was a tremendous explosion. A delayed-action bomb had gone off in Trafalgar Square. In the trio of the minuet which they were playing, the musicians did not lift the bows from their strings. A few of the audience, who had been listening with heads bowed, straightened themselves for an instant and then resumed their posture.

*   *   *   *   *

The writers who surmounted this situation of the world victimized by its own power, were those who best resisted the imprisoning pre-occupation of this age with its own time. They could do this either because, like T. S. Eliot, they had devoted themselves to the task of relating their time to other times, or because they were fertile ana-chronisms, the survival-heroes of a period of luxuriant, cultivated, well-watered individualists, having an increasing worth for our age, as they grew more rare.

The gravest weakness of the writers of what I have here called the Divided Generation was that they were time-bound. They had taken a bet that a world order of peace and social justice would emerge in their time, just as Wordsworth, Coleridge and Shelley had done in their day. They lost, as the Romantics had done, and were forced to spend their next phase searching for an attitude which would be inde-pendent of external events.

T. S. Eliot was the least time-bound of contemporaries. He had always regarded the tradition as the co-existence of the past with the present, like places geographically separated from one another co-existing in place. To him the traditionalist was not the remote heir of a disintegrated inheritance, but a missionary travelling from a civi-lized area – the past – into a fragmentary and incoherent one – the present. His mission was to interpret the integrated past within the fragmentary present, relating himself to both.

The corollary of this general view of co-existent past and present with a tradition where 'existing monuments forming an ideal order' . . . were . . . 'modified by the introduction of the new (the really new) work of art among them,'* was belief in the immortality of the soul. For the living, as for the dead, the present was an episode, a beginning even, and not the edge of time it appears to contemporaries in any age.

Eliot's writing did not (as some critics have asserted) offer an 'escape' into the past from the problems of the present. It confronted the breakdown of present values with past order in the mind of the responsive reader. His work might, indeed, be said to have two aspects: the first, culminating in *The Waste Land*, shows us how deeply we are involved, since we are products of our civilization, in the fragmentariness of our time: the second, culminating in the *Four Quartets*, shows how we are involved in eternity and therefore free from it.

His lesson to a generation unable to put the instruments of power to constructive uses, was to show that, however much the individual might be committed to social tasks, he belonged to an eternal order of events where he was not product and victim of his time.

Edith Sitwell, another poet who now emerged with great force, had something of the time-defeating quality of Yeats: that is to say, a power of invoking a massive and colourful historic past, whether of Egypt, Byzantium, early Christian mysticism, or the Elizabethans. She wrote in long lines, whose slow metric was like a harvesting pulsation under an imagery of mature and golden ripeness. Her fervid poetry, while attaining a wide and beautiful objectivity, yet obviously derived from a profoundly personal existence.

Besides making a great impression during the war years by a poetry which projected the rather isolated qualities of her early writing into an experience deeply shared by her contemporaries, she impressed all who met her or heard her read her poems by her presence, which was that of one of the survivors of a better and richer age.

At this time, my wife and I got to know her well. Her features

* *Tradition and the Individual Talent.*

288

seemed carved as though out of alabaster, in which were cut narrowly watchful eyes, amused, kind, cold, sad, or even at moments incisively shrewd. She wore magnificent dresses and large jewellery – an ivory cross, or jade pendant, or gold set with large and beautiful stones as in a bishop's mitre or cross. In her appearance, as in her poetry, she was triumphantly herself, yet endlessly reaching beyond herself into other people and other times.

We learned to appreciate the sensitive sympathy of Edith Sitwell. Her own well-being was bound up with that of her friends. After experiencing her generosity and sympathy, I was not surprised to learn that she had given up years of her life to nursing a sick friend.

A more familiar aspect of Dr. Edith Sitwell was her humour, often revealed in repartee. One day, after a meeting of some gathering at which she had read her poems, a woman came up to her and said: 'Miss Sitwell, I just want to tell you that I *quite* enjoyed your last book of poems.' Edith Sitwell looked at her remotely, and then, when she was about to go on, interrupted: 'Now please don't say any more. You mustn't spoil me. It wouldn't be good for me to be spoiled.' On another occasion, a correspondent wrote to say that she had a matter of the greatest urgency to communicate to her and her brothers. She had seen a ghost which, to judge from its bewigged eighteenth-century appearance, must be that of one of the Sacheverells. She would be glad to discuss the matter with Edith Sitwell at the earliest opportunity. Dr. Sitwell wrote replying that on receiving Miss X's letter she had immediately got in touch with her brother, Sir Osbert. She and her brother agreed that the ghost must indeed be that of one of the Sacheverells, whom they recognized very well from the description. They joined, though, in begging their correspondent never to mention the matter again as it was extremely painful to them both. As a postscript she added: 'The ghost brings extreme misfortune to whomever sees it.'

One other poet, less often mentioned than these, whose work gained in strength during these years, was Edwin Muir. An unassuming writer, usually writing in familiar metres, Muir might not, at a first glance, seem to command great attention. But in his poetry there is a steady development of certain symbols – the maze, heraldry, the tower, and images derived from Variations on a Time Theme. At different periods these images, objects of his daily contemplation, have a packed force in his work. Muir was perhaps the only contemporary British writer upon whom Franz Kafka (whose work he and his wife, Willa Muir – herself a talented writer – had translated) was a fruitful influence which did not deteriorate rapidly into affectations of style and thought. Indeed, Muir's poetry has something of the obsessive search into the ramifications of an object, which is Kafka's true genius. Muir was also the author of an autobiography called *The Story and the Fable*, of its kind a minor classic.

During these years I had occasionally visited Muir. To see him in his Hampstead home, or later at Saint Andrews, Edinburgh, Prague or Rome, where successively he worked, was to add gratefully to my appreciation of him, without feeling that the years between these journeys were an interruption to our steadily growing friendship. On each occasion I was struck by the integrity of purpose in his work and life, which made him seem a pilgrim from place to place rather than a wanderer like myself. Indeed, he had the purpose which converted a life of shifting jobs into a spiritual pilgrimage. At each place he would tell me of something there which had particularly struck him, and which added to his store of symbols. So that when, in 1950, I visited him in Rome, his work as head of the British Institute there had provided him with the climatic symbol which he witnessed 'everywhere in Rome', of Resurrection.

Nothing, indeed, could be more different than the world of the 1930's, which I have defined here as the period of Intervention and Non-intervention, from that of the rising 1940's. The 1930's saw the last of the idea that the individual, accepting his responsibilities, could alter the history of the time. From now on, the individual could only conform to or protest against events which were outside his control.

The 1930's, which seemed so revolutionary, were in reality the end of a Liberal phase of history. They offered Liberal individualists their last chance to attach Liberal democracy to a people's cause: specifically, to the cause of Spanish democracy. The total armament of the civilized world drowned all individual efforts in a rising flood of mechanized power.

There were a few people who realized what was happening. One

290

was H. G. Wells. After the explosion of the atomic bomb at Hiroshima, Wells, who was then dying, wrote an article in which he declared that he no longer believed in any of the progressive causes to which he had devoted his life. He had abandoned his belief in the inevitability of progress. The world, he declared, had suddenly become very strange, as though events were happening outside history. There was the feeling that anything might happen or that everything might come to an end.

At this time, I met the poet David Gascoyne, who was then in a highly nervous condition, with whom I had a conversation which made the same strange impression on me as Wells's article. Gascoyne said – rather wildly perhaps – that he was convinced that with the falling of the atomic bomb an event had taken place within human consciousness. It was as though the barriers which enclosed people's minds had been broken down and they were aware of living within a situation so overwhelming that they shared a single consciousness.

In other words, the characteristic of the 1930's was that a few people – of whom the members of the International Brigade were the outstanding examples – were aware of an encroaching situation of the domination of the world by power politics, amid the blindness of the majority. In the 1940's most people were aware of a situation, within which the few felt almost powerless. The tragedy of the 1930's was the blindness of the many; the tragedy of the 1940's the ineffectiveness of the few. But perhaps hope lies in a different direction from that in which we have been accustomed to look.

It may be in precisely that which is the cause of discouragement: the awareness of many people of a serious situation only to be solved by meeting almost insuperable difficulties.

Complaints that the atmosphere of the present post-war period is less optimistic than that of the years which followed 1918 mean little, except that today there are fewer illusions. This is to the good, because it was widespread illusions after the First World War which contributed to making the problems of the peace incapable of being solved.

Today, there is more realization of problems than there is faith in solutions. Discouraging as this may seem, it means that if and when solutions are found, the public is prepared to pay a drastic price for

291

them. After the previous war, people expected much of the League of Nations, but were not prepared to abandon national sovereignty. This time, a great many everywhere are prepared to sacrifice a great deal of nationhood and possessions which they formerly clung to, but they do not believe in the United Nations. The most important condition of change – a widespread realism – has been achieved.

*   *   *   *   *

In October 1939, Cyril Connolly, Peter Watson and I planned the review *Horizon*, the first number of which appeared in January 1940. During the summer of 1940, the staff of *Horizon* was, for a few weeks, evacuated to Thurlstone in Devonshire. There, on that beautiful coast (near Salcombe, where I had spent many summer holidays of my boyhood), we received letters from pilots fighting in the Battle of Britain, often saying that they felt that so long as *Horizon* continued they had a cause to fight for.

Such letters could only make us feel unworthy and ashamed. Yet for these young men, *Horizon*, *New Writing*, and one or two other literary reviews, were the means whereby they felt that they, as well as we, survived the war. One such was Gully Mason, who sent us an article describing the life of a miner. We accepted it, and then he wrote asking whether he could come to see us. When he did so, he explained with some embarrassment that perhaps we might be wrong to think of his article as proletarian writing, since, although he worked as a miner, his father owned the mine. Gully Mason was famous for his feats in swimming rivers, climbing, and so forth. He was an example of what was most promising in his generation: a combination of athleticism with a sensitive feeling for the arts. He died in the Battle of Britain. Another pilot, whose gentleness and courtesy impressed me, was Timothy Corsellis. Corsellis was a fighter pilot, who protested, when he was switched to bombing, on the grounds that he wished only to fight against destruction, not to destroy. He was directed to pilot planes across the Atlantic, which he continued to do until he died in an accident. At this time, I was trying to get work in Civil Defence, and Corsellis, who had been an air
292

raid warden for a few weeks, spent a day taking me to his old head-quarters.

All I remember of that day was meeting Corsellis in a bar off Piccadilly where he sat talking to a platinum blonde, and then our bus ride to a large A.R.P. headquarters beyond Hammersmith, where I was introduced to officials. Some years later, I came upon a poem by him addressed to myself, in an anthology of war poets, in which he described our meeting. It concluded with the words: 'Now I see you much as I am.' I was moved by reading this, and I have in my note-books numerous sketches for a poem in which I endeavoured to thank Corsellis. But I never succeeded in writing anything which seemed adequate.

Another visitor to *Horizon* was the famous young pilot, Richard Hillary, whose face was terribly injured by burning. Then there was the Canadian W. J. Sipprell, with a pale, oval face and dark brown eyes, looking strangely like an acolyte in an El Greco painting; and Michael Jones, killed in an accident while training, who stayed with me during one of the worst nights of the Blitz. He went out into the East End of London during the heavy bombing, and returning with shining eyes described the streets full of glass like heaped-up ice, the fires making a great sunset beyond the silhouette of St. Paul's, the East End houses collapsed like playing cards. If I tried to com-memorate some of these men in poems, it was because poetry was exactly what I had in common with them, and it was this that they came to me for. It is right to say that the service they required of my generation was that we should create.

The strength of *Horizon* lay not in its having any defined cultural or political policy, but in the vitality and idiosyncrasy of the editor, Cyril Connolly. I, who started out with concern for planning post-war Britain, defending democracy, encouraging young writers, and so forth, was disconcerted to find myself with an editor who showed little sense of responsibility about these things. His editorial Com-ments were brilliant, wayward, inconsistent, sometimes petulant. But he wrote in a style which was at times like a voice speaking Latin words of honey, and when (for instance) he described a sea anenome on a rock seen through distorting planes of tugging tides, I saw the serious point of what was delightful and absurd about him at Thurlstone: his afternoon setting out, dressed in jersey and shorts, carrying bucket, net and spade, for the rock-and-sand pools along the beach at low tide, into which he would stare, while prodding at the sandy pond-floor with his net. In describing these expeditions, Connolly was a superb mimic. He could *be* a prawn, crab or lobster hiding in the crevice of a rock, as he described his attempts to catch one. He is, I think, the best living parodist, a judgment with which readers of *The Condemned Playground* will probably concur. For him parody is a spontaneous and immediate response bubbling with deceptive amiability from his lips twenty times a day. In the evenings at Thurlstone we would listen to the six o'clock news. In their refined B.B.C. accents, the announcers would cite statements of pilots. 'We gave' (*long pause*) 'Jerry' (*long pause, followed by the next three words spoken very quickly*) 'a jolly good' (*long pause*) 'Pranging'. As soon as the news was switched off, Connolly would continue in an imitation of the B.B.C. announcer's accents an account of his conflict with a prawn.

From Thurlstone I sometimes bicycled to Salcombe, where I would rent a boat for the afternoon. I rowed out of the harbour, eastwards beyond Start Point about a mile out to sea, exactly opposite a place on shore where a stone wall divided the fields, and there I used to row in a wide circle, trailing for fish. This being alone in a boat on a fine summer day, when the sun's rays, absorbed by the sea, surrounded me like a million little green flames within the transparent stone of the afternoon, was a link between my boyhood experiences on the same patch of sea and the peace and solitude of the fires in my few fire-fighting experiences which I shall later describe. Most of the fish I caught were pollock, with occasional mackerel and bass. Connolly, who was a gourmet, particularly disliked pollock, which he called 'poor man's cod'.

In *Horizon*, Connolly's policy was to publish what he liked. This included, in the early numbers particularly, the work of several new young poets: among them, Laurie Lee, W. R. Rodgers, Adam Drinan, Francis Scarfe, and several others, some of whom became well known afterwards. But to prefer the young to the old, or to support a movement, or follow a party, was not *Horizon's* function. Although Connolly was inconsistent, being energetic, enthusiastic, indolent, interested and bored by turns, he held his own views passionately and, on the whole, with judgment; and he faced adverse criticism with an equanimity which astonished me, as I knew him (in personal relationships, at any rate) to care greatly whether he was or wasn't liked. There were days when, if I showed him a poem by some poet whom I thought should be encouraged, he handed it back saying: 'Are you certain that anyone will want to read it in twenty years' time?' On other occasions he seemed to show a more relaxed standard. The point is, though, that *Horizon* was always his own. As an editor he was like a cook, producing with each number a new dish with a new flavour. Sometimes the readers objected, finding it too light, too sweet, too lumpy, or too stodgy, but he had somehow created in them a need to taste more. Or, to change the metaphor, he carried on a kind of editorial flirtation with his readers, so that they were all in some peculiar way admitted to his moods, his tastes, his whims, his fantasies, his generous giving of himself, combined with his temperamental coyness.

We began *Horizon* by inviting some of the best-known living writers to send in contributions. One with a world-wide reputation responded with a lengthy work by no means unworthy of him. When it had been set up in proof, Connolly, on reading it in print, rejected it. Once I was with him in a restaurant when a writer introduced himself with the words: 'Mr. Connolly, why didn't you publish an article by me which you accepted six months ago?' Connolly snapped: 'Because it was good enough to print but not good enough to publish.'

We began editing *Horizon* in the Bloomsbury flat where I had lived with Inez. The long, black-topped inlaid desk which I had built in Hammersmith was used by the secretary and the business manager. Connolly sat reading manuscripts in the editorial chair by the window, occasionally glancing up to see whether any German aeroplanes were coming over, for, during the 'phoney war' period, there were constant false alarms, and we expected a raid which would demolish whole districts of London.

Our most difficult task was to choose a name for the magazine. Connolly thought first of *Equinox*, with the quotation from Marlowe, *Lente currite equi noctis*, on the title page. Yet *Equinox seemed* unoriginal, and the quotation rather discouraging. For some time we weighed the claims of *Orion*. As I remember (though Connolly seems to remember differently) we chose *Horizon* in a moment of despair, when I took a copy of Gide's *Journal* from the bookshelf, and my eye fell on the word *horizon*, which occurred rather frequently. (But when, quite recently, I told Connolly that this was my recollection of the origin of the name *Horizon*, he looked at me amusedly and said: 'Think again, Stephen. If you think hard enough, you'll remember that you thought first of *everything*.')

We inserted a very few quarter-page advertisements in the literary weeklies. Two or three hundred people filled in the little form which was part of the advertisement, and these were the original subscribers.

At this time I lived alone in the flat which had become the office of *Horizon*, and I would be awakened in the morning by the envelopes which contained our filled-in subscription forms, and a cheque for 6s. 6d. falling on to the floor. This reminded me of Virginia Woolf's telling me about the orders arriving at their Richmond house for the first books printed by The Hogarth Press.

The first number of *Horizon* ran into a second edition, in which one or two misprints were corrected. In his editorial Comment for the second number Connolly discussed the reception of the first by the critics: 'To run through the first number, the editorial is escapist and cagey, the poetry out of date (except Auden, which is obscure), Priestley is Priestley, Grigson is spiteful, Bates is Bates. There are too many political articles, and, while full of dull things, the magazine is also much too short. Another line of attack is to concede that the first number is interesting, but to add that it is middlebrow and ''smarty'', and a third is to abandon the contents to their own merit and attack the policy or absence of policy. ''*Horizon* is full of lovely things but . . . should a magazine be just full of lovely things? Shouldn't it stand for something? Be animated by a serious purpose? Be getting somewhere?'' *Reynolds* delivered a homily in which the editors of *Horizon* are identified with the *émigré* writers Huxley, Heard and Isherwood, who have gone to California to ''contemplate their navels''. Others accuse us of going back to the 'twenties, and seldom has a periodical exuded such an atmosphere of sameness and tameness, or so combined Regency smartness with Georgian mediocrity as the ill-fated *Horizon*.'

In the same Comment of February 1940, Connolly wrote: 'the departure of Auden and Isherwood to America a year ago is the most important literary event of the decade.' It did, indeed, signify the end of a literary movement. For them, also, leaving England marked a turning-point.

They were both criticized severely for having left when they did, and their departure helped discredit the movement of the 1930's. But this movement had already been made bankrupt by events. The only important question was whether they could produce better work in the United States than in England. This in the short run was their own affair; in the long run it would be decided by later critics who could compare their work in two continents. Meanwhile the comments of journalists were irrelevant, although one might genuinely regret the unwritten stories of Isherwood about London and Manchester in the Blitz, or about the Occupation of Germany, and the poems of Auden from war-time England. That one can imagine such works and miss them is a tribute to the power and originality of these writers.

*   *   *   *   *

In 1947, 1948 and 1949 I went for periods of the greater part of each year to the United States. There I saw a good deal of Auden and Isherwood. Auden was living in Greenwich Village, that part of New York which seems an outpost of yellowing stuccoed London, where the streets have names and not numbers. He had a room in an apartment house, which bore a remote resemblance to his rooms at Christ Church: there was the same air of concentration amid untidiness, as though he scattered books, papers, ink, cigarette stubs, drinks and cups of coffee around, like pieces in a kaleidoscope which would instantly reassemble in a symmetrical pattern within his own mind. He was worse dressed, slightly more dishevelled, considerably stouter, but with the same pink skin and tow-coloured hair, the same angular alertness of movement. In manner he was perhaps gentler, though also more decided. On his mantelpiece a crucifix denoted the change in his beliefs. As at Oxford, his curtains were still drawn to shut out the daylight, a condition which I found hard to bear, so that one morning, when I had stayed overnight with him, I got up and drew them aside: with the result that they fell clattering to the ground. Auden, who had been asleep, woke up and groaned: 'You idiot! Why did you draw them? No one ever draws them. In any case there's no daylight in New York.'

Auden supported himself in the United States largely by teaching. In the course of my visits to American universities and colleges I met many of his ex-pupils and colleagues. They were impressed by two opposite qualities: one was the conservatism of his approach to texts and the technique of writing; the other, what seemed to them the originality of nearly all his ideas. When he had a class in poetic composition at Bennington College, he expected his students to master the most strict and abstruse verse forms: and when he set an examination to the students at his course of lectures on Shakespeare in New York, the questions consisted largely in asking them to identify quotations. Sometimes his frankness shocked, as when he was reputed to have begun a lecture on *Don Quixote* at Harvard University by saying that, like everyone in his audience, he had never read to the end of it. I have heard such contradictory reports of what he said on different occasions that I conclude the impression he made was sometimes rather vague: but there is no doubt it was stimulating. Moreover, I think Auden has left his mark on the work of the young American poets as much as a teacher, as through the influence of his own poetry. His absence from England was followed by a decline in intellectual effort and technical accomplishment by the younger English poets. Genuinely didactic by nature, he is one of the outstanding teachers of his time.

Although Auden's habits of work had not changed, his pattern of ideas was completely altered. He had shed all preoccupation with politics. In New York he explained to me that his politics in the 1930's had been based on the conviction that the anti-Fascists could really stop the war. When he realized that this view was mistaken, he had dropped the ideas which went with it. His becoming an American citizen had indeed underlined this, because he could never play in the United States a rôle corresponding to his English anti-Fascist one. In America he was an outsider, and he spoke of Americans always in the manner of a shrewd spectator of their affairs. They also spoke of him as a foreigner, criticizing his attempts to introduce Americanisms into his poetry.

He now had two main intellectual interests: one, theology; the other, Italian opera. Just as previously he had fitted the world around him into a Freudian or a Marxist pattern, now he fitted it into a Christian one. But now he accepted a dogma which criticized him and which was not simply an instrument for criticizing others.

As an Anglican, Auden had difficulties to overcome in accepting the moral and ethical judgments of the Church. He was, as I have already noted, peculiarly free from a sense of guilt or of sin, and now when he used these terms they had a curiously theoretical air. With my Puritan upbringing convincing me of a guilt from which I had spent years struggling to be free, it was curious to hear Auden discussing sin as an intellectual position of which one could be convinced by the reasoning of 'Mother Church'.

In so far as Auden had political views they were conservative, whereas mine had scarcely changed though I had withdrawn from politics: 'Of course you are a Protestant,' he said to me once settling the question finally, as when, in Berlin, Chalmers had taken his pipe out of his mouth and said, 'Gandhi'. On another occasion he made a criticism which, while completely justified, emphasized the difference between us: 'I suggest that you attach too much importance to your emotions.' One day, when he had argued more seriously than usual to this effect, I remarked that he was only saying what I had come to think myself. 'I agree with you,' I said, 'and I shall try to change.' At this he buried his head in his hands and exclaimed: 'But don't you realize that I don't want you to change? Why do you take me seriously? I thought you were one of the few people who wouldn't do so. What's so awful in this country is that people will take one seriously.'

He felt so strongly about this that he even complained in a Press interview that he was taken too seriously. The point of his complaint becomes clear, I think, if one substitutes the word 'literally' for 'seriously'. He wanted me to see reasons for entering into intellectual attitudes not temperamentally my own. He did not wish me to abandon what was intrinsic to me. To take him seriously in being persuaded that I could or should really change was both to take him too literally and not to take him seriously enough.

I found the manner of Auden's own changes disconcerting. When, after his travels to Germany he returned to England in 1929, he held the doctrine that 'the poet' must not leave his own country. Now, in America, he had published an essay arguing that the modern creative writer must be international, and probably, celibate; and implying that the literary pilgrimage of Henry James to Europe was now reversed, for today the European writer should come to America. Dogmas grew in this way out of Auden's own actions, tastes and prejudices. I can remember a time when he held it against a friend of mine that he liked the novels of Firbank: that he should do so, he said, was 'symptomatic' of some vital defect in his character. Now Firbank had become for him a saintly innocent of literature, somehow mixed up in the theological pattern. Today he held Italian opera to be superior to Greek tragedy.

Perhaps these tenets so dogmatically held, are examples of Auden's serious-non-seriousness. They are the hypothesis on which his thinking at a given moment of his development rests, and, while everything depends on it, one should not take a hypothesis absolutely.

His development seemed largely a disowning of his own past, or at any rate only an acceptance of that part of it which suited his immediate present. This tendency was shown in his attitude to his work. He produced at the end of the war a volume of *Collected Poems* in which the poems were arranged according to the alphabetical order of the first letter of the first line of each poem. In this way all trace of development from poem to poem was suppressed.

Yet if Auden's changes of view seemed sometimes like the abrupt changes of a kaleidoscope into a new pattern unconnected with any previous one (except that the instrument and the pieces which form the patterns were the same), his own life showed more unity of purpose throughout the twenty years since we were at Oxford than that of any of my friends. Here he was in New York living with the same bareness and simplicity as he had in his rooms at Oxford. He remained devoted to one aim: the writing of poetry, and his development was all within that aim. His life had not, of course, been entirely without unliterary entanglements, but these had not altered his way of living. Everyone else – myself included – had become so much involved in the institutions of living – a career, marriage, children, the war, and so on – that a great gulf divided us from our setting out.

300

The prophecy of Sir John Squire that I would marry and come to consider that a son was worth 'more than four hundred sonnets' no longer seemed so easy to dismiss with a smile. Auden had developed and yet remained the same person.

Auden and Isherwood had gone to America together, but, having got there, each selected that part of the country to live in which was most suited to his temperament – with the result that they were the whole breadth of the continent apart. Auden chose the fog and humidity and darkness of New York, with its exaggerated contrasts of old buildings and ramshackle tenements, out of which, as from a squalid backyard, skyscrapers rocket like sunflowers towards the higher air filled with the sun. Isherwood, with his love of the bronzed, the sandy and the naked, had made his home at Santa Monica near Los Angeles.

Isherwood had worked during the war in a camp for refugees run by the Quakers. He was a pacifist, and was one of the group of Gerald Heard and Aldous Huxley, who became interested in the Hindu philosophy of Vedanta. In their physical environment and in their philosophic development, the vastness of America had offered Auden and Isherwood each his opportunity. In these two simple facts one learns a great deal about America. Isherwood was opposed to the moral dogma of the Church and found in Vedantism an all-embracing mystical conception which, while directing men towards the ascetic ends of pure contemplation, condemned no one and recognized the spiritual significance of every choice contained within human behaviour. He could not accept the Church's condemnation of sins graded in categories. He sought, surely, a novelist's philosophy; for the novelist, least of all artists, can afford to be a dogmatic moralizer.

One day I read in the American anthology *New Directions (eleven)*, a story which Isherwood had already shown me in Berlin, *The Railway Accident*, by Allen Chalmers. This story, written when the writer was a Cambridge undergraduate, and owing much to the influence of *Ulysses*, nevertheless had a strange, sardonic power, creating visual effects of livid brilliance, which still seemed to me compelling. This publication was preceded by a disclaimer from Chalmers quoted by Isherwood, and so curious as to be worth requoting: 'Today

301

Chalmers ... feels that the kind of literature which makes a dilettante cult of violence, sadism, bestiality and sexual acrobatics is peculiarly offensive and subversive in an age such as ours – an age which has witnessed the practically applied bestiality of Belsen and Dachau.' 'Sexual acrobatics' seemed to me, when I read this, amateurish compared with the intellectual acrobatics contained in such a disowning by a still-talented writer of his brilliant early work. For surely literature is a symptom of the state of a society rather than the disease. And nothing could go farther to demonstrate the danger of suppressing symptoms because they seem unpleasant in an age of 'practical' unpleasantness, than that Hitler would have entirely agreed with Chalmers's point of view, as, of course, do the Stalinists. One result of suppressing all the symptoms of 'bestiality and violence' in contemporary German literature (except, of course, when directed against the democracies, as today in Russia when it is against the West) was that the 'practical bestiality' which went on behind the scenes could be ignored by nine-tenths of the populations of the civilized world, until Belsen and Dachau were actually taken by the British and Americans. The case history of Chalmers seemed brought full circle by this denial of his own best talent.

Two other friends whom I visited in America were Franz and Elizabeth, who had a beautiful farmstead, a white-painted New England style house, not far from New York. Elizabeth drove into a neighbouring town each day where she worked in a State Hospital for the neurotic and insane. Since I had last seen them, she and Franz had lived through a disturbed period of underground political work in Austria, when things went from bad to worse, until they expected Franz to be arrested almost hourly. Having escaped from Austria after the Anschluss, at the outbreak of war, they were in France, where Franz was interned as an enemy alien. Fortunately, he managed to get away before the Occupation. At the end of the war they came to Paris where they did relief work.

Now that Elizabeth had returned to America she seemed more fulfilled and happy than I had ever seen her. She was absorbed in her work among the insane, and brought to it the great gift of never allowing insanity to obscure her recognition of the individual personality under the psychotic mask.

302

Devoted to her home, her friends and her work for humanity, Elizabeth's life was beautiful, and this was a fact which all who knew her felt as though it were a part of her physical presence. Her unselfish achievement was not based on a dramatic renunciation. It came more out of a fullness of living than from self-denial.

The position of Franz was far from easy, and his life could have been an exile's tragedy. Events had driven him out of politics, and his marriage had removed him from the world of the workers. Undoubtedly he suffered, and his suffering was reflected in periods of physical illness. But with courage he saw that the loss of his political career provided him with the opportunity to study which he had never had in politics. After several years of reading history and political theory, he was writing a book which promised to be of the liveliest interest. This was a study of the effects of underground activity and exile on the characters of the small group of Socialists with whom he had worked in Vienna.

*   *   *   *   *

The second movement expressing a faith in human values which developed during the war, was of those who believed that a better world could grow out of the war. They dreamed of planned cities which would rise above the bomb-damaged ruins. Thus dreaming, sometimes they seemed almost grateful to the Germans for destroying the slums. There would be better schools, and communal centres, and free medical care for the whole people. They did not seem aware that there might also be unparalleled poverty. An assumption of the planners was that an unplanned community was so wasteful that planning would soon make up for the losses of the war.

I supported the planners, though I reproached myself for not caring more about their plans. For one thing, these plans were hardly linked up with the war. War-time Britain tended to be divided between the military realists occupied in destroying the cities of Europe and the planners, who would come into action when the realists had destroyed enough for the war to be won. Just as planning was not fused with the spirit of the war, so I could not imagine it affecting greatly the spirit of the peace.

303

Lying awake during air raids I would think of the young pilots trained by both sides to believe that the destruction of a city was an abstract task of 'precision bombing' without consideration of the people whose homes were being destroyed; of the young men being trained to the brutal enterprises of Commandos and Paratroopers; and of the children, either at the mercy of the bombers in the cities, or torn away and evacuated into the houses of strangers in the country. It seemed clear that – whatever the plans of governments – the peace would be a period of struggling to impose a pattern of reasonable behaviour on a population which had been systematically demoralized. There would be little respect for private property or for the rights of nations or communities in this world.

How could the war result in anything but more bitterness and hatred, and a general acceptance of further wars, which would destroy all plans? The only plan which would have inspired me with hope would have been one to bring Germany into the community of democratic nations on equal terms as soon as the Nazis had been defeated. But this, which would have given hope of creating a peaceful Germany, I knew to be impossible. If I had any such illusions they were destroyed when, at the end of the war, I offered my services to a Selection Board for considering candidates to work in Germany after the war. The particular job for which I was applying, was to propagate our policy in the German universities, and through the Press and the media of publicity. I was asked by one of the officers of the Selection Board what I thought I could do in Germany. I made a little speech in which I said that German culture had often shown strong leanings towards internationalism. After the last war, for example, German literature, the theatre, the films, and so on, were flooded by foreign influences. Unfortunately, these were often bad, and in their German form became worse, setting up an idea in the German mind of a weak and decadent cultural cosmopolitanism instead of a strong internationalism. I suggested that after the war we should study to strengthen the German need in universities and the arts to have contact with other nations. One of my interviewers said: 'We can assure you, Mr. Spender, that after this war there will be *no* culture in Germany.' And with these words I was dismissed. When I went to Germany a few months later, it was in a temporary capacity and I was there only a few weeks, instead of for the two years which I had offered to the Selection Board.

*   *   *   *   *

Meanwhile, during the four years' lull which included most of my time in the Fire Service, I became involved to some extent with the planners. A group of ordinary firemen started an education scheme among the London firemen, and they invited me to be a discussion group leader. A great virtue of the scheme was the modest and simple way in which it functioned. A few scores of firemen, without being given any rank or relieved from fire-fighting duties, were given facilities to spread the gospel of progressive education, planning and war aims among their fellow firemen. We simply went from station to station, opening discussions on Russia, China, the Law, History, Art, and many other subjects.

I became director of this scheme in No. 34 Fire Force. Every Monday morning I used to meet my fellow discussion group leaders, and we would discuss our projects for the coming week. Finally we were removed from our scattered fire stations, and the educationists of one area were all put into one Fire Station in Holland Park Avenue. In this way I got to know the earnest or adventurous characters who took part in the scheme, because they had a passion either for education or else to get away from the routine of their fire stations. I got to know a great many firemen in the different stations where I spoke. The success of the scheme was assured, if only because the firemen were bored at standing by in their stations. Even a lecture followed by a discussion came as a relief, though some men grudged the turning-off of the Light Programme for an hour or so.

The Fire Service fulfilled one of the aspirations which had been a part cause of my joining the Communists. This was to get to know the workers. Knowing them did not help me understand better what had always seemed to me a mysterious aspect of Communism: the idea that the proletariat had some virtue whereby, when they had made the revolution, all the evils of the bourgeois class would be removed by a classless society.

The workers had, certainly, some of the virtues which were perhaps a result of their situation. The best of these was a seriousness about

305

life, quite distinct from a portentousness which comes from taking only oneself seriously. They really wished to unwind a little knowledge from the tangled skein of disordered and inaccurate information which was the best we could offer them. They liked to discuss a better and juster England. For them, 'progress' was not that optimistic attitude based on a belief in human perfectibility which is justly criticized for its unrealism by those who love to meditate on Original Sin, but making a few important improvements in their living conditions, and working for concrete benefits such as better houses and better education for their children. For them, their own lack of education was not a consequence of their having chosen to be lazy at public school or university: it was an opportunity from which they had been deprived. They wished nothing more than that their children should have a better chance than theirs: and they realized what they had been deprived of by lack of education.

Once or twice I arrived at a station without having prepared anything to say. For lack of a set subject to talk about, I would then, with much misgiving, try to distinguish the kind of writing which is literature from that which is worthless. I pointed out that nature and people are everywhere seen at all times and places by everyone for the first time: and that the good writer is the person who retains in his work this sense of a unique moment of insight into reality. Literature, I went on, releases us from the routine of habit, reminds us of the ever-fresh experience of living, and puts us in a living relation to the past. All this was crude and simplified, but I was amazed to discover how by talking in terms of *their* experiences and perceptions I could always arouse the interest of my fellow firemen. It struck me that, with their closeness to experience and their thirst after a meaning, the poor are disposed to be religious. Yet, whenever it happened that we had a clergyman at a discussion group, he always talked doctrine and theology, or else advanced childish arguments against science.

Whenever the firemen were discussing their situation as workers, or – for that matter – as husbands, they were superior to better-off people, who use their opportunities to spare themselves the trouble of thinking or living at all deeply. Yet beyond their immediate personal situation they were as petty, grabbing, malicious, self-seeking,

306

irresponsible, prejudiced, as members of any other class. It was impossible not to conclude that, given the opportunity to 'improve' themselves, they would be as superficial as the middle-class people of whom they were envious.

Superficiality is surely the supreme vice to which nearly all successful groups fall a prey. By it, I mean accepting opportunities which an improved situation offers, in order to forget less fortunate circumstances which still apply to others. More important perhaps than forgetting others is that successful people forget the complexity even of their own existences by protecting themselves from awareness of catastrophe and death. Seriousness is the power to retain a consciousness of this complexity, and not to use advantages as a means of escaping from it. This does not mean humorlessness. It is possible to be superficial and have no sense of humour. Seriousness includes humour, just as the kind of drama which seems closest to life is neither pure comedy nor pure tragedy, but tragedy which includes the comic.

However, most people are only made serious by the pressure of circumstances. I do not mean to argue that the poor should remain poor because they are better by virtue of their poverty. Yet I am sure it is wrong to assume that proletarian virtues will inevitably remain with the poor when they cease to be oppressed. The selfishness of the Trades Unionists who fight for improved standards of living not only against the rich, but also against the poor of other countries, and against the coloured peoples, should demonstrate this. So that the struggle for better conditions has to be accompanied by a struggle against superficiality. This is even more difficult than the political struggle. For it has to be conducted within each individual soul.

*   *   *   *   *

The top floor of the house in Maresfield Gardens, where my wife and I lived, was a four-roomed attic with sloping ceilings under the roof. In the ground-floor flat of the same house our neighbours had bricked up a room, which they generously allowed us to share with them as an air raid shelter.

In 1944 there was a recurrence of raids, and sometimes, on my

307

leave days, we slept here. Natasha, who was pregnant at the time, seemed completely indifferent to the raids.

One night, when we were in the shelter during an alarm, there was a rushing noise like a train coming down a vertical tunnel through the sky. The very moment when I heard this noise, I had time to think that this must be part of a tremendous raid which would probably destroy the whole of London: the answer to the raids on Berlin, the end I seemed now to have been awaiting all my life.

There was a great thud, when our room rocked, followed by a sound of things collapsing dully and heavily amid a tinkling of falling glass. We ran upstairs to our flat and found the ceiling lying like a blanket of lath and plaster over our bed. I looked out of the window and saw London lying below me, black and calm, with a few isolated fires rising from scattered areas, like tongues of flame fallen from the heavens upon a darkening view of Florence, in some late morbid visioning of Botticelli.

I wanted to go out and see where the bomb had fallen. It was on a building a hundred yards from our house. Owing to the darkness, and still more to the great cloud of dust caused by the explosion, I could see nothing. This left me unsatisfied. I still wanted to see some tangible result of the raid, so I decided to walk to the nearest fire, which from our high-up window illuminated a wide area not far from us.

But when I had climbed down the hill I was lost in a maze of streets whose stuffy, foggy blackness seemed to curtain away all the light of the fire. As I walked I had the comforting sense of the sure, dark immensity of London like a warren, containing a scattered, breeding life concealed in burrows of the ragged, delapidated streets of Kilburn and Maida Vale. They could be destroyed at one place, but then – the wound sealed off – would flow through other channels and streets and tunnels. The houses, with their steep roofs and slummy walls, crouched like indestructible, imbecile peasants under the flogging night. As though kneeling in the darkness, they seemed to take comfort from their own numbers: each separate, obscure, negligible one concealed among so many. The grittiness, stench and obscurity of Kilburn suddenly seemed a spiritual force – the immense force of poverty which had produced the narrow, yet intense, visions
308

of Cockneys living in other times, with their home-made poetic philosophies – William Blake at Lambeth, Keats and Leigh Hunt at Hampstead, all the Cockney characters of Dickens, dancing in the roads, sniffing and snivelling as they ran. Neither Sam Weller nor young Bailey nor Blake's chimney sweepers were far removed from the flaring intensity of the decorations for the Christmas party at the Willesden sub-station – for the London vulgarity had a quality of passion which might break at any moment into the purest flame. I was reminded of the innocent, Cockney lines of Blake:

> 'Then naked and white, all their bags left behind,
> They rise upon clouds and sport in the wind;
> And the angel told Tom, if he'd be a good boy,
> He'd have God for his father, and never want joy.
>
> And so Tom arose, and we rose in the dark
> And got with our bags and our brushes to work.
> Though the morning was cold, Tom was happy and warm:
> So, if all do their duty, they need not fear harm.'

The fire was caused by a burning gas main in the middle of some dripping, empty place, like a dilapidated cistern between streets. People gathered at the end of the streets which were their own homes, to stare with a kind of wordless dignity at the destruction. They were silhouetted by an aura of blue and golden flames.

Soon after this, another event brought me close to death. This was the death of my sister-in-law on Christmas Day, 1945.

For more than five years she had been suffering from the grave illness whose intermittent crises grew ever closer to one another. Between these periods of acute illness, she lived so vigorously, and showed so much confidence in her plans for the future, that it was difficult not to believe a miracle would happen and that she would recover.

But if there was a miracle, it lay in a consolidation of her own faith in life into a certainty which was no longer just of recovery but of a life which extended beyond death. In this, she was greatly fortified by her friend Godfrey Mowatt, that remarkable man who, having been blinded by an accident when he was young, devoted his life to comforting and understanding those who were so ill as to have entered countries of despair with which he was familiar. She died on the icy Christmas Day when cobwebs on which the dew had frozen lay on the hedge outside the window of her Wiltshire house like magnificent bracelets. In the warmth of her room she died, confident that death was only a temporary separation from those she loved, whom she would soon meet again.

*   *   *   *   *

Reading over what I have written, I ask myself whether I would not have done better to write my autobiography as a novel. Many of the experiences would be easier to express in the kind of fiction which people recognize as autobiography, without their being confronted with the immediacy of the writer who says: 'the hero is I'.

Again, experiences are described here which some readers may think should have been confined to the anonymity of the psychological text-book.

Yet I think that I am justified in writing in the first person singular. Fiction and clinically analytic writing extend our knowledge of human personality, but they also offer avenues of escape from the glaring light of consciousness of him who says: 'I am I'. The writer of fictitious autobiography offers the truth about himself within the decent and conspiratorial convention of contemporary fiction, which invites the reader to identify himself with the writer-hero. Reader-writer walk together in a real-seeming dream-alliance leading into gardens inhabited by Stephen Daedalus and Marcel, out of which side-lanes wind obscurely to Dr. Kinsey's Report on the Sexual Life of the Human Male, or Sheldon's analyses of psycho-somatic types.

I am I: hero of a potential autobiographic novel in which I give the hero and the other characters their real names and their attributes: curve on a psychiatrist's chart which I paste on my wall: and in spite of this, in fact because of it, I insist that I am a citizen, that I have views and take sides and accept responsibilities, and even hold opinions about public affairs. I am a citizen who revolts against the concept of himself as 'social man', with a respectable, official outside life, and two secret selves – a fictitious hero and a clinical case-history. It is in the individual who accepts the responsibility of his own complexity, that the diversity of society attains a unity of consciousness where opposites are reconciled.

The main narrative of this book is from my eighteenth year, in which I had attained the climax of a struggle beginning with my adolescence, until my fortieth year. When I was a child I was a naturalist with a long white beard and a clear blue gaze, like a portrait of such a child, which I have seen, by Dürer. That is to say, my early childhood was marked by a quite exceptional harmony, and it is perhaps this which has enabled me to retain throughout life a central calm and happiness, amid violent divisions of my own nature. But at the age of eighteen I could not reconcile my ideals either with myself or with the world. I was tormented by the feeling that nothing was as it should be, single and clear and pure.

My narrative describes how, in Germany and elsewhere, I sought to discover my real self by behaviour which outraged my ideal self. The result of this was a series of relationships undertaken in a spirit of opportunism: yet I was too much an idealist to maintain a cynical attitude.

Then society, appearing in the conscious form of Communism, seemed to offer a way out of my dilemma. It suggested to me that after all I was not myself. I was simply a product of my bourgeois circumstances. By 'going over to the proletariat' and entering a different set of circumstances I could become another kind of social projection. I would be 'on the side of history' and not 'rejected' by it, like one of the disused mines in Auden's early poems.

The Marxist criticism of my own position – sometimes publicly expressed as in Caudwell's *Illusion and Reality*, sometimes the voice of social conscience in myself – told me I was wrong to think of myself as 'separated from society'. The solution of all my problems was to put myself in an 'historically correct position'.

But to believe that my individual freedom could gain strength from my seeking to identify myself with the 'progressive' forces was different from believing that my life must become an instrument of means decided on by political leaders. I came to see that within the struggle for a juster world, there is a further struggle between the individual who cares for long-term values and those who are willing to use any and every means to gain immediate political ends – even

311

good ends. Within even a good social cause, there is a duty to fight for the pre-eminence of individual conscience. The public is necessary, but the private must not be abolished by it; and the individual must not be swallowed up by the concept of social man.

Today, we are constantly told that we must choose between the West and the East. Confronted by such a choice, I can only say that, first and foremost, I am for neither West nor East, but for my self considered as a self – one of the millions who inhabit the earth. The conflict between East and West does not in itself involve a moral choice, if it is only a struggle between external forces: it becomes moral only if it is a choice within myself: that is to say, if having chosen my own self, my humanity, my conscience, I can then judge the rival claims of both sides. I do not *choose* America or Russia: I *judge* between them. If it seems absurd that an individual should set up as a judge between these vast powers, armed with their superhuman instruments of destruction, I can reply that the very immensity of the means to destroy proves that judging and being judged does not lie in these forces. For supposing that they achieved their utmost and destroyed our civilization, whoever survived would judge them by a few statements, a few poems, a few *témoignages*, surviving from all the ruins, a few words of those men who saw outside and beyond the means which were used and all the arguments which were marshalled in the service of those means.

Thus I could not escape from myself into some social situation of which my existence was a mere product, and my witnessing a wilfully distorting instrument. I had to be myself, choose and not be chosen.

* * * * *

When I was young I sought to attain an ideal rightness of my own living, wherein I might feel morally secure. I wanted to *be* my ideal self, and I expected others to correspond to my idealized vision of them. Thus imperfections, doubts, failures, weaknesses in myself and others seemed to prove that neither I nor the world was as I wanted it to be. I imagined that there were people who, through purity and innocence, or through self-discipline and asceticism, or through identifying themselves with a public cause, attained perfection. Especially in my friendships with men, I was drawn towards what I considered truth and disinterestedness in those with whom I sought to identify myself.

But I came to see that direction is everything. Since we live in time we are never complete. Perfection implies arriving at a goal and staying there. But actually we never arrive anywhere, and we never stop until we are dead. Having solved one problem, new ones arise out of the very situation which results from solving it. The greatest of all human delusions is that there is a tangible goal, and not just direction towards an ideal aim. The idea that a goal can be attained perpetually frustrates human beings, who are disappointed at never getting there, never being able to stop. Revolutions and wars are forced because people imagine that there are attainable goals in human affairs, like the Communist goal of the day when the dictatorship of the proletariat will 'wither away'.

Human beings are bound together by the energy of movements in the direction of shared ideals. The ideal is a fictitious vanishing point which draws all who share it towards itself, in the same way as all lines are directed towards the fictitious vanishing point in Renaissance perspective. The direction is powerful just because he who moves in it does not stop. Direction exists in movement, which is living. To stop would be to die.

This way of thinking – that living is movement in a certain direction and that behaviour should be judged by that to which it tends – explained to me problems of art as well as of living. One thing that always puzzled me was the problem of form in poetry, and arising from this, the question of what was meant by free verse, and what the essential difference between poetry and prose. It always struck me that when people talked about some poetic form – the sonnet, for example – they were talking about something which had never been completely achieved; and often they were confronted by the contradiction that the most formally correct works, by all the rules, were not the best examples of the use to which the form could be put. It then occurred to me that form does not lie simply in the correct observance of rules. It lies in the struggle of certain living material to achieve itself within a pattern. The very refusal of a poet to sacrifice what he means to a perfectly correct rhyme, for example, can more powerfully suggest the rhyme than correctness would. For it reveals the struggle towards the form, which because it has direction and movement, and is indeed an expression of will, projects the idea

313

of an ideal form towards which the poem is moving, reaching even beyond the form itself. Thus the tormented statements of Gerard Manley Hopkins, in which living material endeavours to force itself into the mould of the sonnet, suggest the sonnet far more powerfully than the correct sonnets of his friend Robert Bridges. In the same way, the difference between poetry and prose is decided by the direction of language, more than by analysing the prose into its poetic elements. Prose is language used in such a way that the ideas and events or scene within the language are referred to as objects existing apart from the language, so that there is an understanding between the writer and the reader that these things could be discussed in quite other words than those used, because they exist independently of the words. But directly the language tends to create, as it were, verbal objects inseparable from the words used, then the direction of the language is poetic. It is moving towards a condition where, as in poetry, the words appear to become the object, so that they cannot be replaced by other words than the ones used to convey the same experience.

*   *   *   *   *

So I learned both to accept myself and to aim beyond myself. Self-knowledge, I realized, might result simply in a fatalistic self-acceptance. This itself is an illusion, because it is a static idea of oneself based on acceptance of past experience. Being is neither past disillusionment or future illusion, it is a perpetual state of moving from what one was towards a further aim of existence. Strictly speaking, one never *is*, one is only moving. The ideal is the conception of a goal shared by others which unites separately existing individuals within shared values. The goal is the highest conception of the group towards which the individual, from his separate moment, moves. It is the tension between past acceptance and future endeavour, between the isolated individual and the community, between material and form, which is the impulse, the direction, the movement, the closest approximation towards what really *is*.

*   *   *   *   *

My brothers and sister and I were brought up in an atmosphere which I would describe as 'Puritan decadence'. Puritanism names the behaviour which is condemned; Puritan decadence regards the name

314

itself as indecent, and pretends that the object behind the name does not exist until it is named. The Puritans have stern faces; but their eyes have looked on life. The Puritan decadents have unseeing, rhetorical faces, faces of immature boys who are prematurely aged, faces of those upon whose minds some operation has been performed removing those centres which were conscious of the body.

To the son of the Puritan decadent, his body is a nameless horror of nameless desires which isolate him within a world of his own. He is divided between a longing to become like the others who walk about in their clothes without desires and as though they had no bodies, and a sense that nevertheless for him his guilt gives him back his body. But if guilt is knowledge of what is real, nevertheless this knowledge is locked within himself, and as he grows older his relationships with others appear unreal unless he can involve them in a guilt as deep as his own.

During the years of my adolescence, in the solitude of darkness, I would frame long conversations with some friend whom I imagined could share a pure and exalted relationship with me – a relationship in which I could admit the need to love and be loved, and in which my knowledge of myself became my knowledge of him. But in my fantasy this shared knowledge soon changed to shared guilt. I did not know that others felt as I did. My loneliness lay in thinking I was unique, and my desire took the form of longing to prove that I knew someone else completely, who also knew me and who felt as I did. It was distressing to discover that this knowledge had two aspects: of wanting, on the one hand, to share a spiritual revelation; and, on the other, a physical one. But these two extremes were precisely the ones in which I was isolated, and they represented what I wanted to know about another: on the one hand that he had a sense of spiritual vocation; on the other, a body with physical desires like my own. If I had been reassured of this, I would also have had the possibility of discipline: but without knowledge there was no discipline, there were only ferocious imaginative powers feeding upon darkness and emptiness.

Recently I read in Arthur Waley's *The Life and Times of Po Chu-i* the translation of a poem written by the poet's friend, Yuan Chen, in the early part of the ninth century A.D., which expresses the attitude

315

towards friendship which I have tried here to convey. I quote it in full:

> 'Other people too have friends that they love;
> But ours was a love such as few friends have known.
> You were all my sustenance; it mattered more
> To see you daily than to get my morning food.
> And if there was a single day when we did not meet
> I would sit listless, my mind in a tangle of gloom.
> To think we are now thousands of miles apart,
> Lost like clouds, each drifting on his far way!
> Those clouds on high, where many winds blow,
> What is their chance of ever meeting again?
> And if in open heaven the beings of the air
> Are driven and thwarted, what of Man below?'*

What particularly strikes me here is the image of the cloud, which suggests not just the image of the two friends apart, 'each drifting on his own way', but still more, the drifting into one another's consciousness when they were together.

When I write here of 'identification' with another man, I mean identification of our situations, not that I wanted to find someone identical with myself. Even at a very early age, I was struck by the refusal of people to admit the elements of existence out of which they make their lives. Most lives are like dishonest works of art in which the values are faked, certain passages blurred and confused, difficulties evaded, and refuge taken by those bad artists who are human beings, in conventions which shirk unique experiences. As a child, even, I wanted to know someone who saw himself continually in relation to the immensity of time and the universe: who admitted to himself the isolation of his spiritual search and the wholeness of his physical nature. Even then, it struck me that the other children were liars who would not admit their hidden fears, who had already learned from their parents not to ask certain questions, and to dismiss the most urgent problems with an embarrassed laugh.

I retained the sense of this child-like search. If I never met the person who felt exactly the same need for clarity as myself, nevertheless,

* *The Life and Times of Po Chu-i*, with translations of 100 new poems, by Arthur Waley.

I did, piece by piece, construct from moments of happiness and un-happiness, from love affairs and deaths, from books and music and paintings, what added up to a whole experience of the human condition. But people who felt as I did communicated their experience in books, and not in conversations with one another. They were the people whom I knew to be alone. I came to recognize a certain humour, flippancy even, as a sign of the highest seriousness. So that when in this book I touch on the amusing conversation of Virginia Woolf, the malice of Yeats, the wryness of Eliot, the buffoonery of Auden, the farcical play-acting of Isherwood, I am touching on some-thing which indicates its serious opposite, much as in another period the peacock laugh of Shelley, the satiric wit of Byron, and the pun-ning of Keats did.

With one or two friends I entered into an intimacy fulfilling my ideal of complete identification of our situations. I am thinking here of my relationship at one time with a French critic, at another with an American writer. Here, though, with each of these, at the very time when I felt I had attained what I was always seeking, there was a sense of clairvoyant disillusion. It was as if even while he recognized in me, and I in him, the sense of the situation within life which both shared, we recognized also in each other something which was lack-ing. We knew one another too completely, each despised himself and the other: we had arrived at a point beyond which we could not go, and the sad inadequacy of the way in which each lived his life became evident to us.

An analogy for love between human beings might be the conscious-ness of each other by two separate parts of a landscape. The human landscapes look into each other's eyes, each totally aware of the other, each accepting the earth which is the nature of both, and which is the human condition. With that understanding they see what should be planted and what cut down, what irrigated and what drained away, what built and what destroyed. They accept all this in the terrible charity of their knowledge one of the other.

The analogy of the landscape stresses the possibility of two dif-ferent kinds of relationship, one of identity, one of polarity. The two in their complete knowledge might regard one another as the same, and the landscapes might, like the clouds of Yuan Chen's poem, become inseparably one when together, lost in separate isolation when drifting away. Or again, the relationship might be based on the recognition in one another of opposite but complementary qualities: valleys in the one, mountains in the other, etc. The first would be the relationship of male and male, the second of male and female. And in my experience, while I never lost the need to identify myself with someone who recognized himself in the same situation of life as myself, I found that the relationship of identity could be dangerously destructive. There was disillusionment as well as joy in finding in another exactly what I was myself, for I found evil as well as good; and looking back, I see that it was my relationships with women that were the most enduring, because in the relationship of opposites there remained always the mystery of an unknown quantity.

*   *   *   *   *

During my last weeks in the Fire Service I took part in fighting one or two fires.

At this time I had been transferred to a fire station in Holland Park Avenue.

The first fire to which I went was at Kensington. One of my fellow discussion group leaders, called Matters, and myself, were ordered into a block of flats which was on fire. Accompanied by an officer, and carrying the heavy rolled-up hose, we climbed up the stairs inside until we reached the top storey. There we opened the window, from which we could see flames all round us coming from below. The officer said to me: 'Get out of that window and stand on the roof, then direct the nozzle on to the fire.' I did as I was told. The officer, as he started to descend the stairs, turned back and said: 'And if you fall there's only a two-hundred-foot drop.' As soon as he had gone away, Matters said: 'Look here, it's your first fire. You shouldn't be doing that. So let me stand outside. You wait here.' He took the nozzle from me and stood on the roof, while I sat on the window ledge watching him.

He was surrounded by flame and pouring smoke, silhouetted in a heroic posture, and he looked like a bas-relief of a fireman embossed on some medal.

When the fire was put out we 'packed up' and returned to the station. Dressed in our heavy Wellingtons and uniforms, we lounged in the back of the 'appliance' with feelings of elation and relief, the peculiar kind of drunkenness one feels after fire-fighting. Matters said: 'You did very well, considering it was your first fire.' 'Really,' I protested, 'you can't possibly say that. All I did was hand you the nozzle while I sat on the window ledge smoking cigarettes and watching you put out the fire.' It was quite obvious that I had done nothing and there could be no arguing about it. But Matters, in his elation, had simply transferred the credit of his own actions to me. He now went on to divulge that he was not afraid of being killed on a fire, as he was convinced that he would survive after death. He was confident that once out of this world he would have no unpleasantness to be afraid of in the next. He talked about the state of 'awareness' which he would enjoy, and then he went on to speak of his married life, of what he intended to do after the war, and so on. His conversation was quite unlike his usual talk: it was as though the fire had illuminated his mind, and his words as we drove home through the black-out, compared with any I had heard him use before, were from a far profounder level, like arterial compared with venous blood.

At this time, whenever there was an alarm, those of us who were assigned to crews for going out on 'jobs' used to put on our full equipment, and stand around waiting for a call. Although the raids were not severe, they were extremely noisy. The clamour was caused almost entirely by the heavy defence barrage of the London guns. This was a terrifying mixture of gunfire with sounds like immense sheets of lead falling slowly through the sky, rattling and uncreasing as they fell. It was impossible, of course, to distinguish between the noises caused by bombs falling and those of our defence.

One of the least pleasant things some of us had to do was go out into the raid before there was a call, in order to fill our tanks and stand near our pumps. It was then that one noticed how utterly deserted the streets had become, so that, lit by flashes from the continuously firing guns, they were emptied as by some tremendous inundation of waters which had washed all life away. Standing alone amid this turbulent emptiness was more alarming than being on a fire.

In the fire station the men would beat their arms across their chests and say to one another things such as: 'Turned very cold all of a sudden, ain't it, mate?' 'Yus, a nasty spell,' etc. This surprised me, because ever since 'our' bomb had fallen I started trembling uncontrollably when the siren sounded so, of course, like the others, I was shivering now, but for what appeared to be a different reason. They said they felt cold, and undoubtedly this was true, but it never seemed to occur to anyone that there could be any other reason than the weather. Their minds were on the action they were going to take part in, not on analysing their feelings. To admit that they were frightened would not have helped them in what they had to do. To say that they were cold was one way of ignoring that they were afraid.

There was, though, a difference between my attitude towards my war duties and that which was simply taken for granted amongst other people. This was illustrated very effectively by a Transatlantic broadcast in which I once took part. An interlocutor in America asked certain people in England about their war work, which they were expected to describe. I found myself in a studio with about a dozen other people occupied in various kinds of patriotic activity. There was a lady introducer who explained through a microphone to our American interviewer who each of us was, and he then questioned us by means of a loudspeaker. The first person to be introduced was a Mrs. Hargreaves who (the American was told through the microphone in the studio) was a charlady by profession. 'Oh, Mrs. Hargreaves,' said the American voice, 'that is very interesting. And what are you doing now? Do you char for some government office?' 'No,' said Mrs. Hargreaves. 'Then what do you do?' 'I sweep roads.' 'That's very important I'm sure, Mrs. Hargreaves: now, what made you decide to sweep roads?' 'Well, I always did like dirty work, and I decided that this was the dirtiest I could do, and helping the country as well.' Enthusiastic laughter pealed across the Atlantic, and the microphone was passed to a Mrs. Epsom. 'And what do you do, Mrs. Epsom?' 'I'm a bus conductor.' 'Oh, that's very interesting, and what made you become a bus conductor?' 'Well, my hubby and me we talked it over, and we decided that he could help most working in the factory and me by being on the bus.' 'And where is the route of your bus, Mrs. Epsom?' 'At Windsor.'

320

'Windsor? That's where the Royal Family lives, isn't it?' 'Yes, and I do hope that the Queen will have a ride on my bus one day.' 'Well, good luck to you, Mrs. Epsom, and I hope she does.' It was now my turn. After I had been introduced the interlocutor asked: 'What did you do before you were a fireman, Mr. Spender?' 'I wrote poetry.' 'Oh, you wrote poetry? And why should you have decided to become a fireman?' 'Well, I thought that being a fireman gave me the best chance of continuing to write, as when there are no fires there isn't much to do.' Pause. 'And have you been able to write poetry in the Fire Service, Mr. Spender?' 'Well, listening to the Light Programme and watching snooker being played for forty-eight hours out of seventy-two hasn't enabled me to write very much.' Another pause. 'What is snooker? That's a game we haven't heard of in the United States and I'm sure our listeners would be very interested to hear about it.' With a feeling that I had side-tracked the broadcast, I began: 'Well, it's rather like billiards, only with a great many balls.' 'And what do you do with the balls?' Luckily at this moment I was interrupted by the crisp voice of an officer who had been sent to supervise what I said. 'If our American listeners have the impression that London's firemen do nothing but play snooker, Mr. Spender has quite misled them.' Our lady introducer now interrupted cheerfully: 'And I'm sure that our American listeners will want to hear that Mr. Spender is one of London's bravest firemen, and it's only his modesty that makes him talk of snooker.' I retired in disgrace. Fortunately the broadcast was not 'live', and what I said was cut out with a needle made of some precious stone.

*   *   *   *   *

My second fire was more memorable than the first. Several bombs had fallen near St. Mary Abbots Church in High Street, Kensington. We set out from Holland Park Avenue in our appliances. The roads on the way were partly covered with fire bombs, which, in the blackout, burned like hundreds of little lanterns. In the deserted roads this made a charming scene.

On this occasion I was sent alone into a room at the back of the shop. All round me the room was on fire. I directed the jet of water from the nozzle of the hose on to what seemed the fiercest flames, but this had no apparent effect. Nor did there seem any connection between the thin jet of water and the fire. However, the slight uneasiness I felt lest a beam from the ceiling above should fall on to me, was as remote as the knowledge that the jet of water would eventually put out the fire.

Surrounded by a lacquered screen of fire, I felt enormously at peace, settled in the centre of the element, as though rowing in wide circles for hours on end off-shore opposite the wall through the fields near Start Point at Salcombe, or in the centre of the pine forest at Sellin with a sound of crepitating pine needles and oozing gum, more finely etched than silence itself upon the burning copper wall of the day. There was a rustling and crackling all round me, and in my heart I felt the peace which I had always longed to know before I went out on a fire, the knowledge that we were going to have a child. It was as though a cycle of living was completed, and in the fire I stood in the centre of a wheel of my own life where childhood and middle age and death were the same.

*　　*　　*　　*　　*

I have read that it is impossible to remember things which have happened to one, as they really were. Memories – the argument runs – are only present in our minds because they have been transformed from a past actuality into a present myth, which is a new experience only distantly related to the old. We colour our past experiences with those present ones which give them significance, illustrating what we are and not what they were.

This may be so. In writing this book, the memories have forced themselves upon me, rather than been selected. I have written of many presences, ghosts from the past, which surround me, and my aim has been to describe what I am, by making a large sum of a great many ever-present pictures of experience. I want to depict these omnipresent selves rather than a new and emergent self of today. If I have changed, I have done so not so much in having shed some of these presences, as in having rearranged them in their relation with one another, shifting the emphasis slightly, changing a pattern, rather than outgrowing the old, or making an entirely new pattern out of new elements.

*　　*　　*　　*　　*

We lived at Sheringham in Norfolk, where we had a house at the extreme edge of the town on the cliffs and adjoining fields. My childhood was the nature I remember: the thickness of the grass in the pasture fields, amongst whose roots were to be found heartsease (the small pansies which are the colour of the iris in a golden eye), speedwell of a blue as intense as a bead of sky. There were scabious and cornflower and waving grasses and bracken which came as high as my shoulders.

Sometimes, stuck as though glued to the stem of a flower, just below the cup of the petals, there was a chalk blue butterfly – milky blue its widespread wings; and pale russet chalky colour the short under-wings, with small copper rings and spots as though stamped on to them by a minute hammer. In the sun the butterflies expanded and then shut close their wings with the exact movement of a hinge. When the hinge was shut the closed wings were of a knife-blade thickness, so that you could not have split them with the edge of a razor.

In the garden I would lose myself in a forest of hollyhocks. The scent of a rose was a whole world, as though when I buried my nose in the petals the day was instantly canopied with a red sky.

Near Sheringham there were woods and the common, covered with gorse and heather. In the woods at spring there were the pale damp primroses with their scent of sublimated mould and a buttery thickness which one could almost taste. Then in summer there was the heather, brittle flowers like tiny purple beads on gnarled charcoal stems, flooding over the burnt-looking soil, on which bees descended in thousands to lift away the honey. Beyond the heather, near blackberry hedges, the gorse lay like gold armour, or like fleece of fire all round me, on bushes of spiky green thorns.

At evening, floating above the flat Norfolk landscape, there appeared range upon range of mountains with gulfs and valleys between high peaks, which stayed motionless, sculptured on the sky out of clouds. Sometimes, also, at midday, in the sky whose blue was as solid and opaque as the flushed green of a field of young corn, perfect white pictures would appear, as on a screen. 'Look, a milk jug, a white milk jug. It is exactly like a milk jug,' I would cry. 'No, silly,' my sister would say. 'It's a cat, a white cat, can't you see?'

In autumn and winter the prevailing winds which caused the branches of the stunted hedges to bend all in one direction, blew across the cliff-edge fields between Sheringham and East Runton. One day the wind was so strong that I could lean against it; like an invisible door in a wall of air, it would yield slightly if I pushed it, and then spring back against me. Then I started singing into the wind. Then I stopped singing, and I heard a very pure sound of choral voices answering me out of the blowing sky. It was the angels.

My father would take my sister and me to Miss Harcourt's school at East Runton. On the way he would tell us stories. There was the story of the Rubber Man who could climb any building and stretch his neck to see over any wall. This I liked even more than the ones about the parrot my father owned when he was a boy.

My mother, a plaid rug over her knees, lay on a chaise-longue, perpetually grieving over I know not what. Sometimes my eldest brother, Michael, used to go out shooting rabbits with my father. I never remember a time when Michael didn't lead a life quite separate from the rest of us, conspiring with our parents that he should not be regarded as a child.

At Miss Harcourt's there was a girl called Penelope, with whom, at the age of seven, I was in love. There was also a boy called Forbes, with whom I used to fight. Forbes had black wiry hair and flashing black eyes behind his steel-rimmed spectacles. One day, when we were rolling over one another on the ground, he got into a passionate rage of the kind known only to a small child, when his mind becomes a scale in which he measures the whole of his strength against the whole of his weakness. The will of Forbes was breaking against my body as though against a gate. Suddenly afraid, I lay on top of him and held him very closely in my arms, and at that moment I experienced a sensation like the taste of a strong sweet honey, but not upon my tongue, and spreading wave upon wave, throughout my whole body.

Sometimes, when I sat indoors in the kindergarten on a very fine day, I felt as though a wall had been raised between me and nature to which I belonged. I had a sensation of the garden, which I could just see through a window, twisted through with bird song as with forking flame, and of the limbs of trees running like veins through

324

the sky, which poured down on earth in an enormous cataract of blue light.

Then, after the end of the class, I would run into the garden to a place where there was a pond, and, lying on the ground beside it, stare down into that strange life in rust-coloured water where stagnating processes had furred its concrete sides, and even the grass leaves of motionless subaqueous weeds. I soon observed that activity which as little disturbed the gelatinous stillness of the pond as a fly or a leaf fossilized thousands of years ago disturbs the amber in which it is enclosed. Newts moved along the pond-floor, and little water boatmen with their tiny jerking oars cut their courses up and down and across, through the water, as sharp as needles, and straight as ruled lines. Slow beetles stirred, and the snails clinging to the water plants with their mouths, moved a few centimetres up a stalk like a sheep nibbling its way to another pasturage.

The life of the pond was like a theatre whose surface was the front of the stage; and peering down upon this stage I saw naked dramas, glutinous loves, voracious murders, incredibly fertile births, taking place in the utter stillness of unnatural light.

My ambition was to be a naturalist, an old man with a long white beard, like a photograph I had seen of Charles Darwin. When I was eight years old we went for the holiday to the Lake District, which I have described. We walked in the rain through a copse. When the rain had cleared the sun came out in sudden heat and brightness. The copse creaked as all the leaves and flowers unfolded and turned back from the rain towards the sun. The hairy caterpillars I adored so much had tiny drops of vapour on their tufts. There was a rustling sound, as the waters drained away and the odour of the earth rose up to the sky as heavily as incense in a church, or the smell of burning in a room on fire.

All this was during the First World War. One day, while we were in the garden at Sheringham, an enormous, cleanly shaped monster, with smoothly turning propellers paddling in the evening light, glided quite slowly over the roof of our house. My father's secretary, Captain Devoto, ran out of the house and said: 'A Zeppelin.'

My mother's favourite brother, Alfred Schuster, came to visit us at Sheringham, before going to the front. I remember him seated at the dining-room table in his gleaming officer's uniform. When he ate, he skewered the vegetables as well as the mutton from his plate on to his fork. He gave us each a little carved toy of Swiss peasant work. I got a tiny cow with delicate wooden legs.

I remember the winter evenings with the heavy curtains drawn, and, spread over the table, the exciting paint-boxes and paper which called images into being. My mother perhaps wore that amethyst necklace of transparent golden stones (it belongs now to my wife) which I associate with the nearness of her neck when she leaned down to kiss me at night. On one such evening, while she was painting a poster, she stopped working, sighed deeply and said: 'This terrible war.' That remark provoked me to repeat what I had read that morning in my school history book: 'The most terrible war of all time was that of the English against Joan of Arc.' 'This is the most terrible war that has ever been,' she exclaimed with harsh anguish. The next day I learned that our uncle, Alfred Schuster, had been killed.

*　　*　　*　　*　　*

When I was nine I took one of the most important decisions of my life. I decided to go to boarding school.

My brother Michael was a boarder at the Old School House Preparatory School, of Gresham's School, Holt. During the Christmas holidays he came home in grey flannel trousers and a blazer with two interlinked shields embroidered over the breast pocket. He looked almost like a young naval cadet, and talked about the examinations in which he had distinguished himself, the extraordinary skill required to drive a motor-car, and the component parts of water.

I felt that if only I went to boarding school, wore a uniform, and had my hair close-cropped like Michael's, I would become sure and efficient like him. My parents looked at Michael and looked at me, and agreed that such a change was desirable. Perhaps, if I went to school, I would stand up straight, stop being flabby, and learn to pronounce words correctly, not confusing, for example, 'soldier' and 'shoulder'. (Perhaps this mistake had some connection with my frequently being told to hold my shoulders straight, like a soldier.)

So I packed off my caterpillars in a box almost as big as the trunk in which my clothes were put, and went to Holt.

My first impression was of a large grey playing field, round which boys tramped in pairs. Being new, I had no one to tramp with, so I went round looking for Michael. Michael kindly but firmly explained that I must not be seen with him, nor must I call him Michael now, but Spender Major. However, Spender Major said, his friend Hales Major had a brother, Hales Minor, almost as incompetent as I, and perhaps we might make friends. Accordingly, Michael took me along to see Hales Major who was in the school dining-room and assembly hall, playing the Death March of Saul on a rickety upright piano. When he saw me, Hales Major got up, shut the lid of the piano, and looked at me keenly. He was a pleasant-looking boy with an oval face, dark eyes, and hair done rather eccentrically, with a fringe. He just stared at me and laughed and laughed. 'You don't mean to say so,' he exclaimed between laughs. 'So this is Spender Minor.'

Michael excelled at school to exactly the same extent as I failed. There was a kind of symmetry whereby the upward curve of his success was the half of a circle completed by the downward curve of my failure. Once a General Knowledge paper was set for the whole O.S.H. At the top of a chart denoting the results there came the name Spender Major with 90 per cent correct answers, at the bottom was Spender Minor with 0.5 per cent.

The experience which divided my life at the age of nine, from all before and after was the shock of homesickness when I arrived at school. This homesickness took a double form. On the one hand, it was a violent rejection by my senses of everything around me. My palate refused to taste food, my eyes loathed everything they saw. To hear or to feel anything connected with the school was a kind of sick-room duty interrupting my desire to think my own thoughts and be alone. On the other hand, my mind was filled with the overpowering images of home. If I closed my eyes for an instant, there was not a single scene I imagined at home (and I could not stop myself imagining!) which did not overpower me with nostalgia. A corner of the scullery, Ella scrubbing the floor, a sign in the road below my window, creaking in the wind at night: just such irrelevant things provided me with the question I was for ever asking myself: How could I for a single moment ever have imagined that I was unhappy at home and that I wanted to leave?

Each morning, after dreaming of home, I would wake up and for a moment imagine that I was in my own room. Then I opened my eyes wide, and the window of the dormitory was not that of my room at home. This was the worst moment of the day.

Homesickness choked me, making me almost insensible to what was going on around me. I was shut into a world of frustrated passion which I could not communicate to anyone else. To do so would have rendered me incapable of carrying on at all. Had I allowed myself for an instant to show what I felt to the matron, Miss Newcombe (known as the Newt), while she was inspecting my hands or feet, to see whether my finger-nails or toe-nails were clean, I would have been so overcome with tears which could bring no comfort, that I would simply have added exposed helplessness to my already hopeless state. I dreaded a kind remark from Miss Bristowe, the English teacher, who used to look at me sometimes with a gleam of sympathy. I was capable of collapsing in class if she smiled at me with a certain understanding.

I was like an animal or a peasant, deprived of his familiar surroundings. I wrote desperate letters to my parents, but they thought it wise to ignore my appeals to be taken back home. They looked to school to provide me with the discipline which they themselves had failed to teach me.

Occasionally some other boy who felt much as I did, would tell me that the term was only ninety-one days long. He might as well have told me it was only eternity. For to someone, especially a child, who is passionately obsessed, a moment can be packed with what seems an eternity of longing.

Why did I not run away? Because I feared the cold upper-class shockedness my parents would have felt if a son of theirs had run away from school. Berthella would have said: 'So you've come home, boy. Well, now you're here, you'd better stay.' And that would have been the end of that. But my parents would have felt I was unnatural, and in order to comfort themselves and myself would have pretended that I was ill. At the best, they would have sent me to a doctor.

It may be objected that I exaggerate my feelings in remembering them. This is certainly not the case. When I was nine, I often asked myself whether I would experience anything worse than school; and subsequently, during the worst situations I have been in, I have always been able to console myself by thinking: 'This isn't nearly as bad as the beginning of term at The O.S.H.'

Perhaps the worst feature of school was that one could not escape into the mind of any other boy. Some of the boys, like Hales Major, were naturally kind: one or two, like Christopher Bailey, were extremely intelligent. But I knew that if I committed the indiscretion of showing what I really felt in conversation with them, I would encounter simply the blank walls of the school. They would betray me to the spirit of the school. The deep treachery of childhood infected the whole place, like a Fascist state where you discover every neighbour to be – even if he is not aware of it himself – an agent of the interests of the police.

The headmaster, not just of the junior school but of the whole of Gresham's School, was Howson, the great Howson, always known as Howson of Holt. He certainly transformed Gresham's School from a grammar school into the great public school which it now is. But it was not this aspect of him which I knew, and I must describe our meeting in the way in which it impressed itself on me.

Early in the term, the little new boys from the preparatory school had to go up to the main school buildings and meet Howson. We bicycled the mile or so which divided the main from the junior school. Then we were shown into a classroom where our little group of the smallest boys in the whole school – none of us was older than ten – sat and waited for Howson. The headmaster came in. As far as I remember, he had a rotund face with a purplish complexion, and he was rather short. He sat down and said to the boy opposite him, from where he faced us: 'How did you get here?'

'We came on bikes,' said the boy, whose name was Seyd.

'*Sir*, sir, and there's no such word as bikes!' roared the headmaster.

'Yes, sir,' said Seyd.

'What do you say? What do you say?'

'Bicycles. We came on our bicycles.'

'*Bicycles, sir!*'

Howson's thought now seemed to enter a mighty passage, like the entrance of the whole orchestra at the end of a fugal introduction, while he explained to us what our generation was doing to the English language.

When this was over there were a couple of bars of silence, and then he took up another great theme, characteristic of him, I suppose, in its bare simplicity. 'Hands up those of you who are only children, without brothers or sisters!'

Two or three boys put up their hands. The headmaster then said that the only child was a miserable, pitiable creature, born of selfish parents, unlikely to play the game.

This was one of the very rare occasions in my school career in which I happened to be on the right side. But just as I was savouring the sweet injustice of being favoured, another question was fired at us: 'Hands up those who have never been beaten by their fathers!'

Two or three, of whom I was one, put up their hands.

The headmaster let himself go. Fathers who did not beat their children, he said, were not men. Children who were not beaten by their fathers would not be men. Beating was the best treatment a boy could receive.

At this moment I noticed hanging on a coat hook on the classroom door two canes. I felt faint and forgot the rest of the great man's words.

On my second morning at school I was told to go and take a cold shower. I entered a room where I saw a number of boys, some of them pubescent, completely naked. It was the first time I had ever seen any nakedness, outside my own family, and it made a strong impression on me.

In the agitation of the first few days of school I forgot my caterpillars, but now I used to go out into the yard, where I kept them in a box, to look at them. Their rustling lives among leaves and behind walls of perforated zinc, seemed the only existence around me unaffected by regimentation. But very soon my nature studies were organized, and I lost interest in them.

A nice young master explained nature to us. He said that trees grow because birds ate pips which, passing through their bodies, were excreted within globules of dung acting as a manure. His nature lessons were interrupted, because, before he got to frogs and pollen, he himself, practising what the frogs and pollen would have preached

330

to us, fertilized another master's wife and left the school under a pregnant cloud.

The one reality I could hold on to was my own inner life, my capacity to enact dramas for myself, to speak to those who would never listen to me in an impassioned language of hidden love. I would lie in bed imagining the drama of the Crucifixion so vividly that I had to imagine that Christ was tied by ropes to the cross, because, when I had thought about them deeply, I could not bear the nails. I had then a power not only to imagine shapes (suggested, for example, by the clothes over a chair) so vividly that they seemed indistinguishable from the reality, but also to listen to sounds which I first thought of and then listened to, as they formed tunes of their own which seemed to develop independently of my thinking them. For instance, if I was in a train I could think a tune, which seemed played upon a single wire, giving out long-drawn thin notes. As I listened, for a time I controlled the notes to go up or down the scale, as I chose. But after a time I ceased to think of the tune. It separated from my thinking and I could hear it everywhere in the train, whether I wished to do so or not. I could not escape from it. However, with a considerable effort of will, I could regain control of it, making it change key or be loud or soft.

My difficulty was to connect my interior world with any outward activity. At what point did my inner drama enter into relation with the life which surrounded me?

For an answer to this question I listened carefully to the conversation of the grown-ups, searching as it were for the key which would open the door of my interior world on to reality. I soon became fascinated by the mysterious word 'genius'. 'So-and-so,' I heard, 'never shone, was always in trouble, obtained no recognition – but then, with him all this did not matter, because he was a genius.'

The boys, of course, used the word 'genius' (which preoccupied people more thirty years ago than it does today) differently from this. They meant either all-round ability, or else excellence in one particular direction. Either, 'he's an absolute genius, he plays the piano, knows six languages, is wonderful at mathematics, and in the Eleven'; or: 'he's a mathematical genius', or 'a musical genius', and so forth.

But Miss Bristowe, teaching us about Coleridge, Keats, Chatterton and Byron, meant the quality of Romantic poets whereby they broke all the rules, diving as it were into the depths of their own isolated being, and fetching up pearls of the creative imagination which had no apparent relation to existing knowledge.

In my prison of school this idea was like the thought of Leonora inspiring Florestan with the brush of an angel's wing which is a flute, as he lies in his prison. It gathered together my experiences of the chalk blue butterfly, the heartsease and scabious in the fields, and told me that these were the knowledge I needed more than that which enabled people to pass examinations. And that my incommunicable visions were struggling through a night beyond which they would find the day.

*   *   *   *   *

During this, my first term, I became involved in a terrible row in which I was outlawed from school discipline.

What happened was this. At 11 a.m. each morning, during 'break', plates of bread, cut into pieces of a quarter of a slice each, were put out on tables. Each boy was allowed to eat one such quarter slice, and no more. Certain of the older boys who had bicycled up to the senior school for classes, arrived rather later than the rest of us for break and their bread. One day, five or six of the smaller boys were particularly hungry, and ate more than one of the quarter slices each. The result was that when the older boys returned from the upper school there was not enough bread to go round among them. They complained to the kitchen maids, who defended their mathematics, and it became obvious that some of us had taken more than one piece of bread.

The whole junior school was assembled, and the housemaster, Dr. Wynne Wilson (related to many bishops, and an authority on divinity and bicycling), called upon the boys who had eaten more than one quarter slice to put up their hands. This a few of us did. Then addressing the rest of the school, Wynne Wilson said we were worse than Huns, we were Food Hogs. We were so wicked that he himself could not punish us. So he gave the other boys leave to do whatever they liked with us. We were outlawed for that afternoon.

I did not observe what happened to the others, because several boys set on me. They tied some rope, which they had found, round my hands and feet, and then pulled in different directions. After this I was flung down a hole at the back of the platform of the school dining-room, called the Kipper Hole, because heads of kippers were thrown there.

My chief preoccupation during all this time was whether I would get to my music lesson in time. The school had impressed on me strongly that salvation lay in obeying rules, conforming and being inconspicuous.

Finally, I tore myself away from my attackers and got on to my bicycle. I arrived in a sad state at the house of the music master, Mr. Greatorex.

Mr. Greatorex was one of those masters who attain at school an astonishing reputation. At the Old School House the boys used to discuss whether or not he was 'the eighth greatest musician in England'. Whatever his status, he was undoubtedly a fine pianist and organist. He had a sour, rather morose air covering an underlying generosity and kindliness, and this confused him in my mind with certain romantic portraits of Beethoven. To everyone it seemed that his being at Gresham's and not on the pedestal of greatness in the world was an unexplained mystery.

He used to come to the O.S.H. to teach us singing. He had a manner perhaps more brusque than that of other masters, but less frightening. It had more of the warm great world than of the refrigerated school. While he conducted our singing, I used to stare at his domed bald head with the clusters of hair on each side and at the back, and pray that when I grew up I would be bald. For the child unquestioningly attributes beauty to whom he loves. Thus Greatorex seemed to me one of the most beautiful people I had ever seen.

So now, bending down over my handle bars, I bicycled, almost blinded by tears, to his house where he was to give me my piano lesson.

I sat at the keyboard and tried to begin to play. All I hoped was that somehow I would get through my lesson without disgracing myself. But without saying a word, Greatorex put his arm round my shoulders. Then he said: 'Tell me what is the matter.'

When he had heard my story he said quietly: 'Listen. You are unhappy now, and you may as well realize that you will be unhappy for a long time, perhaps throughout all your time at school. But I can assure you that a time will come, perhaps when you are about to go to University, when you will begin to be happy. You will be happier than most people.'

I never forgot Greatorex's remark, slipped like a banned letter into the concentration camp of my childhood; and when I was grown up, I wrote and thanked him for having made it, and confirmed that it was true.

*   *   *   *   *

In the dormitory, in the watches of the night, I thought that one day I would write a book which would contain the truth to which I bore witness. What I would say was perfectly clear to me. It was this: everyone is occupied in blindly pursuing his own ends, and yet beneath his aims, and beneath his attempts to escape from solitude by conforming with the herd-like behaviour of those around him, he wants something quite different from his aims, and quite different from the standards of human institutions, and this thing which he wants is what all want: simply to admit that he is an isolated existence, and that his class and nation, even the personality and character which he presents to his fellow beings, are all a mask, and beneath this mask there is only the desire to love and be loved just because he is ignorant, and miserable, and surrounded by unknowns of time and space and other people.

In the night of my childhood, I saw that the smallness and brevity of a human life, compared with the infinitude of time and the immensity of the universe, dwarf each separate person, and the most the cleverest can know is that he knows nothing. Within each there is a world of his own soul as immense as the external universe, and equally with that, dwarfing the little stretch of coherent waking which calls itself 'I'.

Standing midway between vast interior and exterior natures, each one is equal with the others, in enclosing within his own littleness a spark of consciousness of all. He does not even know himself or others, so that he can never even say with conviction: 'I am better than the others'; and yet, alas, he knows enough to be able to think: I am worse.'

All men know is that conditioning in time and space and human psychology which all share in common, and which throw them into life like shipwrecked people upon a sea. In their situation the only sanity must lie in helping one another, and above all for each generation to remember that the New World is simply their children, who form the next.

Undoubtedly certain old poems, certain texts, certain laws even, said all this with sacred authority: to hear them, as I lay awake, was like seeing cold water falling through the night which had the power to wash and shape the stone which was my heart. When I read of the lives of those saints of utterly simple purpose who had put aside all evasion and lived for humanity, making their own material welfare the lowest common multiple of the material existence of the poor, I felt a deep obeisance of my nature, and I knew that their illogicality was right.

So I thought that under all causes and all appearances, there was an extreme simplicity, like that of a lost child or a sick person. What really mattered were extreme situations, in the light of which ordinary ones should be judged: the beginning of creation, the end of the world, extreme poverty or suffering, great love, death. Life acquired significance – I thought, when I was nine or ten – in so far as isolated moments of living were stretched upon these extremes, penetrated by the awareness of ultimate ends. Health and well-being and comfort should not simply be an escape into the body or the money from the realities which are always present, and which all finally have to face.

Of course these ideas were childish, and when I thought that I would one day write a book which stated them very simply, I was a child. Yet now I am a middle-aged man, in the centre of life and rotted by a modicum of success, surrounded on the one hand by material responsibilities and on the other by material achievements, it seems to me that the boy I was, was aware of the dangers I have fallen into now – for didn't I read in many legends of purposes forgotten, of forests full of thorns, of grails unnoticed? My mistake was to think that my own nature would make everything easy. Perhaps

335

I was less a child when the purpose was clearer, and now that I am old I am encumbered by many childish things. Yet the fact remains that I am and was the same person: when I was a child there were moments when I stood up within my whole life, as though it were a burning room, or as though I were rowing alone on a sea whose waves were filled with many small tongues of fire: and where I thought of my son, and my daughter, and my ancestors, and when I remembered how my mother, the night before she died, said to Ella, who was lighting the little gas fire in her bedroom, 'Tell them I have had a very happy life.'

(1947 – May 30 1950)

INDEX

337

French Revolution, 1, 203
Freud, Sigmund, 42, 137
Friends' House, 16
Frognal, 20, 25, 63, 76, 88, 280
Front Populaire (*see also* Popular Front), 142
Fry, Roger, 140, 144, 151

Galsworthy, John, 23
Gamp, Mrs. 83
Gargoyle Club, 258
Garnett, David, 140
Garsington, 159, 166
Gascoyne, David, 218, 291
Gauguin, Paul, 33, 34
Gedaechtniskirche, 133, 252
General Election of 1923, British, 7, 89
Geneva, Lake of, 30
'Georgians, The', 138–9
German Jews, 12–13, 190
German Literature, Contemporary, 302
German Modernism, 108
German Nationalists, 130, 133
German Social Democrats, 130
Germans, 12, 13, 188, 190, 265, 303
Germany, 12, 15, 28, 77, 78, 80, 89, 104, 106–8, 111, 114–116, 119, 129–34, 142, 147, 188, 190, 234, 253, 262, 264, 267, 281–2, 285, 297, 300, 304, 311
German-Soviet Pact, 254
German Universities, 304
Gertler, Mark, 166
Gibraltar, 215
Gide, André, 240–1, 247, 296
Ginger, 278
Giotto's Tower, 2
Gladstone, Rt. Hon. W. E., M.P., 1
Glasgow razor-slashers, 213, 229
Goebbels, Joseph, 132
Goering, Hermann, 188, 192
Goethe, Wolfgang, 147, 159, 185, 251
Goethehaus, 199
Goldberg Variations, 207

Golden Age, 2
Gold Rush, The, 65
Gongora y Argote, Luis, 205, 209
Good Companions, The, 99
Goodman, Richard, 36
Goyen, William, ix
Graben, 199
Grant, Alexander, 38
Grant, Duncan, 140, 144, 151
Graves, Robert, 95
Gray, Thomas, 92
Great Barrier Reef, 46, 47
Great Britain, 114, 137, 154, 202, 207, 221, 224, 234, 237, 247, 267, 297–8, 303, 306
Greatorex, W. J., 333–4
Greece, 94, 162, 178–81
Greek Tragedy, 300
Green, George, 219–20
Green, Henry, 95
Green, Julian, 153
Greene, W. Graham, 159
Greenland, 46, 47, 282
Greenwich Village, N.Y., 297
Gresham's School, Holt, 49, 326–34
Grey, Sir Edward, 79
Grigson, Geoffrey, 296
Group Theatre, The, 249
Gruning family, 12
Grünewald, 125–6
Guadalajara, Battle of, 226, 227

Hales, 327, 329
Hamburg, 101, 104, 106–13, 117, 120–1, 130, 204, 264, 282
Hamilton, Hamish, ix
Hamilton, Sir Ian, General, 85
Hammersmith, 10, 204, 208, 211, 255–6, 293, 295
Hampstead, 6, 13, 21–2, 25, 26, 279, 290, 309
Hapsburgs, 160
Harcourt, Miss, 324
Hardy, Thomas, 23, 147
Hargreaves, Mrs., 320
Harvard University, 298
Hayward, John, ix

347